DEFINING MÉTIS

DEFINING MÉTIS

CATHOLIC MISSIONARIES AND THE IDEA OF CIVILIZATION IN NORTHWESTERN SASKATCHEWAN, 1845–1898

TIMOTHY P. FORAN

ump

UNIVERSITY OF MANITOBA PRESS

20   19   18   17   1   2   3   4

University of Manitoba Press
Winnipeg, Manitoba, Canada
Treaty 1 Territory
uofmpress.ca

Cataloguing data available from Library and Archives Canada
ISBN 978-0-88755-774-3 (PAPER)
ISBN 978-0-88755-513-8 (PDF)
ISBN 978-0-88755-511-4 (EPUB)

Cover design by Marvin Harder
Interior design by Karen Armstrong
Maps by Weldon Hiebert. Maps contain information licensed
under the Open Government Licence–Canada.
On the cover is a view of of the Saint-Jean-Baptiste mission at
Île-à-la-Crosse drawn by Henri Julien (1903), based on an 1874 sketch by
Sara Riel. Centre du patrimoine, La Société historique de Saint-Boniface,
SHSB 14879.

Printed in Canada

The University of Manitoba Press acknowledges the financial support for
its publication program provided by the Government of Canada through
the Canada Book Fund, the Canada Council for the Arts, the Manitoba
Department of Sport, Culture, and Heritage, the Manitoba Arts Council,
and the Manitoba Book Publishing Tax Credit.

Funded by the Government of Canada | Canadä

CONTENTS

LIST OF ILLUSTRATIONS

PREFACE

This book is about Roman Catholic missionaries and the ways that they thought and wrote about Indigenous people in the latter half of the nineteenth century. Its focus is very different from the one I had intended when I began my research in 2006. In the early spring of that year, I learned that the Société historique de Saint-Boniface (Winnipeg) had recently acquired and accessioned a collection of French-language Catholic mission records from the Métis community of Île-à-la-Crosse in northwestern Saskatchewan. The collection spanned nearly a century and a half, from the establishment of a Catholic missionary presence at Île-à-la-Crosse in 1845 to the completion of the last mission journal in 1988. It contained a wealth of information on the local community: a running chronicle of daily life, genealogies of congregant families, sacramental records, and more. Never before had the collection been available to lay researchers, so if I hurried, I would be the first to use it as a corpus of primary sources. Here, I thought, was a golden opportunity to produce a sweeping ethnohistorical study of a Métis community using methods that were tried, tested, and true: scholars have long relied—and continue relying—on mission records to yield qualitative and quantitative information on the historical Métis.

My initial enthusiasm turned to confusion, however, when I examined the collection and found very few references to a local Métis population—the putative subject of my study—until the mid-1870s. Up to then, missionary record-keepers seemed to have referred to all local Indigenous people as "des sauvages," subcategorizing them according to linguistic criteria as "des Cris"

(Cree speakers) and "des Montagnais" (Chipewyan speakers). This made no sense to me: I had expected these records to corroborate Brenda Macdougall's identification of Île-à-la-Crosse as "one of the oldest, most culturally homogeneous Metis communities in western Canada"—a place where Métis ethnogenesis had preceded the arrival of Catholic missionaries by generations.[1] Yet these records contained few explicit references to "des métis" until more than a full generation *after* the missionaries' arrival.

As I attempted to account for this apparent incongruity, my attention turned toward missionary record-keepers themselves and away from the people whom they purported to describe. I became increasingly interested in the missionaries' use of the categories *sauvage* and *métis* and in the forces that shaped their understanding and application of these categories. Pursuing this line of research meant delving deeper into the archival record and consulting letters, journals, and reports written by the missionaries of Île-à-la-Crosse and by their *confrères/consœurs*, superiors, and lay associates across North America and Europe. A careful reading of these sources convinced me that missionary-made categories of indigeneity reveal far more about missionary assumptions, motives, and world views than they do about actual Indigenous collectivities. Indeed, the categories *sauvage* and *métis* appear to have shifted and evolved in response to broad changes affecting the Catholic apostolate on the local, regional, and global levels.

Although constructed by missionaries and imbued with missionary meaning, these categories acquired influence well beyond missionary circles. The Canadian state appropriated them to classify and govern Indigenous people: in northwestern Saskatchewan, for instance, missionary-made categories played a critical role in drawing legal and administrative distinctions between Indians and Half-breeds after the onset of federal intervention in local affairs in 1898—the end year of this study. Additionally, these categories suffuse works of history, anthropology, and other social sciences whose authors have drawn on mission records—with varying degrees of critical awareness—to elucidate aspects of Indigenous people's past and present. This practice is sure to continue, even to intensify, on the heels of the 2015 research recommendations of the Truth and Reconciliation Commission of Canada and recent case law inviting re-examination of Métis identity and citizenship.[2] I hope, therefore, that this book will enhance researchers' understanding of missionary-made categories by situating them within the context in which they were originally constructed, applied, and understood.

From *sauvage* to *métis*: The Evolution of Missionary-Made Categories at Île-à-la-Crosse

On 24 May 1845, *abbé* Jean-Baptiste Thibault wrote an uncharacteristically forceful letter to his bishop. The normally stolid missionary reported that he had just visited the Hudson's Bay Company (HBC) post at Île-à-la-Crosse, where he had encountered eighty "Montagnais" families who earnestly desired religious instruction. Unfamiliar with their language, Thibault had endeavoured to teach them the Paternoster, the Ave Maria, the Credo, and the Gloria Patris in French. Then, before resuming his itinerant mission, he had promised these "bons sauvages" that he would send them priests who would learn their language and provide them with regular spiritual care. Thibault insisted on the urgency of the situation: Île-à-la-Crosse was ripe for mass conversion, and the Catholic Church needed to seize the opportunity before its Protestant rivals did. He therefore urged his bishop to waste no time in dispatching missionaries to Île-à-la-Crosse and assured him that these missionaries would be welcomed enthusiastically by the locals. "Never," asserted Thibault, "was a *sauvage* people better disposed to embrace the faith than are the Montagnais."[1]

Fifty-four years later, the resident priest at Île-à-la-Crosse bemoaned the faithlessness and degeneracy of the local population. A year after assuming direction of Saint-Jean-Baptiste mission, Father Jean-Marie Pénard undertook "a little inquisition" among his regular congregants—to whom he referred collectively as "our métis"—in early January 1899.[2] In reporting the findings of his investigation, Pénard noted "such a state of degradation and immorality among the poor métis of Île-à-la-Crosse that [I] found [my]self wondering why the good Lord had yet to inflict the punishment of Sodom

on this miserable place." Then, somewhat ironically, the inquisitor posed a
rhetorical question: "How did our poor métis get to this point?"[3]

During the half century bracketed by Thibault's optimistic report and
Pénard's troubled musing, Catholic missionaries re-labelled, re-classified, and
re-appraised the people of Île-à-la-Crosse. To a certain extent, this revision
paralleled the evolution of local identities and the shift of local demographic
patterns resulting from migration, disease, and famine.[4] Yet it also reflected an
epistemological change among missionary commentators themselves, namely
their adoption of a new and more inclusive conception of *métis*. In applying
the term *métis* to the resident population of Île-à-la-Crosse, Catholic missionaries set aside the linguistic, social, cultural, and geographic criteria that
had previously informed their application of this term. They broadened their
conception of *métis* to include a community whose language, lifestyle, and
location had once been considered hallmarks of "la sauvagerie." Underlying
this reconceptualization was a series of local, regional, and national developments as well as intellectual currents circulating within a global network of
Catholic missions. This book seeks to delineate these converging forces and to
examine the ways in which they contributed to the revised conception of *métis*.

This line of enquiry engages two distinct historiographies—Métis
historiography and Catholic missionary historiography—and potentially
broadens the investigative scope of both. Despite their frequent reliance on
Catholic mission records, historians of the Métis have seen little need to
interrogate missionary epistemologies. For the most part, they have assumed
constancy in the observational practice of missionaries and have scrutinized
mission records to yield empirical knowledge of the nineteenth- and early
twentieth-century Métis. In his seminal work, *Le métis canadien: son rôle dans
l'histoire des provinces de l'Ouest* (1945), Marcel Giraud based his treatment of
"the psychology of the métis, their private lives, and their moral development"
almost exclusively on letters, journals, and reports written by Catholic
missionaries.[5] Giraud ascribed a privileged perspective to missionaries because
of their enduring roles as confessors, educators, and advisers to the Métis: "The
duties of the missionary and the trust that he shared with the métis allowed
him to understand their reactions, to know their nature, and to participate in all
aspects of their lives."[6] From this rare and intimate vantage point, missionaries
produced an allegedly authoritative commentary on behavioural and
psychological patterns exhibited by the Métis. Giraud drew abundantly from
this commentary but provided scarce contextualization of its production. With
the exception of prelates, the names of particular commentators were relegated

to the footnotes. Their origins, education, affiliations, and clerical status (i.e., regular vs. secular clergy, priest vs. prelate) eluded consideration altogether. So too did their reasons for writing, their intended audience, and their use of epistolary codes and conventions.[7] Emphasizing content to the exclusion of authorship, intention, and form, Giraud fused missionary commentators into an undifferentiated, unchanging, and unbiased record-keeping body.

In the wake of Giraud's study, historians of the Métis developed increasing reservations about the interpretive value of mission records. These reservations emerged from a secular current in post–Second World War scholarship and an accompanying reconsideration of missionary-Indigenous relations. As Philip Goldring has noted, historians and anthropologists began to conceptualize missionaries as part of "a bureaucratic élite which deliberately erode[d] traditional native identities."[8] These scholars honed an acute sensitivity to the cultural bias pervading missionary writings and approached these texts with cautious scepticism.[9] Nevertheless, historians of the Métis remained confident in the empirical soundness of a particular class of Catholic mission record. Embracing quantitative methodologies pioneered by French *Annalistes* and American proponents of "the new social history" in the 1960s and '70s, these historians seized upon mission censuses together with routinely generated records of baptism, marriage, and burial in order to delineate patterns of family formation, fertility, mortality, and migration.[10] Mission registers were deemed particularly useful in examining micro-level processes and were thus consulted extensively in studies of individual Métis communities—notably Diane Paulette Payment's study of Batoche (1990), Gerhard J. Ens's study of Saint-François-Xavier and St. Andrew's parishes in the Red River Colony (1996), and Brenda A. Macdougall's study of Île-à-la-Crosse, Portage La Loche, and Green Lake (2005, 2006, 2010).[11] Beholden to the scientific claims of statisticians and database aficionados, these studies devoted scant attention to the missionaries who served as enumerators and registrars. Census-taking and record-keeping were assumed to be standardized, objective, and impersonal processes that registered unequivocal data on Métis communities.

Catholic missionary history holds the potential to problematize this assumption by training a critical lens on the authors of the above-mentioned records and by addressing their origins, motives, and world views. The post–Vatican II era witnessed radical change in historical writing on the Catholic apostolate in northern and western Canada. In the mid-1960s, the church ceded its interpretive monopoly on the missionary past and opened its archives to laypeople pursuing diverse research interests.[12] There subsequently emerged a new generation of scholars who approached missionary themes from a self-consciously secular perspective and who drew on theoretical and methodological insights from a number of fields—including administrative history,[13] biography,[14] missiology,[15] education,[16] and medicine.[17] These scholars effectively transformed the Catholic missionary from a heroic figure of hagiographic lore into an object of critical scrutiny. Yet while this transformation has raised questions about the missionary's relationship with the Métis, it has not extended historical inquiry beyond a traditional empiricist focus on observable interaction and praxis. Following in the footsteps of their clerical predecessors, secular historians of the Catholic apostolate have generally limited their discussion of the Métis to behavioural dimensions of religious involvement (such as reception of the sacraments, church attendance, and communal devotion) and to services rendered to missionaries (particularly as guides, hunters, trappers, interpreters, and language instructors).[18] The constancy of this focus has resulted in the perpetuation of an orthodox, one-dimensional image of the Métis as "missionaries' assistants," their "reliable and trustworthy guides," and their "teachers of *sauvage* languages."[19] In some cases, this image has been essentialized by reference to a Lower Canadian legacy underlying the "natural" affinity between the Métis and French-speaking Catholic missionaries. For instance, in his survey of Catholic missionary activity in Rupert's Land and the North-Western Territory during the latter half of the nineteenth century (1995), Robert Choquette contends that the Métis "readily reverted to the faith of their fathers when the priests appeared among them.... Catholic missionaries therefore had a ready-made constituency ... throughout the North and the West; the fact that both the priests and the Métis were French-speaking only reinforced this tendency."[20] Similarly, in her account of the Catholic apostolate in the Athabasca and Mackenzie river basins during the same period (1995), Martha McCarthy posits a deep-seated predisposition of the Métis to collaborate with French-speaking Catholic missionaries: "Sharing the same language and faith, if only to a small extent in both instances, the Métis were natural allies of the French Catholic Oblates."[21]

Implicit in both of these historiographies is the notion of a singular, empirically existing, and readily identifiable Métis population that was susceptible to discovery and description by Catholic missionaries. The present study complicates this notion by contending that Catholic missionaries did not simply discover and describe a Métis population, but rather that they played a critical role in its conceptual production and in the delineation of its collective characteristics. They were empowered to play this role in the absence of a civil administrative infrastructure that could accumulate and organize knowledge about the Indigenous peoples of Rupert's Land and the North-Western Territory. After the Dominion of Canada acquired these territories in 1870, the state drew heavily on Catholic missionary knowledge to identify, classify, and govern its newest Indigenous charges. In the process, missionary-made categories of indigeneity were co-opted into a project of intensive government administration.[22] Catholic missionaries were acutely conscious of their contribution to this project. As early as March 1873, Bishop Vital-Justin Grandin of Saint-Albert—whose canonical jurisdiction included all of present-day Alberta and most of northern Saskatchewan—instructed his missionaries to be increasingly diligent in registering vital events among their congregants. Grandin anticipated that mission records would soon acquire an importance beyond their traditional ecclesiastical function: "Because a regular government will soon be established here, our registers are about to become much more important."[23] The bishop reissued this instruction repeatedly over the following years, adding stipulations in the late 1870s and '80s that his missionaries conduct enumerations of "the *sauvage* population" and "the métis population" in their pastoral care, and that they keep genealogical records of their congregants whenever possible.[24] Grandin reminded his missionaries in November 1887 that these records had a direct bearing on the administrative categorization and on the legal entitlement of their congregants: "The *liber animarum*, the *codex historicus* or daily journal of all that happens in your mission, and the registers of baptisms, weddings, and burials . . . are the only available sources that can provide the necessary information for issuing Scrip."[25]

At the time of their appropriation and redeployment by the Canadian state, missionary-made categories of indigeneity had undergone decades of evolution. The present study charts the course of this evolution through the lens of one particular community—Île-à-la-Crosse—from the establishment of a Catholic missionary presence there in 1845 to the onset of federal intervention in local affairs in 1898. The latter year marked the transformation of the local mission school into a state-sponsored boarding school entitled to an annual per capita grant for its "Indian boarders."[26] During the intervening half century, Catholic missionaries produced a running commentary on Île-à-la-Crosse as well as on its inhabitants, its visitors, and its passers-through. This commentary—whose aggregate components are inventoried further below—serves as the main body of primary source material for this study. The commentary is analyzed within an interpretive framework that is based on the epistemological premise of microhistory, which holds that the study of a single community can elucidate the workings and interplay of much larger historical forces.[27] Unlike most works of microhistory, however, the present study focuses principally on the authors of the primary source material rather than on the community that they purported to describe. The observers have thus become the observed, and their written observations are conceptualized as windows on their own assumptions, motives, and world views.

The authors of this primary source material were members of the congregation of Missionary Oblates of Mary Immaculate.[28] Founded in January 1816 by *abbé* Charles-Joseph-Eugène de Mazenod in Aix-en-Provence (the department of Bouches-du-Rhône, southeastern France), this congregation emerged from a powerful evangelical undercurrent within post-Revolutionary Catholicism.[29] Mazenod's immediate objective in founding the congregation was to re-evangelize the rural communities of Provence, many of which had been deprived of the spiritual, liturgical, and educational services of the Catholic Church since the outbreak of the French Revolution over twenty-five years earlier. According to Mazenod, the inhabitants of these communities had been left to languish in moral and spiritual poverty. They were therefore identified collectively as *les pauvres* (the poor) and ascribed a perilous degree of detachment from the institutional church. "The people are wallowing in abysmal ignorance of all things relating to their salvation," affirmed Mazenod in his congregation's *Constitution and Rules* (1818). "The result of this ignorance has been the weakening, if not the total collapse, of the faith and the corruption of morals. It is therefore pressing that all of these stray sheep be brought back into the fold and that these degenerate Christians be reacquainted with Jesus Christ."[30] It was the Oblates' urgent calling to assist in the redemption of *les pauvres*—a calling enshrined in the congregation's motto: *Evangelizare pauperibus misit me* (He has sent me to evangelize the poor).[31] To this end, Oblates travelled the Provençal countryside and officiated at Masses, administered the sacraments, and taught catechism in the late 1810s and early '20s. Their preferred method of evangelization was the *mission paroissiale* (parish mission)—a localized revivalist campaign based on a model developed by Saint Vincent de Paul in the early seventeenth century. The *mission paroissiale* drew together the inhabitants of a particular parish for three to six weeks of intensive instruction, preaching, and catechizing. Participants were encouraged to bare their souls in the confessional and to repent of their sins. They were also encouraged to join in a solemn procession that culminated in the planting of a large wooden cross, which was meant to remain a permanent feature of the local landscape.[32]

Having established an expansive mission circuit throughout rural Provence by the mid-1820s, the Oblates of Mary Immaculate underwent institutional consolidation over the following decade. Through the influence of his uncle, Bishop Fortuné de Mazenod of Marseilles (1823–37), Mazenod assumed administrative responsibility for the *grand séminaire* (diocesan seminary) of Marseilles in October 1827. This charge enabled him to design and to implement a program for preparing candidates for the priesthood and, more specifically, for mission work. At the core of his program was an ultramontane ecclesiology predicated on submission to papal authority and profound distrust of liberalism, secularism, and individualism—ideologies that had been challenging the church's social and moral power since before the Revolution. Mazenod's project of inculcating an ultramontane mindset was reflected in his choice of textbooks, notably the selected writings of Saint Thomas Aquinas, whose dictum "ostenditur quod subesse Romano pontifici sit de necessitate salutis" (to be subject to the Roman Pontiff is necessary for salvation) would later be marshalled in support of the doctrine of papal infallibility at the First Vatican Council (1870).[33] Mazenod replicated this training program on the French island of Corsica after Bishop Xavier Toussaint Raphaël Casanelli d'Istria of Ajaccio (1833–69) granted him the administration of the *grand séminaire d'Ajaccio* in September 1834.[34] With two sources of recruitment and training at his disposal, Mazenod considered expanding the Oblates' apostolic field beyond the borders of France. His prospects of securing the necessary diplomatic and financial support improved considerably in December 1837 when he succeeded his uncle as Bishop of Marseilles.[35]

The initial impetus for the Oblates' expansion beyond France was an invitation from Bishop Ignace Bourget of Montreal (1840–76) to establish missions in his vast diocese. Accepting this invitation eagerly, Mazenod dispatched six missionaries from the Oblate General Administration in Marseilles on 30 September 1841. These Oblates subsequently established their principal residence at Longueuil—across the Saint Lawrence River from Montreal—in August 1842.[36] Similar invitations from other prelates prompted Mazenod to dispatch Oblates to Great Britain and Ireland in 1843, the Red River Colony in 1845, the Oregon Territory in 1847, Ceylon (present-day Sri Lanka) in 1847, Texas in 1849, the Colony of Natal (in present-day South Africa) in 1852, the Colony of Vancouver Island in 1858, and the Colony of British Columbia in 1859.[37] Thus, throughout the 1840s and '50s, Oblates became increasingly committed to establishing and consolidating *des missions étrangères* (foreign missions).[38] Embracing this new dimension of the

Oblate apostolate, Mazenod amended the congregation's *Constitution and Rules* and added instructions on the operation of *les missions étrangères* in 1853. In these instructions, he proclaimed that the Oblates had been blessed with a natural extension of their ministry to *les pauvres*: "*Missions étrangères* ... are indeed a source of spiritual wealth that accrues to multitudes of souls. ... [These missions] constitute tangible evidence of the divinity of the Catholic Church and also of the zeal of our Congregation for the glory of God and of its unfailing charity toward the most abandoned souls."[39]

Among the first of *les missions étrangères* was that at Île-à-la-Crosse, founded within five years of the Oblates' initial foray beyond France. This mission took root in one of the oldest continuously occupied communities in present-day western Canada. Situated at the confluence of the Canoe, Deep, and Beaver Rivers and at the headwaters of the Churchill River system, the community of Île-à-la-Crosse stood—and continues to stand—on a peninsula jutting from the southwestern shore of Lac Île-à-la-Crosse. Historically, it included small encampments around the lakeshore.[40] This area had been a contact zone between distinct ethnolinguistic groups for at least a century before the arrival of the Oblates. By the mid-1700s, it had become a point of intersection and overlap in the territories of the Woods Cree and the Chipewyan (or Denésoliné, a subgroup of the Dene).[41] Cree and Chipewyan families established seasonal encampments on the peninsula and along the shoreline of Lac Île-à-la-Crosse, which sustained them with whitefish and waterfowl.[42] Other ethnolinguistic groups began trickling into the area after 1775, when Thomas Frobisher and James Frobisher—private entrepreneurs based in Montreal—visited Île-à-la-Crosse and ascertained its strategic potential in the rapidly expanding fur trade. The Frobishers recognized that Île-à-la-Crosse could serve as a gateway into the fur-rich subarctic because of its proximity to the watershed separating the Churchill River system (that flows eastward into Hudson Bay) and the Athabasca River system (that flows northward into the Mackenzie River system, thence to the Arctic Ocean).[43] Within fifteen years of this discovery, three rival fur companies—the HBC, the North West Company (NWC), and the New North West Company (XYC)—had constructed posts at Île-à-la-Crosse and had begun manning them with personnel recruited from the British archipelago and the Saint Lawrence Valley.[44]

Following the merger of the HBC and the NWC in 1821, Île-à-la-Crosse acquired a critical role in the commercial operations of the newly reconstituted HBC.[45] It became the headquarters and the central depot of the English River District—a trading jurisdiction comprising most of present-day northwestern

Saskatchewan.[46] The spot was eminently suited to this role because of its location on the tortuous chain of lakes, rivers, and portages that connected York Factory (on Hudson Bay) and Fort Garry (in the Red River Colony) to the Athabasca and Mackenzie River basins. Each year from mid-spring to early autumn, these waterways and portages were plied by boat brigades transporting furs, supplies, trade goods, and—of course—young men.[47] In her extensive research on Île-à-la-Crosse, Brenda Macdougall has identified successive waves of "outsider male fur trade employees"—principally French-Canadian, British, and Red River Métis—who arrived in the English River District over the course of the late eighteenth and nineteenth centuries. Through intermarriage and the forging of interpersonal relationships, these outsider males were incorporated into local Indigenous family networks that were defined by matrilocal residency patterns. This process of incorporation gave rise to Métis ethnogenesis in the region by the early nineteenth century.[48] Thus, according to Macdougall, Île-à-la-Crosse holds the distinction of being "one of the oldest, most culturally homogeneous Metis communities in western Canada."[49]

To the Oblates, however, Île-à-la-Crosse was not immediately recognizable as a Métis community. In fact, the term *métis* appeared rarely in Oblate commentary on Île-à-la-Crosse until the mid-1870s.[50] This rarity reflected the Oblates' conception of *le peuple métis* as an Indigenous collectivity exhibiting clear markers of a Lower Canadian paternal heritage—namely communication in a dialect of French and membership in the institutional Catholic Church. Oblates had formed this conception in the Red River Colony, where they had established an administrative headquarters in 1845.[51] There they had encountered a self-conscious *métis* community that was francophone and that had been receiving the ministrations of the church since the arrival of ordained clergy from the Diocese of Quebec in 1818.[52] Yet while perceiving the Red River Colony as the principal homeland of *le peuple métis* during the 1840s, '50s, and '60s, Oblates also acknowledged the existence of *métis* communities beyond the colony. In 1868, Oblate Bishop Alexandre-Antonin Taché noted that at least one of these communities had been founded by French-speaking, or partially French-speaking, Catholic Iroquois:

> A small colony of Iroquois came from Canada to the Rocky Mountains. There they formed unions with women from local indigenous tribes and, curious to relate, the children born of these unions are classed among our métis. Not a drop of white

blood flows in their veins. Yet the descendants of those fierce warriors, who made our ancestors quake with fear during the early settlement of Canada, are now considered Canadian métis. From Canada, these poor Iroquois brought the same Catholic faith that had rescued them from barbarism. Isolated in the Rocky Mountains amid infidel tribes, they did not neglect the precious gift that they had received; rather, they passed it on to the children whom they had fathered through their alliances with these tribes, and so a few hundred of these Iroquois métis awaited only the arrival of priests to complete their religious education.... It is this circumstance that connects them to our Canadian métis, with whom they mix and unite as a single people.[53]

In identifying an apparent idiosyncrasy in his and his *confrères'* application of the term *métis*, Taché highlighted a critical nuance: the term was not necessarily—nor even predominantly—a signifier of mixed-bloodedness. Its racial meaning was preceded in importance by its religious and linguistic meaning.

Upon their arrival at Île-à-la-Crosse, Oblates encountered a community that exhibited neither of the defining characteristics of *le peuple métis*. Many of its members were native speakers of Chipewyan—a language that francophone traders and missionaries called "le Montagnais" although it bore no resemblance to the Montagnais, or Innu-aimun, language of Quebec and Labrador.[54] Others spoke a dialect of Cree as their mother tongue; this dialect had become the lingua franca of Île-à-la-Crosse. None of the community members had had recourse to the sacramental, liturgical, or educational services of the institutional church, as there had been no ordained clergy in the English River District prior to *abbé* Jean-Baptiste Thibault's visit in May 1845.[55] In light of these considerations, Oblates referred to members of the community collectively as *des sauvages*. Indeed, Mazenod considered Île-à-la-Crosse the prototypical *mission sauvage* and lauded its missionaries as exemplary respondents to the Oblate calling. "My dear children, I consider you true apostles," wrote Mazenod to the Oblates of Île-à-la-Crosse in 1860. "Our Divine Saviour has chosen you to be the first to announce the good news of salvation to those poor *sauvages* who, until your arrival, were languishing in the deepest darkness under the demon's thrall."[56] The term *sauvage*—like the term *métis*—did not necessarily convey racial meaning. Rather, its primary connotation was remoteness from *la civilisation*, and more particularly from *la civilisation chrétienne*. This meaning was evident in an essay penned in the early 1860s by Bishop Henri Faraud—one of the first Oblates deployed to Île-à-la-Crosse:

> Whatever the origins of the *sauvages*, they are our brothers in Jesus Christ. They were created in the likeness of God; they are a portion of humanity and, as such, their fate is a worthy concern for more advanced peoples. Do we not all share a common origin? . . .
>
> A man is not *sauvage* simply because he dwells in the wilderness: he is *sauvage* because he has no knowledge of the true God. Until religion enlightens him and refines his ways, he allows himself to be guided by his animal instincts and desires.
>
> But when Christianity penetrates the abode of *la sauvagerie*, man acquires a sense of truth and goodness, he cultivates the arts, and civilization emerges.
>
> All the peoples of the earth were barbarians once; they all began more or less in the *sauvage* state. . . .
>
> Were our fathers, the Gauls, not also *sauvages* once? . . .
>
> In time, barbarism . . . will disappear from this part of the New World, just as it disappeared from Britain and Gaul and from Upper and Lower Canada.
>
> *La civilisation chrétienne*, which has regenerated so many people since the coming of Jesus Christ, will one day reach even the most remote regions of North America.[57]

According to Faraud, *sauvages*—in common with all of humankind—possessed an innate capacity for moral, spiritual, and intellectual improvement. They could be redeemed from the "*sauvage* state" just as Faraud's own Gaulish ancestors had been redeemed centuries earlier. Their redemption could only be effected, however, through their full incorporation into the institutional Catholic Church. Within the Oblates' ultramontane paradigm, the institutional Catholic Church was the one and only source of true civilization—*la civilisation chrétienne*. The church alone could inculcate and reinforce "civilized" habits of thought, behaviour, and expression that conformed with the divinely willed order of things.[58] Thus, as applied by Oblates, the term *les sauvages* referred primarily to a transitory moral and spiritual state rather than to a fixed racial or biological one.[59]

Like the term *pauvre*, the terms *sauvage* and *métis* had particular meaning within the context of the Oblates' institutional vocabulary: each term connoted a degree of proximity to the institutional Catholic Church and, by extension, to *la civilisation chrétienne*. The Oblates' application of these terms implied an assessment of the status and progression of Catholicism among Indigenous peoples. The present study examines this commentary as a reflection of broader developments in the Catholic apostolate over the latter half of the nineteenth century. It does this through four chapters, each of which provides a chronological examination of a particular aspect of the Oblate mission experience at Île-à-la-Crosse. Chapter 1 situates the mission at Île-à-la-Crosse within the general context of the Catholic apostolate to Rupert's Land and the North-Western Territory (subsequently western and northern Canada). It charts the evolution of the mission's strategic and administrative role within the apostolate. Chapter 2 examines the relationship between the Oblates of Île-à-la-Crosse and the HBC, devoting particular attention to the implications of the Company's changing political and commercial fortunes. Chapter 3 considers the conceptualization and implementation of the Oblates' residential education program at Île-à-la-Crosse—a program intended to effect a thorough transformation of Indigenous childhood and to integrate future generations into *la civilisation chrétienne*. Finally, Chapter 4 examines the evolution of Oblate categories of indigeneity as a function of developments discussed in the three preceding chapters. It concludes with the Oblates' acknowledgement of Île-à-la-Crosse as a *métis* community, but one that differed markedly from the *métis* communities that they had encountered at the beginning of their apostolate.

This study draws on primary source material that was produced in compliance with the official regulations of the Missionary Oblates of Mary Immaculate. In his amendment to the *Constitution and Rules* (1853), Mazenod issued clear instructions on the conduct of correspondence between the constituent parts of the Oblate hierarchy. "No matter the distance," stipulated Mazenod, "a regular epistolary exchange between subjects and superiors will be established on the following bases: as far as possible, each missionary will write once a month to his resident director [i.e., the local Oblate superior], once per quarter to his vicar of missions [the regional Oblate superior], and at least once a year to the Superior General [Mazenod and his successors]."[60] Thus, in his capacity as vicar of missions in Rupert's Land from 1851 to 1868, Alexandre-Antonin Taché received regular letters and reports from the Oblate personnel at Île-à-la-Crosse.[61] These letters and reports contain detailed information on the progress of the mission and on the spiritual, moral, and physical condition of the local community. Most of these documents are now held in the Fonds

Taché in the archival collection of the Société historique de Saint-Boniface (Winnipeg), where they have been consulted extensively for the present study.[62] Between 1868 and 1891, Île-à-la-Crosse was included within the jurisdiction of the Vicariate of Saint-Albert, which was administered by Vital-Justin Grandin.[63] Grandin consequently maintained a regular correspondence with the Oblates of Île-à-la-Crosse. Substantial portions of this correspondence are now held in the Alberta-Saskatchewan Oblate collection at the Provincial Archives of Alberta (Edmonton), and have been drawn upon for this study. Moreover, Grandin produced a voluminous commentary on the mission at Île-à-la-Crosse while serving as resident superior there (1857–60, 1864–68) and during his semi-regular pastoral visits (1868–91).[64] He dispatched much of this commentary to the Oblate General Administration, where it was subsequently transcribed into typewritten form and included in a twenty-six-volume collection titled Les Écrits de Grandin.[65] A copy of this collection is currently housed at the Research Centre for the Religious History of Canada (Saint Paul University, Ottawa), and has been consulted for this study. Finally, the holdings of the Archives Deschâtelets (previously in Ottawa; transferred to Richelieu, Quebec, in 2014) include outward correspondence from individual Oblates who resided at Île-à-la-Crosse during the period under consideration. This correspondence is analyzed in detail in the following chapters.

Besides instructing Oblates to maintain regular correspondence with their superiors, the Oblate General Administration urged them to prepare letters and reports for publication in two French Catholic periodicals: *Missions de la Congrégation des missionnaires oblats de Marie Immaculée*, and *Les Annales de la Propagation de la Foi.* The former was a quarterly founded in 1862 by Mazenod's successor, Oblate Superior General Joseph Fabre (1861–92). Its foundational purpose was to facilitate communication between far-flung members of the congregation and to create a sense of community that transcended vast geographical distances.[66] The latter periodical was founded in 1827 as the official organ of l'Œuvre de la Propagation de la Foi—the principal underwriter of Oblate missionary activity in Rupert's Land and the North-Western Territory (and subsequently western and northern Canada). The avowed aim of this periodical was to solicit funds for *les missions étrangères* and to inspire missionary vocations among a French Catholic readership.[67] Both periodicals have yielded extensive primary source material for this study. Additionally, Oblate prelates were required to provide l'Œuvre de la Propagation de la Foi with financial reports, receipts, and inventories each year. Many of these records have been deposited in the Archives de la Propagation de la foi de Paris (Paris), which subsequently provided microfilm copies to the Research Centre for Religious History of Canada.[68] These microfilm copies have provided primary source material for Chapters 1 and 3.

According to another regulation of the congregation, the resident superior of each *mission étrangère* was required to keep a *codex historicus*—a contemporary chronicle of daily life at the mission and its outlying satellite posts.[69] Yet no such chronicle exists for the mission at Île-à-la-Crosse during the period under study. The original *codex historicus* was destroyed in the fire that engulfed the mission on 1 March 1867.[70] Subsequently, no *codex historicus* was kept until 1898, when federal intervention in the local mission school compelled Oblates to update and regularize their records.[71] This task fell to thirty-three-year-old resident superior Father Jean-Marie Pénard, who composed the nominal "Codex historicus de l'Île-à-la-Crosse, 1845–1897" on the basis of primary sources that he acknowledged in the body of his text and in marginalia.[72] These sources included handwritten records kept by local mission personnel, published reports in *Missions de la Congrégation des missionnaires oblats de Marie Immaculée* and *Les Annales de la Propagation de la Foi*, and oral accounts from elderly lay residents of Île-à-la-Crosse.[73] In addition, Pénard initiated the practice of keeping a *liber status animarum* (book of the state of souls), which listed all Catholic families and individuals living within the pastoral jurisdiction of the mission. Pénard organized this document by family name, beginning each section with commentary on the family's founding couple and subsequently listing their descendants. He indicated each individual's year of baptism and—if applicable—his or her year of marriage, the name(s) of his or her spouse(s), and the year of his or her obsequies.[74] In 2005, both of these records—the "Codex historicus" and the "Liber status animarum" (or "Arbre généalogique")—were transferred from the Oblate-operated Archdiocese of Keewatin-Le Pas (headquartered at The Pas, Manitoba) to the Société historique de Saint-Boniface, where they have been consulted extensively for the present study.[75] However, neither has been used as a primary source for the period before 1890—the year in which Pénard was first posted to Île-à-la-Crosse.[76]

Finally, this study draws on primary sources that were produced outside of the Oblates' institutional and administrative apparatus. These sources serve principally to contextualize and to cross-reference Oblate commentary. They include—from the Archives des Sœurs Grises de Montréal (Montreal)—chronicles and reports written by female religious who staffed the mission school and the infirmary at Île-à-la-Crosse between 1860 and 1898.[77] They also include microfilm copies of correspondence between mission personnel and the federal Department of the Interior. This correspondence is included in the Black Series at Library and Archives Canada (Ottawa).[78] Lastly, this study incorporates HBC records from the English River District, including post journals, inward and outward correspondence, accounts books, servant rosters, and district reports. These documents were accessed through the Hudson's Bay Company Archives microfilm collection at Library and Archives Canada.[79]

On the basis of these primary sources, this book presents a qualitative investigation of Oblate perceptions of their ministry at Île-à-la-Crosse in the latter half of the nineteenth century. It examines the forces that shaped these perceptions and that impelled their evolution over a fifty-three-year period. In particular, this study examines the relationship between the Oblates' evolving objectives, concerns, and priorities, and their construction of categories of indigeneity at Île-à-la-Crosse.

CHAPTER 1

Saint-Jean-Baptiste in an Evolving Mission Network

The centennial of Saint-Jean-Baptiste mission at Île-à-la-Crosse occasioned the publication of the first book-length history of a Catholic mission in western Canada—Germain Lesage's *Capitale d'une solitude* (1946). Commissioned by the Vicariate Apostolic of Keewatin, the book presented a collective portrait of the priests, nuns, and lay brothers who had staffed Saint-Jean-Baptiste over the previous century. Its avowed aim was to inspire missionary vocations by introducing Catholic readers to paragons of service, devotion, and charity: "Légeard, the long-suffering one, faithful servant of the Sacred Heart"; "Rapet, the kind-hearted one"; "Pénard, the philosopher, historian, and linguist"; "Dubé, a father to the schoolchildren"; "Labelle, the jack of all trades"; "Bowes, the builder"; "Agnès, Dandurand, Nadeau, Eugénie, model mothers with boundless hearts."[1] Saint-Jean-Baptiste thus served as a showcase in which to display the diverse talents and qualities required for the extension of God's kingdom on earth. It represented the ideal harmonization of these talents and qualities, a harmonization that gave rise to a "Christian city" within a vast expanse of pagan wilderness. The isolation—or "solitude"—of this city underscored the sacrifice of its founding citizens and reminded readers that the work of evangelization was far from complete, for beyond loomed a hinterland where the light of Christ had still to penetrate.[2]

While arguably effective as a rhetorical strategy, Lesage's emphasis on isolation obscures the historical connectedness of Saint-Jean-Baptiste to regional, national, and global processes. The mission belonged to a network that conveyed people, information, funds, and freight over vast distances. This network operated under ecclesiastical aegis and existed for the fulfillment of Christ's mandate to evangelize the nations.[3] It was sustained—and gradually extended—through collaborative interaction between lower clergy in the mission field, local superiors, regional prelates, and international administrative and financial bodies. This chapter examines the role of Saint-Jean-Baptiste within this network during the latter half of the nineteenth century, charting the mission's rise as a central node (1846–66) and its decline into marginality (1867–98). In the process, the chapter speaks to a broader transformation of the Catholic mission network in which Saint-Jean-Baptiste was embedded.

The founding of Saint-Jean-Baptiste represented a critical step in the extension of the Catholic mission network into Rupert's Land and the North-Western Territory.[4] Since his installation as the first resident bishop in the region in 1822, Joseph-Norbert Provencher had confined his personnel to the environs of his administrative headquarters at Saint-Boniface in the Red River Colony.[5] The principal reason for this confinement was the HBC's ban on missionary activity in its chartered territory beyond the colony—a subject that will receive further consideration in the next chapter. This ban was lifted in 1839 when the governor and committee of the HBC invited the Wesleyan Methodist Missionary Society to establish posts at Norway House, Moose Factory, Cumberland House, and Fort Edmonton. The following year, the Company permitted the Anglican Church Missionary Society (CMS) to deploy a catechist to The Pas on the Saskatchewan River.[6] Determined to curb the spread of evangelical Protestantism in the interior, Provencher adopted a program of expansion beyond the confines of the Red River Colony. On 20 April 1842, he dispatched Jean-Baptiste Thibault—a thirty-two-year-old secular priest from Lévis, Lower Canada—on horseback across the western plain in search of a strategic location for a missionary beachhead.[7] Thibault established his residence seventy-five kilometres west of Fort Edmonton on the southern shore of Lac Sainte-Anne.[8] From there, he reconnoitred eastward along the North Saskatchewan River between Fort Edmonton and Fort Carlton.[9]

Thibault's attention shifted northward after his visit to Fort Pitt in the winter of 1843–44. There he encountered "a few *sauvages* from Île-à-la-Crosse" who expressed keen interest in receiving his ministrations.[10] Yet due to pressing obligations at Lac Sainte-Anne and Saint-Boniface, Thibault was unable to travel to Île-à-la-Crosse until the following year.[11] He arrived by canoe on 9 May 1845, and was warmly received by seventy-three-year-old Roderick McKenzie—Chief Factor of the English River District at Île-à-la-Crosse.[12] Over the next two weeks, Thibault visited approximately eighty "Montagnais" families living within the vicinity of the HBC fort.[13] He taught them to recite prayers in French and marvelled at their eagerness for further instruction. "All of them, from the youngest to the oldest, show an incredible zeal to learn to serve God," he reported to Provencher on 24 May. "Although my work is sometimes very hard, I must admit that it is greatly softened by the sense of consolation I feel among *sauvages* who are so docile and so eager to know the way to heaven."[14] Envisaging mass conversion, Thibault urged his bishop to deploy missionaries to Île-à-la-Crosse without delay.[15] On 26 May, he took leave of his catechumens and continued northward to Portage La Loche.[16]

Thibault's report persuaded Provencher to establish a permanent mission at Île-à-la-Crosse. In April 1846, the bishop commissioned the two youngest priests in his jurisdiction to lay the foundations of the mission—twenty-seven-year-old Louis-François Laflèche (a secular priest from Sainte-Anne-de-la-Pérade, Lower Canada) and twenty-two-year-old Alexandre-Antonin Taché (an Oblate from Rivière-du-Loup, Lower Canada).[17] The latter commission marked a departure from Provencher's exclusive reliance on secular clergy to undertake missionary work.[18] The bishop believed that the launch of *missions sauvages* beyond Red River required a degree of discipline, cohesion, and financial stability that only a religious community could provide.[19] He had consequently appealed to the Missionary Oblates of Mary Immaculate in May 1844. Having only recently established an institutional presence in Canada—at Longueuil (1842) and Bytown (1844)—the Oblates did not have sufficient numbers to deploy a hefty contingent into Rupert's Land and the North-Western Territory. Nevertheless, Joseph-Eugène-Bruno Guigues—the superior of Oblates in Canada—received instructions from the Oblate General Administration to choose two of his personnel from Longueuil to serve under Provencher.[20] Mindful of the HBC's aversion to "foreign priests," Guigues narrowed his choice to the few Canadian recruits in his otherwise entirely French community.[21] Taché seemed an obvious candidate for, despite his extreme youth, he had already displayed an aptitude for teaching and an earnest desire to serve in the west.[22] He reached Saint-Boniface in the company of his new superior, Pierre Aubert, on 25 August 1845. The two Oblates spent the following months ministering to the local Catholic population until Taché received his assignment to Île-à-la-Crosse.[23]

On 8 July 1846, Taché and Laflèche boarded HBC barges at Fort Garry and set out upon the tortuous waterways that conveyed the Portage La Loche Brigade to Île-à-la-Crosse each summer.[24] Having obtained free passage through an agreement between Provencher and George Simpson—governor of the HBC's trading territories in British North America—the young missionaries descended the Red River into Lake Winnipeg and sailed northward to the source of the Nelson River. After a brief sojourn at Norway House, they crossed the northern end of the lake to Grand Rapids and proceeded up the Saskatchewan River to Cumberland House. They then ascended the rapids of the Sturgeon-Weir and crossed over Frog Portage to the English River (known today as the Churchill River). On 10 September, Taché and Laflèche reached Île-à-la-Crosse after travelling 1,600 kilometres in just over two months.[25] With winter steadily approaching, the missionaries postponed constructing a residence and accepted McKenzie's offer of temporary room and board at the HBC fort—a cluster of houses and stores enclosed within a palisade. There they spent five months studying Cree and Chipewyan under the tutelage of McKenzie's resident interpreter.[26]

In spring, Taché and Laflèche began physical work on the mission and entrusted their labours to the patronage of Saint John the Baptist.[27] They settled into a crude log cabin that McKenzie had offered them as a gesture of goodwill. Located approximately one and a half kilometres south of the HBC fort, the cabin stood on the long-abandoned site of the NWC fort near the tip of the peninsula. It measured eleven by seven metres and had yet to be caulked, such that the elements found their way into every nook and cranny. The missionaries therefore spent two weeks filling chinks with mud and hay, then plastering the interior with a mixture of earth and ash.[28] At one end of the cabin, Laflèche built sleeping quarters and an alcove for the sacrament. The remainder of the "maison-omnibus" served as kitchen, refectory, parlour, confessional, choir, and nave.[29] These functions tended to intersect and to blend awkwardly, as Oblate missionary Vital-Justin Grandin later recalled in his description of Masses officiated by Taché in 1848:

> The missionaries celebrated Mass in the same apartment in which they cooked their meals, boiling their fish in a cauldron suspended over the chimney fire. . . . So, after communion, the celebrant would turn toward the congregation to say "Dominus vobiscum" ["The Lord be with you"] only to see his surplice-clad cantor gripping the cauldron with the help of a rag and swirling it around to prevent its contents from burning, all the while offering the congregational response ["Et cum spiritu tuo," meaning "And with your spirit"]. . . . Father Laflèche thus fused the rather disparate roles of cantor and cook while Father Taché did his best to keep a straight face.[30]

In order to lessen their reliance on the provisioning services of the HBC, Taché and Laflèche cleared a garden plot and sowed potatoes, which grew well in the sandy soil of Île-à-la-Crosse.[31] They also learned to fish in the lake where, according to Taché, "great hauls of fish crowd into our nets."[32] Their efforts to consolidate the mission were redoubled with the arrival of another Oblate in July 1848. Hailing from the Vaucluse in southeastern France, twenty-five-year-old Henri Faraud had served in the Red River Colony for a year before Provencher assigned him to Île-à-la-Crosse.[33] A skilled carpenter and woodworker, Faraud spent several months renovating the "maison-omnibus" by rebuilding its roof, panelling its interior, installing locks on its doors, and adorning its alcove with a wooden tabernacle and candlesticks.[34]

While still in the initial phases of consolidation, Saint-Jean-Baptiste served as a launching pad for Catholic missionary activity further afield. Taché and Laflèche reached an agreement whereby the former would undertake a series of excursions to outlying HBC posts while the latter—whose mobility was becoming increasingly restricted by rheumatism—would remain at Île-à-la-Crosse.[35] Thus, in late February 1847, Taché procured snowshoes, a sled, harnesses, and four emaciated dogs from McKenzie. He then ventured 165 kilometres southward to the HBC post at Green Lake, where he baptized a small party of Cree speakers. Taché returned to Île-à-la-Crosse on 5 March, only to embark four days later on a much longer expedition to the post at Reindeer Lake—a journey of approximately 550 kilometres to the northeast.[36] He travelled in the company of four HBC servants whom McKenzie had instructed to guide the young missionary. After sixteen days of arduous sledding, Taché reached Reindeer Lake and took up residence in the home of HBC clerk Charles Thomas. Over the next two months, he evangelized forty Cree- and Chipewyan-speaking families living in the vicinity of the post. Taché returned to Île-à-la-Crosse by canoe on 15 June.[37] Two months later, he departed for Fort Chipewyan on the shore of Lake Athabasca—approximately 715 kilometres northwest of Île-à-la-Crosse. Travelling by canoe in the company of "two *sauvage* guides," Taché traversed Lac Île-à-la-Crosse and headed northwestward across Clear and Buffalo Lakes, ascended La Loche River and entered Lac La Loche. He disembarked at the southeastern end of the portage, walked its twenty-kilometre trail, and re-embarked by canoe down the Clearwater and Athabasca Rivers.[38] Taché arrived at Fort Chipewyan on 2 September and was received as a guest of Chief Trader Francis Ermatinger.[39] The young missionary devoted the next three and a half weeks to evangelizing local families and reportedly performed 194 baptisms.[40] He left Fort Chipewyan by canoe on 27 September and reached Île-à-la-Crosse on 15 October—four days before ice sealed the lakes and rivers.[41]

Over the course of this intensive tour, Taché had laid the foundations of a satellite mission at each HBC post on his itinerary—namely Green Lake, Reindeer Lake, Portage La Loche, and Fort Chipewyan. These posts were subsequently visited on a semi-regular basis by missionaries from Saint-Jean-Baptiste.[42] Taché returned by dogsled to Green Lake in early January and to Reindeer Lake in early March 1848. In late August, he returned by canoe to Portage La Loche en route to Fort Chipewyan.[43] At Ermatinger's request, he prolonged his visit to the latter post by several weeks until the departure of the winter mail party on 2 January 1849.[44] This prolongation enabled Taché to grasp the strategic value of Fort Chipewyan as a potential staging point for missionary expansion to Fond-du-Lac on the eastern end of Lake Athabasca and Fort Resolution on Great Slave Lake. The task of consolidating this important position fell to Faraud, who consequently left Île-à-la-Crosse in late August and travelled by canoe to Fort Chipewyan to build a permanent chapel and residence there.[45] Meanwhile, the addition of two new Oblates to the personnel of Saint-Jean-Baptiste resulted in more regular visits to the other satellite missions. Shortly after their arrival at Île-à-la-Crosse in July 1850, twenty-five-year-old Jean Tissot (from the French department of Haute-Savoie) and twenty-six-year-old Augustin Maisonneuve (from the department of Ardèche) relieved Taché of his ministry at Green Lake, Reindeer Lake, and Portage La Loche.[46] Their presence provided much-needed reinforcement after Laflèche's rheumatism compelled him to quit Saint-Jean-Baptiste in June 1849.[47]

As Saint-Jean-Baptiste extended its influence beyond Île-à-la-Crosse, it required increasing financial support from its chief benefactor—l'Œuvre de la Propagation de la Foi. Founded in 1822 by a group of laypeople in Lyons, this society endeavoured to assist Catholic missions throughout the world by prayer and funding. To this end, it drew on hundreds of thousands of associates from virtually every diocese in France. These associates made weekly contributions to a general fund that was managed by two central councils—one in Lyons, the other in Paris. Monies from this fund were then disbursed to individual bishops, vicars, and prefects apostolic according to their stated needs.[48] Provencher was among the earliest beneficiaries. Since 1828, he had received an annual allocation from l'Œuvre for the undertaking of missionary activity in the vicinity of Saint-Boniface.[49] As the Catholic mission network expanded northwestward in the mid-1840s, Provencher repeatedly

requested that this allocation be increased in order to cover mounting travel
and provisioning expenses.[50] His requests were denied on the grounds that
civil unrest in France—culminating in the revolution of 1848—was hindering
the administration of l'Œuvre and reducing donations from its associates.[51]
Provencher's allocation was consequently frozen at its 1845–46 level, and
all of his nascent missions beyond Red River faced the prospect of closure.
In January 1849, Taché and Faraud received orders from Saint-Boniface to
restrict their ministry to the immediate vicinity of Saint-Jean-Baptiste and to
abandon all satellite missions until l'Œuvre could provide sufficient funding
for their maintenance.[52]

This funding was ultimately secured through the intercession of the Oblate
General Administration in Marseilles.[53] In the aftermath of Laflèche's departure, the Oblate General Administration took an increasingly active interest
in Saint-Jean-Baptiste and its satellite missions, as these were now staffed
entirely by members of the congregation.[54] Bishop Charles-Joseph-Eugène de
Mazenod of Marseilles—founder and first Superior General of the Oblates—
personally recommended these missions to l'Œuvre and affirmed that they
were worthy of financial support. In February 1850, Mazenod informed the
central councils of Lyons and Paris that these missions were the unique charge
of his congregation and that they were maintained by the selfless dedication
of his "beloved sons . . . who live in a frozen land and so far apart from one
another that we must incur enormous expense to provision them. God alone
can fathom the suffering that these men endure for His glory and for the
salvation of those poor, abandoned souls."[55] Through Mazenod's commenda-
tion, the Oblate missions of Rupert's Land and the North-Western Territory
obtained a permanent annual allocation that was entirely separate from the
one granted to Provencher.[56] To ensure the regular replenishment and periodic
augmentation of this fund, Mazenod instructed his missionaries to send letters
and reports to the central councils of Lyons and Paris. These texts could then
be published in *Les Annales de la Propagation de la Foi*—the official organ of
l'Œuvre—and circulated among the French Catholic reading public in order
to elicit general interest, financial support, and vocations.[57]

Informing Mazenod's advocacy was a realization of the growing importance
of Saint-Jean-Baptiste within the broader Oblate apostolate. The mission was
quickly becoming the de facto administrative headquarters of Catholic missionary activity in Rupert's Land and the North-Western Territory. Its rise
to prominence was accelerated in November 1849, when Provencher recommended to the Canadian bishops that Taché be nominated as his coadjutor

with the right of future succession.[58] Mazenod welcomed this nomination, as it endowed his congregation with jurisdiction over a vast mission territory.[59] When Rome ratified the nomination and appointed Taché Bishop of Arath *in partibus infidelium*—a titular see—on 14 June 1850, Mazenod ordered him to accept the appointment and insisted on personally consecrating the young bishop. Obediently, Taché left Saint-Jean-Baptiste in June 1851 and travelled to France, where he was consecrated by Mazenod in the cathedral of Viviers on 23 November 1851.[60] Besides conferring episcopal ordination on Taché, Mazenod appointed him vicar of missions (i.e., Oblate superior) of Rupert's Land and the North-Western Territory, thereby detaching the region from the Oblate Province of Canada.[61] Taché returned to Saint-Jean-Baptiste on 11 September 1852 and undertook the administration of his vicariate from there.[62] He remained at the mission after succeeding Provencher as Bishop of Saint-Boniface upon the latter's death on 7 June 1853. Entrusting diocesan affairs to Thibault and Laflèche, Taché postponed relocating to Saint-Boniface until he was canonically compelled to take possession of his cathedral in November 1854.[63] After his enthronement, Taché returned frequently to Saint-Jean-Baptiste and continued supervising its consolidation over the next two years.[64] Yet his perambulation between Saint-Boniface and Île-à-la-Crosse soon presented serious logistical problems, thus prompting him to write to the Oblate General Administration in June 1856 to request the appointment of an Oblate coadjutor with permanent residence at Saint-Jean-Baptiste.[65]

Acceding to Taché's request, the Oblate General Administration narrowed its choice of candidates to Oblates residing at Saint-Jean-Baptiste and its satellite missions in January 1857. Four newcomers had lately reinforced this contingent. The first was thirty-year-old Henri Grollier (from the department of Hérault), who had accompanied Taché on his return voyage from France in 1852.[66] Grollier had spent only a week at Saint-Jean-Baptiste before continuing northward to assist Faraud in consolidating Nativité (Fort Chipweyan) and Notre-Dame-des-Sept-Douleurs (Fond-du-Lac) missions.[67] The second newcomer was twenty-eight-year-old Valentin Végréville (from the department of Mayenne), who had arrived at Saint-Jean-Baptiste in mid-July 1853 and who had subsequently established Saint-Raphaël mission at Cold Lake—approximately 180 kilometres southwest of Île-à-la-Crosse.[68] Thirty-three-year-old René Rémas (from the department of Mayenne) was the third newcomer. After a brief posting at Saint-Jean-Baptiste in October 1853, Rémas had ventured 320 kilometres southwestward to lay the foundations of Notre-Dame-des-Victoires mission at Lac La Biche.[69] The most recent arrival was twenty-seven-year-old

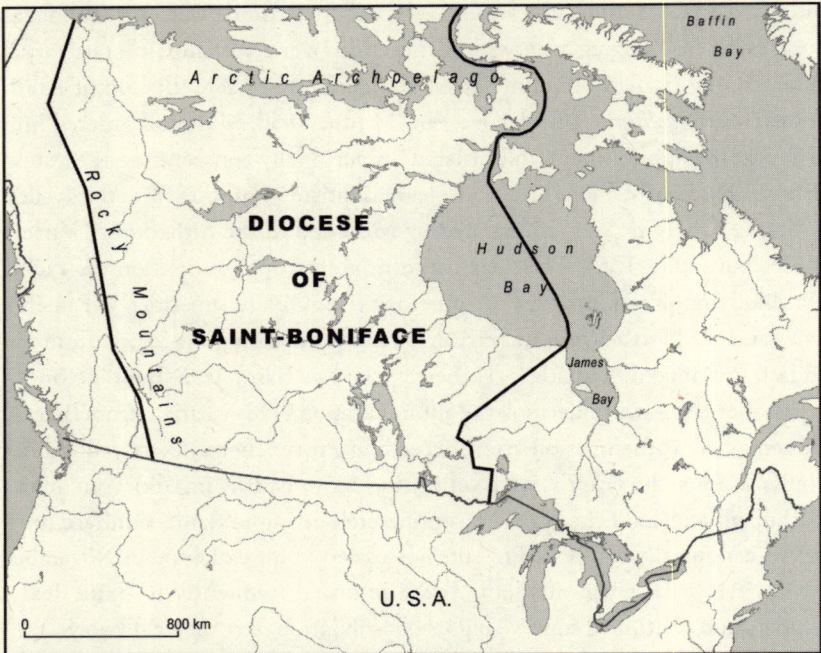

Figure 1. The Diocese of Saint-Boniface, 1854.

Vital-Justin Grandin (from the department of Mayenne). Grandin had passed through Saint-Jean-Baptiste in July 1855 en route to la Nativité and Notre-Dame-des-Sept-Douleurs, where he assisted Faraud and Grollier.[70] Despite having comparatively little experience in the mission field, Grandin was deemed *dignissimus inter dignos*—worthiest among worthies—by the Oblate General Administration and appointed Bishop of Satala *in partibus infidelium* by the Holy See on 10 December 1857.[71] He initially refused the appointment on account of his youth, frail constitution, and pronounced speech impediment. Yet Mazenod considered the matter non-negotiable and summoned Grandin to Marseilles to receive consecration. The chastened appointee left Saint-Jean-Baptiste in late August 1859 and was consecrated by Mazenod on 30 November. Grandin was installed as coadjutor upon his return to Saint-Jean-Baptiste on 4 October 1860, effectively elevating Île-à-la-Crosse to the status of episcopal see.[72]

While assuming an increasingly important administrative role in the Catholic apostolate, Saint-Jean-Baptiste experienced a dramatic material evolution. Impelling this evolution were Oblate lay brothers—unordained members of the congregation charged with the temporal affairs of the mission.[73] In July

1849, Saint-Jean-Baptiste welcomed the first Oblate lay brother ever deployed into Rupert's Land and the North-Western Territory—thirty-one-year-old Louis Dubé (from Saint-André de Kamouraska, Lower Canada).[74] Upon his arrival at the mission, Dubé assumed the duties of gardener, fisherman, house-keeper, and cook. His *confrères* soon delighted at the service of appetizers and desserts at mealtimes and drolly nicknamed their residence "château Saint-Jean" in acknowledgement of Dubé's refining influence.[75] The lay brother sowed new crops in the garden, and in autumn 1852 he harvested three bushels of barley as well as a substantial yield of oats, peas, onions, rutabaga, and broad beans.[76] He procured cattle from the HBC fort and was tending two cows, eight heifers, two bulls, and five calves by January 1853. This livestock enabled Dubé to supplement his *confrères'* diet with cheese, butter, and occasionally beef.[77] A second lay brother—twenty-five-year-old Patrick Bowes (from Kingston, Upper Canada)—arrived at Saint-Jean-Baptiste on 16 July 1855.[78] An accomplished carpenter and woodworker, Bowes constructed a wooden church measuring eighteen metres in length and featuring a steeple, a sculptured altar, and twelve glass windows along its nave.[79] After completing the structure in spring 1856, Bowes travelled to Lac La Biche, where he applied his carpentry skills to the consolidation of Notre-Dame-des-Victoires. He returned to Saint-Jean-Baptiste in July 1858 and began construction of a two-storeyed residence for the local mission personnel.[80] A third lay brother—twenty-four-year-old Louis Boisramé (from the department of Mayenne)—arrived at the mission on 4 October 1860 to assist Dubé and Bowes in fishing, gardening, tending livestock, and chopping and hauling firewood.[81] Yet while these lay brothers brought material improvement to Saint-Jean-Baptiste, their numbers remained too limited to release ordained Oblates from the duty of manual labour.[82] Hence, in April 1861, Végréville wrote to Taché complaining that his days were spent gardening or chopping firewood rather than in prayerful contemplation or in the study of Cree and Chipewyan.[83] The following month, Grandin reported that all Oblates at Saint-Jean-Baptiste—lay brothers and ordained priests alike—were preoccupied with gardening and with building a cowshed.[84] In hopes of entrenching a clear division between temporal and spiritual ministries, Grandin appealed for vocations to the Oblate brotherhood in a letter published in *Les Annales de la Propagation de la Foi* in 1863: "For our consolation and for the betterment of our work, may the Lord increase the number of good brothers who assist us. Their mission is a humble one, but it is very beautiful and very important."[85]

Though short of Oblate manpower, Saint-Jean-Baptiste was enhanced by the arrival of three Sisters of Charity of Montreal—known colloquially as

Grey Nuns—in autumn 1860.[86] Having established an institutional presence at Saint-Boniface sixteen years earlier, the Grey Nuns accepted the invitation of the Oblate General Administration to expand beyond Red River and to establish a daughter convent at Île-à-la-Crosse.[87] They agreed to labour *gratis pro Deo* in the fields of education, health care, and social work, stipulating only that the Oblates provide them with food, clothing, and ownership of a local residence.[88] Accordingly, two of their members—twenty-seven-year-old Sister Agnès (*née* Marie-Rose Caron from Louiseville, Lower Canada) and twenty-two-year-old Sister Philomène Boucher (from Saint-Rémi, Lower Canada)—were dispatched to Île-à-la-Crosse from the motherhouse in Montreal on 4 June 1860.[89] Agnès and Boucher were joined at Saint-Boniface by twenty-three-year-old Sister Pepin (*née* Marie-Anne Lachance from La Malbaie, Lower Canada).[90] The three young nuns travelled under the escort of Grandin and twenty-seven-year-old Jean Séguin (from the department of Puy-de-Dôme), a recently ordained Oblate assigned to Saint-Jean-Baptiste.[91] After an arduous ten-week journey along the HBC transport system, the party reached Île-à-la-Crosse on 4 October.[92] The nuns took up residence in a two-storeyed structure lately completed by Dubé and Bowes. Measuring eleven by seven metres, the structure contained a refectory, a kitchen, a dormitory, and a common room. It was blessed on the feast day of Saint Bruno (6 October) and was consequently entrusted to his celestial patronage.[93] "Le couvent Saint-Bruno" (Saint Bruno Convent) was delineated as a feminine space into which Oblates were to consign duties and chores that required "more experienced hands and maternal care."[94] Hence, Dubé hauled cauldrons, kettles, spits, pans, dishes, cups, and cutlery to the convent and relinquished housekeeping responsibilities to its newly installed residents.[95] Grandin, Végréville, and Faraud ceased administering homeopathic remedies at Saint-Jean-Baptiste and referred cases of physical affliction to the convent.[96] Faraud himself became a regular patient at Saint-Bruno as his worsening rheumatism occasioned long periods of bed rest and constant medical attention between 1860 and 1863.[97]

Beyond tending to the alimentary and medical needs of mission personnel, the Grey Nuns engaged directly in the work of evangelization by providing local children with a Catholic education—an undertaking that will receive detailed consideration in Chapter 3. On 25 November 1860, the nuns opened a convent boarding school for nine girls and six boys.[98] These schoolchildren were divided into two cohorts—a *pensionnat supérieur* (comprising children of HBC officers) and a *pensionnat inférieur* (comprising children of HBC servants and three orphans).[99] The ranks of both *pensionnats* increased steadily over the following years as the Grey Nuns welcomed children from HBC posts throughout the English River District together with a growing number of orphans and foundlings. Enrolment rose to seventeen in 1862, nineteen in 1863, twenty-two in 1864, twenty-eight in 1865, and thirty in 1866.[100] Assembled in the common room at Saint-Bruno, these pupils followed a morning curriculum—consisting of reading, writing, and arithmetic—under Pepin's tutelage. In the early afternoon, they attended catechism class taught by one of the ordained Oblates of Saint-Jean-Baptiste. Later in the afternoon, the girls received instruction in cooking, cleaning, and sewing from Agnès while the boys learned carpentry, husbandry, and maintenance from Dubé.[101] At eight o'clock in the evening, the girls retired to their dormitory at Saint-Bruno and the boys to their dormitory in the Oblate residence, where they remained under Dubé's supervision.[102]

The development of a solid and diversified infrastructure at Saint-Jean-Baptiste strengthened the entire network of Catholic missions in Rupert's Land and the North-Western Territory. Through their labours at Saint-Jean-Baptiste, Grey Nuns and Oblate lay brothers provided farm produce, clothing, and equipment for missionaries in outlying areas. With assistance from their female pupils, the nuns produced stockpiles of butter, cheese, and berry preserves at Saint-Bruno.[103] They made cassocks from coarse wool (obtained at the HBC fort), as well as hats, coats, mittens, trousers, and boots from animal skins.[104] The lay brothers kept a store of dried pork, beef, and fish, as well as barrels of potatoes, wheat, oats, barley, onions, and rutabaga. They made fishnets, snowshoes, dogsleds, and harnesses with assistance from male pupils.[105] Shortly after his arrival at Saint-Jean-Baptiste in September 1862, forty-five-year-old Joseph Salasse (an Oblate lay brother from the department of Savoie) procured a hand-powered mill from the HBC fort and began grinding flour at the mission.[106] Thus, by the early 1860s, Saint-Jean-Baptiste had become sufficiently endowed to serve as a central provisioning depot for a vast territory. The mission outfitted Taché and Grandin on their annual episcopal visits to Portage La Loche, Green Lake, and Cold Lake between 1860 and 1866.[107] It also outfitted thirty-year-old Julien Moulin (an ordained Oblate from the department of Ille-et-Vilaine) on his overland expedition from Green Lake to Fort Carlton, where he founded a mission in December 1860. Saint-Jean-Baptiste continued to provision Moulin's mission throughout the 1860s.[108] Concurrently, Saint-Pierre mission (Reindeer Lake) drew many of its supplies from the same source. Appointed resident superior at Saint-Pierre in August 1861, Végréville placed immediate strain on the stores of Saint-Jean-Baptiste by requisitioning foodstuffs, clothing, and equipment for himself and his two subordinates—thirty-one-year-old Alphonse Gasté (an ordained Oblate from the department of Mayenne) and thirty-three-year-old Jean Pérréard (an Oblate lay brother from the department of the Rhône).[109] Until his reassignment in April 1864, Végréville dispatched Gasté and Pérréard to Saint-Jean-Baptiste periodically to restock on essential supplies.[110] For their part, Oblates in the Athabasca and Mackenzie River basins (northeast of Portage La Loche) also drew on the stores of Saint-Jean-Baptiste. Although detached from the jurisdiction of the Bishop and Coadjutor Bishop of Saint-Boniface by the canonical erection of the Vicariate Apostolic of Athabasca-Mackenzie (13 May 1862), these Oblates remained dependent on provisions from Saint-Jean-Baptiste.[111] Hence, while visiting Saint-Jean-Baptiste en route to la Nativité in late July 1862, twenty-three-year-old Émile Petitot (an ordained Oblate from the department of Côte-d'Or) and twenty-two-year-old Émile Grouard (an ordained Oblate from the department of Sarthe) procured butter, flour, potatoes, and dried meat for themselves and their *confrères* in the north.[112]

In addition to producing supplies for outlying missions, Saint-Jean-Baptiste served as a point of transshipment for manufactured goods and liturgical articles sent from Saint-Boniface. The mission was able to perform this function because of its strategic location on the main route of HBC barges plying between Red River and Portage La Loche.[113] In accordance with an agreement brokered between HBC Governor George Simpson and Taché in 1853, the HBC delivered freight directly to Saint-Jean-Baptiste each July or August.[114] This freight consisted of items that had been ordered the previous year by the Oblate superior of Saint-Jean-Baptiste and his *confrères* in outlying posts. These missionaries sent their orders to Taché, who subsequently arranged for the shipment of specified items from Great Britain and France by way of York Factory (on Hudson Bay) and Norway House (on Lake Winnipeg). Once received at the episcopal palace in Saint-Boniface, the items were inventoried, packaged, and loaded aboard HBC barges bound for Portage La Loche.[115] At Saint-Jean-Baptiste, Oblate lay brothers unloaded the items and checked them against an accompanying copy of the inventory. Pieces addressed to the Vicariate Apostolic of Athabasca-Mackenzie were reloaded and shipped north to Portage La Loche, thence hauled to the Clearwater River and shipped up the Athabasca River.[116] Pieces addressed to Reindeer Lake and Fort Carlton were held in storage at Saint-Jean-Baptiste until they were claimed and removed by Oblates stationed in those areas.[117] Pieces addressed to Notre-Dame-de-la-Visitation (Portage La Loche), Saint-Raphaël (Cold Lake), and Saint-Julien (Green Lake) also were stored at Saint-Jean-Baptiste and were carried to their respective destinations by Oblates on pastoral visits. Because these missions were served directly from Saint-Jean-Baptiste, they drew from a common repository of liturgical articles. Oblates lugged vestments, chalices, ciboria, patens, hosts, and flagons of wine to these missions for the celebration of Mass, then returned these items to storage at Saint-Jean-Baptiste.[118]

As a further consequence of its location on an HBC thoroughfare, Saint-Jean-Baptiste served as the communications hub between Saint-Boniface and the far-flung missions of Rupert's Land and the North-Western Territories. Ordained Oblates stationed in the Saskatchewan, English, Athabasca, and Mackenzie River basins were required to send written reports to Saint-Jean-Baptiste at least twice a year. Each Oblate was expected to provide detailed information on the progress of the faith among his neophytes and to comment on his own spiritual and physical condition. He was then to transmit his report to Saint-Jean-Baptiste by the courier system that served the HBC posts of the English River and Athabasca Districts in the winter and summer. Alternatively, he could entrust his report to a fellow Oblate or to an HBC servant travelling to Île-à-la-Crosse.[119] Once all of the reports had been received at Saint-Jean-Baptiste, they were read by Grandin or—in the event of his absence—by his deputy.[120] Grandin or his deputy then prepared a general report on the progress of the apostolate to Rupert's Land and the North-Western Territory. Administrative records—such as inventories, receipts, and lists of necessary provisions—were appended to the general report. So too were documents marked for forwarding to France—principally reports to the Oblate General Administration and letters to l'Œuvre de la Propagation de la Foi.[121] The completed dossier left Saint-Jean-Baptiste by barge in late August or by dogsled in early January.[122] After its delivery to the episcopal palace in Saint-Boniface, the dossier was scrutinized by Taché and/or by his counsellor, Joseph Lestanc (an ordained Oblate from the department of Finistère).[123] Documents destined for France were removed and inserted into Taché's correspondence with the Oblate General Administration and l'Œuvre.[124] The remainder of the dossier provided information upon which Taché ordered supplies for distant posts, deployed reinforcements into the mission field, and issued instructions to his coadjutor. In his written response to Grandin, Taché included a list of supplies bound for Saint-Jean-Baptiste the following summer, directives on supervising missionaries, and administrative news from France. His letter left

Saint-Boniface by courier in December or by barge in June.[125] After reaching
Saint-Jean-Baptiste, the letter was read by Grandin and its contents were
relayed to missionaries in outlying posts by circular.[126]

The combination of its strategic location and its diversified infrastructure
made Saint-Jean-Baptiste the central meeting place for Oblates serving in
Rupert's Land and the North-Western Territories. Beginning in 1860, the
mission hosted an annual retreat in October. This event drew Oblates—
ordained priests and lay brothers alike—from distant missions to spend eight
days in communal worship and reflection.[127] Although intended primarily
as a devotional and reflective exercise, the retreat also served an important
administrative function, as it facilitated interpersonal communication
between Oblates. It enabled superiors to obtain first-hand information on
particular missions while allowing subordinates to receive clarification on
matters of discipline and organization. Hence, in 1860, Taché availed himself
of the retreat at Saint-Jean-Baptiste to consult with his personnel about the
missions of the Athabasca and Mackenzie River basins. It was during this
consultation that he and Grandin resolved to petition the Holy See to detach
the northern missions from the Diocese of Saint-Boniface and to consign them
to a new vicariate administered by a resident *évêque-roi* (bishop-king)—an
office to which they subsequently nominated Faraud.[128] Four years later, the
retreat at Saint-Jean-Baptiste was attended by the Oblate Superior General's
delegate, thirty-eight-year-old Florent Vandenberghe (an ordained Oblate
from Belgium).[129] Over the course of the retreat, Vandenberghe collected
testimony from Taché, Grandin, Moulin, Gasté, Dubé, and Pérréard in order
to prepare a comprehensive report on *missions sauvages* for the Oblate General
Administration.[130]

Thus, by the mid-1860s, Saint-Jean-Baptiste had come to occupy a piv-
otal role in the Catholic apostolate to Rupert's Land and the North-Western
Territory. In addition to serving as the administrative headquarters of the
Coadjutor Bishop of Saint-Boniface, the mission had become a centre of
education and health care, a provisioning depot, a point of transshipment, and
a rallying place for Oblates dispersed throughout the region. As a corollary of
its strategic importance, Saint-Jean-Baptiste had assumed an exalted position
in the consciousness of Oblates. They referred lyrically to the mission as the
"cradle of bishops," as four prelates had begun their missionary careers there:
Taché, Bishop of Saint-Boniface; Grandin, Bishop of Satala *in partibus infidelium* and Coadjutor Bishop of Saint-Boniface; Faraud, Bishop of Anemour *in
partibus infidelium* and Vicar-Apostolic of Athabasca-Mackenzie (consecrated

on 30 November 1863); and Laflèche, Bishop of Anthedon *in partibus infidelium* and Coadjutor Bishop of Trois-Rivières (consecrated on 25 February 1867, succeeded to the see on 30 March 1870).[131] In his published overview of the Oblate enterprise in Rupert's Land and the North-Western Territory—*Vingt années de missions dans le Nord-Ouest de l'Amérique* (1866)—Taché presented Saint-Jean-Baptiste as the congregation's crowning achievement. He paid it homage in describing his visit there in autumn 1864:

> At the first light of dawn, our canoe entered the lake of Île-à-la-Crosse and soon the immense cross, the soaring steeple, the church building, the entire mission of Saint-Jean-Baptiste reflected the rays of a magnificent September sun. A flood of light spilled upon us, and our soul was filled with the most delightful emotions. There, on the shores of that tranquil lake, on a spot that would enchant many a visitor, stood that establishment which has already done so much good and which will do even more in the future. . . . From all directions a festive fusillade assured us that our joy and contentment were reciprocated; cheerful schoolchildren greeted us waving small flags. . . . The Reverend Father Visitor [Vandenberghe], having arrived at Île-à-la-Crosse over a month earlier, awaited us alongside six other Oblates—two bishops, two priests, and two lay brothers. He told us that he could never have imagined finding a mission so complete, a work so perfect, isolated in these woods and lying so far beyond the boundaries of the civilized world. His words brought us great satisfaction.[132]

To a degree, Taché's panegyric reflected a sense of individual accomplishment in the mission's progress. As its co-founder, Taché acknowledged that he felt personally invested in Saint-Jean-Baptiste: "This heart once beat so fervently on that distant shore. This heart has loved it so! And how this body has suffered on that shore, watering it with its sweat! We lived there for ten years and . . . we once believed that we would breathe our last there. All of this entitles us to call it *ad propria* ['our own,' or 'our home' in this context]."[133] Yet far from mere self-congratulation, Taché's panegyric reflected a sentiment that was widespread among his fellow Oblates. Grouard and Petitot had both marvelled at Saint-Jean-Baptiste while passing through in July 1862. In their respective letters to Taché, the former Oblate praised the mission's scenic charm while the latter praised its ideal strategic positioning.[134] Three and a half years

later, twenty-nine-year-old Jean-Marie Caër (an ordained Oblate from the
department of Finistère) expressed astonishment upon arriving at Saint-Jean-
Baptiste. He reported to the Oblate General Administration that the mission
emanated "a certain air of civilization that I have not encountered in any other
mission since my departure from Saint-Boniface."[135]

This sense of collective wonder was short-lived. It perished in the fire that
ravaged Saint-Jean-Baptiste on Friday, 1 March 1867.[136] While taking their
evening meal at Saint-Bruno, Grandin, Caër, Dubé, Bowes, and Boisramé
were alerted by a schoolboy that their residence had caught fire. The Oblates
rushed from the refectory and proceeded to fight the blaze, but their efforts
were thwarted by a southward wind that fanned the flames toward a warehouse stocked with gunpowder. Fearing mass injuries and loss of life, Grandin
ordered the mission personnel and schoolchildren to assemble on the frozen
lake at a safe distance from the imminent explosion:

> We distanced ourselves from the scene of the fire. The sisters,
> the children, the neighbours—we all just stood there on the ice,
> condemned to watch the destruction of so much hard work and
> so many hopes. . . . We heard something detonate: it was the gun-
> powder exploding and sending flaming debris in all directions.
> Fortunately, no one was hurt. . . . By nine o'clock, all was over, that
> is to say that everything had been destroyed. . . . We did not even
> have a blanket to shield ourselves from the cold of twenty to thirty
> degrees. The fire had melted the snow, so our feet were soaking and
> not a single one of us could change shoes.[137]

Although there were no casualties, the conflagration had claimed the Oblate
residence and the schoolboys' dormitory together with everything inside—
bedding, clothing, furniture, and a library that had taken two decades to
compile. It had also claimed stores of farm produce, dried meat, manufactured
goods, and liturgical articles.[138] Left with few alternatives, Grandin installed
his four *confrères* and nineteen schoolboys in a hastily refurbished warehouse
and supplied them with blankets borrowed from the HBC fort. Then, after
sending orders to Father Julien Moulin to leave Saint-Pierre (Reindeer Lake)
and assume temporary direction of Saint-Jean-Baptiste, Grandin set off on 15
March to procure emergency provisions and solicit relief funds.[139]

Grandin's efforts on behalf of Saint-Jean-Baptiste stretched over a year and
drew on an array of benefactors. At Saint-Boniface, he persuaded Taché and

Lestanc to reorganize and repackage the annual consignment to the missions of Rupert's Land and the North-Western Territory so as to provide Saint-Jean-Baptiste with bare essentials. In notifying the Oblate personnel of Saint-Pierre of this measure, Grandin warned of looming shortages throughout the entire mission network: "Monseigneur Taché is going out of his way to alleviate the suffering of the priests and brothers of Île-à-la-Crosse. He is unpacking and repacking all of the bales destined for the other missions to offset losses and relieve the poor victims of the fire."[140] From Saint-Boniface, Grandin travelled to Canada and thence to France, where he appeared in person before the Paris council of l'Œuvre de la Propagation de la Foi in October. He informed the council that Saint-Jean-Baptiste had suffered 60,000 francs in damages and was in urgent need of a special allocation.[141] After consulting with its counterpart in Lyons, the council advanced Grandin 12,000 francs and promised an additional allocation of 38,080 francs the following year.[142] While still in Paris, Grandin appealed for reinforcements from the Oblate General Administration (which had relocated from Marseilles in 1862).[143] He consequently obtained four recruits for Saint-Jean-Baptiste: twenty-five-year-old Prosper Légeard (an ordained Oblate from the department of Mayenne); forty-six-year-old François Leriche (an Oblate lay brother from the department of Mayenne); twenty-five-year-old Célestin Guillet (an Oblate lay brother from the department of Mayenne); and twenty-six-year-old Auguste Némoz (an Oblate lay brother from the department of Isère). These recruits accompanied Grandin as he sailed from Brest on 25 April 1868.[144]

The travellers reached Saint-Jean-Baptiste on 29 August.[145] They lent immediate assistance to their *confrères*, who had been absorbed in reconstruction over the previous year.[146] Leriche—a former blacksmith and farrier—set up a forge and wrought hinges, nails, locks, latches, and tools. He also mended pots, pans, and other kitchen utensils from Saint-Bruno.[147] Légeard and Némoz assisted Bowes in cutting and planing lumber for the new Oblate residence—a task that was facilitated by Grandin's procurement of a "sawing machine."[148] Besides relieving Dubé of his responsibility for tending livestock, Guillet began tanning hides and making soap from rendered beef fat.[149] Yet even as Saint-Jean-Baptiste underwent renewal, Grandin expressed misgivings about the mission's ability to resume its multifarious functions. He opined that the mission had sustained too much infrastructural damage to accommodate large numbers of visitors and to continue producing, storing, and transshipping supplies. His principal concern, however, was for the welfare of the resident personnel—half of whom still slept in a cramped, weather-beaten warehouse. Inadequate lodgings and limited food supplies obliged Grandin to consider transferring several of these missionaries elsewhere.[150] Doubtful that Saint-Jean-Baptiste could continue serving as his administrative headquarters, Grandin left on 1 October 1868.[151]

Three weeks later, Grandin took up residence at the mission of Saint-Albert—approximately 640 kilometres southwest of Saint-Jean-Baptiste.[152] Founded in January 1861 by Taché and thirty-three-year-old Albert Lacombe (an ordained Oblate from Saint-Sulpice, Lower Canada), Saint-Albert showed strong potential as a base of operations.[153] Its location on the Sturgeon River—a tributary of the North Saskatchewan—allowed for relatively easy provisioning from Fort Edmonton. It also provided access to a string of nascent missions along the North Saskatchewan—Saint-Joachim (established in 1860), Saint-Paul-des-Cris (established in 1865), Saint-François-Régis at Fort Pitt (established in 1865), and the mission at Fort Carlton (established in 1860)—as well as overland access to Blackfoot territory in the south.[154] Besides its geographical advantages, the mission boasted a diversified infrastructure that included a water gristmill, a large farm, and a school-cum-infirmary staffed by Grey Nuns (established in 1863).[155] As Grandin's place of residence, Saint-Albert became the de facto seat of a new vicariate erected by the Oblate General Administration and consigned to Grandin's charge on 20 March 1868. This vicariate comprised the northern and western portions of the former Diocese of Saint-Boniface, extending diagonally from the foot of the Rocky Mountains to Hudson Bay. On 22 September 1871, the Holy See recognized Saint-Albert as the administrative centre of this vast territory by elevating the mission to the status of episcopal see and appointing Grandin first Bishop of Saint-Albert.[156]

Concurrent with its loss of administrative pre-eminence, Saint-Jean-Baptiste ceased functioning as a provisioning depot and a point of transshipment to outlying missions. It was divested of this function in 1868 when the HBC—preparing the transfer of its chartered territory to the Dominion of Canada and seeking to streamline its commercial operations—declined responsibility for the transport of mission freight. Henceforth, mission freight had to be conveyed from Saint-Boniface either by Red River cart along the Carlton Trail or by steamboat along the Saskatchewan River as far as Fort Carlton, Fort Pitt, or Fort Edmonton. From these posts, the freight could be shipped to its destination.[157] Grandin and Faraud were compelled to organize this transshipment and to establish supply routes in their respective jurisdictions. On 1 July 1869, the two prelates reached an agreement whereby

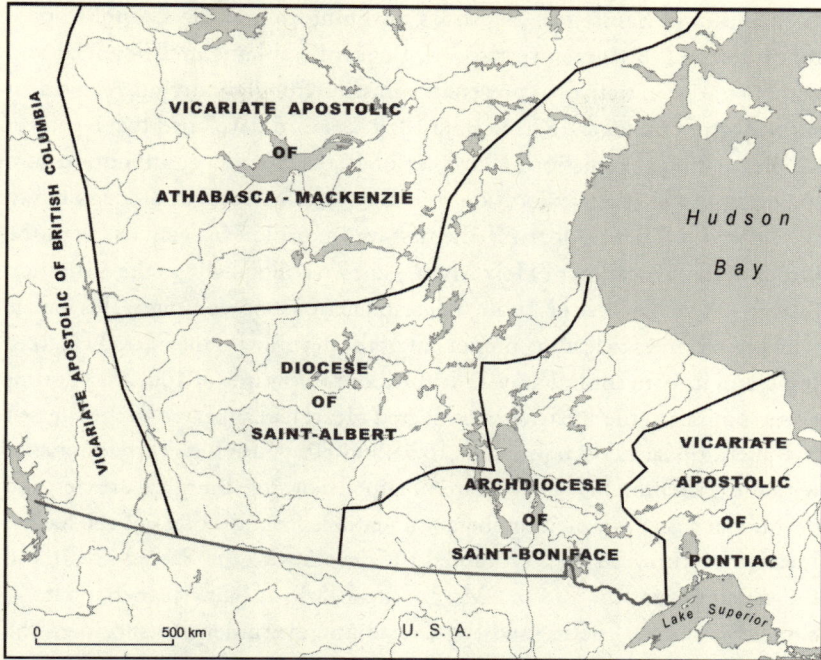

Figure 2. The Diocese of Saint-Albert and neighbouring jurisdictions, 1871.

Faraud would establish his headquarters at Notre-Dame-des-Victoires (Lac La Biche)—a mission that was technically within Grandin's jurisdiction.[158] Notre-Dame-des-Victoires subsequently became the entrepôt of the Vicariate Apostolic of Athabasca-Mackenzie. At his vicarial residence, Faraud received freight transported overland from Fort Pitt and supervised its shipment to the northern missions by way of the Little La Biche River and the Athabasca River.[159] Saint-Julien (Green Lake) acquired a similar function in the Diocese of Saint-Albert. This mission became the point of transfer between Fort Carlton and the missions of Saint-Jean-Baptiste, Notre-Dame-de-la-Visitation, and Saint-Raphaël.[160] Mission freight was transported by cart from Fort Carlton to Saint-Julien, where it was loaded onto barges and shipped north to its destination.[161] Thus, by the early 1870s, Saint-Jean-Baptiste had been displaced as the Oblates' central depot. Contemplating this displacement in a letter to the Oblate General Administration, Légeard noted: "Saint-Jean-Baptiste was once the most important of our establishments in the Northwest, but it will soon be little more than a simple, unremarkable *mission sauvage*."[162]

Mindful of Saint-Jean-Baptiste's declining role in the Catholic apostolate to the Northwest Territories, Légeard implemented financial and administrative initiatives to prevent the mission from foundering. As resident superior from October 1870 to June 1879, Légeard developed two means of supplementing the mission's allowance of 10,000 francs per annum—a sum drawn from the annual allocation of l'Œuvre de la Propagation de la Foi to the Diocese of Saint-Albert.[163] The first was to exploit his contacts with the Order of the Visitation of Holy Mary—known colloquially as the Visitation Sisters—in the Diocese of Autun (department of Saône-et-Loire). This female religious order was a leading proponent of the devotion to the Sacred Heart of Jesus, and its convent in Paray-le-Monial drew upwards of 100,000 pilgrims every summer to the site where the Sacred Heart had appeared to the Blessed Marguerite-Marie Alacoque in the 1670s and '80s.[164] Through correspondence with the Visitation Sisters, Légeard obtained clothing, liturgical articles, and devotional tracts as well as monetary donations from devotees of the Sacred Heart. In return, Légeard promoted the devotion to the Sacred Heart and the veneration of the Blessed Marguerite-Marie at Saint-Jean-Baptiste.[165] Secondly, Légeard petitioned the Canadian government to subsidize the convent boarding school. He consequently obtained grants of $300 in 1875 and in 1876, but was denied further subvention in 1877 on the grounds that the school was not located within the limits of Treaty Six.[166]

These pecuniary gains enabled Légeard to effect considerable material improvement at Saint-Jean-Baptiste. In January 1872, he obtained the transfer of Bowes—the self-styled "factotum to the missions"—from Saint-Albert, where the lay brother had served as resident carpenter for the previous two years.[167] Bowes reached Saint-Jean-Baptiste on 14 June in the company of twenty-five-year-old Léon Doucet (an ordained Oblate from the department of Loiret).[168] With assistance from Doucet and Némoz, Bowes constructed a three-storeyed residence roughcast with lime, sand, and gravel. The residence—lauded by Légeard as "the most beautiful in all the Northwest"—was entrusted to the Grey Nuns and inaugurated as their convent, refectory, and infirmary on 10 August 1874. The Oblates and schoolboys took up residence in the former "couvent Saint-Bruno" after it had been reinsulated by Bowes. The lay brother also constructed a new schoolhouse—Notre-Dame du Sacré-Coeur (Our Lady of the Sacred Heart)—that opened its doors on 14 September 1874.[169] The following spring, Légeard began refurbishing the church with new windows, a bell, external siding, internal wood panelling, and several coats of paint. He also purchased and installed a harmonium to accompany the singing of hymns during Mass.[170] Légeard's extensive renovation campaign was cut tragically short. While drafting plans for an orphanage-cum-hospice in January 1879, the thirty-five-year-old Oblate took ill and was committed to the Grey Nuns' infirmary, where he died five months later.[171] In tribute, the Oblate General Administration commissioned Louis Soullier—Oblate Assistant General—to write Légeard's biography.[172] Soullier eulogized Légeard as a model Oblate whose administrative skill and financial acumen had left a tangible legacy at Saint-Jean-Baptiste: "The traveller who wanders through the district of Île-à-la-Crosse can everywhere see traces of Father Légeard's fruitful ministry and rare virtues; he can everywhere hear testimonies to the universal and profound reverence that Father Légeard's memory inspires."[173]

Despite having honoured Légeard's life's work, the Oblate hierarchy opted to drain his beloved mission of resources and personnel over the following decade. This measure was a response to rapid demographic growth in the southern portion of the Diocese of Saint-Albert. Although Grandin had foreseen Euro-Canadian immigration as an inevitable consequence of the Rupert's Land transfer (1870), he had not anticipated its scale, its geographic concentration, or its overall impact on his diocese.[174] He had only recently established missions in the prairie grasslands—Notre-Dame-de-la-Paix (founded in 1873) near the confluence of the Bow and Elbow Rivers, and its satellite posts on the Siksiká (Blackfoot) reserve at Blackfoot Crossing, the Piikani (Peigan) reserve near the entrance of the Crowsnest Pass, and the Kainai (Blood) reserve between the St. Mary's and the Belly Rivers (all founded after the signing of Treaty Seven, 1877).[175] These missions acquired critical strategic importance when the Canadian Pacific Railway reached the Rocky Mountains in 1883, thereafter delivering a stream of settlers to the prairies and foothills.[176] From their southern bases, Oblates scrambled to minister to Catholic newcomers and to lay the foundations of churches, schools, and hospitals. To expedite their efforts, Grandin initiated a southward redeployment of personnel and resources. He justified this decision in a circular to his clergy in 1887, explaining that the south had become "the most important part of my diocese" and that the development of its missionary infrastructure was now his chief priority:

> In the part that I consider important, there is now a fairly considerable population; there are at least eight cities and many other sizeable communities. The poor *sauvages* have been confined to reserves to make room for the whites. There they await their complete destruction, which is happening quickly due to a way of

life that is unfamiliar to them and to the general immorality of *la civilisation moderne*. Thus, in order to save at least their souls and to minister to white newcomers, we must multiply our missions and our schools. . . . As you can see, dear Fathers, this part of my diocese is indeed the most important part. It is here that the bishop must reside.[177]

This administrative shift resulted in drastic financial reductions for Saint-Jean-Baptiste. The Diocese of Saint-Albert ceased subsidizing the construction of new buildings and the renovation of old ones at the mission, thus leaving local Oblates to fend for themselves.[178] Moreover, the mission's regular allocation—10,000 francs per annum in the 1870s—was permanently reduced by half and local Oblates were forbidden from making "extraordinary purchases" of "ornaments, statues, stained-glass windows, or anything of the like."[179]

Besides its financial constraints, Saint-Jean-Baptiste became chronically understaffed as a result of Grandin's prioritization of southern missions. Between 1880 and 1887, the bishop withdrew all Oblate lay brothers who had served under Légeard and reassigned them to newer missions in the south.[180] In their place, he transferred twenty-six-year-old Félix-Victor Marcilly (an Oblate lay brother from the department of Meurthe-et-Moselle) to Saint-Jean-Baptiste in 1880.[181] The following year, the mission received a second Oblate lay brother—twenty-eight-year-old Fabien Labelle (from Saint-Vincent-de-Paul, Quebec).[182] Grandin consigned the mission to the pastoral care of twenty-five-year-old Joseph Rapet (an ordained Oblate from the department of Var) in July 1881.[183] To assist Rapet in his ministry, the bishop appointed twenty-five-year-old Louis Dauphin (an ordained Oblate from the department of Mayenne) in June 1882 and twenty-seven-year-old Jules Teston (an ordained Oblate from the department of Drôme) in January 1884.[184] Grandin recognized that this corps was much too small to fulfill its spiritual and material responsibilities, which extended beyond Saint-Jean-Baptiste to include Notre-Dame-de-la-Visitation (Portage La Loche) and Saint-Julien (Green Lake) as well as nascent missions at Canoe Lake and Waterhen Lake.[185] In February 1884, the bishop acknowledged the need for an additional four Oblates at Saint-Jean-Baptiste and its satellite missions, but maintained that he could not spare the manpower to meet this need.[186] The situation worsened when Dauphin was compelled to quit Saint-Jean-Baptiste in September 1886 due to a heart condition.[187] His departure left Rapet and Teston heavily overburdened with travel duties and pastoral work. The pair devised a rota whereby Rapet would remain at Saint-Jean-Baptiste while Teston would journey to Saint-Julien by way of Canoe Lake and Waterhen Lake. Upon Teston's return, Rapet would embark for Notre-Dame-de-la-Visitation.[188] Although feasible in principle, this arrangement was frequently interrupted by the vicissitudes of mission life. For instance, during epidemic outbreaks in 1886, 1887, and 1889, Rapet and Teston were compelled to undertake simultaneous journeys in order to administer extreme unction in several different places. Saint-Jean-Baptiste was consequently left without ordained clergy for several weeks on end.[189]

Although conscious of personnel shortages and poverty at Saint-Jean-Baptiste, Grandin could offer only limited succour on account of the recent upheaval of his primary benefactors—the Oblate General Administration and l'Œuvre de la Propagation de la Foi. Crisis gripped both organizations in the wake of the French legislative election of 1877 and senate election of 1879. Republican victories in these elections led to the passing of two bills—introduced and championed by Education Minister Jules Ferry—that effectively dissolved all "unauthorized congregations" in March 1880.[190] Oblates were among the prohibited communities and were forcibly expelled from seventeen establishments across France, including their general headquarters on rue Saint-Pétersbourg in Paris.[191] Concurrently, the proceeds of l'Œuvre decreased as its associates were inundated with appeals from France's beleaguered congregations.[192] These developments had immediate implications for the Diocese of Saint-Albert. As early as December 1880, Grandin bewailed the shortage of funds and recruits that had resulted from events overseas:

> The persecution against the Church, which will soon spread throughout Europe and which is an acknowledged fact in France, leaves me more distressed and ashamed than I could possibly say. It afflicts us even here, not only by closing our novitiates and scholasticates, that is to say, our seminaries, but especially by reducing our financial resources. Our benefactors, overwhelmed by a host of charities that they must suddenly support in France, can no longer offer their customary support for my missions.... They tell me: "We are truly sorry, Monseigneur, that we cannot continue helping you. But before spreading the faith abroad, we must do what we can to maintain it at home."... Nevertheless, our expenses are increasing as our missions multiply and expand.... I really do not know how to deal with so many pressing needs.[193]

Among the repercussions of this "persecution" was the deferment of Grandin's administrative scheme for Saint-Jean-Baptiste and its outposts. Since February 1880, the bishop had been planning to divide his diocese and to consign the northeastern missions to a local vicar who would be entitled to new recruits from the Oblate General Administration and to an annual allocation from l'Œuvre. Yet in view of developments in France, Taché and Faraud dissuaded Grandin from pressing for a new vicariate.[194] "Circumstances hardly favour your plan . . . given the state of anarchy that prevails in France," asserted Faraud in February 1881. "It is difficult to imagine any increases in manpower or money. And that, after all, is the crux of everything for us: no missionaries, no money—no missions."[195] In deference to his fellow prelates, Grandin delayed pursuing the division of his diocese until April 1887, after a moderate republican government had permitted the Oblate General Administration to reoccupy its headquarters in Paris.[196] The restored administration granted its approval to Grandin's proposal and the Vicariate Apostolic of Saskatchewan was canonically erected on 20 January 1891.[197]

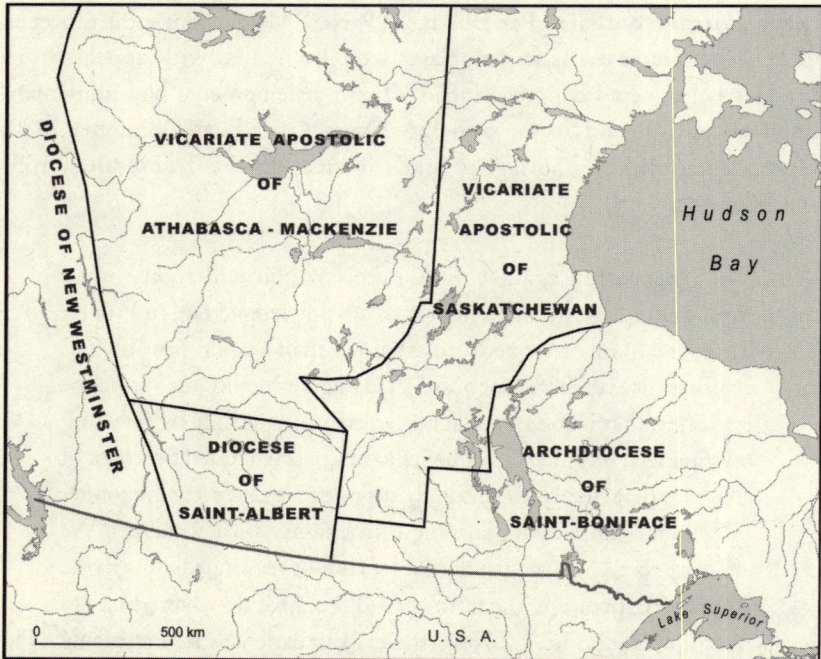

Figure 3. The Vicariate Apostolic of Saskatchewan and neighbouring jurisdictions, 1891.

Yet despite Grandin's hopes, the creation of a new vicariate brought little financial relief or personnel reinforcement to Saint-Jean-Baptiste and its outposts. Although the vicariate did receive an annual allocation from l'Œuvre and a small contingent of missionaries from the Oblate General Administration, these resources were concentrated in Prince Albert, Battleford, and other burgeoning settlements along the North Saskatchewan River.[198] After fixing his vicarial residence at Prince Albert in September 1891, forty-three-year-old Albert Pascal (an ordained Oblate from the department of Ardèche) endeavoured to establish parishes in "the fertile and temperate zone of the vicariate" where English-, French-, German-, and Polish-speaking Catholics were immigrating each year.[199] This region claimed most of Pascal's attention while the north—which he described as "a wild country . . . ill-suited to settlement on account of its severe climate and poor soil"—was left largely as it had been in the final years of Grandin's administration.[200] However, Pascal did attempt to ease the travel burden on Oblates serving at Saint-Jean-Baptiste and its outposts. In July 1892, the vicar assigned resident missionaries to Saint-Julien and to Notre-Dame-de-la-Visitation. He entrusted the former post to Teston and the latter to twenty-eight-year-old Jean-Marie Pénard (an ordained Oblate from the department of Morbihan).[201] Although this arrangement relieved Rapet of his circuit between Île-à-la-Crosse and Portage La Loche, it also deprived him of an ordained companion and increased his pastoral responsibilities at Saint-Jean-Baptiste.[202] Rapet's workload was compounded by his duty to travel annually to Saint-Julien, Notre-Dame-de-la-Visitation, and other posts in order to administer the sacrament of confirmation—normally a prelatic function, but one that Pascal performed with decreasing regularity in the northern missions after 1893.[203]

Desperate to procure a second priest for Saint-Jean-Baptiste, Rapet and Pénard wrote multiple appeals to Pascal and travelled to his vicarial residence to press their case in March and again in June 1894.[204] They eventually persuaded Pascal to send twenty-five-year-old Henri Jouan (an ordained Oblate from the department of Morbihan), who reached Saint-Jean-Baptiste on 31 March 1895.[205] Shortly after his arrival, Jouan attempted to launch an itinerant mission along a circuit that ranged from Buffalo Lake in the north to Waterhen Lake in the south.[206] This mission proved abortive, however, as Jouan contracted tuberculosis and was committed to the Grey Nuns' infirmary on 10 June 1896.[207] His illness progressed over the following year and he died on 14 September 1897.[208] Although anticipating a critical strain on the local ministry as a result of Jouan's death, Pascal considered himself powerless to forestall the situation due to the restricted number of ordained Oblates at his disposal. The vicar could do little but implore the Oblate General Administration to send him reinforcements: "Dear Father Jouan, in whom we had placed such high hopes, has died at the very beginning of his priestly and apostolic career, leaving us ... broken-hearted and inconsolable. And he has yet to be replaced!! His death has left Saint-Jean-Baptiste mission at Île-à-la-Crosse in a state of unimaginable need."[209]

As a makeshift remedy, Pascal opted to shuffle the *in situ* personnel of the northern missions. In the vicar's estimation, the forty-two-year-old Rapet was no longer a suitable superior for Saint-Jean-Baptiste, as he had grown weary and sullen after seventeen years in that position. Thus, in December 1897, Pascal reassigned him to Notre-Dame-de-la-Visitation and consigned Saint-Jean-Baptiste to the younger, more vigorous Pénard. Accordingly, the two Oblates exchanged posts the following month.[210] Pénard registered profound trepidation in assuming his new charge. He had been thrust to the helm of a mission that was falling into severe disrepair and that was burdened by a debt of more than 7,000 francs.[211] "When I became fully aware of the situation," he informed the Oblate General Administration, "I found myself sinking into despondency. I felt like a drowning man, grasping frantically for something to hold on to and finding nothing."[212]

Saint-Jean-Baptiste's rise as a centre of evangelization (1846–66) and gradual relegation to the status of a remote, ramshackle outpost (1867–98) reflected sweeping changes to the Catholic mission network in which it was embedded. In the late 1840s and '50s, Saint-Jean-Baptiste played a critical role in extending this network beyond the Red River Colony and into Rupert's Land and the North-Western Territory. Founded in an HBC trading hub, the mission served as a base of operations from which Oblates branched out along pre-existing water and land routes to establish outlying satellite posts. By 1860, Saint-Jean-Baptiste had generated several far-flung missions and served as the central node through which personnel, information, funds, and freight were conveyed to these missions. Because of its centrality in the expanding network, Saint-Jean-Baptiste emerged as the administrative headquarters of the Coadjutor Bishop of Saint-Boniface, as well as a centre of education and health care, a major provisioning depot, and a gathering place for Oblates dispersed throughout the region.

After the mid-1860s, however, Saint-Jean-Baptiste was shaken by a series of crises emanating from different parts of the mission network. Locally, the fire of 1867 weakened the physical infrastructure and compromised the administrative capacity of Saint-Jean-Baptiste, thus precipitating the transfer of the Coadjutor Bishop of Saint-Boniface to the more westerly mission of Saint-Albert. The fire sent reverberations throughout the network by forcing a temporary concentration of resources and manpower on the burnt-out mission. When the HBC overhauled its transport system in the late 1860s and 1870s, the southern portion of the network came under strain as Oblates scrambled to establish transshipment centres along the Saskatchewan River and to integrate these centres into the network via new supply routes. In the process, Saint-Jean-Baptiste was divested of its function as a central provisioning depot and point of transfer.

Yet the gravest crisis began in the late 1870s with the encroachment of Euro-Canadian settlement into the arable river valleys of the prairies and foothills—areas the mission network had barely penetrated. In order to minister to Catholic newcomers in these areas, Oblates sought to expand and to consolidate the southern portion of the mission network by establishing churches, schools, and hospitals in the 1880s. Their efforts were hindered, however, by contemporary developments in France, where state regulations against "unauthorized congregations" prevented the deployment of Oblate reinforcements and restricted the flow of finances from l'Œuvre de la Propagation de la Foi. Left with few alternatives, Oblate prelates resolved to develop the southern portion of the mission network at the expense of the northern portion. They concentrated their resources and personnel on nascent Euro-Canadian parishes, while older missions in the north—including Saint-Jean-Baptiste—grew chronically underfunded and understaffed.

By the time of Pénard's appointment as resident superior of Saint-Jean-Baptiste in January 1898, the mission bore little resemblance to the "work so perfect" that Taché had extolled over three decades earlier. No longer did it inspire the sense of pride and accomplishment expressed succinctly in the epithet "ad propria." On the contrary, the mission filled the young Oblate with an overwhelming sense of despair and desolation.

CHAPTER 2

Oblate Perceptions of the Hudson's Bay Company

In his pioneering survey, *Moon of Wintertime: Missionaries and the Indians of Canada in Encounter since 1534* (1984), John Webster Grant defined the Hudson's Bay Company (HBC) as "the unquestioned master of the north" in the mid-nineteenth century and warned that "any account of mission work that left it out of the picture would be like *Hamlet* without some reference to the state of Denmark."[1] Although historians of the Oblate apostolate have endeavoured to heed Grant's warning, they have been surprisingly reluctant to acknowledge the presence of something rotten. These historians have consistently described the relationship between Oblates and the Honourable Company as strategic, harmonious, and mutually advantageous. According to their interpretation, the HBC benefited from the Oblates' inculcation among neophytes of respect for contractual obligations and obedience to duly constituted civil authority, while the Oblates depended on the transportation, provisioning, and communications services of the HBC to expand and sustain their mission network.[2] Within this context of institutional symbiosis, personal affinities developed across ethnolinguistic and denominational lines as Anglo-Protestant traders and Franco-Catholic missionaries formed friendships based on "an immutable mutuality of experience acquired and shared in the field."[3] By dint of living at the same posts and interacting with the same Indigenous populations, HBC officers and Oblates developed mutual trust and respect which they expressed in letters, journals, and memoirs as well as through personal favours.[4] Robert Choquette has insisted that this rapport remained unaffected by the contemporaneous raging of an "anti-Catholic crusade in the English-speaking countries of the Western world."[5] Impervious to the "No-Popery" that infused British and American Protestantism in the mid-nineteenth century, HBC officers were pragmatic businessmen who appraised everything on the basis of its commercial worth to the Company. They valued Oblates as loyal supporters of Company rule and as low-maintenance clients because of their vow of poverty, their efforts to become self-sufficient, and their freedom from the obligation to provide for wives and children.[6]

In addition to providing a uniformly sanguine depiction of relations between Oblates and the HBC, historians of the Oblate apostolate have observed standard chronological boundaries. They have commonly restricted their focus to the period before the transfer of Rupert's Land to the Dominion of Canada (1870). Hence, after its cession of civil authority, the Honourable Company promptly vanishes—like the Dane's ghost—from historical accounts of the Oblate apostolate.[7] This disappearance belies the continuity and complexity of relations between the HBC and the Oblates. Although their government-subject relationship did come to an end in 1870, the HBC and the Oblates continued to interact long into the post-Confederation period. Their interaction was particularly long-lived in the boreal forest region, where the relatively slow rate of Euro-Canadian settlement left Oblates little alternative but to continue relying on the Company for a variety of services—including provisioning, freighting, transportation, and long-range communications. In the case of Île-à-la-Crosse, the HBC fort and the Oblate mission remained the only European/Euro-Canadian institutions with a permanent presence until the onset of federal intervention in local affairs in 1898. The present chapter examines the evolving relationship between these two institutions, from the Oblates' arrival in 1846 to the establishment of a federal presence fifty-two years later. In the process, this chapter illuminates a gradual transformation in Oblate perceptions of the HBC and its role in the Catholic apostolate.

As Oblates struggled to establish a presence at Île-à-la-Crosse in the mid-1840s, they recognized that the success of their endeavour depended on the fiat of the HBC. Indeed, it was only as a result of recent change in HBC policy that Oblates had managed to venture beyond the Red River Colony in the first place. Since 1818 (and possibly earlier), the Company had enforced a ban on missionaries in its chartered territory for fear that they would transform nomadic hunters into sedentary agriculturalists and foment sectarian tension among the Indigenous labour force.[8] Yet the HBC came under increasing pressure to adopt a more liberal policy toward missionaries in the late 1830s. British humanitarian organizations—principally the Aborigines' Protection

Society (established in 1837)—lobbied Parliament to discontinue the HBC's Licence for Exclusive Trade if Indigenous peoples were to remain cut off from "the benevolent purposes of Christianity . . . [and] kept as closely as possible to the barbarous and savage state."[9] Thus in 1839, when John Rowand—Chief Factor of the Saskatchewan District—reported that his servants desired access to clergy, Governor George Simpson and the London Committee had little alternative but to acquiesce.[10] Simpson sought initially to engage a single missionary organization that would be amenable to direction and supervision by the HBC. To this end, he approached the Wesleyan Methodist Missionary Society and offered accommodation at Company posts as well as transportation, communications, and provisioning services free of charge.[11] His hopes for a Wesleyan monopoly were short-lived, however, as Catholic and Anglican clergy at Red River wasted no time in requesting passage into the new mission field.[12] Anxious to avoid charges of thwarting missionaries, Simpson acceded to these requests but insisted that Catholic, Anglican, and Wesleyan clergy abide by three cardinal rules. First, they were to refrain from "injuring the Company's commercial interests" by interfering with Indigenous hunting practices or by assisting free traders—"those fur traffickers who illegally invade the Company's rights of trade."[13] Second, each denomination was to obtain permission from the governor and the London Committee before establishing itself in a particular district. Third, each denomination was to avoid expanding into a district in which another denomination had previously established itself.[14]

Seizing upon this change in policy, Bishop Provencher asserted a preemptive claim to Île-à-la-Crosse—a claim based on Jean-Baptiste Thibault's visit in May 1845.[15] To the prelate's delight, Simpson ratified the claim in May 1846 and offered free transport for two priests to Île-à-la-Crosse.[16] Additionally, Simpson assured Provencher that the priests would be lodged at the HBC fort while their future residence was under construction.[17] Fathers Louis-François Laflèche and Alexandre-Antonin Taché were accordingly conveyed to Île-à-la-Crosse on HBC barges and were received by Chief Factor Roderick McKenzie with "incomparable kindness and gracious hospitality."[18] McKenzie provided the young missionaries with a private room, daily meals, and warm clothing during the winter of 1846–47. He also offered the services of his resident interpreter, under whose guidance Laflèche and Taché began their studies in Cree and Chipewyan.[19] Far from merely obeying Simpson's orders to "make them comfortable & . . . keep them in good humour," McKenzie expressed genuine fondness for his guests and actively sought out their company and conversation.[20] As a token of his friendship, he commissioned the building of a log cabin for the missionaries in spring 1847. After its completion, McKenzie reportedly remarked: "I shan't enter the cost of the cabin on the company books: it is such a sorry thing I would be afraid of being reproached."[21]

Besides helping the missionaries settle at Île-à-la-Crosse, the HBC facilitated their expansion into outlying areas. In February 1847, McKenzie commissioned one of his servants to convey Taché by dogsled to the post at Green Lake.[22] Around the same time, McKenzie wrote to his junior officers at Rapid River (Lac la Ronge) and Reindeer Lake and instructed them to arrange for Taché's safe passage to these posts. The officers dutifully dispatched four guides to Île-à-la-Crosse, where Taché was collected on 9 March. After replenishing their provisions at Rapid River, the travellers pressed northeastward and reached Reindeer Lake on 25 March.[23] Charles Thomas—resident clerk at Reindeer Lake—offered Taché a private room furnished with the post's only table and chair. Thomas also offered his services as French-Cree translator to the young Oblate.[24] Similar hospitality awaited Taché at Fort Chipewyan, where he lodged at the residence of Chief Trader Francis Ermatinger for most of September 1847. The two men developed a friendly rapport and Ermatinger urged Taché to return the following autumn for a longer stay.[25] In his published account of these visits, Taché expressed profound gratitude to HBC officers: "In general, the members of the Honourable Hudson's Bay Company have not only rendered us great service, but they have also shown themselves to be our sincere and devoted friends. The praise that we have given Mr. McKenzie could be given in equal measure to the amiable Mr. Ermintinger [*sic*] and to many others in the Company's employ. . . . The officers of the Honourable Company have earned our gratitude and our respect."[26] In the years following Taché's initial excursions, HBC officers continued to provide the Oblates of Île-à-la-Crosse with safe passage to outlying posts and to offer them lodging. Thomas personally accompanied Taché on his second journey from Île-à-la-Crosse to Reindeer Lake (March 1848) and again assigned him a private room at the post.[27] Likewise, Ermatinger accompanied Taché on his second journey to Fort Chipewyan (September 1848) and extended the same courtesy to Father Henri Faraud the following year.[28] After McKenzie's retirement in June 1850, his successor—Chief Trader Georges-Fleury Deschambault—maintained the practice of appointing guides and arranging accommodation for itinerant Oblates.[29] Deschambault's goodwill was undoubtedly strengthened by the fact that he and Taché were blood relatives and had both grown up in Boucherville, Lower

Canada. "Mr. Deschambault is full of kindness, consideration, and generosity toward us," wrote Taché to his mother on 5 January 1853. "A thousand leagues from Boucherville, the spiritual chief (Ayamihew-Okima) and the temporal chief (Okima) are both from Boucherville. Is this not yet another circumstance arranged by Providence for my personal satisfaction?"[30]

After laying the foundations of Saint-Jean-Baptiste and its satellite missions, Oblates relied on the HBC's transport system to consolidate their position. In June 1853, Taché and Simpson entered into a formal arrangement whereby the HBC would transport freight to Saint-Jean-Baptiste at the rate charged to officers and servants of the Company.[31] Oblates subsequently adapted to the Company's provisioning cycle. Each January, the superior of Saint-Jean-Baptiste compiled a list of supplies required at the mission and its outposts. He then sent the list to Red River, where the vicar of missions ordered the supplies through an agent of the HBC. Imported goods arrived at York Factory the following summer or autumn. They were then hauled by barge up the Nelson River to Norway House, where they remained in storage over the winter. In early June, the Portage La Loche Brigade collected the supplies and carried them westward across Lake Winnipeg, past Grand Rapids, and up the Saskatchewan River to Cumberland House. From there the brigade ascended the Sturgeon-Weir River and crossed over Frog Portage to the English River. It usually reached Saint-Jean-Baptiste by late July or early August.[32] In addition to delivering freight, the brigade provided a communications relay to Saint-Boniface and also to Notre-Dame-de-la-Visitation (Portage La Loche) and points further north. It carried official reports, personal letters, and word of mouth to and from Saint-Jean-Baptiste.[33] The mission also sent and received mail by the HBC courier who passed through Île-à-la-Crosse each winter—usually in January or February.[34]

Concurrently, Oblates drew on the labour of HBC servants to develop the infrastructure of Saint-Jean-Baptiste and to meet the basic material needs of its inhabitants. In the late 1840s, the HBC outsourced servants to the mission on an ad hoc basis for small-scale projects. These projects consisted mostly of odd jobs for the fort's resident joiner and blacksmith.[35] Yet as Saint-Jean-Baptiste grew in population and importance in the 1850s, Oblates requested a wider range of services from local HBC personnel—including the chopping and hauling of firewood, the harvesting and threshing of cereal crops, the tending of livestock, and the daily provision of whitefish.[36] Thus, in 1855, the HBC initiated the practice of transferring servants to the mission, where they served one-year contracts as *engagés* (employees) under the supervision of lay brothers.[37] Oblates paid the *engagés'* wages from the annual allocation from l'Œuvre de la Propagation de la Foi.[38] They supplemented these wages with items known as *butin*—principally tea, sugar, tobacco, chocolate, peppermint, dyed cloth, powder, and shot—which they drew directly from mission stores.[39] By the early 1860s, Saint-Jean-Baptiste contracted three *engagés* per year at £22 each and provided permanent employment to former HBC servant Pierre Malbœuf.[40] Originally from Saint-Hyacinthe, Lower Canada, Malbœuf had served as a crewman in the Portage La Loche Brigade before entering the Oblates' employ as resident fisherman at Saint-Jean-Baptiste.[41]

Beyond providing essential material services, the HBC set the basic seasonal rhythm of the Oblates' evangelical activity. This rhythm emerged from long-established provisioning and trading cycles. Since the 1830s, groups of Cree- and Chipewyan-speaking hunters and their families had gathered at Île-à-la-Crosse each September in the wake of the Portage La Loche Brigade. They sought—and usually obtained—advances for their furs before travelling to their winter hunting and trapping grounds. They returned to Île-à-la-Crosse with their pelts once the waterways were free of ice—generally in late May or early June—at which point local HBC personnel began preparing the year's fur packet for shipment to York Factory.[42] These biannual gatherings enabled Oblates to make regular contact with large numbers of prospective converts and to provide them with spiritual and liturgical services. Thus, beginning around 1850, Oblates scheduled periods of intensive missionizing to coincide with these gatherings at Île-à-la-Crosse. They held the *mission de l'automne* (autumn mission) in the second half of September and the *mission du printemps* (spring mission) in the first half of June.[43] Over the course of each *mission*, Oblates preached in Cree and Chipewyan, administered the sacraments, taught prayers and hymns, oversaw devotional exercises, regularized marriages, and attempted to alter behaviour that they deemed immoral—undertakings that will receive further consideration in Chapter 4.[44] By the early 1860s, the biannual *mission* at Île-à-la-Crosse had become a focal event of the Oblate calendar in Rupert's Land and the North-Western Territory. It drew Oblates from far afield to join in a collective operation that lasted twelve to eighteen days and that required considerable physical and mental exertion.[45] In 1861, for instance, Father Valentin Végréville journeyed from Saint-Pierre (Reindeer Lake) to assist in the *mission du printemps* and fell into an exhausting daily routine upon arrival: "I would not go to bed until eleven o'clock at night and I would wake at four in the morning.... I relied on God to provide the necessary physical strength and courage. And I knew that the mission would not last long."[46]

Yet while adapting to rhythms and routines set by the HBC, Oblates expressed profound disapproval of certain Company-sanctioned practices at Île-à-la-Crosse. They deemed these practices prejudicial to their apostolate and generally incompatible with Catholic morality. Particularly troubling to Oblates was the Company's purveyance of alcohol and its endorsement of drinking on festive occasions—namely Christmas and New Year's Day. By the time of the Oblates' arrival at Île-à-la-Crosse, a seasonal custom had taken root whereby the fort dispensed port wine and spirits to HBC officers, servants, and their families for the purpose of toasting.[47] Oblates denounced the custom on the premise that drinking led to depravity, dissipation, and sin. Taché expressed this view to HBC Governor Simpson in 1853 and entreated him to discontinue the importation of alcohol altogether in the interests of morality and public order.[48] Equally distressing to Oblates was the Company's laxity in policing the sexual mores of its personnel. In 1866, for instance, Bishop Vital-Justin Grandin reported that four HBC servants at Île-à-la-Crosse were engaged in extramarital relationships with "harlots" who had lately arrived with the Portage La Loche Brigade. Grandin asked Taché to discuss the matter personally with William Mactavish, Governor of Rupert's Land: "Please, Monseigneur, speak to the Governor on my behalf and implore him to order all clerks, guides, and boatmen to stop taking on board all of the harlots whom they encounter on their way. These women can only cause trouble in the barges. . . . I always thought that concubinage was grounds for dismissal from the Company's service."[49] Underlying the appeals of Taché and Grandin was the belief that the HBC possessed sufficient power to effect moral improvement among the inhabitants of Île-à-la-Crosse but did not exercise this power with due diligence or paternal care. This power needed to be guided by moral purpose and brought into line with the goals of the Oblates apostolate.

Oblates sought especially to marshal this power in support of their education project. Beginning in the early 1860s, they elicited cooperation from high-ranking officers of the HBC in publicizing the convent boarding school at Île-à-la-Crosse and in recruiting pupils. Every year, a chief factor, chief district officer, or other commissioned officer assisted in organizing the *examen public* (public exam) in the common room at Saint-Bruno. He invited local parents to attend the *examen* and welcomed them personally to the convent on the predetermined day. There followed a program of readings, recitations, and songs by schoolchildren, after which the attending HBC officer awarded prizes and delivered a speech on the value of a mission education.[50] Chief Factor William Joseph Christie assumed this role while visiting Île-à-la-Crosse in 1865 and again in 1873.[51] Christie's speeches—both delivered in fluent French—reportedly left a deep impression on his listeners. According to Father Prosper Légeard, these speeches provided powerful encouragement for local parents to send their children to Saint-Bruno: "When they see the most prominent man in the region, when they hear him speaking as we do, they begin to reflect on the value of education. So, when officers of the company are here, we take full advantage to hold a formal exam of our schoolchildren. These exams have played a large part in giving the school at Île-à-la-Crosse its excellent reputation."[52] While grateful to HBC officers for placing their social status and political influence at the service of Saint-Bruno, Oblates believed that the school was naturally entitled to such a high level of Company support. One of Saint-Bruno's foundational objectives was to impart skills of literacy and numeracy to future HBC officers.[53] In its first year of operation, the school enrolled sons of three officers: Deschambault, Pierriche Laliberté (resident postmaster at Portage La Loche), and Bernard Rogan Ross (Chief Trader in charge of the Mackenzie River District).[54] It also enrolled three children of William Spencer (clerk in charge of Rapid River and Cold Lake) over the course of the 1860s.[55] Thus, from the perspective of Oblates, the HBC held a considerable stake in Saint-Bruno and stood to gain long-term benefits from the school.

Another endeavour in which Oblates perceived a mutuality of interests between themselves and the HBC was their campaign against free traders. Having failed to obtain the renewal of its Licence for Exclusive Trade in 1859, the Company faced an onslaught of independent competitors in the early 1860s.[56] One of these competitors—Charles McDermott of Red River—established a small operation in the vicinity of Île-à-la-Crosse in autumn 1861.[57] His presence caused consternation among the Oblates, who regarded his operation as a moral and physical threat to the community. Oblates were particularly alarmed by the conduct of the young men in McDermott's party. "The young people who have accompanied young McDermot [*sic*] are becoming a public menace; women are no longer safe here," lamented Faraud in spring 1862.[58] Father Julien Moulin made a similar, if more explicit, charge against the newcomers: "A few of Makdermot's [*sic*] people seduced some Montagnaise women and resorted to violence to have their evil way with them. . . . We can safely say that all of these people have been a scourge on this country."[59] While outraged at instances of sexual predation and violence, Oblates feared a more insidious and ultimately more destructive evil. According to Faraud, McDermott's party had imported alcohol as an article of trade and had thus

initiated a process that would have devastating consequences for the local
population: "I am certain that our poor missions will soon suffer greatly, if they
are not destroyed altogether, because of the opposition [i.e., free traders] and
their traffic in drink."[60] In hopes of staving off the moral and physical danger
posed by free traders, Oblates urged hunters and trappers in the vicinity of
Île-à-la-Crosse to continue dealing exclusively with the HBC and to shun
commerce with newcomers. Oblates conveyed this message through public
preaching during their biannual *missions* and through private conversation
with local hunters and their families.[61]

Thus, by the mid-1860s, Île-à-la-Crosse had become the site of a complex
and mutually reinforcing relationship between the Oblates and the HBC.
Oblates depended on the Company for the temporal sustenance of their
mission and for the basic rhythm of their evangelical activity. They invoked
the Company's authority to enforce their vision of moral order and to
legitimize their education project. In turn, Oblates served the interests of the
HBC by providing schooling for future officers and by voicing disapproval
of free traders. This symbiosis between Oblates and the Company gave rise
to expressions of mutual goodwill and appreciation. For instance, during his
residence at Île-à-la-Crosse (1849–51, 1852–64), Deschambault frequently
invited Oblates to the fort and treated them to long, lingering dinners.[62] He
also supplied the mission with fresh meat at no charge when the local fishery
foundered in the summer and autumn of 1861.[63] For their part, Oblates sent
gifts of milk, butter, cheese, eggs, and berry preserves to the fort and also loaned
their sled dogs when HBC personnel were in need of them.[64] Moreover, when
travelling from Île-à-la-Crosse to an outlying mission or trading post, Oblates
and HBC personnel frequently carried each others' provisions, letters, and
even oral messages.[65]

Yet while engaged in a mutually supportive relationship with the HBC
at Île-à-la-Crosse, Oblates perceived a very different situation developing
at other trading posts. These posts had become theatres of rivalry between
Catholic and Anglican missionaries since the expiry of the HBC's Licence for
Exclusive Trade, at which point the Company had ceased regulating the establishment of new missions and had adopted a policy of impartiality in religious
matters.[66] The rivalry began in the Mackenzie River District, where Oblates
had held a foothold at Fort Resolution (Saint-Joseph mission) since 1854.[67]
When Anglican Archdeacon James Hunter arrived in the district in August
1858, Oblates hastened to expand beyond Fort Resolution and to establish
themselves at other trading posts so as to counter the advance of Anglicanism.

Spearheading this expansion was Father Henri Grollier, who founded three missions in rapid succession: Sacré-Cœur de Jésus at Fort Simpson (1858); Sainte-Thérèse-d'Avila at Fort Norman (1859); and Notre-Dame de Bonne-Espérance at Fort Good Hope (1859).[68] As he endeavoured to consolidate these posts and to continue founding new ones, Grollier reported that his efforts were being thwarted by the "fanaticism" and "anti-Catholic hatred" of local HBC officers. He complained in 1861 that the officers in charge of Fort Resolution, Fort Norman, Fort Yukon, and Fort McPherson (Peel's River) had refused him room, board, and transport while extending every courtesy imaginable to Anglican missionary William West Kirkby.[69] On the basis of Grollier's complaints, Bishop Grandin wrote to Governor Mactavish and to Bishop Taché on 20 September 1861 and formally accused HBC officers in the Mackenzie River District of championing the Anglican cause.[70] Chief Trader Ross subsequently assured the bishops that he and his officers abided by their "obligations to the Company to treat all religions alike" and suggested that Grollier's experience had resulted from personal differences with particular officers.[71] Grandin was not convinced by Ross's claims of neutrality. During his three-year tour of the northern missions (1861–64), the bishop reported sceptically on his encounters with HBC officers in the Mackenzie River District. "All of these gentlemen are friendly enough to me, and Mr. Ross assures me that they will be friendly to all missionaries who in turn are friendly to them," he wrote to Taché in April 1862. "One must take all this with a grain of salt. . . . They are humiliated to see us succeed where Protestant ministers fail; after all, they are the ones who brought the ministers here and they share a common cause."[72]

Oblates expressed similar suspicions about HBC officers in the English River District. They were particularly wary of Chief Factor Roderick McKenzie's son, Samuel. As resident postmaster at Rapid River (1843–51, 1853–62), Samuel McKenzie had assisted Anglican missionary Robert Hunt in founding and consolidating Stanley Mission at Lac la Ronge—approximately 170 kilometres down the English River from Île-à-la-Crosse.[73] In January 1861, Grandin learned that McKenzie and Hunt intended to establish a satellite mission at Reindeer Lake, where Oblates had been exercising a ministry for the previous fourteen years.[74] Determined to strengthen the Oblates' position and to forestall an Anglican incursion into the area, Grandin obtained authorization from Deschambault to establish a mission near Lac-du-Brochet House—an HBC fort on the northern extremity of Reindeer Lake. The bishop assumed that the fort would provide provisioning, transportation, and communications services to the new mission.[75] To his dismay, Grandin learned in April 1861 that McKenzie—in concert with Chief Trader Robert Campbell of the Athabasca District—had petitioned Governor Mactavish to close Lac-du-Brochet House on the grounds that it was draining furs from the Athabasca District. In reporting the matter to Taché, Grandin ascribed sectarian motives to the petitioners and suggested that McKenzie was waging a furtive campaign against Catholicism. Grandin cited evidence of this campaign in McKenzie's alleged mistreatment of Catholic servants and traders at Rapid River: "Mr. Samuel McKenzy [sic] is always a true gentleman whenever we stop by his home, but he exercises tyrannical power over his hired men and the *sauvages* when it comes to all things religious. . . . He assaults the consciences of those hired men and *sauvages* who do not share his religious convictions. A young French Canadian who had his child baptized by Father Végréville was, for this reason, given a tongue-lashing and deprived of potatoes for his journey."[76] Although the petition was denied in July 1861, Oblates continued to perceive McKenzie as a threat to their mission near Lac-du-Brochet House. Shortly after reaching the mission site on 4 October 1861, Fathers Valentin Végréville and Alphonse Gasté heard rumours of McKenzie's plan to establish a new post with a resident Anglican catechist at Lac La Hache (known alternately as Wollaston Lake)—approximately 130 kilometres west of Lac-du-Brochet House.[77] These rumours continued to circulate over the following year, prompting Végréville to declare in November 1862 that the HBC intended to undercut the Oblate mission near Lac-du-Brochet House: "The company . . . is doing everything it can to promote heresy. It has sent someone to man the post at Lac La Hache for no other purpose than to provide for the schoolmaster [i.e., the Anglican catechist] and to divert the *sauvages* away from us."[78]

Oblate unease deepened in June 1864 when Samuel McKenzie replaced Deschambault as Chief Trader in charge of the English River District.[79] After taking up residence in the HBC fort at Île-à-la-Crosse, McKenzie came into regular contact with the Oblates of Saint-Jean-Baptiste. This contact was generally courteous, and both parties strove to conduct themselves with diplomatic tact. Grandin enjoined his personnel from expressing displeasure with the new chief trader and urged them to continue cooperating with all HBC officers.[80] For his part, McKenzie made weekly visits to the mission and even attended Sunday Mass on occasion, though he also held private services at the HBC fort for his family and other Protestants—mostly junior officers and their families.[81] Beneath this polite exterior, however, there simmered intense apprehension and distrust. In February 1865, Grandin reported to Taché: "Although all is well on the surface, I could not be more displeased with our *bourgeois*. This is a man who despises us and everything that we do. And despite the pleasant words that he exchanges with me and our people, I am convinced that he would ruin us completely if he could. I am as friendly and as helpful as can be to him; he, in turn, is friendly to me and does little favours for me. Big favours, however, are impossible to obtain from him."[82] One such "big favour" was the feeding of schoolchildren at Saint-Bruno. Since the local fishery had begun foundering a month earlier, Oblate lay brothers and *engagés* had experienced increasing difficulty in securing daily sustenance for the Grey Nuns' twenty-eight pupils. Grandin therefore asked McKenzie to provide rations for the "children of the fort"—pupils whose fathers worked for the Company and resided in the vicinity of Île-à-la-Crosse.[83] The bishop claimed that a precedent existed for such assistance, as Deschambault had previously provided the children of HBC officers and servants with meat, potatoes, and fish during times of scarcity.[84] However, McKenzie declined to follow the example of his predecessor and instead recommended that the children be released from the mission and sent back to their parents' homes, where they would be better fed. Grandin interpreted this recommendation as an expression of contempt for the Oblates' education project and a renunciation of the HBC's traditional support. "Our schools, far from being detrimental to the Company, can only help it," mused the bishop in March 1865. "Mr. McKenzie seems to believe the opposite."[85]

With their confidence in the HBC waning, Oblates began seeking alternative means of provisioning Saint-Jean-Baptiste. In October 1864, Grandin and Taché resolved to open an ox-cart road from Fort Carlton to Green Lake so that mission freight could be transported overland from Saint-Boniface to Saint-Julien (Green Lake), thence hauled by barge down the Beaver River into Lac Île-à-la-Crosse and finally to Saint-Jean-Baptiste.[86] They enlisted assistance from Pierriche Laliberté (resident postmaster at Portage La Loche) in obtaining Company authorization for the project and also in recruiting labourers and overseeing the work.[87] Hewing began in May 1866 and continued into the autumn of that year.[88] It was postponed the following spring, however, as Oblates were compelled to concentrate their manpower and financial resources on reconstructing Saint-Jean-Baptiste in the wake of the fire.[89] As a result of this setback, the road was not completed until August 1870.[90] Spanning nearly 180 kilometres through forest and over muskeg, the "Green Lake Road" could be travelled by ox cart in approximately one week in optimal summer conditions. From the road's northern terminus at Green Lake, one could reach Île-à-la-Crosse by barge in three days if water levels were sufficiently high.[91] Oblate lay brothers and *engagés* began hauling mission freight on this route in the early 1870s.[92] The HBC soon took interest in the "Green Lake Road" as it provided a potential alternative to the Portage La Loche Brigade for shipping freight to the English River, Athabasca, and Mackenzie River Districts. By 1872, the Company had incorporated the route into its transport system and had assumed responsibility for its general maintenance.[93] The Company periodically rented out oxen, carts, and barges to Saint-Jean-Baptiste, but Oblates retained supervisory control over the transport of mission freight on the new route.[94]

While affording Oblates a degree of independence from the HBC, the new provisioning system generated disruption in the rhythm of their evangelical activity. In the early 1870s, the HBC reduced the amount of freight conveyed annually to the northern districts by the Portage La Loche Brigade. This freight was increasingly transported from Red River by ox cart across the plains or by steamboat up the Saskatchewan and North Saskatchewan Rivers to Fort Carlton, thence carted along the newly hewn road to Green Lake.[95] There it was loaded onto small barges and transhipped at intervals over the course of the summer.[96] As a corollary of this southward realignment of the system, the biannual *mission* at Île-à-la-Crosse fell into rapid decline. In 1875, Légeard reported that the *mission de l'automne* "was virtually nonexistent," as Cree- and Chipewyan-speaking hunters and trappers no longer gathered for prolonged periods. "What are the causes of this change?" asked Légeard.

> They are the following: in the past, the Company's barges would leave each spring for York Factory on Hudson Bay to collect goods to trade with the *sauvages* and would ordinarily return in the first half of September. The arrival of the barges was a major event in this country: the *sauvages* would all gather here to obtain their advances, that is to say, the clothing, ammunition, and other things that they needed for the winter. We would take advantage of their presence to provide them with the exercises of the *mission* over twelve or fifteen days, after which time they would all make their way to their respective wintering places.
>
> Things have changed a great deal. Now that goods are transported from Red River through Green Lake, the barges no longer go all the way to the sea. They arrive here at different times all summer

long, completing a single back-and-forth trip between Île-à-la-Crosse and Green Lake in a week or two. The *sauvages* can afford to take their time because they are guaranteed to find whatever they need whenever they need it. . . . What are the consequences? Some *sauvages* have stopped coming to the *mission*, while others come in scattered groupings and only stay a few days. Under these circumstances, it is impossible to hold a proper *mission*.[97]

The decline of the biannual *mission* spurred Légeard to devise new strategies for reaching Cree- and Chipewyan-speaking hunters and their families. As resident superior of Saint-Jean-Baptiste, he coordinated pastoral visits to outlying communities and founded permanent satellite missions in wintering grounds at Canoe Lake (la Bienheureuse-Marguerite-Marie) and Waterhen Lake.[98] Légeard also endeavoured to establish a more regular presence at the older missions of Saint-Julien (Green Lake), Saint-Raphaël (Cold Lake) and Notre-Dame-de-la-Visitation (Portage La Loche). He appointed Oblates to reside at these posts on a seasonal basis and instructed them to conduct itinerant ministries in surrounding areas.[99]

Légeard anticipated further disruption to the Oblate apostolate as a consequence of the HBC's reduction of operational expenses. Faced with intensifying competition from free traders and decreasing financial profits in the early 1870s, the Company began reducing the number of its servants in the English River District and overhauling the customary "debt system" whereby Cree- and Chipewyan-speaking hunters and trappers received advances for their furs each autumn.[100] In 1873, Légeard predicted that these initiatives would drain Saint-Jean-Baptiste of its congregation. He forecasted the dispersal of former HBC servants and the estrangement of Cree- and Chipewyan-speaking hunters and trappers from Île-à-la-Crosse.[101] Légeard's apprehensions deepened after thirty-eight-year-old Ewen McDonald assumed direction of the English River District in 1877.[102] McDonald placed severe restrictions on advances to hunters and trappers even as fur-bearing animals became increasingly scarce throughout the region.[103] Expecting widespread suffering to result from these restrictions, Oblates and Grey Nuns increased enrolment at the convent boarding school and dispensed material relief from mission stores. Légeard accounted for these costly measures in a report to Augustin Maisonneuve—commissary to the Vicariates of Athabasca-Mackenzie and Saint-Albert—dated 8 October 1878:

The *bourgeois* announced to the *sauvages* that he would not give
them advances this autumn, or rather that he would advance paltry
amounts and only to some. The great majority of *sauvages* have
therefore gone off to their wintering places without *butin* for their
families, without nets, without ammunition, etc. We found this
treatment very harsh, but the Company has its reasons for acting
this way and I do not wish to discuss these reasons here. To assist
these poor people ... we gave them everything that we could possibly part with.... This may have been imprudent on our part, but
I do not believe so. In any case, we did it as an act of charity. ...
The result is that our store is quite empty and we must now request
additional supplies for next year.[104]

Bishop Grandin also expressed alarm at McDonald's austerity. After visiting Saint-Jean-Baptiste in June 1880, the prelate reported that McDonald
continued to withhold advances regardless of worsening poverty among local
Cree- and Chipewyan-speaking families.[105] Yet owing to the limited financial
resources at his disposal, Grandin would not countenance another large-scale
relief effort. Instead, he suggested petitioning the Canadian government to
disallow free trade in the English River District, which he considered "the
true cause of impoverishment of this country and of the *sauvages*." Grandin
called for a return to the reciprocal obligations that had existed under the HBC
monopoly and predicted dire consequences if these relations were not restored:
"Things being what they are, everyone will simply take whatever he can get
from the *sauvages* and when these poor, unfortunate people have shot the last
caribou and the last fox, they'll simply be left to die of hunger and cold."[106]

Over the following decade, Oblates perceived continuing divergence between the welfare of their congregants and the interests of the HBC. They came
into protracted conflict with McDonald's successor—Chief Factor Joseph
Fortescue—over the rights of Catholic servants to observe feast days and to
participate in devotional exercises at Saint-Jean-Baptiste.[107] The conflict began
in early June 1886, after Fortescue had engaged several Chipewyan-speaking
men to serve aboard the HBC barges that plied from Green Lake to Portage
La Loche. Having issued orders that these men were to set out from Île-à-la-
Crosse on 7 June, Fortescue was incensed to learn that Fathers Joseph Rapet
and Louis Dauphin had counselled them to remain at Île-à-la-Crosse until
the end of the *mission du printemps* the following week. The chief factor consequently wrote to HBC Trade Commissioner Joseph Wrigley in Winnipeg

and complained that Oblates were undermining Company operations in the English River District.[108] Fortescue redoubled his complaint two years later, after the crewmen of an HBC barge had defied his orders to set out from Île-à-la-Crosse for Green Lake on 10 May 1888—the moveable feast of Ascension Day.[109] Rapet had reportedly forbidden the crewmen to work on the feast day and had insisted that they attend church services at Saint-Jean-Baptiste instead.[110] "This is becoming intolerable," fumed Fortescue in a letter to Wrigley. "As a protestation we shall have to get rid of all our Roman Catholic servants and simply employ none but Protestants if we cannot command our men in our own Posts."[111] Wrigley subsequently instructed Fortescue to assume a more conciliatory tone and insisted that the Company could not forego the Oblates' goodwill at a time of increasing competition from free traders. In response to this admonition, Fortescue assured Wrigley that he would endeavour to improve his relations with the missionaries.[112]

Yet even as he urged conciliation with Oblates, Commissioner Wrigley devised a series of sweeping administrative reforms that would only alienate them further. In May 1889, he appointed fifty-three-year-old Henry John Moberly to manage the English River District for a period of three years and instructed him to dismiss "refractory servants," reduce wages, eliminate the debt system, and strengthen opposition to free traders. Wrigley promised Moberly a promotion to the rank of chief factor if he implemented these reforms successfully by the end of his three-year term.[113] Moberly therefore wasted little time in executing his agenda. In August 1891, he reported to Wrigley's successor—Commissioner Clarence Campbell Chipman—that he had reduced the number of servants in the district, stopped "Indian Debts," and established outposts near the wintering grounds of the Cree and the Chipewyan where there was little likelihood of encountering competitors.[114] Oblates decried these reforms as detrimental to their apostolate and ultimately prejudicial to the commercial interests of the HBC. According to Father Jean-Marie Pénard, Moberly's attempts at downsizing—particularly his elimination of the debt system—had had the unintended effect of encouraging hunters and trappers to align themselves with free traders based in Prince Albert (approximately 285 linear kilometres southeast of Île-à-la-Crosse). This settlement was eclipsing Île-à-la-Crosse as a centre of trade and was steadily drawing hunters and trappers out of the orbit of Saint-Jean-Baptiste.[115] Moreover, Oblates claimed that Moberly's extensive cost-cutting measures were causing a loss in revenue for the mission. To supplement their diminishing allocation from l'Œuvre de la Propagation de la Foi, the Oblates of Saint-Jean-Baptiste had been

accepting furs as stipends for Mass intentions and as charitable donations since
1887.[116] Each spring or early summer, they delivered these furs to the HBC
fort in exchange for payment in kind or cash. In June 1891, however, Rapet
discontinued this custom and withheld his furs on the grounds that Moberly
did not offer reasonable rates.[117] Six months later, Pénard and Brother Fabien
Labelle hauled the furs to Prince Albert and sold them there at "a fairly good
price."[118]

Beyond expressing dissatisfaction with Moberly's business administration, Oblates levelled charges of moral depravity and licentiousness against
the chief trader. They were especially critical of his endorsement of drinking
and dancing at the HBC post. In his entry in the "Codex historicus de l'Île-à-
la-Crosse" for 1891, Pénard ascribed to Moberly a desire to corrupt the local
population through these activities: "Throughout the entire year, this individual
pursued his mission of debauching our people, sometimes pushing them to
drink, sometimes dragging them to his parties. Sadly, his efforts were often
successful."[119] Pénard identified Moberly as the willing instigator of "scandals"
and "disturbances" that plagued Île-à-la-Crosse over the course of that summer: "During the summer, serious disturbances erupted on the point [i.e., the
peninsula of Île-à-la-Crosse] and Father Rapet was obliged to respond with
severity. Yet he was unable to put a complete stop to this trouble because the
notorious Moberly, *bourgeois* of the Company, sought to neutralize the influence of the missionaries by all means available to him. Thus, despite all of the
Fathers' efforts, dancing and drunkenness ran rampant and Master Moberly
delighted in it. This undermined his commerce with the *sauvages*, but Moberly
cared far more about the affairs of the devil than those of the Company."[120]
Rapet and Pénard complained about Moberly's conduct to Inspecting Chief
Factor James McDougall during the latter's visit to Île-à-la-Crosse in February
1892. To ascertain the validity of the Oblates' complaint, McDougall arranged
and presided over a formal inquiry at the HBC fort on 1 and 2 March.[121] After
the first session, however, Rapet and Pénard were convinced that McDougall
was seeking to discredit their testimony and to exonerate Moberly. The Oblates
consequently boycotted the second session: "Faced with such flagrant bad faith,
the priests decided to let the visitor deal with his *bourgeois* as he saw fit and to
wash their hands of the whole inquiry."[122] The subsequent worsening of relations between Oblates and Moberly prompted direct intervention by Vicar
Apostolic Albert Pascal. During his first official visit to Saint-Jean-Baptiste
in June 1892, Pascal attempted to mediate between Rapet and Moberly.[123]
His efforts yielded a tentative agreement whereby Oblates would resume the

custom of delivering their furs to the HBC fort and Moberly would cease his endorsement of drinking and dancing.[124]

In the aftermath of Pascal's intervention, Oblates became somewhat more favourably disposed to the HBC.[125] Contributing to this development was Moberly's resignation and his replacement by forty-nine-year-old Chief Trader William Cornwallis King in September 1894.[126] During the first year of his tenure at Île-à-la-Crosse, King took steps to redeem the Company's reputation and to establish an amicable relationship with Oblates. He discontinued the practices of dispensing alcohol and holding dances at the HBC fort on festive occasions, thus prompting Rapet and Pénard to marvel at the "perfect tranquility" that reigned over Île-à-la-Crosse on New Year's Day, 1895.[127] Additionally, King offered the mission a reduced rate on freighting services from Green Lake to Île-à-la-Crosse and periodically lent barges to Oblate lay brothers.[128] In return for these services, Rapet and Pénard made a concerted attempt to persuade Cree- and Chipewyan-speaking hunters and trappers to trade once again with the HBC. "Thanks to their efforts," reported Pénard, "by Christmas [1894], nearly all of the *sauvages* had reconciled with the Company, which once again became the master of the fur trade in this region."[129] Oblates continued supporting the commercial interests of the HBC over the following year as the Company faced increasing competition from free traders, two of whom—a Mr. Tupper from Edmonton and a Mr. Peterson from Battleford—established small operations at Île-à-la-Crosse.[130] Through public preaching and private counsel, Oblates discouraged local hunters and trappers from trading with "strangers about whose morality and background we know nothing."[131]

The reconciliation was short-lived, however, as Oblates soon developed grave doubts about King's sincerity and integrity. By January 1896, Rapet and Pénard had come to suspect that the chief trader's goodwill was a mere pretence to regain Oblate support in the struggle against free traders. "The *bourgeois*, Mr. King, is determined to stay on good terms with the mission; he knows that he needs us," noted Pénard in the "Codex historicus." "Nevertheless, relations between the mission and the fort are a little cold; Mr. King cannot restrain himself from occasionally revealing the hatred that he bears the Catholic religion."[132] Oblate suspicions deepened as King continued to commit "impairs," or blunders, over the following year.[133] Finally, in summer 1897, Pénard reported that King had abandoned all pretence of friendship and had brazenly exposed his "ill will toward the mission."[134] This development occurred in the context of a construction project that had been ongoing at Saint-Jean-Baptiste for several months. With permission from their vicar apostolic, Rapet and Pénard had drafted plans for a new church and had recruited workers from the local population.[135] King had reportedly promised to assist the Oblates by procuring and delivering construction supplies at a reduced rate.[136] However, when these supplies reached Île-à-la-Crosse in August, King allegedly refused to deliver them to the mission at the agreed-upon price. Instead, he charged a considerable markup and declared that Oblates would no longer receive preferential rates on provisioning or freighting services.[137] Oblates interpreted this new policy—and particularly its abrupt implementation by King—as an expression of hostility to their apostolate. "War has been declared between the mission and the Hudson's Bay Company," reported Pascal to the Oblate General Administration in February 1898. "Those amiable gentlemen have adopted a policy designed to ruin and destroy our most remote posts."[138]

Unable or unwilling to pay the prices demanded by King, the Oblates of Saint-Jean-Baptiste sought to complete their construction project with assistance from free trader Antoine Marcelin. Originally from Pont-Château, Quebec, Marcelin had been trading in the vicinity of Muskeg Lake—approximately 124 linear kilometres southwest of Île-à-la-Crosse—since winter 1890.[139] He had first attempted to trade at Île-à-la-Crosse in early March 1897, but had reportedly been under-equipped in *butin* to compete with the HBC and other free traders.[140] Nevertheless, Marcelin had made a favourable first impression on Rapet and Pénard, who acknowledged him as the only "practising Catholic" among local traders.[141] Marcelin further endeared himself to the Oblates during his second trading expedition to Île-à-la-Crosse the following autumn when he donated handsaws, a circular saw, and a planing machine for the construction of the new church. He also donated fifty dollars and a large consignment of *butin* to pay day workers.[142] Rapet and Pénard accepted these donations gratefully and arranged for Marcelin to provide additional construction supplies—including hardware and a steam-driven log saw—in exchange for Mass intentions.[143] After assuming direction of Saint-Jean-Baptiste in January 1898, Pénard commissioned Marcelin to provide continued services for the mission. Over the course of the following year, Marcelin oversaw the purchase of provisions in Prince Albert and Winnipeg as well as their shipment to Saint-Jean-Baptiste. He also provided mission personnel with transportation by barge between Green Lake and Île-à-la-Crosse.[144]

By December 1898, Marcelin had assumed the role of "supplier to the mission" and had effectively obviated the Oblates' material dependence on the HBC. His services enabled Pénard to terminate a business relationship that had endured for over fifty-two years between Saint-Jean-Baptiste and the HBC fort.[145] In reporting on this rupture with the Company, Pénard asserted that King had forfeited the Oblates' support through his oppressive administration and that he would consequently incur heavy commercial losses:

> Indignant with King's conduct, the *sauvages* are distancing themselves from the Company and growing ever closer to the free traders, especially to Mr. Marcelin, who is kind and generous to the mission and who is a very good Christian. On balance, Mr. King has done a great service to the mission by forcing it to shake off the Company's yoke. Before winter's end, I hope that the high and mighty autocrat of the North will realize that it needed the mission far more than the mission ever needed it.... The good old Company will soon understand that the Catholic religion is not to be trifled with; whoever does so invites serious trouble.[146]

Between Taché's grateful acknowledgement of his "sincere and devoted friends" and Pénard's indignant castigation of "the high and mighty autocrat of the North" there lay decades of diverging goals and interests. Driving this divergence were profound structural changes in the regional economic landscape—namely the decline of the HBC's monopoly and the emergence of competitive fur buyers. In the beginning of their apostolate at Île-à-la-Crosse in the late 1840s and '50s, Oblates took full advantage of the order, stability, and predictability afforded by a mercantile monopoly. The HBC's vast transport system provided them with a secure lifeline to Saint-Boniface in the Red River Colony and to the Oblate General Administration and l'Œuvre de la Propagation de la Foi in France. The transport system also enabled Oblates to consolidate their mission network by facilitating regular back-and-forth travel between Saint-Jean-Baptiste and its outlying satellite posts. Moreover, Oblates synchronized the rhythm of their local ministry with the HBC's provisioning and trading cycles. They scheduled their principal missionizing campaigns—the *mission de l'automne* and *mission du printemps*—to coincide with the biannual gathering of Cree- and Chipewyan-speaking hunters and their families at Île-à-la-Crosse. Finally, Oblates mobilized the social and political influence of HBC officers in support of their education project. They assigned these officers a critical role in publicizing the convent boarding school and in recruiting pupils from local families. Thus, by the mid-1860s, Oblates had become heavily dependent on the Company for the temporal sustenance of their apostolate. Acutely conscious of this situation, Oblates endeavoured to buttress the Company's commercial dominance by urging Indigenous Catholics to avoid contact with free traders.

Despite their efforts, however, Oblates could do little to stem the rising tide of competition. In the late 1860s and 1870s, pressures from independent fur buyers prompted the HBC to implement various streamlining and restructuring initiatives. Among these initiatives was the modification of the transport system through the incorporation of a southern supply route and the adoption of steam power. This initiative had profound repercussions on the Oblate apostolate, as it broke traditional provisioning and trading cycles, thereby disrupting the biannual *mission*. Further disruption resulted from the Company's reductions of its labour force and from its progressive restriction of credit over the course of the 1870s and '80s. Oblates bemoaned these changes because they provoked the displacement of many regular congregants from Saint-Jean-Baptiste. More gravely, Oblates perceived that the Company was abdicating its traditional responsibility to safeguard the physical, moral, and spiritual welfare of Indigenous peoples. Its officers flouted this responsibility by interfering with the devotional practices of Indigenous Catholics and by inciting them to dissolute behaviour.

While conscious that market forces were contributing to the erosion of traditional patterns of interaction, Oblates suspected the workings of another force—an insidious anti-Catholicism. Having expressed apprehensions about the Protestantism of "les bourgeois" since the 1860s, Oblates ascribed a sectarian basis to the gradual worsening of relations between the fort and the mission over the following decades. By the 1890s, Oblates had become convinced that the Company sought to sabotage their apostolate by corrupting Indigenous Catholics and by withholding essential services to Saint-Jean-Baptiste. A striking corollary of this conviction was the Oblates' reimagining of the free trader. Once vilified as the enemy of order and the embodiment of greed, the free trader was now transformed into a benevolent entrepreneur whose presence enabled Catholics to liberate themselves from the Company's heretical tyranny.

CHAPTER 3

Oblates and the Beginnings of Residential Education

Since the mid-1980s, historians have devoted considerable attention to the role of Oblates in the establishment and administration of schools in northern and western Canada. For the most part, their investigations have focused on the period after the signing of the first seven numbered treaties (i.e., post-1877), when Oblates—together with Anglican, Methodist, and Presbyterian missionary organizations—entered into a "joint venture" with the federal government to provide residential education for Indigenous children.[1] The forging of this relationship has generally been regarded as the beginning of Oblate involvement in a project of comprehensive social, cultural, and linguistic assimilation—a project comparable in intent and implementation to the United States' "policy of aggressive civilization." Like their missionary counterparts in the United States, Oblates in northern and western Canada were commissioned by the federal state to operate residential institutions in which Indigenous children were to be isolated from the influence of their families and "educat[ed] in industry and the arts of civilization."[2] Yet while acknowledging the Oblates' role as executors of this assimilative project, some historians have cast doubt on their commitment to its underlying objective. Martha McCarthy, for instance, has suggested that Oblates in the Vicariate of Athabasca-Mackenzie were drawn reluctantly into the project in the aftermath of treaty negotiations: "It was only when the treaties made it mandatory for the government to provide schooling for the Dene that the policy of 'aggressive civilization' was promoted, using denominational schools to accomplish this aim more economically than the government could. Thus, even if the Oblates ...

had had any different notions of education, they would have had to conform to government regulations in order to obtain vital financial support."[3] J.R. Miller has similarly cast Oblates as ambivalent collaborators. According to Miller, Oblates were critical of the virulent assimilative thrust of federal policy, but ultimately accepted residential schooling as an opportunity to subsidize their evangelical work and to assist Indigenous peoples in adjusting to coexistence with a Euro-Canadian settler population.[4] Oblates nevertheless held lingering reservations about implementing the most aggressive federal directives and were particularly reluctant to enforce an outright ban on the use of Indigenous languages in residential schools.[5]

While shedding light on complexities and tensions in the relationship between Oblates and the federal government, the prevailing historiographical focus on the post-treaty period has tended to obscure—if not to negate—the agency of Oblates in formulating an assimilative project predicated on residential education.[6] Decades before the advent of federal intervention in their mission field, Oblates had devised a program of social, cultural, and linguistic transformation that relied on the convent boarding school as its operative instrument. They envisaged the convent boarding school as a highly disciplined space in which Indigenous children would be weaned from beliefs and behaviours deemed characteristic of *la sauvagerie* and prepared for inclusion in *la civilisation chrétienne*. The present chapter examines the articulation and implementation of this project through the lens of the convent boarding school at Île-à-la-Crosse, from its founding in 1860 to its integration into the federal residential school system in 1898. In their capacity as administrators and principals of this school, Oblates produced a vast commentary on the role of residential education in their civilizing project. This commentary is analyzed in this chapter for its insights into the Oblates' conception of *la civilisation chrétienne* and its accompanying behavioural expectations. Oblate commentary is also analyzed for its insights into the strategies they adopted in order to sustain a residential education program without state assistance.

In laying the foundations of a convent boarding school at Île-à-la-Crosse, Oblates acted in accordance with a mandate from the founder and first Superior General of their congregation, Charles-Joseph-Eugène de Mazenod. As an addendum to the second edition of the Oblates' *Constitution and Rules* (1853), Mazenod issued instructions on the operation of *les missions étrangères* and included a directive on the establishment and supervision of schools:

Far from eschewing the work of preparing *sauvages* to participate in social life, members of this Society will embrace this work as an excellent way to contribute to the good of the Mission and to render their apostolate more fruitful.... Given that the prosperity of civil societies is intimately linked to the instruction of youth, we must—as far as possible—open a school in each Mission. There, under the guidance of a schoolteacher, children will acquire the rudiments of Christian doctrine as well as temporal knowledge and all that they need to know of the arts of everyday life.[7]

Mazenod envisioned a strictly administrative—rather than pedagogical—role for the Oblates. Loath to divert his missionaries' time and energy from their regular ministry, the Superior General encouraged the recruitment of full-time teaching personnel from outside the ranks of the congregation. In January 1857, he approved Bishop Alexandre-Antonin Taché's proposal to negotiate a contract with the Sisters of Charity of Montreal—or Grey Nuns—to staff a series of convent boarding schools in Rupert's Land and the North-Western Territory.[8] According to Taché, the Grey Nuns were particularly well-suited to this task, as they had been exercising a teaching vocation at Saint-Boniface since 1844 and had expressed willingness to expand beyond the confines of the Red River Colony.[9] With Mazenod's blessing, Taché met with Mother Superior Julie Hainault Deschamps in summer 1857 and reached an agreement whereby the Grey Nuns would staff daughter convents at Lac Sainte-Anne, Île-à-la-Crosse, and Lac La Biche.[10]

Underlying Taché's choice of personnel was the belief that childrearing—the teaching, disciplining, and socialization of children—fell within the natural purview of the "missionary woman." Despite having renounced physical motherhood through her vow of chastity, the female religious was assumed to possess the quintessentially maternal qualities of nurturance, tenderness, and patience. Taché believed that these qualities could be harnessed toward the inculcation of civilized habits of thought and behaviour in Indigenous children.[11] His belief was shared—and likely reinforced—by the Grey Nuns themselves, many of whom conceptualized their role in the western mission field as that of adoptive mothers. Hence, while travelling by barge to Île-à-la-Crosse in August 1860, Sister Agnès (Marie-Rose Caron) wrote to Taché to assure him that "my motherly heart will embrace all of those little *sauvages*."[12] As the

first superior of Saint-Bruno, Agnès instructed her two subordinates—Sister
Philomène Boucher and Sister Pepin (Marie-Anne Lachance)—to adopt a
motherly approach to the teaching and supervision of Indigenous schoolchildren.[13] She outlined this approach in her chronicle, "Annales de l'établissement
des Sœurs Grises à l'Île à la Crosse," prepared in 1883:

> We had to make up for all that was missing from their first educa-
> tion; we had to become like mothers to them and get back to the
> basics. Our first task was to get them to acquire the habit of wash-
> ing themselves and combing their hair each morning. Until then,
> their single greatest pleasure had been to run recklessly through
> the woods. . . . We therefore had to teach them to play calmly and
> quietly, without harming one another or themselves. We also had
> to teach them better conversational manners, as they thought it
> ridiculous to speak politely. Such were the children whom the
> Sisters found in their care when they arrived at Île-à-la-Crosse
> in November 1860. It may not have been an attractive posting for
> everyone, but oh how we loved those poor children of the woods![14]

In becoming "like mothers," Agnès and her *consœurs* adhered to a gendered
division of roles and responsibilities in the civilizing project. Their duties
reflected contemporary French and French-Canadian conceptions of the
mother as the ideal educator and the natural agent for instilling norms of
civility, composure, and cleanliness.[15]

   To further harness the civilizing potential of motherhood, Oblates
enjoined the Grey Nuns to devote particular attention to the education of
young girls and thus to ensure the transmission of *la civilisation chrétienne*
and its sociocultural characteristics to future generations.[16] In December
1861, Bishop Vital-Justin Grandin reported to l'Œuvre de la Propagation
de la Foi that the Grey Nuns had been called to Île-à-la-Crosse specifically
to mould future wives and mothers: "Their calling is to civilize our *sauvages*
by training young girls and, ultimately, mothers of families."[17] Accordingly,
the first cohort of schoolchildren at Saint-Bruno contained more girls than
boys—nine of the former, six of the latter.[18] Among the girls were Julie and
Esther, both Chipewyan-speaking orphans; Marie and Thérèse, daughters of
Charles Lafleur (an HBC apprentice in the English River District); Sophie, a
daughter of Antoine Morin (an HBC guide in the English River District); and
Catherine, a daughter of Pierriche Laliberté (postmaster in charge of Portage

La Loche).[19] From the first day of class (25 November 1860), these girls were trained and readied for their future roles as wives, mothers, and homemakers through a curriculum based on contemporary French and French-Canadian domestic norms. They received instruction in cooking, cleaning, laundering, knitting, sewing, and embroidery from Agnès and were assigned daily chores in the kitchen and in the refectory.[20]

Through intensive schooling, the girls of Saint-Bruno were expected to become the vanguard of a regenerated and emancipated womanhood. For at least a decade before the establishment of the school, Oblates had bemoaned the status of Cree- and Chipewyan-speaking women living in the vicinity of Île-à-la-Crosse. Oblates had commonly described these women as degraded victims of fathers, husbands, and sons who would sell them, beat them, and ultimately abandon them.[21] In his first published letter from Île-à-la-Crosse (1851), Taché had even equated local womanhood with slavery: "It is painful to see woman—who was created to be man's companion—become his slave, subjugated by the superior strength that he was given in order to protect her, rather than torture her. . . . We have seen some local men knock their spouses unconscious and treat them with barbaric severity."[22] According to Taché, Chipewyan-speaking women bore a particularly onerous burden as the conditions of their "slavery" were aggravated by extreme poverty and frequent starvation:

> While the fate of this tribe is unhappy in general, that of the women in particular is filled with privations and sufferings that are virtually unheard of among civilized nations. "I will multiply your pain," said God to Eve, and this terrible anathema still applies here with all of its original force; misery is heaped upon misery, creating a terrible mass of tribulation. Christian women, if you do not understand all that Religion has done for you, come to the school of the infidel peoples and you will see what you would have become without the saving influence of Christianity![23]

Informing Taché's ascription of the terms "civilized" and "barbaric" was a normative assumption about the place of women in society. This assumption held that women needed to be cared for and protected in order to fulfill their God-given roles as helpmates and homemakers.[24] Only through Christian education could women gain an awareness of their place in the divine order and acquire the skills necessary to assume that place. Thus, in December 1861,

Grandin declared that the founding of Saint-Bruno represented a major first step toward "the elevation of women . . . who are so despised and degraded in this country."[25]

The school was also intended to effect a transformation of local manhood by producing conscientious husbands and fathers. With the exception of a Chipewyan-speaking orphan known as Francis, the first contingent of schoolboys consisted of sons of local HBC personnel: Antoine, son of Pierriche Laliberté; Gabriel, son of Charles Lafleur; Baptiste, son of Antoine Morin; and Joseph and Zacharie, likely sons of James Bruce (an HBC boat builder).[26] These boys were entrusted to the supervision of Oblate lay brother Louis Dubé, who conveyed them at 5:30 each morning from the Oblate residence at Saint-Jean-Baptiste to the common room at Saint-Bruno. There the boys spent the morning learning basic arithmetic and acquiring skills in written and spoken French—a language that none of them spoke natively.[27] Their teacher—Sister Pepin—struggled to assert authority over the boys, prompting her sister superior to marvel at her fortitude and devotion:

> What patience was needed to discipline those boys! They were accustomed to doing whatever they pleased; in this country a ten- or twelve-year-old boy is too big—"too much of a man!" as they say here—to submit to his parents. . . . It is easy to imagine how those children, having been raised according to such principles, reacted upon finding themselves under the authority of a Sister. And in their eyes, the only difference between a Sister and their mother was a habit. We therefore needed to be very cautious and very gentle with them. We needed to assert authority without hurting or humiliating them. Above all, we needed help from above and the blessing of our heavenly Father, for although we may sow, it is God alone who gives growth. Sister Pepin, to whom the principal task of teaching had fallen, knew this well. . . . And while this devoted Sister cared for the children, . . . we prayed that God would bless her efforts and crown them with success.[28]

In the afternoon, Pepin dismissed the schoolboys and they performed manual labour under Dubé's direction. Their tasks were meant to prepare them for lives as industrious heads of households. Hence, the youngest boys worked in the barn milking cows, mucking out stalls, and distributing fodder. Older boys were assigned more strenuous tasks, such as chopping and hauling firewood and maintaining mission buildings. In the spring, the boys tilled the soil around the mission and sowed barley, wheat, and potatoes. They assisted in harvesting these crops in the late summer and autumn.[29] Eighteen months after the implementation of this daily regimen, Father Henri Faraud reported that a gradual transformation was underway among the schoolboys: "These children . . . are slowly becoming pious, losing those *sauvage* characteristics that are so detestable among the children of the North, and will eventually become dutiful and conscientious fathers."[30]

Yet while confident in the transformative power of Saint-Bruno, Oblates expressed concern about the rate of the schoolchildren's progress. In June 1861, Father Valentin Végréville reported that the children had made little headway in learning French and recommended that they be subjected to a more intensive pedagogical program:

> It is urgent that the children learn to speak French. This, in my opinion, must be our priority. It is true that we are already work-ing toward this end by speaking only French to them, but this is not enough. The children only speak Cree among themselves, and thus more than three-quarters of their conversations take place in *sauvage*. The result is that they have made very little progress in French conversation. . . . Until there develops a core of French-speaking children, neither the Sisters nor the Oblates should content themselves with merely supervising the children. Rather, we must involve ourselves in their games, place ourselves in greater contact with them, and not tolerate their speaking *sauvage* among them-selves. We must force them to speak French by various means. . . . We will need to make sacrifices to achieve this goal, but our school will otherwise remain inconsequential. The sooner we make these sacrifices, the sooner we will reap the benefits: once a small French-speaking core has formed, newly arrived children will be drawn to it without realizing it and without our having to force things.[31]

Father Julien Moulin echoed Végréville's recommendation seventeen months later, noting that the schoolchildren persisted in speaking Cree among them-selves: "I do not think that the children are sufficiently supervised at mealtimes or at other times. We cannot seem to stop them from speaking Cree among themselves, and this is harming their education a great deal. . . . I think that we are giving them too much freedom."[32] Moulin further opined that the children had made little progress in reading and writing. After more than two years of schooling, they could barely hold a pen, let alone compose a legible sentence.[33] More worrisome than the pupils' slow progress was their teachers' apparent disappointment and despondency. In his capacity as principal of Saint-Bruno from July 1861 to July 1863, Faraud registered concern that the Grey Nuns were beginning to doubt their own abilities and to waver in their commitment to the civilizing project. He confided to Taché that he suspected the nuns of wishing to return to Saint-Boniface and Montreal.[34]

According to most Oblate commentators, the principal impediment to the schoolchildren's progress was frequent contact with their Cree- and Chipewyan-speaking relatives. Starting in November 1860, Oblates had endeavoured to alleviate strain on mission food stores by permitting the schoolchildren to spend Sundays and Thursdays with their families.[35] While accepted as an economic necessity, this strategy prompted concerns that the children would remain impervious to *la civilisation chrétienne* because of their regular re-immersion in *la sauvagerie*. Hence, in spring 1861, Végréville and Moulin recommended a decrease in the number of "congés," or holidays, allotted to the schoolchildren so as to mitigate the influence of their families.[36] This recommendation proved impossible to implement, however, as a series of crises shook Saint-Bruno over the following decade and compelled its administrators to return the children to their families for extended periods. The first of these crises occurred in spring 1866 when the local fishery failed completely. Unable to secure daily sustenance for all schoolchildren, acting principal Father Jean-Marie Caër cancelled classes for two months and sent away children who had relatives in the vicinity of Île-à-la-Crosse.[37] The second crisis occurred the following year when the schoolboys' dormitory burned to the ground. In the immediate aftermath of the fire, Oblates attempted to lodge nineteen schoolboys in a small warehouse with beds stacked four high. They soon ascertained that this situation was untenable and returned most of the boys to their families.[38] The final crisis occurred as the new dormitory was nearing completion in August 1869. While preparing to resume his supervision of the schoolboys, Dubé suffered a bout of paralysis and was committed to the Grey Nuns' infirmary.[39] His incapacity prompted Grandin to introduce a day-student system whereby the children of local HBC personnel—"children of the fort"—were permitted to attend classes during the day and return to their families in the evening. This system remained in operation until April 1871, when Father Prosper Légeard restored the original "système de pensionnaires" whereby all pupils boarded at the mission.[40]

Beyond their persistent linguistic and cultural influence on schoolchildren, local families prompted concern among Oblates because of their apparent ambivalence—and occasional hostility—toward Saint-Bruno. Under the terms of the "système de pensionnaires," the families of schoolchildren were expected to pay an annual "pension"—a fee in cash or in kind—to cover their children's material needs.[41] Yet payment of the "pension" became increasingly rare after the first school year. By the winter of 1862–63, the schoolchildren were being fed, clothed, and sheltered entirely at the expense of the mission.[42] This situation aggravated the strain on mission food stores and increased the burden of manual labour borne by Grey Nuns, Oblate lay brothers, and *engagés*. "I find it totally unreasonable that we are expected to feed all the children of the Company men," grumbled Faraud in late November 1862. "Our own men must devote so much time to fishing that it is impossible to get them to do anything else around here."[43] In March 1864, Moulin reported that the mission was compelled to provide at least twenty fish per day for the sustenance of the schoolchildren in addition to the usual thirty-five required for the sustenance of Oblates, Grey Nuns, *engagés*, and sled dogs. The following year, Grandin reported that the schoolchildren required at least thirty-six fish per day. Besides forcing Oblates to devote more time and energy to fishing, this situation presented complications for the Grey Nuns, as their kitchen was under-equipped for the preparation of such large meals: the nuns relied on a "chimney system," in which fish was cooked slowly and in relatively small quantities.[44] According to Oblates and Grey Nuns, this lack of material support from local families was symptomatic of their general disengagement with Saint-Bruno. Reinforcing this perception was the reluctance of several families to enrol their young children in the school.[45] In an effort to extol the benefits of a mission education and to garner community support for Saint-Bruno, Oblates and Grey Nuns launched a publicity campaign centred on the annual *examen public*.[46] The priests and nuns reported mixed results from this campaign: although it boosted enrolment and encouraged payment of the "pension," the campaign did not dispel all misgivings among local families. Hence, in her chronicle entry for the year 1871, Agnès noted that the enrolment of a record thirty-five "pensionnaires" coincided with vociferous criticism from local families over the treatment of their children: "Some families were beginning to appreciate the benefits of education, so they took the initiative themselves to enrol their children. Nevertheless, these poor *sauvages* retained their old habit of finding fault in our treatment of their children even though we were exhausting ourselves and sacrificing so much for their benefit. . . . Yet to draw as many children as possible to our little school, good Sister Pepin resigned herself to all reproaches, all difficulties, and all suffering."[47] Such "reproaches" were especially common when schoolchildren fell ill or perished at Saint-Bruno—as occurred in January 1865, when six-year-old François Beaulieu died of pleurisy, and in March 1875, when four-year-old Patrice Stevenson died after an outbreak of chicken pox.[48] Cases of juvenile illness and death provoked some local families to accuse Oblates and Grey Nuns of being negligent, unloving, or excessively severe with their charges. While these accusations dwindled during periods of relative good health among school-children, they left a legacy of uncertainty among Oblates and Grey Nuns as to the local community's goodwill and support for Saint-Bruno.[49]

Oblates perceived another obstacle to the operation of Saint-Bruno in the internal dynamics of the mission personnel. Even while publishing descrip-tions of their relationship with Grey Nuns as a seamless cooperation between missionary congregations, Oblates struggled with scruples and apprehensions in their daily interactions with the nuns.[50] These scruples and apprehensions stemmed in part from the clerical vow of chastity and its accompanying gendered divisions of space, labour, and power. In the early 1860s, the Oblate General Administration instructed Oblates to avoid frequent, prolonged, and unnecessary contact with Grey Nuns, but it issued no specific protocol on daily interaction between members of these two communities. Such interaction was to be regulated according to the discretion of local superiors.[51] This situation created serious administrative concerns at Saint-Bruno, especially during the intermittent principalships of Father Julien Moulin (November 1862 to January 1863, July 1863 to September 1864, and March 1867 to October 1870).[52] Moulin attempted to impose unprecedented restrictions on personal contact and communication between Oblates and Grey Nuns. For instance, he sought to discontinue the practice whereby Oblates consulted directly with the nuns in preparing the annual list of supplies required at the mission. He urged the nuns to compile their own list and recommended the complete material separation of the two communities.[53] More drastically, Moulin in-structed Oblate lay brothers to conduct their daily exchanges with the nuns through handwritten messages delivered by schoolboys. Even the most prosaic exchanges were to be conducted in writing—including commentary on pupils, updates on the fishery, and requests for services and supplies.[54] When Bishop Grandin returned to Île-à-la-Crosse after completing his three-year tour of the northern missions in August 1864, he was shocked at the isolation and divisiveness that had arisen under Moulin's supervision.[55] Grandin reported to

Bishop Taché and to Father Florent Vandenberghe—delegate of the Oblate Superior General—that the nuns had encountered inordinate difficulty in conveying requests for such basic necessities as water, food, and firewood, and that they had become sorely alienated from the Oblates. Grandin therefore requested Taché and Vandenberghe promulgate binding rules and regulations on interaction between the two communities: "I implore you, Monseigneur and Reverend Father, to draft rules and provide instructions so that these two communities—which are capable of doing so much good together—need no longer experience such deplorable circumstances. . . . It seems to me that if the [Grey Nuns'] superior general, or even the provincial, knew about these troubles, she would have no choice but to recall her sisters."[56] In the absence of such rules, Grandin feared that the relationship between Oblates and Grey Nuns could be irreparably damaged at the whim of an injudicious superior. His fears were rekindled in August 1868, when he returned to Île-à-la-Crosse after a year-long sojourn in Canada and France.[57] Despite having admonished Moulin for his earlier administrative gaffes, Grandin discovered yet again that the Grey Nuns had chafed under Moulin's austere direction: "The sisters suffered from this administration: their relationship with the director of the mission was so awkward that they were afraid to ask even for bare essentials."[58] Given Moulin's "tiresome severity" and "unpleasant bearing," Grandin resolved to replace him as superior of Saint-Jean-Baptiste and principal of Saint-Bruno as soon as a suitable candidate could be found.[59]

Grandin's resolution suggests that the presence of Grey Nuns generated tension not only between religious communities but also among Oblates themselves. Indeed, during the 1860s, several Oblates of Saint-Jean-Baptiste expressed concerns and misgivings about their *confrères'* relations with the nuns. In April 1863, for instance, Moulin reported that Faraud was spending excessive amounts of time at the convent. Faraud visited at least once a day in order to give Cree and Chipewyan language lessons to the nuns. He in turn received private English lessons from Sister Pepin. According to Moulin, word of these intimate sessions could be exploited by Protestant detractors who spread scandalous rumours about the sexual hypocrisy of Catholic missionaries. "The Anglican ministers of the Mackenzie River District are telling everyone that we're all married," noted Moulin. "This habitual exchange with the sisters might lend credence to such rumours and make us lose our standing among the *sauvages*."[60] Three and a half years later, Grandin expressed similar concerns about the conduct of Father Jean-Marie Caër during the latter's brief tenure as superior of Saint-Jean-Baptiste and principal of Saint-Bruno (June to September 1866). Having spent the summer of 1866 at Saint-Boniface, Grandin returned to Île-à-la-Crosse on 21 September and was promptly briefed on an unsettling situation. He subsequently informed Taché of what he had learned:

> Having spoken with all of the brothers and sisters, I am convinced that this poor priest [Caër] cannot be left alone with the sisters. According to our three lay brothers [Louis Dubé, Patrick Bowes, and Jean Pérréard], who are surely exaggerating, he spends more time at the convent than here [at the Oblate residence], and allows himself such familiarity with the sisters that the brothers are scandalized and the sister superior [Agnès] deeply troubled. This good sister assured me that the priest always has a good reason for visiting the convent, but he stays too long and spends hours on end with Sister Pepin during her classes. . . . I forbade him to spend so much time with the sisters.[61]

"Familiarity with the sisters" became a recurring theme in the conflict that simmered between Grandin and Caër over the next two years. This conflict reached boiling point in September 1868 when Caër—ostensibly on behalf of the nuns—reproached Grandin for habitually standing too close when speaking with them. In reporting the matter to Taché, a flabbergasted Grandin insisted that he could not keep a greater distance on account of his "lazy ears" and suggested that Caër had simply delivered the reproach out of spite. "Could the sisters really have wanted to relay such a message to me through an inferior, through someone like Father Caër?" asked Grandin with rhetorical incredulity. "He must have relished telling me, after all of the times that I admonished him for his imprudence, after all of my insistence that the sisters see him exclusively in the confessional. . . . I believe that he is the source of all of this."[62] It was therefore with a sense of relief that Grandin learned of Caër's resolution to leave the Missionary Oblates of Mary Immaculate in spring 1869 and to seek admittance to a Carthusian monastery in France. Grandin marked his departure with a terse farewell: "May he be a better Carthusian than he was an Oblate!"[63]

While never entirely placid or unguarded in the presence of Grey Nuns, the Oblates of Saint-Jean-Baptiste registered a marked improvement in their relationship with the nuns over the course of the 1870s. This improvement resulted in part from a joint effort by Grandin and Sister Ursule Cécile

Charlebois—Assistant General of the Grey Nuns—to clarify and codify rules on interaction between the two communities. Grandin accompanied Charlebois on her visit to Île-à-la-Crosse in late August 1871, and together they devised "sensible regulations" for local use, which included an outright ban on unsupervised contact between individual Oblates and individual nuns outside of the confessional.[64] Responsibility for implementing these regulations fell to a young Oblate who inspired tremendous confidence in his superiors. Having assumed direction of Saint-Jean-Baptiste and Saint-Bruno the previous autumn (October 1870), Father Prosper Légeard quickly garnered praise for his administrative and interpersonal skills. "All of my hopes for this priest are being realized," reported Grandin after his visit to Île-à-la-Crosse in August 1871. "One can confidently assign any task to him; he gets along exceedingly well with his *confrères*, the sisters, and the local people."[65] In pursuing his mandate to regularize and to improve relations with the Grey Nuns, Légeard endeavoured to enhance their material position and their standard of living at Île-à-la-Crosse. He drafted plans and oversaw the construction of two buildings that he entrusted to the nuns in 1874. The first was a two-storeyed structure measuring ten by seven metres. It was subdivided into a classroom, a parlour, and a dormitory. The second was a three-storeyed structure measuring fifteen by ten metres. It was subdivided into a private chapel, an infirmary, a kitchen, a refectory, and a dormitory.[66] This second structure—commodious by the standards of the time and place—was dubbed "the little château" by Agnès and her *consœurs*.[67]

Another reason for rapprochement between Oblates and Grey Nuns was their adoption of a shared devotion in the early 1870s. Through Légeard's pastoral guidance, both communities began venerating the Sacred Heart of Jesus and its most celebrated interlocutor, the Blessed Marguerite-Marie Alacoque.[68] Légeard had developed a personal devotion to the Sacred Heart and to the Blessed Marguerite-Marie while studying at the Oblate scholasticate of Sacré-Cœur in the Diocese of Autun (department of Saône-et-Loire) from June 1864 to October 1865. This diocese was home to a burgeoning pilgrimage site at Paray-le-Monial, where the Blessed Marguerite-Marie had experienced her divine visions in the 1670s and '80s, and where her remains lay displayed in a reliquary.[69] "You should have a great devotion to this *Bienheureuse* [the Blessed Marguerite-Marie]," Légeard had written to his younger sister, Hortense, in 1865. "I do not doubt that through her intercession, your love for the Sacred Heart of Our Lord will grow. . . . One does not suffer when one truly loves the Heart of Christ, for it transforms the worst bitterness into sweetness and radiates joy amid pain and humiliation."[70] Légeard made the very same recommendation to the Oblates and Grey Nuns of Île-à-la-Crosse a few years later. As their confessor and spiritual director, he urged the missionaries to dedicate their labours to the Blessed Marguerite-Marie and to pray constantly for her intercession.[71] His efforts appeared to bear fruit in the miraculous healing of Sister Sara Riel in autumn 1872. The twenty-four-year-old Riel— younger sister of the famed Louis Riel—had arrived from Saint-Boniface the previous year and had since experienced a rapid decline in her physical health. By 23 November, she was bedridden with severe pneumonia and was apparently in extremis. Légeard, after administering the sacrament of extreme unction, advised the dying nun to pray to the Sacred Heart through the intercession of the Blessed Marguerite-Marie. Riel followed his advice and soon experienced a rapid recovery. Oblates and Grey Nuns hailed this recovery as a genuine miracle and both communities endorsed Riel's decision to pay homage to her heavenly benefactress by adopting a new name—Sister Marguerite-Marie.[72]

In the wake of this healing, Oblates and Grey Nuns invoked the Sacred Heart and the Blessed Marguerite-Marie to protect and to promote the convent boarding school at Île-à-la-Crosse. The most committed proponents of this movement were Riel (Sister Marguerite-Marie) and Légeard. When Sister Pepin was reassigned to Saint-Boniface in August 1873, Riel and twenty-six-year-old Sister Angèle Langelier (lately arrived from the Montreal motherhouse) assumed joint responsibility for teaching the schoolchildren. Riel's first initiative as a teacher was to usher the schoolchildren to the mission church on 12 September 1873, where they consecrated themselves and their studies to the Sacred Heart.[73] She subsequently painted images of the Sacred Heart, which she hung on the classroom walls and distributed to the children.[74] For his part, Légeard made use of his personal contacts with the Visitation Sisters of Paray-le-Monial to procure devotional material—including sheet music for hymns to the Sacred Heart, printed images of the Blessed Marguerite-Marie in ecstasy, and banners emblazoned with a bleeding heart and the motto "Honneur, amour, réparation au S.C. de Jésus" (Honour, love, reparation to the S.H. of Jesus). He even obtained a bona fide relic—a lamp that had burned on the spot where the Blessed Marguerite-Marie had experienced her visions.[75] Finally, Légeard obtained permission from Grandin to re-consecrate the convent boarding school at Île-à-la-Crosse. It became known officially as l'École de Notre-Dame du Sacré-Cœur (Our Lady of the Sacred Heart School) in August 1874.[76] Légeard expressed confidence that this re-consecration would bring "extraordinary grace" to the school and to its pupils: "I am certain that they will receive all of the blessings that Christ Himself has promised to those who honour His divine heart."[77]

This re-consecration was an expression of renewed commitment to residential education in the early 1870s. A sense of urgency infused Oblate writing on the subject after the transfer of Rupert's Land and the North-Western Territory to the Dominion of Canada. Underlying this sense of urgency was a collective fear that Indigenous peoples would shortly be displaced and marginalized by large-scale Euro-Canadian immigration and settlement. As early as 1873, Légeard predicted that "the coming of the whites" would have dire consequences for Indigenous peoples. "Civilization has reached the edges of our region, or at least the edges of the prairies," he reported to the Oblate General Administration in August of that year. "This is all well and good, but it will hardly help our *sauvages* and our métis, who will all disappear little by little. The strangers are watching and waiting for the moment when a treaty is reached between the *sauvages* of the prairies and the Canadian government; then they will pounce on the Saskatchewan Valley and other places."[78] Grandin made a similar prediction two years later in a circular issued to the Oblates and Grey Nuns of the Diocese of Saint-Albert. He insisted, however, that the ills of *la civilisation moderne* could be tempered through the initiative of missionaries:

> The different tribes of *sauvages* who inhabit the immense territory of North America can, through the patient and devoted zeal of missionaries, convert to the faith and become good Christians. But by continuing their wandering and unhappy ways, these poor Indians cannot be brought to a civilized life and will forever remain *sauvages*.
>
> Owing to the annexation of their territory to Canada, they find their hunting grounds increasingly taken over by strangers; their hunting is dwindling and will soon fail altogether; widespread misery will follow and will be compounded by the immorality that civilized people all too often exemplify. The *sauvages* will be lost, both physically and morally.
>
> For a long time now, missionaries have foreseen this tragedy and have wanted to prevent it, or at least postpone it, at all costs. Extensive experience has shown us that *sauvages*, taken in as children, can be educated and civilized. Young Indians raised in our orphanages or even entrusted to Catholic families have effectively

ceased being *sauvages*; they can now live honestly from the fruit
of their own labours and can become members of society. We
currently have no means to undertake this important work other
than the support provided by the Propagation de la Foi. Thus, we
have been able to prove that the civilizing of the *sauvages* can be
accomplished through their little children, but we lack the means
to accomplish this work on a larger scale.[79]

In other words, the imminent physical and moral degeneration of Indigenous
peoples could be forestalled—or at least mitigated—by missionary intervention
in Indigenous childhood. Whereas the behaviours and lifestyles of adults were
deemed fixed and unalterable, those of children were considered eminently
mutable. Missionaries could harness this mutability to effect a transformation
among Indigenous peoples and thereby prepare them for the encroachment
of Euro-Canadian settlement.[80] The convent boarding school seemed a
particularly well-suited institution for this purpose; indeed, it had been at the
core of the Oblates' civilizing project for over a decade. In order to meet the
vicissitudes of the 1870s, however, this institution would need to be thoroughly
revamped. It would need to intensify its assimilative capacity. It would need to
enrol, lodge, feed, and clothe greater numbers of children. Above all, it would
need to obtain a significant increase in funding.

In hopes of meeting this financial challenge, Oblates turned to their long-
established underwriter—l'Œuvre de la Propagation de la Foi. At the dawn of
the 1870s, this society remained the principal financier of Oblate missionary
activity in the Northwest Territories and Grandin commended it to Pope Pius
IX as "the temporal benefactress of the Diocese of Saint-Albert."[81] In 1872,
Grandin requested that l'Œuvre increase his annual allocation so that he could
improve the existing schools in his diocese and establish several new ones. To
publicize this project and elicit donations from associates of l'Œuvre, Grandin
embarked on an extensive lecturing tour through several dioceses in France the
following year.[82] He also made use of l'Œuvre's official periodical—*Les Annales
de la Propagation de la Foi*—to reach the broader French Catholic reading
public. In the 1872 edition of *Les Annales*, Grandin extolled the civilizing
potential of the convent boarding schools through a panegyric on the Grey
Nuns' establishment at Île-à-la-Crosse:

For the past ten years, the Sisters of Charity—also known as the
Congregation of Grey Nuns of Montreal—have lent us their zeal

and devotion. These Sisters work tirelessly in several of our missions, but the good that they accomplish is more perceptible at Île-à-la-Crosse than anywhere else.... Over forty children, thirty of whom are *pensionnaires* and a good number born to *sauvage* parents, receive a very sound and thorough education there. Several of these children write and speak French so well that, while attending their *examens*, one forgets one's exile from beautiful France. These *pensionnaires* are divided into two houses: the little boys live with the priests, the little girls with the Sisters. We often speak of civilizing the *sauvages*. I can see no better way of doing this than by taking them in as small children. Those who leave our schools are no longer *sauvages* in their habits, and we foresee them establishing truly Christian families.

Our schools are not terribly costly, but we cannot increase them because we alone pay for them, the parents being unable to help. But if instead of thirty *pensionnaires* we could lodge and feed a hundred, we would be able to recruit them immediately: the *sauvages* whose children are in our care are proud that, as they say, their children have become French. Scores of other parents pester us to accept their children so that they too can become French. Let our schools and our missions multiply, and the *sauvages* will disappear without ceasing to exist.[83]

Grandin's panegyric—tailored specifically for a French Catholic readership—presented the convent boarding school at Île-à-la-Crosse as a model to be replicated throughout the Diocese of Saint-Albert. This replication would accelerate an ongoing civilizing process that transformed "sauvages" into Frenchmen and Frenchwomen—a process that had already created an oasis of French Catholicism in the wilderness of British North America. This replication could only occur, however, through an increase in financial support from l'Œuvre de la Propagation de la Foi.

Through his entreaties, Grandin did obtain incremental gains in his allocation from l'Œuvre over the course of the 1870s.[84] Yet he confided to his *confrères* that these gains were sorely insufficient to effect any substantial improvements in residential education in the Diocese of Saint-Albert.[85] By spring 1875, Grandin had resolved to solicit additional funding outside the auspices of l'Œuvre. He eagerly endorsed a proposal by Légeard for the sponsorship—or "l'adoption"—of schoolchildren at Notre-Dame du

Sacré-Cœur (formerly Saint-Bruno) by private benefactors in Europe.[86] Légeard recommended that the Oblates of Saint-Jean-Baptiste use their personal and professional contacts to find a sponsor for every schoolchild. Sponsors could be individuals, families, schools, seminaries, convents, parish congregations, or even commercial enterprises. Each sponsor would donate at least fifty francs per year to feed, clothe, and shelter a schoolchild. In return, sponsors would receive special mention in the schoolchildren's daily prayers. An additional honour would be reserved for sponsors of orphans and found-lings (who generally incurred greater expenses than did the "children of the fort"): "We will give to the orphans whom we receive *the name* of the sponsor, or at least the name of one of the people who contributes to this good work."[87] Grandin's elder brother—a Parisian layman—received this honour in 1875 after he agreed to sponsor a Chipewyan-speaking foundling who had lately been admitted to Notre-Dame du Sacré-Cœur. At his baptism, the child was given the name Joseph Grandin.[88]

Although intended originally for the maintenance of schoolchildren at Notre-Dame du Sacré-Cœur, Légeard's proposal became the basis of a large-scale project to finance residential education throughout the Diocese of Saint-Albert. In March 1878, Grandin announced his intention to create a new charitable association that would be known as l'Œuvre des écoles du Nord-Ouest. This association would consist of sponsors—or "adoptants"—who would collectively assume the costs of boarding, feeding, and clothing Indigenous schoolchildren in the diocese. Sponsors would be divided into four classes. A first-class sponsor would donate 400 francs per year and, in return, would have the privilege of bestowing his or her surname on a beneficiary. A second-class sponsor would be a group of four to eight members who would each contribute between fifty and 100 francs per year. They would decide among themselves which member would bestow his or her surname on a beneficiary. Third- and fourth-class sponsors would be groups of ten and twenty members who would each contribute "a few francs or pennies" per year.[89] To avoid overburdening France with an additional charitable association, Grandin sought to establish l'Œuvre des écoles du Nord-Ouest among Catholics in the United Kingdom and justified this decision on the grounds that the Indigenous peoples in his diocese were British subjects. He enlisted support for his project from prominent British Catholics—including Father Robert Cooke (superior of the Oblates' Anglo-Irish Province) and Dr. Henry Edward Cardinal Manning (Archbishop Westminster and titular head of English Catholicism).[90] Yet while preparing a journey to London to meet with potential sponsors in June 1878,

Grandin was stopped in his tracks by the intervention of the Paris council of l'Œuvre de la Propagation de la Foi. Members of this council had read published reports of Grandin's intention to establish a "sister organization" to the Propagation de la Foi in England and had become wary of a possible competitor.[91] Léon Colin de Verdière—the seventy-seven-year-old president of the Paris council—consequently wrote to Grandin and threatened to with-hold his allocation until he renounced l'Œuvre des écoles du Nord-Ouest. "We have full confidence," added Colin de Verdière with Parisian aplomb, "that in renouncing this project, which completely violates the rules of l'Œuvre [de la Propagation de la Foi], you will allow us to continue providing the Diocese of Saint-Albert with an assistance that has always been a source of great consola-tion for us."[92] Seeking to defend his project before the Paris council, Grandin insisted that l'Œuvre des écoles du Nord-Ouest would pose no threat to l'Œuvre de la Propagation de la Foi because the two organizations would have different functions and would draw their funds from different sources.[93] The council was unmoved by this argument; it promptly reissued its threat to cut off Grandin's annual allocation.[94] Unable to forgo this allocation—insufficient though it was—Grandin officially abandoned his plan to establish l'Œuvre des écoles du Nord-Ouest on 24 June 1878.[95] He subsequently confided to Taché that l'Œuvre de la Propagation de la Foi had asserted a paralyzing grip on the Diocese of Saint-Albert: "Under this exclusive system of la Propagation de la foi, we are condemned to stagnate, unable to grow, unable to break free of the confines in which we find ourselves."[96]

No longer able to rely exclusively on the largesse of Catholic benefactors in Europe, Oblates in the Diocese of Saint-Albert turned to a new poten-tial source of funding—the government of the Dominion of Canada. In January 1875, Grandin wrote to Alexander Morris—Lieutenant Governor of Manitoba and the Northwest Territories—and informed him that the Oblates and Grey Nuns were operating convent boarding schools at Île-à-la-Crosse, Lac La Biche, and Saint-Albert. Grandin affirmed that these schools were in-tegral elements of an ongoing civilizing project and insisted that the Dominion government had a vested interest in supporting them so as to facilitate the transformation of *sauvages* into productive citizens. "We must acknowledge," noted Grandin, "that the only way to civilize the *sauvages* is to take them in as small children. I, along with all of my missionaries and all of the pious nuns who devote themselves to teaching our children, have no doubt that Her Majesty's Government will assist us in this civilizing venture."[97] The following year, Grandin commended these three schools to Lieutenant-Colonel James

Farquharson Macleod—stipendiary magistrate for the Northwest Territories and former assistant commissioner of the North West Mounted Police—and urged him to use his government connections to obtain federal funding for them. The bishop assured Macleod that the convent boarding school was the most effective and the most economical means of redeeming the *sauvages*:

> At Saint-Albert, at Île-à-la-Crosse, and at Lac La Biche, we are raising at least sixty children. . . . I can assure you that these children, from whichever nation they hail, are no longer *sauvages* when they leave our schools. Obviously they could not join the high societies of civilized countries, but they can certainly take their place with honour among the métis and the ordinary settlers of this country. Experience has proven that civilization kills the *sauvages*, but more than twenty years of experience has convinced me that our manner of civilizing does not kill. If, instead of three orphanages, we had ten or more, and if, instead of raising only fifteen or twenty children in each of these establishments, we could enrol a hundred or more, civilization would soon make the *sauvages* disappear without killing them. When they leave our establishments, these children have nothing of the *sauvage* left in them but their blood. They have even forgotten their natural language, so much so that returning to the *sauvage* lifestyle is no longer possible for them; we inspire such strong aversion to that lifestyle that they are humiliated when we remind them of their origins. You see, Colonel, our objective is not to produce <u>monks or partisans of our Religion</u>; our objective is uniquely <u>to produce men</u>. Thanks to the combined efforts of priests, lay brothers, and Sisters of Charity in their complementary spheres, we can succeed in this work more easily and more economically than anyone else. Bound by vows of celibacy and therefore having no one else to provide for, we think only of our mission. We see only our mission. We live only for our mission.[98]

Grandin thus presented the convent boarding school as an ideal adjunct to the Canadian state. By sponsoring this institution, the state could hasten the transformation of *sauvages* into industrious, conscientious, and self-sufficient individuals—"men"—who would contribute meaningfully to a settler society and raise civilized children. The bishop emphasized two particular benefits of the convent boarding school in order to garner the support of government officials. First, graduates of this institution could never revert to "the *sauvage* lifestyle" because they had been thoroughly acculturated to European/Euro-Canadian modes of thought and behaviour and because they had been inculcated with contempt for ancestral ways. Second, the operational costs of the convent boarding school were comparatively lower than those of Protestant educational institutions. Oblates and Grey Nuns laboured *gratis pro Deo* and were unencumbered by the obligation to provide for spouses and children. They therefore offered the promise of a better return on state investment in residential education.

To assist Grandin in his bid for federal support, Légeard petitioned for subsidies to Notre-Dame du Sacré-Cœur. On 3 April 1874, a federal order-in-council authorized the payment of $300 per year to each "Indian school" attended by at least twenty-five pupils in the Diocese of Saint-Albert. Légeard subsequently notified the Lieutenant Governor of the Northwest Territories that Notre-Dame du Sacré-Cœur was attended by upwards of forty pupils and that it was duly entitled to an annual subvention. Accordingly, the convent boarding school received a payment of $300 in 1875 and another in 1876.[99] The following year, however, the school was denied further subvention on the grounds that it lay outside the limits of Treaty Six—negotiated and signed at Fort Carlton and Fort Pitt in late August and early September 1876 by Crown officials and representatives of bands of Plains Cree, Woods Cree, Saulteaux, and Chipewyan.[100] In an effort to obtain a renewal of federal funding, Légeard wrote to David Laird—Lieutenant Governor of the Northwest Territories—on 25 March 1878, and drew his attention to the clause in Treaty Six that obliged the Crown to "maintain schools for instruction . . . whenever the Indians of the reserve shall desire it."[101] The most effective way to fulfill this obligation, insisted Légeard, was to support Notre-Dame du Sacré-Cœur:

> It is true one could tell us we are not properly speaking on the ground comprised in the Treaties made by the Government with the Indians of the North West, but a Government as liberal as the one that rules Canada actually will not look so narrowly, I hope, from the moment the question is the promotion of education in a portion of these countries of the North West he [*sic*] desires so much to civilize. He will not I trust refuse to come to the help of the most ancient school now existing in the North West, the only one in the English River District. More so I will take leave to make Your Honor observe that this school is open to all of any religion.

It is true we only have Catholic children actually, but at different periods we had few Protestant ones, their parents were in the Company service and they entrusted them to our care. Moreover allow me to say that although we are not really in the territories included in the Treaty, we depend from [sic] them in some way. At the time of the Treaty made in 1876 between Her Majesty, Our Most Gracious Queen, and the Indians of the Plains at Carlton and at Fort Pitt, the Government engaged himself to give to each band who adheres to the Treaty school and teachers. The Indians of Green Lake who have taken the Treaty at Carlton, and the Chipewyans at Fort Pitt would have the right to ask for a school, and the Government I am sure would do all in his power to satisfy them, but the band of Green Lake and that of Cold Lake are really not in number sufficient to have a school each, they will not ask for one, but finding a school all organized, as much as they can they will ask us to instruct their children as they have done and as they would do more than ever if they knew we could accept them. We have some of Green Lake, and lately a request has been made from Cold Lake to place a child in the summer. For all these reasons it would be preferable it seems to me to support a large school where the teaching is better organized, where there is more emulation, than to try to establish many small schools that would not maintain themselves certainly.[102]

Légeard's letter—written in English and sprinkled liberally with Gallicisms—outlined the practical advantages of off-reserve education for the Cree and Chipewyan children of Green Lake and Cold Lake. These children would have better educational opportunities at Notre-Dame du Sacré-Cœur than at smaller—and as yet nonexistent—schools on their reserves. They would be better taught, better supervised, and better accommodated at "the most ancient school now existing in the North West." Légeard noted also that the children would receive a solid grounding in both French and English, as the Grey Nuns had been giving English lessons at Notre-Dame du Sacré-Cœur since autumn 1873.[103]

Another advantage identified by Légeard was the large contingent of "Half-breed children" at Notre-Dame du Sacré-Cœur. Légeard's letter to Laird contains the earliest pronouncement by an Oblate that the majority of the schoolchildren were of mixed European and Indigenous ancestry. This majority had purportedly remained consistent since the early 1860s: "During the first years also Half-breed children were more admitted than Indian ones, room missing absolutely to receive many Indian children, and so much the more that from the opening of the school, all the pupils were boarders." According to Légeard, this core of mixed-blood pupils would exercise a "civilizing influence" on Cree and Chipewyan children recruited from Treaty Six territory.[104] Informing Légeard's projection was a growing tendency among Oblates to advertise the instrumentality of mixed-blood children in their correspondence with government officials. In April 1875, for instance, Grandin had written to Laird—then federal Minister of the Interior—and had characterized mixed-blood children as "people who are more advanced in civilization." The bishop ascribed to them a salutary role in the civilizing project:

> I have the advantage of operating three orphanages in my diocese where we are raising around fifty métis and *sauvage* children. We often speak about civilizing the *sauvages*. . . . Fifteen years of experience have left me with little doubt that this can be accomplished by raising them from childhood. Not all of them need to receive a complete education, but at least they will cease speaking their *sauvage* language and become accustomed to work. The *sauvage* lifestyle will no longer be possible for them, so they will merge with the métis to whom we will marry them without much difficulty. I have no doubt that, in the end, they will establish good families who will have nothing *sauvage* about them but their blood. If I had more orphanages and could enrol more little *sauvages*, we could greatly advance the work of civilization. Surely this work is worthy of government support.[105]

Implicit in the statements of Légeard and Grandin was the notion of a spectrum of moral, social, and cultural development between *la sauvagerie* at one pole and *la civilisation* at the other. "Half-breeds" or *les métis* occupied an intermediate—and potentially transitory—position between these poles. They could assist in impelling "little *sauvages*" along the spectrum toward *la civilisation* by serving as role models and by reinforcing new standards of thought and behaviour. Their mere presence enhanced the civilizing potential of convent boarding schools.[106]

Yet despite repeatedly touting the merits of convent boarding schools, Oblates failed to obtain the level of federal funding that they considered

necessary for the maintenance and growth of these institutions. They were
particularly aggrieved by the refusal of Lawrence Vankoughnet—Deputy
Superintendent General of Indian Affairs—to consider renewing the annual
subsidy to Notre-Dame du Sacré-Cœur in 1879 and again in 1880 on the
grounds that the school was located outside Treaty Six territory. Their requests
for smaller one-time grants were also denied for the same reason, such that
Notre-Dame du Sacré-Cœur received virtually no federal assistance at the
dawn of the 1880s.[107] Oblate displeasure with this situation soon festered into
resentment and suspicion when Anglican schools in the Lesser Slave Lake
and Peace River regions began receiving federal support in the mid-1880s,
despite being located well outside treaty limits. Grandin expressed his ire at
this apparently inequitable financial arrangement in a memoir penned in 1890:

> The school of Île-à-la-Crosse has existed for thirty years; enrol-
> ment there has averaged twenty-five to thirty children during this
> period.... Since the establishment of a regular government, I have
> been begging incessantly for government support for that school.
> ... My requests have always been refused on the pretext that the
> *sauvages* of Île-à-la-Crosse were not part of the treaty. I neverthe-
> less remained convinced that, as a gesture of goodwill, the gov-
> ernment would do something about this situation.... No sooner
> had Protestant schools been established at Lesser Slave Lake and
> Peace River than they began receiving government assistance. That
> seems fair enough, but why not do the same for the school at Île-
> à-la-Crosse? Everyone knows the reason, and the gentlemen at
> the Department of Indian Affairs better than anyone: it's because
> this establishment is Catholic.... This is an undeniable crime.[108]

The bishop perceived this "undeniable crime" as evidence of an insidious plot
on the part of federal bureaucrats to discriminate against Catholic schools in
favour of Protestant ones. He perceived further evidence of this plot in the
administration of day schools and boarding schools on the reserves lately
established under Treaty Six. According to Grandin, "Treaty Indians" had
been guaranteed freedom of conscience and were therefore entitled to schools
operated by the denomination of their choosing. He claimed, however, that
officers, agents, and employees of the Department of Indian Affairs (established in 1880) systematically violated the treaty rights of Catholic Indians
by prohibiting Oblates from establishing schools on their reserves and—more

commonly—by moving Catholic Indians away from pre-existing convent boarding schools.[109] Grandin informed the Oblate General Administration that the latter practice had effectively ruined several Catholic schools his diocese by 1887: "Although the government itself is quite liberal, we have become convinced that far too many of its agents are much the opposite. For shameful reasons that are well-known to us, they have moved the *sauvages* far away from several of our establishments and in so doing they have rendered these establishments as useless as if they had burned them to the ground."[110] Grandin attributed this trend partly to the discriminatory hiring practices of the Department of Indian Affairs. In November 1887, he informed his clergy that the department was staffed almost entirely by like-minded Protestants who were hostile to Catholic interests: "None of these employees, at any level of the department . . . can escape the influence of his religion, goaded on as he is by his friends and especially by the ministers of his cult. The latter, enjoying political support, are empowered to do whatever they like against us. . . . There is no denying it: we are targets of a steadily intensifying persecution."[111]

As their hopes of obtaining necessary financial support dwindled in tandem with their confidence in the federal bureaucracy, Oblates abandoned their resolve to maintain Notre-Dame du Sacré-Cœur as a large-scale residential institution. Three local developments contributed to this decision. The first was the loss of mission personnel occasioned by the deaths of Légeard (1 June 1879) and Riel (25 or 27 December 1883).[112] Both deaths had serious repercussions on the quality of instruction and the level of surveillance at Notre-Dame du Sacré-Cœur, but Légeard's was especially devastating as it portended the dissolution of an extensive network of private benefactors.[113] The second development was the depletion of the natural resource base in the immediate vicinity of Île-à-la-Crosse. By the mid-1880s, the inhabitants of the Catholic mission and the HBC fort had drastically altered the surrounding landscape after decades of felling trees, sowing and harvesting crops, and husbanding livestock.[114] Under these circumstances, Grandin doubted that his clergy could continue supplying the quantities of firewood and food required for the maintenance of a large *pensionnat*. "Local resources are steadily diminishing," the bishop observed to HBC Chief Factor Lawrence Clarke in October 1884. "Fishing is becoming erratic; hay and firewood are harder than ever to procure. Soon we will need to import provisions just to feed the schoolchildren. It will be impossible for me to maintain this establishment under such conditions."[115] The third development was the evacuation of the mission during the Northwest Rebellion in spring 1885.[116] The immediate impetus for this evacuation was a rumour—relayed on 28 April by a panic-stricken HBC clerk—that a horde of marauding *sauvages* was coming to capture the mission and the fort at Île-à-la-Crosse. Alarmed at this rumour, Father Joseph Rapet and Factor Roderick Ross resolved to relocate their respective personnel and dependents to a guarded encampment on Île Sainte-Croix—an islet in the rapids of the English River.[117] Preparations for the relocation were frenzied and slapdash: mission stores were dumped into ox carts and barges; fishing nets were abandoned in the lake; fields were left unploughed; seeds were left unsown. After more than a month in self-imposed exile, the "refugees" returned to Île-à-la-Crosse on 30 May and found that neither mission nor fort had been touched by rebel hands. They also found that their exile had taken a serious toll on their material position, making it impossible for Oblates and Grey Nuns to continue providing daily food and fuel for a large contingent of schoolchildren. Rapet was therefore left with little alternative but to re-introduce the day-student system for children with relatives in the immediate vicinity of Île-à-la-Crosse. Only six orphans—three girls and three boys—would remain in residence at the mission; the other thirty would return to their families every evening. Thus, when classes resumed on 1 June 1885, Notre-Dame du Sacré-Cœur began operating primarily as a day school.[118]

The abandonment of the large-scale *pensionnat* was a source of bitter disappointment to Oblates. In January 1889, a sullen Rapet informed the Oblate General Administration that a day school could provide only a limited education to local girls and boys, whom he described as "children who have no taste for studying and whose sole desire is to leave school as soon as possible." Nevertheless, he conceded that the Grey Nuns were making tolerable progress with their day pupils.[119] Rapet and his *confrères* attributed this progress to Sister Marguerite Brabant, who had arrived from Saint-Boniface in July 1888 and who had begun teaching at Notre-Dame du Sacré-Cœur the following autumn.[120] In the "Codex historicus de l'Île à la Crosse," Father Jean-Marie Pénard described Brabant as "métisse by origin" and posited a natural affinity between her and the day pupils: "As a métisse herself, she understood the métis well and knew how to deal with them."[121] While registering tepid satisfaction with the progress of the day pupils, Oblates pinned greater hopes on the small contingent of orphans who remained under the constant supervision of mission personnel. These orphans were deemed more readily civilizable because of their isolation from family members and their perpetual immersion in the company of clergy. Additionally, Oblates persisted in the belief that the rearing of "*sauvage* orphans" entitled the mission to a modicum of federal financial assistance. Hence, over the course of the late 1880s and 1890s, Rapet and Vicar Apostolic Albert Pascal petitioned repeatedly for funding from the Department of Indian Affairs.[122]

Their efforts finally bore fruit in autumn 1897. In preparation for the negotiation of Treaty Eight (1899), the Department of Indian Affairs initiated a major expansion of funding for schools in the northern portions of the Northwest Territories and British Columbia.[123] Within this context, the department recognized Notre-Dame du Sacré-Cœur as a boarding school and agreed to disburse per capita grants of seventy-two dollars per annum for twelve of its "Indian boarders." The school received its first federal payment of $864 the following spring.[124] In reporting this development to the Oblate General Administration, Pénard noted that Notre-Dame du Sacré-Cœur had begun generating regular revenue for the first time in its history and that it would eventually cease being a burden on the debt-ridden mission. To hasten its progress toward financial viability, Pénard considered increasing the enrolment of "*sauvage* orphans" over the following years: "If we could manage to boost the number of government-sponsored boarders, the orphanage . . . could actually be of some help to the rest of the mission."[125]

For nearly four decades before its integration into the federal residential school system, the convent boarding school at Île-à-la-Crosse had served as the operative instrument in the Oblates' civilizing project. The school had been devised to transform local Indigenous children into full members of *la civilisation chrétienne*. It was meant to reorder their social lives and to reshape their patterns of thought and behaviour in accordance with contemporary French Catholic norms. Through a pedagogical regimen based on French and French-Canadian notions of childrearing and socialization, Indigenous children were expected to become dutiful Catholics and fluent speakers of French. Their gender relations were to be reconfigured in preparation for their roles as Catholic wives, mothers, husbands, and fathers—the progenitors of civilized families. Schoolgirls were to become the vanguard of a regenerated and emancipated womanhood, possessed of domestic skills and fully cognizant of a mother's civilizing vocation within the home. Schoolboys were to be taught care and respect for their future helpmates, whom they would support through diligent work outside the home. Both sexes were to undergo an inward moral improvement and an outward refinement of manners through constant supervision, intervention, and role-modelling by missionaries.

Yet after formulating this civilizing project in the late 1850s and 1860s, Oblates encountered continual challenges in implementing it over the following decades. Among these challenges was the ambivalence—if not outright resistance—of local Indigenous families. Oblates noted that many families were incorrigibly reluctant to contribute to the material welfare of the school and to enrol their children as *pensionnaires*. Another challenge was the Oblates' perpetual struggle to maintain a productive relationship with their closest collaborators, the Grey Nuns. This relationship was fraught with tension arising from the imperative of celibacy and the ambiguous division of space, responsibility, and power at the convent boarding school. Finally—and perhaps most critically—Oblates encountered tremendous difficulty in securing the financial resources necessary to maintain the school. Despite their repeated entreaties, Oblates were never able to obtain a sufficient increase in their allocation from l'Œuvre de la Propagation de la Foi. Nor were they able to supplement this allocation with donations from other corporate benefactors. Their petitions for federal funding were equally unfruitful as the Dominion of Canada declined responsibility for schools located outside of treaty limits. By summer 1885, the school's material needs had far outpaced its financial resources. Under the circumstances, Oblates had little alternative but to convert Notre-Dame du Sacré-Cœur into a day school and to retain only a small contingent of orphans as boarders.

Thus, when Notre-Dame du Sacré-Cœur became a federal boarding school in 1898, it was a much attenuated version of the institution that Oblates had envisaged four decades earlier. In deviation from the original civilizing project, missionaries were compelled to relinquish their hold on most of their pupils each evening and let them return to their families.

CHAPTER 4

Oblates and the Categorization of Indigeneity

During the second half of the nineteenth century, Oblate missionaries to Rupert's Land and the North-Western Territory occupied a liminal space between the western societies that produced them and the Indigenous societies that they sought to evangelize. This position enabled them to serve as two-way conduits, transmitting western religious and cultural values to Indigenous peoples while at the same time transmitting knowledge of Indigenous peoples to interested parties in Europe, the United States, and Canada. While the former transmission was an inherent goal of the Oblate apostolate, the latter was a response to growing demand from outside the ranks of the congregation. There emerged at least two distinct markets for information on the Indigenous peoples of Rupert's Land and the North-Western Territory in the late nineteenth century. The first of these markets was fuelled by the burgeoning scholarly disciplines of anthropology and ethnography. Oblates—together with missionaries from other communities and denominations—were enlisted as "men on the spot" to contribute field data to both human sciences.[1] For instance, the Smithsonian Institution in Washington, DC, relied on Oblates for ethnographic and linguistic data on the Dene (or "Tinneh"), the Cree, and the "Metifs of Red River" throughout the 1860s and '70s.[2] Concurrently, French scholarly societies—notably the Société d'anthropologie de Paris and the Société philologique de Paris—drew on the Oblates' transcriptions of Indigenous oral traditions and also on their lexicons, grammars, and primers in Indigenous languages.[3] The second market for Oblate knowledge was fuelled by the expansionist aspirations of the Canadian state. This market was inaugurated in 1858 when Simon James Dawson—chief surveyor of the Canadian Exploring Expedition—requested that Bishop Alexandre-Antonin Taché of Saint-Boniface prepare a detailed report on Rupert's Land and its inhabitants. In his preface to the official version of Taché's report (1859), Dawson ascribed unrivalled expertise to the Oblate prelate: "Bishop Taché has been in the country for fourteen years, and has travelled far and wide among the native tribes, and in the exercise of his high office must have had the best opportunities of observing their habits and character. His remarks are therefore of the greatest value."[4] Oblate knowledge was increasingly solicited over the following decade as Canadian politicians debated the merits of annexing Rupert's Land and the North-Western Territory. In an avowed effort to inform this debate, Taché prepared and published his *Esquisse sur le Nord-Ouest de l'Amérique* (1869), which contained seven chapters of detailed information on soil, climate, flora, fauna, transportation, and population.[5] His discussion of the latter subject was subdivided according to the various "nations" that inhabited the vast region.[6]

This purveyance of knowledge of Indigenous peoples has received consistent acknowledgement from historians of the Oblate apostolate since the early 1970s, when Gaston Carrière first called attention to the enormity of the Oblates' ethnographic and linguistic output.[7] Yet Oblate knowledge itself—its production, its content, and its organization—has received scant critical attention. For the most part, historians of the Oblate apostolate have assumed that this knowledge derived from prolonged empirical observation and that its interpretive value lies solely in its factual content. Hence, in her discussion of the writings of Father Émile Petitot on the Dene of the Athabasca and Mackenzie regions, Martha McCarthy notes that much of this corpus is "valuable" because it contains accurate ethnographic and linguistic information. However, she issues a word of warning about a particular theme that recurs in some of Petitot's writings and that compromises their reliability:

> [Petitot] was convinced that [the Dene] were the descendants of the Ten Lost Tribes of Israel. He saw similarities in Dene myths to Bible stories of the Flood, of Noah and the Ark, of giants, the Tower of Babel and the subsequent confusion of languages. . . . Petitot's writings on the Dene and their traditions and beliefs are one of the major sources of contemporary knowledge about them. His enthusiasm for conversion, however, added to his conviction that the Jewish foundation he saw in Dene life would facilitate

their acceptance of Catholicism, led him to extremes. Other Oblates rejected many of his notions about the Jewish traits of the Dene. Though his statements are often valuable, they should be taken cautiously and interpreted in the light of later scholarship.[8]

Implicit in McCarthy's warning is the prescription that Petitot's "valuable" statements be disentangled from his valueless statements (i.e., those whose factual content has been invalidated by later scholarship). Yet even while opting to dispense with the latter statements, McCarthy alludes—perhaps inadvertently—to their interpretive potential: statements about the Dene's Jewish origins are reflective of Petitot's own "enthusiasm for conversion" and of his confidence in the Dene's readiness to become devout Roman Catholics. Thus, while these statements reveal little about the Dene themselves, they reveal a great deal about Petitot, as they provide a window on his cultural and intellectual conditioning, his belief system, and his professional objectives.[9] These statements are a salutary reminder that Oblate perceptions and representations of Indigenous peoples were necessarily informed by an underlying missionary agenda.

This chapter explores the role of this agenda in shaping Oblate perceptions and representations of Indigenous people. In particular, the chapter examines ways in which the Oblates' objectives, concerns, and priorities informed their construction of categories of indigeneity at Île-à-la-Crosse between 1846 and 1898. As these underlying motivations evolved over this fifty-two-year period, so too did Oblate-made categories of indigeneity. In the course of this process, the Indigenous inhabitants of Île-à-la-Crosse were reassigned from the category *sauvage* to that of *métis*.

In their earliest writings on Île-à-la-Crosse, Oblates referred to local Indigenous peoples collectively as *des sauvages*. This practice was evident in Taché's published account of the welcome that he and Father Louis-François Laflèche received upon their arrival in 1846: "The two men of prayer arrived at Île-à-la-Crosse on 10 September. How could we possibly describe what was happening in their souls as they shook hands with hundreds of poor *sauvages* who hungered for knowledge of God and who gave wholehearted thanks that the work begun by Father Thibault would continue?"[10] In a letter to his mother dated 26 May 1854, Taché provided a somewhat more tempered assessment of the moral and spiritual development of the local population: "Our *Sauvages* are very well disposed [to the faith]; pray that their favourable dispositions continue and deepen."[11] Underlying this broad application of the term *sauvage* was the consideration that local Indigenous peoples had yet to be fully incorporated into institutional Catholicism, which Oblates deemed the precondition for membership in *la civilisation chrétienne*.[12] Father Jean-Baptiste Thibault had initiated their incorporation during his visit to Île-à-la-Crosse in May 1845 when he had baptized 218 *sauvages*, several of whom he registered as having French surnames—including Boucher, Bouvier, Desjarlais, Morin, and Roy.[13] Taché and his *confrères* continued this intensive baptizing over the following decade, such that an estimated 617 *sauvages* had received the sacrament at Île-à-la-Crosse by 1 January 1856.[14] Yet the administration of baptism was merely the beginning of an incorporation process that Oblates expected to last several years, and possibly even generations. Neophytes—those who had lately been baptized—had still to imbibe the spiritual and moral teachings of the institutional church in preparation to receive dispensations of grace through the six remaining sacraments.[15] Their progression toward full membership in *la civilisation chrétienne* would require regular and intensive ministration by ordained clergy.

While ascribing uniformity to *les sauvages* of Île-à-la-Crosse on the basis of their common neophyte status, Oblates divided them into subcategories on the basis of their different linguistic exigencies. This division reflected one of the foundational objectives of the Oblate apostolate—namely that all peoples receive the ministrations of the Catholic Church in their native language. Since founding the congregation in 1816, Charles-Joseph-Eugène de Mazenod had instructed his missionaries to follow apostolic tradition by acquiring local vernaculars in order to preach persuasively and to guide laypeople to a deeper acceptance of Catholicism.[16] Hence, the first Oblates were required to become proficient in the Provençal dialect of Occitan before undertaking mission work in Aix, Marseilles, or the surrounding countryside.[17] Mazenod extended this requirement to *les missions étrangères* and elaborated on it in the second edition of the Oblates' *Constitution and Rules* (1853): "To facilitate the infidels' introduction to necessary truths, missionaries will take it upon themselves to compose—in the indigenous language—a summary of Christian doctrine in the form of question and answer. Neophytes will learn this summary by heart; it will be explained to them gradually and in terms appropriate to their capacity. Missionaries will also convey these truths through hymns, which will be sung to their congregations; they will compose illustrated catechisms; in short, they will use every means at their disposal to communicate Christian doctrine to neophytes and to engrave it in their memories."[18] Mazenod's directive established "the indigenous language" as the primary strategic consideration in *les missions étrangères*. Proficiency in Indigenous languages was the *conditio sine qua non* for inculcating the tenets of Catholicism through sermonizing, catechesis, and hymnody. Bound by this imperative, the first Oblates at Île-à-la-Crosse categorized their neophytes according to spoken language, identifying two target groups for their ministrations: speakers of Cree and speakers of Chipewyan.

Acquiring the vernaculars of these target groups was a protracted process that demanded considerable effort on the part of Oblates. There existed no dictionaries, grammars, or primers to facilitate this process in 1846, so the first Oblates at Île-à-la-Crosse were compelled to procure teaching and interpretive services from native speakers of Cree and Chipewyan. Taché and Laflèche received their first lessons in these languages from three Chipewyan-speaking oarsmen during their long journey from Fort Garry to Île-à-la-Crosse in summer 1846.[19] They continued their studies at Île-à-la-Crosse under the tutelage of the HBC's resident interpreter—a native Cree-speaker who was reportedly fluent in Chipewyan, but who spoke no French.[20] While studying with this tutor over the following two years, Taché reported ambivalently on his personal progress. He learned Cree with relative constancy and ease—a feat that he attributed to the grammatical regularity and semantic transparency of the language. Indeed, Taché accorded eloquent praise to Cree, asserting that it surpassed European languages in its "energy, variety, and neatness of expression."[21] Yet Chipewyan beset him with "almost insurmountable difficulties"—difficulties that he attributed to the complexity of its pronunciation patterns:

> It is impossible to imagine such an assortment of bizarre and raspy sounds: sudden stops in the middle of words; frequent aspiration; gutturals accompanied by sibilants; long series of consonants, interspersed with barely audible vowels. The sum effect provokes laughter among all who hear it for the first time. Therein lies the great difficulty of learning this language . . . a task that has thus far daunted even the most courageous. One can find documents on most other *sauvage* languages, but nothing is available on this one, apart from the documents that we ourselves have prepared. We have had to develop around twenty arbitrary characters to indicate sounds that cannot be rendered in our alphabet.[22]

Notwithstanding inherent difficulties, the acquisition of Chipewyan was made somewhat easier through the efforts of Father Henri Faraud, who quickly distinguished himself as a gifted linguist.[23] Immediately after his arrival at Saint-Jean-Baptiste in July 1848, Faraud began learning the two local languages from his *confrères'* tutor. In the process, he developed and refined the notes that Taché and Laflèche had compiled over the previous two years. Faraud gradually transformed these notes into Cree and Chipewyan dictionaries, grammars, and vocabularies—each of which was eventually copied and placed at the disposal of other Oblates.[24] Moreover, Faraud provided personal language instruction to the Oblate reinforcements who were deployed to Saint-Jean-Baptiste and its satellite missions over the course of the 1850s and early 1860s.[25] Hence, in November 1862, Father Julien Moulin marvelled at Faraud's "tremendous knowledge of local languages" and noted: "He could not be more gracious in teaching them to others. Each day he gives me a two-hour language lesson and he is always willing to do more."[26]

Yet despite the efforts of the first contingent of Oblates, later arrivals to Saint-Jean-Baptiste still struggled to acquire—and maintain—proficiency in Cree and Chipewyan. Even with textual resources and a personal tutor at his disposal, Moulin experienced great difficulty in learning these languages. In June 1863, Faraud reported that his student had made little headway after four years of intensive study: "Father Moulin is still struggling with his language studies; he is still in the beginning stages."[27] Moulin professed embarrassment about his slowness, particularly because he considered it a hindrance to his ministry and to the spiritual growth of his neophytes. His embarrassment was most acute when administering the sacrament of penance—a process requiring direct and spontaneous communication between priest and penitent. By his own admission, Moulin struggled to understand confessions in Cree and in Chipewyan, and was incapable of imposing penance or of providing counsel in either language.[28] Similarly, Bishop Vital-Justin Grandin agonized over his own difficulties in acquiring Chipewyan. The bishop feared that his linguistic shortcomings prevented him from asserting proper authority and from project-ing credibility among Chipewyan-speaking neophytes. Much to his chagrin, some of these neophytes chided him for his awkward, halting speech. "You're such an idiot," they reportedly told him. "You sound like a stuttering child."[29] Compounding Grandin's difficulties were the many episcopal duties that di-verted his time and attention away from the study of Chipewyan. Preoccupied with administrative affairs and continual travel in the 1860s, Grandin admitted that proficiency in Chipewyan was an ever-elusive goal for him.[30]

Because of their continued difficulty in acquiring and maintaining proficiency in Cree and Chipewyan, the Oblates of Saint-Jean-Baptiste relied on long-term assistance from native speakers of these two languages. By June 1864, they were receiving frequent language lessons from a Chipewyan-speaking widow known as "the aged Catherine," reportedly one of the first people baptized at Île-à-la-Crosse. Living with her daughter, her son-in-law, and her grandchildren some eighty kilometres northeast of Saint-Jean-Baptiste, Catherine welcomed Oblates into her family home and treated them as "well-behaved schoolboys."[31] Among her pupils was Father Laurent Le Goff (an ordained Oblate from the French department of Finistère), who produced several works in Chipewyan in the 1870s—including a collection of hymns and sermons (1873), a sacred history (1876), and a grammar (1877). Catherine collaborated in the composition of each of these works.[32] Her contribution was described in Le Goff's personal memoirs:

> The aged Catherine and I had an understanding that we would not try to force our ideas on one another, but would instead work together in the interests of truth and true doctrine. I would compose out loud and Catherine would listen intently. Whenever the right word eluded me—which happened all the time—I would try to explain my meaning to her. Being very intelligent, she would quickly understand and provide the very word that I had been seeking. Whenever I used a word that might shock or offend, she would stop me immediately and offer a better one. Whenever my phrasing became awkward or irregular, she would stop me and have me begin again. And thus, over time, this kindly old woman taught me to develop a truly montagnais turn of phrase.[33]

While receiving instruction and editorial assistance in Chipewyan from Catherine, Oblates obtained comparable services in Cree from another local widow—Marie-Rose Piwapiskus (also known as Marie-Rose Petit-Fer, or Marie-Rose Iron).[34] Descended from a Plains Cree family settled at Canoe Lake (approximately forty kilometres southwest of Île-à-la-Crosse), Marie-Rose had been catechized by Taché in the early 1850s and had subsequently acquired a reputation among Oblates for intelligence and piety. She began providing Oblates with Cree-language instruction in 1869 and continued this service for nearly fifty years.[35] During the same period, Marie-Rose also ran a small day school at the mission of Canoe Lake—la

Bienheureuse-Marguerite-Marie (founded in 1871). There she taught prayers, hymns, and catechism in Cree to local children in exchange for an annual stipend disbursed by the Oblate superior of Saint-Jean-Baptiste.[36] Her efforts produced impressive results and garnered high praise from the Oblates. In spring 1876, Father Prosper Légeard reported—with evident admiration—that many of Marie-Rose's pupils knew the catechism by heart. "This is the first time," noted Légeard, "that we see in one of our satellite missions *sauvage* children who know the catechism inside and out. No one else would have thought of attempting this difficult task, and now our little schoolmistress—with her goodwill and perseverance—has done it."[37]

The Oblates' continual pursuit of proficiency in Cree and Chipewyan reflected the centrality of language in the local ministry. Indeed, language was the organizing principle around which all evangelical activity was structured at Saint-Jean-Baptiste. In Ordinary Time—comprising thirty-three or thirty-four weeks of the liturgical year—Oblates followed a weekly schedule that was designed specifically to meet the linguistic exigencies of the local community.[38] The focal event of this schedule was dominical Mass, which Oblates sang three times each Sunday: once in the morning with a homily in French (for mission personnel and schoolchildren); once in the afternoon with a homily in Chipewyan; and once in the evening with a homily in Cree. On weekdays, Oblates catechized schoolchildren in French at Saint-Bruno and catechized non-enrolled children and adults in Cree and Chipewyan at the mission and at the HBC fort.[39] This schedule was modified slightly during Lent—a liturgical season lasting approximately six weeks—when Oblates guided neophytes through the Stations of the Cross and offered penitential prayers in French, Cree, and Chipewyan each Friday afternoon.[40] An altogether different schedule was adopted during the biannual *mission* when large numbers of Cree- and Chipewyan-speaking families travelled to Île-à-la-Crosse and swelled the congregation of Saint-Jean-Baptiste in late September and early June. Each *mission* proceeded according to a relatively standard program.[41] It began shortly after the Cree- and Chipewyan-speaking visitors had set up camp around the mission and the fort, effectively transforming the peninsula into a "village of tents."[42] Over the following twelve to eighteen days, Oblates undertook an intensive missionizing campaign that they structured according to the dictates of language. Father Valentin Végréville outlined this structure in his account of the *mission du printemps* of 1861, which he conducted in concert with Grandin and Moulin:

We began with a procession that was truly worthy of France.... There was strong participation in the singing; we opened with the *Pange Lingua*; then, a hymn in Montagnais carried us up to the small altar near the cross; finally, a hymn in Cree brought us the rest of the way to the church building....

Monseigneur Grandin ... announced the following exercises: I would celebrate Mass for the Cree and give a homily in Cree; Monseigneur would celebrate Mass for the Montagnais and preach in Montagnais. In the evening before sunset, I would address the Montagnais and Monseigneur would address the Cree. At ten o'clock the next morning and again at three o'clock in the afternoon, we would ring for the children. The Montagnais would attend catechism in the sisters' residence; Father Moulin would instruct the Cree....

As soon as a Montagnais left my confessional, a Cree ... would take his place; then another Montagnais would come, and so on and so forth all day and every day.... After my sermon at seven o'clock every evening, I would prepare marriages and attend to all other matters that required personalized attention.[43]

When not engaged in their primary occupations of preaching, catechizing, and administering the sacraments, the Oblates of Saint-Jean-Baptiste set aside hours of the *mission* to pursuing Cree- and Chipewyan-language literacy programs. By the early 1860s, Oblates had adopted the syllabic script developed by Wesleyan missionary James Evans for use among the Western Woods Cree. After adapting this syllabary to the Chipewyan language, they endeavoured to teach their neophytes to read and to write it.[44] To this end, they gathered Cree- and Chipewyan-speaking families in the common room at Saint-Jean-Baptiste and assisted them in transcribing prayers, hymns, and sermons onto scraps of paper or pieces of bark. "We had to write a great deal during our *missions*," noted Grandin, "and our *sauvage* room would be transformed into a veritable study hall. Many young people would copy out prayers and hymns in there, and one of us would always be present to assist them with the writing."[45] In the early 1870s, Oblates began supplementing these handwritten notes with hymnals, catechisms, and prayer books printed in Cree and Chipewyan syllabics.[46]

Given the strategic and organizational importance of language in the local ministry, the Oblate hierarchy assigned congregants of Saint-Jean-Baptiste to one of two categories—*Cris* and *Montagnais*—on the basis of their linguistic affiliation. Hence, in January 1870, Bishop Grandin reported to l'Œuvre de la Propagation de la Foi—the chief financial sponsor of his missions—that the congregation of Saint-Jean-Baptiste comprised 150–200 Cree and "a much larger number of Montagnais."[47] He continued applying this two-part categorization over the course of the 1870s, noting as late as July 1880 that "the *sauvages* of Île-à-la-Crosse are becoming Christianized, Cree and Montagnais alike" and adding that "the priests are beloved by the local *sauvages* and speak their languages perfectly."[48] Grandin's language-based categorization was a necessary concomitant of his administrative responsibility. As Vicar of Missions and Bishop of Saint-Albert, Grandin was responsible for coordinating pastoral and liturgical services for several different language groups dispersed across a vast territory.[49] This charge compelled him to ascertain the linguistic needs of particular missions and to develop appropriate strategies to meet these needs. Accordingly, Grandin oversaw the regular shipment of Cree- and Chipewyan-language reference and devotional materials to Saint-Jean-Baptiste throughout the 1870s.[50] Concurrently, he ensured that the mission was always staffed by at least two ordained Oblates, one of whom was proficient in Cree, the other in Chipewyan. He instructed these Oblates to schedule regular visits to Cree- and Chipewyan-speaking families in the broad vicinity of Saint-Jean-Baptiste.[51]

Yet while the Oblate hierarchy continued to invoke language as the prime criterion for categorizing Indigenous laypeople, Oblates stationed at Saint-Jean-Baptiste began employing new criteria in the mid-1870s. These new criteria emerged from changing patterns of mobility, residence, and trade among the congregants of Saint-Jean-Baptiste—developments that Oblates perceived as cleaving a division across lines of language. Oblates feared that a section of their congregation was becoming detached from the civilizing influence of institutional Catholicism. This section comprised Cree- and Chipewyan-speaking hunters and their families who had customarily travelled to Île-à-la-Crosse each September and June in tandem with the provisioning and trading cycles of the HBC. After surrendering its monopoly trading privileges, the Company broke these cycles through its implementation of various streamlining and restructuring initiatives—notably by restricting the issuance of "Indian debt" (i.e., credit in the form of supplies) and by modifying the transport system through the incorporation of a southern supply route and the adoption of steam power.[52] Concomitantly, Île-à-la-Crosse began drawing fewer Cree- and Chipewyan-speaking hunters and their families each year. Those who did make the journey arrived at scattered intervals and rarely stayed longer than three or four days.[53] Under these circumstances, the Oblates of Saint-Jean-Baptiste opined that Cree- and Chipewyan-speaking hunters and their families were no longer receiving the ministrations of the church with sufficient regularity or continuity. In 1875, for instance, Légeard reported to the Oblate General Administration that these families were forgoing the sacraments and that their children went uncatechized.[54] Furthermore, he asserted that these *sauvages* were losing whatever moral and spiritual values they had once espoused, and that they were drifting toward materialistic greed as their furs fetched rising prices from competitive buyers: "These *sauvages* . . . all have their noses in the air. Until recently, they had only been able to trade with the Company. Now that free traders are here, these poor children of the woods—these big children—think of nothing but their pelts and the prices that they fetch."[55]

In contrast to these *sauvages* who appeared to be drifting physically and spiritually from the orbit of Île-à-la-Crosse, the Oblates of Saint-Jean-Baptiste identified another section of their congregation that they believed was still amenable to the civilizing influence of institutional Catholicism. This section comprised Cree- and Chipewyan-speaking families residing permanently at Île-à-la-Crosse or within a distance that allowed them to attend Mass at Saint-Jean-Baptiste *die dominica aliisque diebus festis de praecepto* ("on Sundays and other Holy Days of Obligation").[56] Among these were the families of local HBC servants, whom Oblates labelled "people of the fort."[57] Also included were the families of "free people"—individuals who were free of contractual obligations to the Company and whose families subsisted principally by fishing, trapping, and gardening.[58] These two groups were settled on the peninsula near the fort and the mission, and also along the surrounding shoreline of Lac Île-à-la-Crosse. In autumn 1876, Légeard enumerated their combined population at 159 and noted that they shared devotional traits that distinguished them from Cree- and Chipewyan-speaking hunters and their families.[59] For instance, the families of "people of the fort" and "free people" attended church services on a weekly basis, received the sacraments with due frequency, and committed their faithful departed to consecrated ground in the local Catholic cemetery.[60] Légeard identified this cemetery as a community space from which non-resident *sauvages* were generally excluded: "Our *sauvages*, being dispersed throughout the woods, are typically buried wherever they die. Only the people of the fort and the *sauvages* who live nearby are buried in our cemetery."[61]

In the course of cataloguing the devotional traits that distinguished resident from non-resident congregants, Légeard provided the first Oblate-authored reference to Île-à-la-Crosse as a predominantly *métis* community. He made this reference in his report to the Oblate General Administration for the year 1876: "Saint-Jean-Baptiste mission (Île-à-la-Crosse). . . . We are very pleased with our little population. These poor people, most of them métis, have their faults, but they listen to our instructions, they receive the sacraments diligently, and they attend services faithfully. What gives us the greatest hope for the future is that there is not a single house at Île-à-la-Crosse that is without an image of the Sacred Heart. This divine heart will surely grant them the blessings that are promised to all who honour it."[62] Légeard identified the veneration of the Sacred Heart as a local devotion—one that was as yet restricted to the métis of Île-à-la-Crosse. He reported, however, that he and his *confrères* sought to encourage its observance among the *sauvages* in outlying areas. Their efforts had thus far been impeded by the limited supply of Sacred Heart paraphernalia at their disposal—notably medallions, prayer cards, and devotional images paint-ed by Sister Sara Riel (also known as Sister Marguerite-Marie). "Currently, each of our métis families belonging to the mission of Île-à-la-Crosse pos-sesses a fairly large image of the Sacred Heart painted on paper by the Sister who was healed," wrote Légeard to a Visitation Sister of Paray-le-Monial. "As for our *sauvages*, they too wish to have images of the Sacred Heart. We have not yet been able to oblige them because our dear Sister Marguerite-Marie is very busy teaching classes each day and has had little time to paint these images."[63] Thus, by the second half of the 1870s, the veneration of the Sacred Heart—together with its material accoutrements—had become one of the devotional traits cited by the Oblates of Saint-Jean-Baptiste in distinguishing a local *métis* population from an outlying *sauvage* population. Collectively, these traits signalled a greater amenability to clerical influence and a more thorough integration into institutional Catholicism.[64]

Yet within a decade of applying the term *métis* to the resident population of Île-à-la-Crosse, Oblates began reconceptualizing the term and reappraising the religious and moral character of those to whom they applied it. Spurring this process were developments in the southern missions of the Diocese of Saint-Albert—particularly those scattered along the fertile Saskatchewan River Valley and its tributary river valleys. In the late 1870s and early '80s, Oblates stationed at these missions reported increasing impiety and immorality among their métis congregants. Bishop Grandin attributed this degeneration to the incursion and spread of *la civilisation moderne* through the medium of Euro-Canadian and European settlers.[65] Unlike the *sauvages*, who were somewhat insulated from *la civilisation moderne* on their reserves, the métis were left vulnerable to its most nefarious influences—including material greed, sexual dissipation, and intemperance.[66] According to Grandin, many were absorbing the virulently anti-Catholic and anti-clerical attitudes that had accompanied white settlement. These attitudes received tangible expression during the Northwest Rebellion in spring 1885 when—in Grandin's account—the métis congregants of Saint-Laurent-de-Grandin, Saint-Antoine-de-Padoue (Batoche), and Sacré-Coeur (Duck Lake) apostatized en masse and embraced the prophetic leadership of Louis Riel.[67] In a particularly violent episode on 2 April 1885, insurgents shot and killed two ordained Oblates at Frog Lake—thirty-four-year-old Félix-Adélard-Léon Fafard (from Saint-Cuthbert, Lower Canada) and twenty-seven-year-old Félix Marchand (from the French department of Ille-et-Vilaine).[68] Underlying this attack on ordained clergy was the corrupting, immoral, and irreligious influence of *la civilisation moderne*.[69] "The métis . . . have suffered greatly from the changes that have come to their country," reported Grandin to the Oblate General Council in April 1887:

> They were not sufficiently prepared for this *civilisation moderne* that came down on them so suddenly. . . . Now they are manipulated by agitators who, for their own selfish ends, pull them away from the priests, from the Church, and from God. I can tell you that this was the entire reason for the recent civil war. . . . We suffered greatly during this civil war, and we continue to suffer in its aftermath, especially in the district of Saint-Laurent-de-Grandin. At one point, nearly all of our métis in that area had apostatized, at least outwardly. We were able to return them to order relatively quickly because they were unaware of their apostasy. Nevertheless, the painful effects of this war will linger for a very long time.[70]

In Grandin's interpretive scheme, the Northwest Rebellion—"this civil war"—had confirmed a widening chasm between "our métis" and institutional Catholicism. Swayed by unscrupulous and acquisitive settlers, the rebels had rejected the piety, morality, and deference that Oblates had striven to inculcate over the previous four decades.[71]

Locally, however, the Northwest Rebellion did not underscore alienation between métis and missionaries at Île-à-la-Crosse. On the contrary, the Oblates of Saint-Jean-Baptiste remained confident in the loyalty and steadfastness of their métis congregation throughout the spring of 1885. They instead directed their fears toward an unseen—and, unbeknownst to them, probably non-existent—horde of marauding *sauvages* that was rumoured to have set its sights on the HBC fort and the Catholic mission.[72] Panic gripped Île-à-la-Crosse on 28 April when an HBC clerk arrived from Green Lake and warned of the horde's approach from the south. Similar warnings followed over the next two days as terrified "refugees" arrived from Green Lake and Muskeg Lake, among whom was thirty-five-year-old Father Mélasyppe Paquette (an ordained Oblate from Sainte-Marie-de-Monnoir, Lower Canada).[73] These refugees joined fifty-nine inhabitants of the mission and the fort in their flight to the safety of a small island—Île Sainte-Croix—in the rapids of the English River. There they entrusted themselves to the care and protection of a band of Chipewyan-speaking hunters.[74] On 24 May, the exiles erected a large wooden cross on which they inscribed a narrative of their ordeal: "It was on this island that the Fathers, Sisters, Brothers, and the *Bourgeois*, imperilled by the approach of the rebellious and persecuting Cree, found refuge among their faithful Montagnais. This cross was erected in memory of their stay as an act of thanksgiving to God."[75] Conspicuously absent from the inscription was any mention of the métis. This absence reflected the Oblates' perception of their local congregation as docile and detached from the Northwest Rebellion. In his chronicle of the exile, Father Jean-Marie Pénard noted that the métis of Île-à-la-Crosse rejected the insurrection tacitly and dreaded the prospect of being drawn into the fray:

> Total fear gripped the place. Our métis, not being very brave by nature, were afraid of incurring ~~the reprisal~~ the hate and vengeance of Riel by declaring themselves on the side of order (to which they were all inclined, less by conviction than by prudence). In general, they all dreaded the coming of Riel, not so much because of the harm that he might inflict on the company or the mission, but rather because he might press them into his service and compel them to fight the English, whose bullets they feared terribly. In short, a sense of worry and fear prevailed among the métis.[76]

Although written thirteen years after the events in question, Pénard's chronicle drew on firsthand accounts from Oblates who had been present at Saint-Jean-Baptiste during the evacuation—namely Fathers Louis Dauphin and Joseph Rapet, and Brothers Fabien Labelle, Félix-Victor Marcilly, and Auguste Némoz.[77] Their perception of the métis as tractable and orderly was corroborated by their memory of finding the mission and the fort unpillaged, unplundered, and unburned upon their return from self-imposed exile on 30 May 1885.[78]

It was only in the aftermath of the rebellion that the Oblates of Saint-Jean-Baptiste began reappraising the moral and religious character of their métis congregants.[79] This reappraisal paralleled the development and exacerbation of serious administrative problems in the Diocese of Saint-Albert. At the core of these problems was a critical shortage of Oblate manpower caused by the recruitment crisis in France and by the pastoral exigencies of Catholic settlers in the prairies. Left with few alternatives, Bishop Grandin redeployed most of his *in situ* personnel to the southern portion—"the most important part"—of his diocese over the course of the 1880s.[80] Concurrently, those Oblates who remained at Saint-Jean-Baptiste and its satellite missions were compelled to assume increasing workloads and to undertake constant travel. By June 1885, three ordained Oblates—Fathers Louis Dauphin, Joseph Rapet, and Jules Teston—shared responsibility for ministering to the métis of Saint-Jean-Baptiste and to the *sauvages* of Notre-Dame-de-la-Visitation (Portage La Loche), Saint-Julien (Green Lake), la Bienheureuse-Marguerite-Marie (Canoe Lake), and Waterhen Lake. They were also required to venture beyond these posts and to visit Cree- and Chipewyan-speaking families in outlying camps.[81] In September 1886, Grandin opted to remove Dauphin from this mission circuit and to redeploy him to Saint-Louis mission at Onion Lake (approximately twenty kilometres northwest of Fort Pitt).[82] According to Pénard, Dauphin's departure marked the beginning of a process of religious and moral degeneration at Île-à-la-Crosse:

> His parting ... was a great misfortune for the mission of Île-à-la-Crosse and for the mission of Green Lake. This priest was well-loved by the Cree and the métis, over whom he had a powerful influence; the young people especially feared and respected him. It is not an exaggeration to say that these two missions would not have fallen into their current state of degradation had Father Dauphin remained at Île-à-la-Crosse. It was precisely at the time of his departure that we began seeing the young métis go awry and give themselves over to disorder with total abandon. None of the priests who succeeded Father Dauphin at Île-à-la-Crosse have managed to reclaim such influence over them.[83]

Beyond depriving "the young métis" of an apparently exemplary pastor and
role model, Dauphin's departure put inordinate strain on the remaining
mission personnel, encumbering Rapet and Teston with additional travel
and pastoral duties. The pair endeavoured to coordinate their itineraries so
that one of them was always present at Saint-Jean-Baptiste, but their efforts
were often thwarted by unforeseen circumstances. Between 1886 and 1889,
for instance, a series of epidemics forced Rapet and Teston to undertake
simultaneous journeys in order to minister to the sick and dying in scattered
locations. Saint-Jean-Baptiste was consequently left without ordained clergy
for several weeks at a time.[84] Despite appealing repeatedly for reinforcements,
the Oblates of Saint-Jean-Baptiste remained acutely understaffed until the
arrival of Pénard in May 1890 and Father Henri Jouan in March 1895.[85]
Still, for several months after their arrival, Pénard and Jouan could make only
limited contributions to the ministry owing to their lack of proficiency in the
local languages.[86] Moreover, Jouan's missionary career was cut short by critical
illness in June 1896.[87] Thus, stretched to the limits of their pastoral capacity,
the Oblates of Saint-Jean-Baptiste sensed a weakening of their moral and
religious influence over the métis of Île-à-la-Crosse. "Those poor métis," noted
Pénard, "are slipping further and further from the missionaries' influence and
into religious indifference."[88]

In slipping from the Oblates' supervision and guidance, the métis of Île-à-
la-Crosse were deemed to be growing increasingly vulnerable to the corrupting
influence of *la civilisation moderne*. Oblates expressed mounting apprehension
about the presence and conduct of "strangers" in the immediate vicinity of
Île-à-la-Crosse in the late 1880s and early '90s. Their concerns were initially
directed toward Protestant—or generally non-Catholic—free traders whose
business practices they considered immoral and whose personal proclivities
they deemed licentious.[89] By 1892, however, Oblates perceived even the HBC
as a source of immorality and irreligion in the local community.[90] That year they
lodged a formal complaint against resident Chief Trader Henry John Moberly
for allegedly inciting the métis to drunkenness and debauchery at *soirées* in
his home. When Moberly was exonerated of this charge by Inspecting Chief
Factor James McDougall in March 1892, the Oblates of Saint-Jean-Baptiste
concluded that the HBC had forfeited any moral credibility that it may once
have held.[91] Relations between Moberly and the Oblates reached their nadir
in early January 1894 when the chief trader and his wife hosted a particularly
bacchanalian New Year's celebration. "The *bourgeois* encouraged a few métis
to drink," recounted Pénard.

He encouraged them to dance with his wife and his daughters. The women of the point [i.e., the peninsula of Île-à-la-Crosse] refused to attend the ball, even though the *bourgeois* had invited them. Nevertheless, he managed to get a few of them to come to the fort on some pretext or other, then he locked them in to prevent their leaving. But they refused to join in the dancing. The *bourgeoise* [Moberly's wife] encouraged them to drink, as her husband had done with the men, but she did not succeed. She was therefore left to drink all by herself, which she managed to do exceedingly well. She drank so much, in fact, that while admiring her rosy complexion in a mirror, her legs buckled and she fell to the floor in a state that propriety militates against describing. It was the most noteworthy part of the evening.[92]

In counterpoising the local women's resolute sobriety with the *bourgeoise*'s wanton drunkenness, Pénard stressed that the métis and métisses had been exposed to corrupting influences against their will. Indeed, the women had been lured under false pretences to the fort and trapped there for the duration of the revelry. While the veracity of Pénard's account is questionable—he had presumably not been present at the Moberlys' party—its underlying meaning is evident: forces of moral corruption were exerting a powerful pull on the métis of Île-à-la-Crosse.

Hoping to counter this pull, the Oblates of Saint-Jean-Baptiste ministered with an increasingly firm hand over the course of the 1890s. They responded to "scandals" and "disturbances" among their local congregants by issuing ever-harsher reprimands and by imposing ever-stricter punishments. Oblates were particularly obdurate in their opposition to social dancing—an activity that the prelates of Saint-Boniface and Saint-Albert had banned on the grounds that it was conducive to frivolity, impiety, and carnal sin.[93] "Since the founding of this mission," recalled Pénard, "all of the missionaries have strictly forbidden dances in which men and women dance together . . . experience having demonstrated incontestably that serious disturbances always accompany such dances, and that the love of religion and church attendance always decline as the love of dancing and carousing increases."[94] After learning that several of his local congregants had attended social dances in early January 1890, Rapet reprimanded them from the pulpit during Sunday Mass.[95] He delivered further scolding from the pulpit in summer 1891 during an apparent rash—"une irruption"—of dancing and drunkenness at Île-à-la-Crosse.[96] As these "scandals" and "disturbances" flared continually into the late summer and early autumn, Rapet and Pénard threatened to take severe disciplinary action against any congregant who attended a dance or who consumed alcohol.[97] Pénard followed through on the threat in late September after returning from a pastoral visit to a Chipewyan-speaking family in an outlying camp:

> Upon his return to Île-à-la-Crosse, Father Pénard learned that the people of the point had—at the incitement of the *bourgeois*—taken advantage of his absence to hold a great ball. Under the circumstances, this ball was a gesture of sheer contempt for the priest's authority and a profoundly scandalous act. The guilty parties evidently assumed that their numbers were too great for Father Pénard to follow through on his threats. . . . But he did not hesitate an instant to execute his threats to the fullest extent. He expelled from the church every man and every woman who had attended the ball, in all around fifteen people. He would have expelled Moberly, too, if the latter hadn't been a Protestant. . . . Our people . . . were stunned and distressed by the brazen ease with which he executed his threats; most of them were instantly filled with regret. . . . Unfortunately, it was not so easy to stop the spread of immorality on the point.[98]

The pronouncement of such a penalty—an *interdictum* against fifteen people—was totally unprecedented at Saint-Jean-Baptiste. Never before had the Oblates punished so many congregants so summarily and so severely.[99] According to Pénard, the pronouncement had an immediate effect on the offenders. Most took steps to gain readmission into the church by confessing their transgressions and by performing penance.[100] Nevertheless, Pénard reported that their contrition faded quickly and that "scandals" and "disturbances" resumed with even greater intensity at Île-à-la-Crosse. He and Rapet consequently redoubled their public reproaches, pronouncing a second interdict in 1895 and a third in 1898.[101] "As things stand at present," noted Pénard in the latter year, " the director of the mission needs to have a firm hand if he wishes to check the gangrene of corruption that is wearing away at the spiritual edifice of Île-à-la-Crosse."[102]

As an extension of casting the métis as casualties of "the gangrene of corruption," Pénard cast them also as agents of this insidious malady. Through them, moral corruption and impiety could spread to the *sauvages*. Hence, by the time of his appointment as superior of Saint-Jean-Baptiste in January 1898, Pénard had become convinced that the *sauvages* should be kept away from Île-à-la-Crosse, "where their contact with the métis is always detrimental to them in terms of their morality."[103] The safest and most effective way of ministering to the *sauvages* was to meet them at outlying satellite missions or in their wintering grounds.[104] To this end, Pénard devised a travel rota whereby he, Rapet, and Teston would undertake itinerant ministries from their respective bases at Saint-Jean-Baptiste, Notre-Dame-de-la-Visitation, and Saint-Julien. Besides shielding the *sauvages* from corrupting influences, this strategy would have the added advantages of providing them with more regular pastoral care and better religious instruction.[105] Pénard believed that the strategy would prove particularly beneficial to Chipewyan-speaking hunters and their families, whom he regarded as morally good but highly impressionable and abysmally ignorant of their religious duties. "Our Montagnais are much better than our métis," he plainly informed the Oblate General Administration. "But they lack firmness and they are not sufficiently well-instructed in their religious duties. . . . I have noticed that many of the most elementary obligations, even those stemming from natural law, are more or less unknown to them; they are inclined to consider these truths as mere novel inventions."[106]

In contrast to the *sauvages*, the métis were fully conscious of their religious duties and responsibilities. They had gained this consciousness through their regular contact with missionaries and through their regular reception of the spiritual and liturgical services of the institutional church. Pénard suspected, however, that this consciousness was no longer underpinned by genuine religious belief. The progressive erosion of métis belief had resulted in a hollow, perfunctory profession of Catholicism.[107] "Our métis . . . seem to shake off their moral apathy on solemn occasions," observed Pénard, "and one can almost believe that their faith and their conscience have awoken at last and that things will change. And then nothing; we return to the same old routine of disturbances and scandals. Thus, even in those moments of apparent awakening, one might wonder if they actually have faith."[108] Troubled by the seeming incongruity between outward religious observance and disordered personal lives, Pénard launched an investigation—"une petite inquisition"—among his regular congregants in early January 1899.[109] He reported being shocked at his findings:

This inquisition—which he did not have the courage to pursue to its end, resentment and disgust having seized him

beforehand—revealed to him such a state of degradation and immorality among the poor métis of Île-à-la-Crosse that he found
himself wondering why the good Lord had yet to inflict the punishment of Sodom on this miserable place. For a long time, the priest
had had some suspicions, but he had certainly not suspected such a
general and complete state of degradation. How did our poor métis
get to this point? That is a question that remains without a satisfac-
tory answer. In all of the reports filed by the missionary superiors
of Île-à-la-Crosse right up to 1876, this mission and the local
Christians all received good grades. Were these priests mistaken?
We do not believe so. Indeed, the people who were adults back
then are still very good Christians today. The degradation began
in their children's generation, that is to say among people who are
now thirty years of age and younger. . . . Because this immorality is
now so widespread and so entrenched, local children will grow up
amid corruption and will be even worse than their parents. All of
this would cause us to despair if we did not have faith in God's help.

On the day of Epiphany [6 January 1899], the priest delivered
a thundering sermon on this subject, threatening the vengeance
of God if things did not change. He could see many of the young
people grinning during his address. This proved to him that their
faith had sunk to the same level as their morality; that is to say
that there is very little left. And yet, their external devotions seem
to indicate that they still have faith. It defies understanding.[110]

Here, then, was a community set so inexorably on a course of moral and
religious degeneration that it risked incurring divine wrath in the form of
fire and brimstone—"the punishment of Sodom."[111] On the basis of records
left by his predecessors—namely Taché, Faraud, Grandin, Moulin, Caër,
Légeard, and Rapet—Pénard determined that the "degradation" had begun
approximately twenty years earlier and that it was proceeding incrementally
with each generational cohort. Yet while confident that he could chart the
course of this degeneration, Pénard was admittedly baffled by the effects it
produced: it eroded the moral and spiritual core of the métis while leaving
their outward religious behaviours unchanged.

In their extensive commentary on the Indigenous congregants of Saint-Jean-Baptiste, Oblates constructed and ascribed categories of indigeneity on the basis of their own objectives, concerns, and priorities as Catholic missionaries. For the first three decades of their apostolate (1846–76), Oblates grouped all Indigenous congregants into a general category—*sauvage*—in recognition of their common neophyte status and their pressing need for the sacramental, liturgical, and educational services of the institutional Catholic Church—the fount and nurturer of *la civilisation chrétienne*. Oblates divided this category into two subcategories—*Cris* and *Montagnais*—on the basis of the linguistic considerations around which they were required to organize the local ministry. Thus, while Oblate-made categories of indigeneity reflected the presence of distinct language groups within the congregation, they did not reflect the presence of distinct ethnic, cultural, or racial groups. Families of mixed Indigenous and European ancestry were subsumed within either subcategory of *sauvage*.

In the mid-1870s, these categories underwent revision in response to the emergence of a chasm within the congregation of Saint-Jean-Baptiste. Forcing this chasm were changes in the HBC's operational and trading strategies, which disrupted traditional patterns of mobility among Cree- and Chipewyan-speaking hunters and their families. These families became an increasingly rare presence at Île-à-la-Crosse, prompting concern among Oblates that they were evading the ministrations of the Catholic Church and entrenching themselves in the moral and spiritual space of *sauvagerie*. By comparison, families residing within the immediate vicinity of Île-à-la-Crosse appeared to remain amenable to the civilizing influence of institutional Catholicism. These families were steadily acquiring a set of shared devotional traits that differentiated them from *sauvages* in outlying areas—notably regular fulfillment of the dominical obligation, dutiful reception of the sacraments, burial in consecrated ground, and veneration of the Sacred Heart. In the course of cataloguing these devotional traits in 1876, Father Proper Légeard provided the first Oblate-authored reference to Île-à-la-Crosse as a predominantly *métis* community.

Yet while they persisted in categorizing the residents of Île-à-la-Crosse as métis over the following decades, Oblates began reconstructing the category and shifting the criteria for inclusion within it. Prompting this reconceptualization was the Oblates' perception of moral and spiritual degeneration in métis communities on the prairies. In the aftermath of the Northwest Rebellion, Oblates attributed the apostasy of these communities to the corrupting influence of *la civilisation moderne* imported by Euro-Canadian and European settlers. *La civilisation moderne* spread steadily and relentlessly

northward, reaching Île-à-la-Crosse in the late 1880s and early '90s through
the conduit of free traders and agents of the HBC. Despite their efforts to
stem the contagion, Oblates found that their ability to do so had been hindered
by reductions in their manpower and increases in their travel obligations.
They sought to compensate for their much-reduced pastoral and supervisory
capacity by introducing coercive measures designed to deter the métis from
indulging in immoral and irreligious behaviour—notably drinking and dancing. These measures had little effect, however, as Oblates reported throughout
the 1890s that the métis committed "scandals" and "disturbances" with increasing frequency, and that they were deviating from their former path of piety,
morality, and modesty.

By the time of Father Jean-Marie Pénard's appointment as resident
superior of Saint-Jean-Baptiste, Oblates had integrated the inhabitants of
Île-à-la-Crosse into a newly revised category of indigeneity. Those subsumed
within this category had once been pious and promising Catholics, but they
were now being corrupted by the encroachment of *la civilisation moderne*.

CONCLUSION

La civilisation moderne:
The World Came Seeping In

In haranguing his congregation with threats of fire and brimstone, Father Jean-Marie Pénard lent his voice to a growing Oblate chorus. By January 1899, the Oblate prelates of Manitoba and the Northwest Territories had united in calling for spiritual and moral reform among "our métis." The prelates had even formed a syndicate to implement a "philanthropic plan to redeem the Half-breeds"—a project developed by Father Albert Lacombe and Father Adéodat Thérien (an ordained Oblate from Sainte-Anne-Des-Plaines, Quebec) in the early 1890s.[1] Lacombe and Thérien envisaged "a refuge" that would draw métis families from across Manitoba, the Northwest Territories, Montana, and North Dakota. These families would settle on contiguous plots of land that they would cultivate under the watchful eye of a resident Oblate. According to Thérien, each family would create "a home near the magnificent church tower and near the school where the métis child—so neglected, so deceived—will receive the benefits of *la civilisation chrétienne*. And, in the not so distant future, I see on that solitary shore a Catholic people, active, hard-working, harvesting surpluses, raising livestock, enjoying the benefits of industry; a people regenerated, ennobled by the salutary influence of work, and blessed by the exercise of our holy religion."[2] Through application to the federal government, the Oblate syndicate obtained a twenty-one-year lease on four townships of Dominion Lands in 1895.[3] Located approximately 160 kilometres northeast of Saint-Albert, the land under lease was christened Saint-Paul-des-Métis and received thirty métis families in 1896.[4] Bishop Vital-Justin Grandin of Saint-Albert dedicated the final years of his life to developing this farming colony and commending it to private benefactors in France and central Canada. He assured these benefactors that Saint-Paul-des-Métis would be a sanctuary from the evils of *la civilisation moderne*, which had wrought such havoc on the faith and the morals of the métis scattered throughout Manitoba and the Northwest Territories. "These poor métis," sighed Grandin while soliciting charity in 1898. "They once gave us such consolation; they were the instrument of Providence for the conversion of the *sauvages*, the bridge between civilization and barbarism.... They were not sufficiently prepared for *la civilisation moderne* that came down on them so suddenly and with all of its usual abuses."[5]

Beyond its prima facie commentary on the sufferings of "these poor métis," Grandin's appeal contained a self-reflective admission: the Oblate apostolate itself had been beleaguered and overwhelmed by social, economic, and political changes in northern and western Canada during the last quarter of the nineteenth century. In the process, Oblates had lost much of their former spiritual and moral influence among Indigenous people. Grandin attributed this loss to *la civilisation moderne*, which he conceptualized as the spawn of irreligious forces unleashed by the Enlightenment and emboldened by the French Revolution—liberalism, secularism, and individualism—and the antithesis of *la civilisation chrétienne*.[6] Since the transfer of Rupert's Land and the North-Western Territory to the Dominion of Canada (1870), Grandin and his *confrères* had grown increasingly sensitive to the encroachment of *la civilisation moderne*. Agents of this virulent force lurked at every turn and assumed a variety of guises: the Euro-Canadian or European migrant who settled on Indigenous lands and exhausted the natural resource base; the Protestant HBC officer who sabotaged the Catholic mission network; the federal bureaucrat who schemed against Catholic educational interests; the French anticlerical republican who persecuted the church in its European heartland; the grasping fur trader who worshipped none but Mammon. Out of this increasing sensitivity there emerged a profound ambivalence toward European and Euro-Canadian society. On the one hand, Oblates continued to insist that membership in *la civilisation chrétienne* required conformity to particular European habits of thought, behaviour, and expression. On the other hand, they identified Europeans and Euro-Canadians as agents of *la civilisation moderne*, and therefore as corrupting influences on Indigenous people.

Try as they might, Oblates could do little to brace their Indigenous flock against the world that was seeping in. Even their "philanthropic plan to redeem the Half-breeds" was eventually submerged and swept away in the flood. Oblates had nevertheless built a sturdy bulwark around Saint-Paul-des-Métis: they forbade white people from settling in the colony; they banned intoxicating liquors there; and they threatened would-be squatters, trespassers, and traffickers with prosecution. They also insisted on retaining control of the colony's land, granting the métis only usufructuary rights in order to prevent them from selling to acquisitive Europeans or Euro-Canadians.[7] Yet the colony was beset with staffing and financial problems from the outset. Neither the Oblate General Administration nor local Catholic prelates could spare the manpower to meet Lacombe and Thérien's requests for farming, carpentry, and blacksmithing instructors.[8] Neither the federal nor the territorial government provided regular financial support for the colony. Private benefactors offered only sporadic assistance, and most of their contributions went to the construction and maintenance of a large church, presbytery, and boarding school.[9] When a fire destroyed the school and claimed the life of a boarder on 15 January 1905, Saint-Paul-des-Métis faced imminent collapse. Thérien blamed the métis themselves for the disaster, alleging that a cabal of their "treacherous and ungrateful" children had set the blaze intentionally.[10] He and his *confrères* struggled to maintain their philanthropic plan in the wake of the fire but ultimately admitted defeat in June 1908 when they requested termination of the land lease. They nevertheless hoped to mitigate the influence of *la civilisation moderne* on the local métis by encouraging French-Canadian and Franco-American Catholics to take up homesteads in the area. Through clerical agents known as *missionnaires-colonisateurs*, the Oblate prelates of Manitoba, Saskatchewan, and Alberta devoted whatever financial resources they could muster to advertising the agricultural potential of Saint-Paul-des-Métis and other métis communities to prospective homesteaders in Quebec and in French-Canadian expatriate communities in the northeastern United States.[11]

While growing ever warier of the encroachment of *la civilisation moderne* into their mission field, Oblates revised the meaning and scope of the term *métis* within the context of their apostolate. Before the 1870s, they had employed the term in reference to an Indigenous collectivity defined by its common use of French and by its common profession of Catholicism. These characteristics had distinguished the métis as eminently suited to integration into *la civilisation chrétienne*. In the decades after 1870, however, Oblates began to perceive the métis as the segment of their flock that was most vulnerable to *la civilisation moderne*. Two considerations underlay this perceived vulnerability. The first was the Dominion government's exclusion of "Half-breeds" from the treaty and reserve system, which left them exposed to the corrupting influence of settlers, speculators, and traders. The second was an administrative crisis in the Catholic mission network: white settlement placed increasing strain on the Oblates' diminishing resources, prompting a redeployment of personnel and finances from long-established Indigenous missions to nascent Euro-Canadian parishes. Under these circumstances, Oblates feared that they were losing the ability to countervail the influence of *la civilisation moderne* on the métis. This fear impelled a reconceptualization of the métis as an Indigenous collectivity requiring extraordinary ministrations—including closer supervision, harsher ecclesiastical discipline, and exemplary punishment. Thus, the Oblates' revision of the term *métis* was as much a product of disruption in their apostolate as it was a reflection of objective change in an historical Métis population.

This evolutionary trajectory of the term *métis* is discernible in Oblate commentary on the Indigenous inhabitants of Île-à-la-Crosse. From the founding of Saint-Jean-Baptiste in 1846, Oblates were undoubtedly conscious of a large mixed-blood contingent in the community, given the pervasiveness of European surnames and the historical role of Île-à-la-Crosse as a contact zone between distinct ethnolinguistic groups. Yet they ascribed no intrinsic meaning to mixed-bloodedness, and referred to members of the community collectively as *des sauvages* on the basis of linguistic and religious considerations. Oblates did not begin differentiating between a local *métis* population and an outlying *sauvage* population until the mid-1870s, by which time some residents of Île-à-la-Crosse had acquired a degree of proficiency in French (through the convent boarding school) and virtually all had been incorporated into the institutional Catholic Church (through the reception of the sacraments and the regular ministration of a resident priest). During the latter half of the 1870s, Oblates represented the métis of Île-à-la-Crosse as pious and promising Catholics and as models of civilized thought and behaviour for the *sauvages* in surrounding areas. The *métis* were thus conceptualized as both beneficiaries and agents of *la civilisation chrétienne*.

Within a decade of re-labelling the community, however, Oblates began investing it with characteristics of vulnerability to *la civilisation moderne*. This development paralleled the erosion of the Oblates' pastoral and supervisory capacity. As Saint-Jean-Baptiste experienced drastic reductions in personnel and funding over the course of the 1880s and '90s, Oblates sensed a weakening of their moral and religious influence over the métis of Île-à-la-Crosse. Concomitantly, they expressed mounting apprehension about the influence of free traders and agents of the HBC, whom they began to perceive as sources of vice and corruption. By the late 1890s, Oblates had reconceptualized Île-à-la-Crosse as a community gripped by the same moral and spiritual crisis that pervaded all métis communities in western and northern Canada.

ACKNOWLEDGEMENTS

This book began its life as a doctoral dissertation researched, written, and defended at the University of Ottawa. I could never have conceived of it, let alone have completed it, without the wisdom, guidance, and extraordinary forbearance of my thesis supervisor, Nicole St-Onge. After completing my dissertation, I was fortunate to have continued working closely with Dr. St-Onge and also with Brenda Macdougall, both of whom I consider exemplary scholars; I extend to them my heartfelt thanks. I am indebted to Keith Thor Carlson (University of Saskatchewan) for his unfailing encouragement and kindness. I am also indebted to the University of Manitoba Press, and especially to Glenn Bergen, David Carr, David Larsen, and Jill McConkey.

Many scholars have contributed to this book by answering my endless questions and by providing much-needed advice. I am particularly grateful to Chris Andersen, Damien-Claude Bélanger, Marie-Pierre Bussières, Heather Devine, Richard Connors, Mike Evans, Kouky Fianu, Corinne Gaudin, Raymond Huel, Father Pierre Hurtubise, Paul Laverdure, Carolyn Podruchny, and the profoundly missed Vasilis Vourkoutiotis. My deep appreciation goes to Maureen Epp for her feedback and her splendid copyediting work. Generous funding for this research was provided by the Social Sciences and Humanities Research Council of Canada, and also by the Faculty of Graduate and Postdoctoral Studies and the Department of History at the University of Ottawa.

A number of archivists and librarians facilitated my research through their extensive knowledge and their generous provision of access to information. I am beholden to Gilles Lesage and Jacinthe Duval of the Société historique de Saint-Boniface (Centre du patrimoine), Diane Lamoureux and Claude Roberto of the Provincial Archives of Alberta (Grandin Archives), Jean-Marie LeBlanc of the Research Centre for the Religious History of Canada, Father André Dubois of the Archives Deschâtelets, Sister Julienne Massé and François Nadeau of the Archives des Sœurs Grises de Montréal, Ellen Alers of the Smithsonian Institution Archives, and the staff of Library and Archives Canada.

Another set of debts is owing to family members, friends, and colleagues who provided invaluable feedback and moral support. I am particularly grateful to Peter Bangs, Robert Englebert, Mandy Fehr, Hardy Firla, Ken Foran, Margaret Foran, Mike Foran, Ron Foran, Gretchen MacMillan, Émilie Pigeon, Donald B. Smith, and Neil Soiseth. I have benefitted enormously from the wisdom and kindness of several colleagues at the Canadian Museum of History and the Canadian War Museum, especially amid the intensity of exhibition development. I extend my sincere thanks to Jennifer Anderson, Morgan Baillargeon, Jameson Brant, Kerri Davis, Alan Elder, Xavier Gélinas, Judith Klassen, Jean-François Lozier, Kathryn Lyons, Peter MacLeod, David Morrison, Glenn Ogden, Forrest Pass, Jean-Luc Pilon, Nadja Roby, Karen Ryan, and Jamie Trepanier.

My final debts are the largest, and I acknowledge them here with humble and heartfelt gratitude. Sylvie Perrier was unfailingly present and engaged during the hardest stretches of the writing process; this process would not have come to fruition without her. My sister and best friend, Jill Foran, was an untiring and uncomplaining sounding board for all of my best ideas. Jessica Shaw has been a source of happiness, hope, and much-needed perspective. My parents, Frank and Pat Foran, have always been pillars of strength but were especially supportive during my doctoral program and the very hard transition that came after it.

Finally, I thank Olivia Faucher for everything. Seasons change, but my appreciation and gratitude remain.

The Evolution of a Catholic Mission Network: Saint-Jean-Baptiste and its Outposts, 1852–72

The Roman Catholic apostolate to Rupert's Land and the North-Western Territory was conceived and initiated by the Missionary Oblates of Mary Immaculate—a religious community founded in southern France in 1816 and granted papal approval in 1826. With assistance from the Hudson's Bay Company (HBC), the Oblates established a major mission at Saint-Boniface in the Red River Colony in 1845. The following year, they established another at Île-à-la-Crosse in the English River District (present-day north-western Saskatchewan). The first mission became the official headquarters of Catholic evangelization throughout the HBC's chartered territory. The latter—entrusted to the patronage of Saint John the Baptist and named in his honour—became the actual headquarters for Oblate expansion into the English (the present-day Churchill), the Athabasca, the North Saskatchewan, and the South Saskatchewan River basins. Strategically located in an HBC trading hub, Saint-Jean-Baptiste provided a base of operations from which Oblates branched out along pre-existing water and land routes to establish satellite missions. Between the late 1840s and the early 1860s, Saint-Jean-Baptiste dominated an extensive network of missions and acted as the central node through which personnel, information, funds, and freight were conveyed. Because of its centrality in this network, Saint-Jean-Baptiste served as the residence of the Coadjutor Bishop of Saint-Boniface, a centre of education and healthcare, a major provisioning depot, and a gathering place for Oblates dispersed throughout the region.

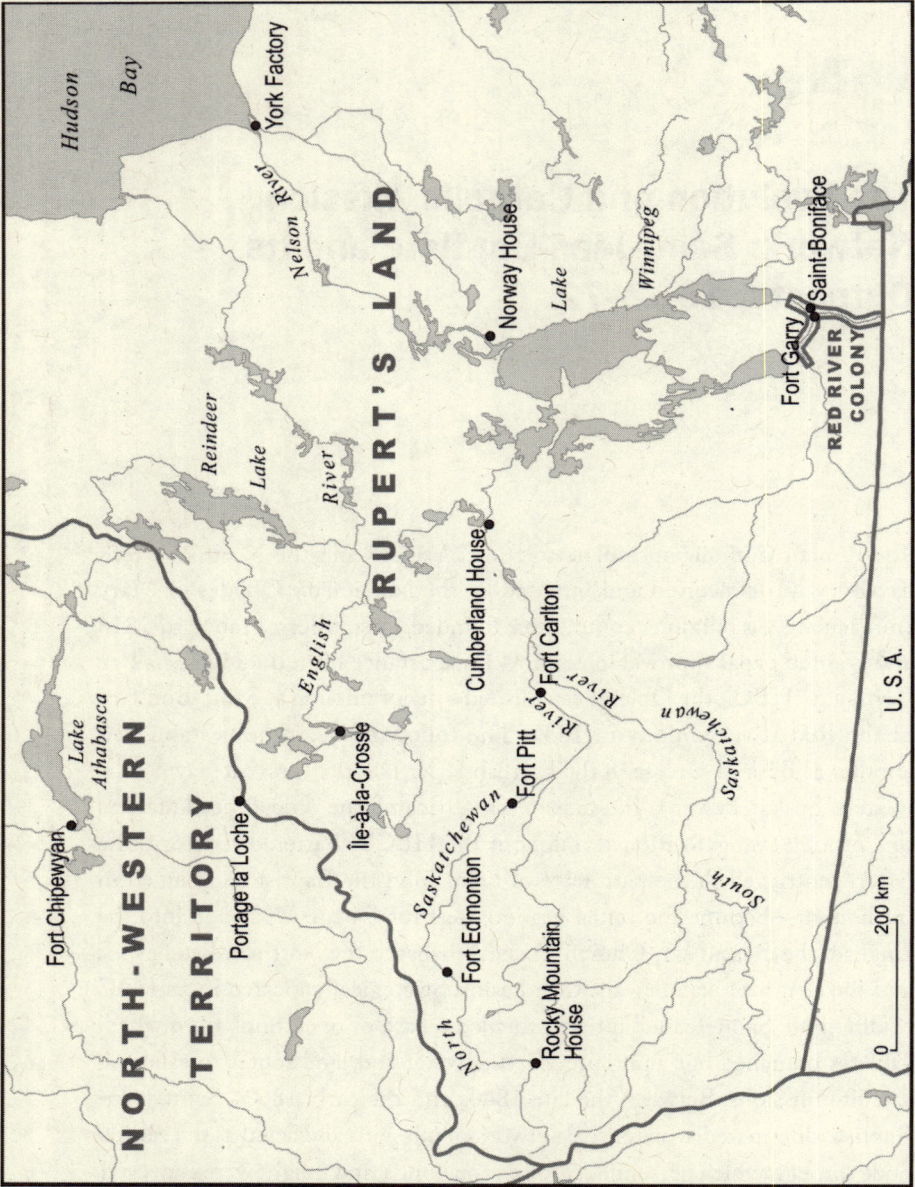

Plate 1: Rupert's Land and the North-Western Territory, 1845

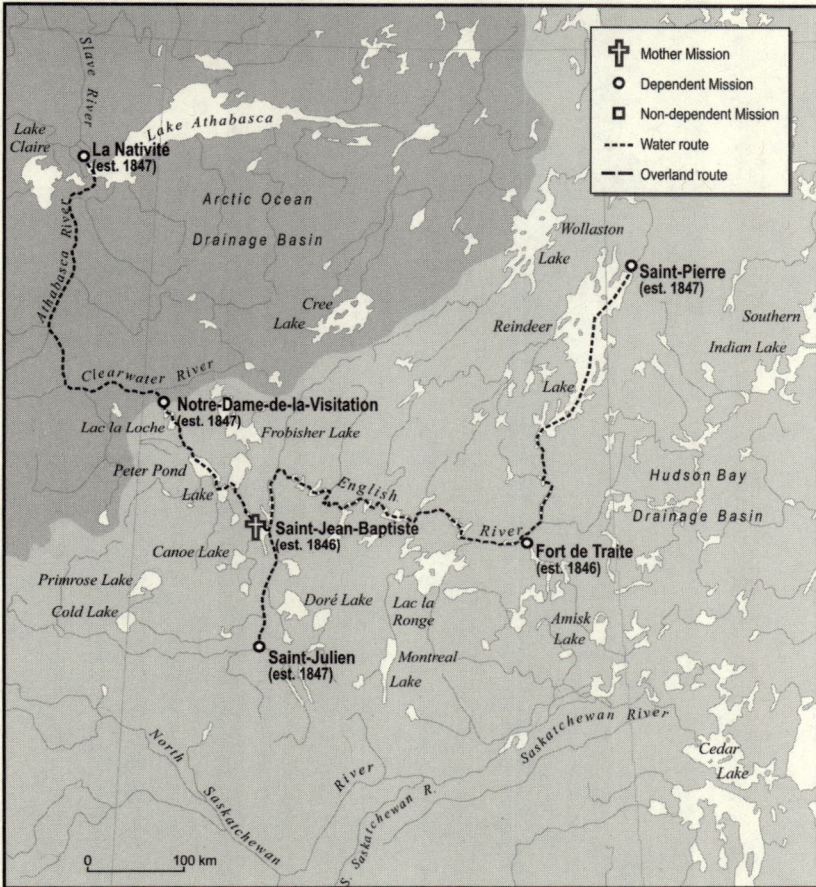

Plate 2: 1852

Within a year of establishing Saint-Jean-Baptiste, Oblates undertook a series of excursions by dogsled, canoe, and barge to outlying HBC posts where they laid the foundations of new missions. These missions were subsequently integrated into a coherent network through regular visits and material provisioning from Saint-Jean-Baptiste. Administrative responsibility for this network was vested in the Coadjutor Bishop of Saint-Boniface, who established his residence at Saint-Jean-Baptiste in 1852.

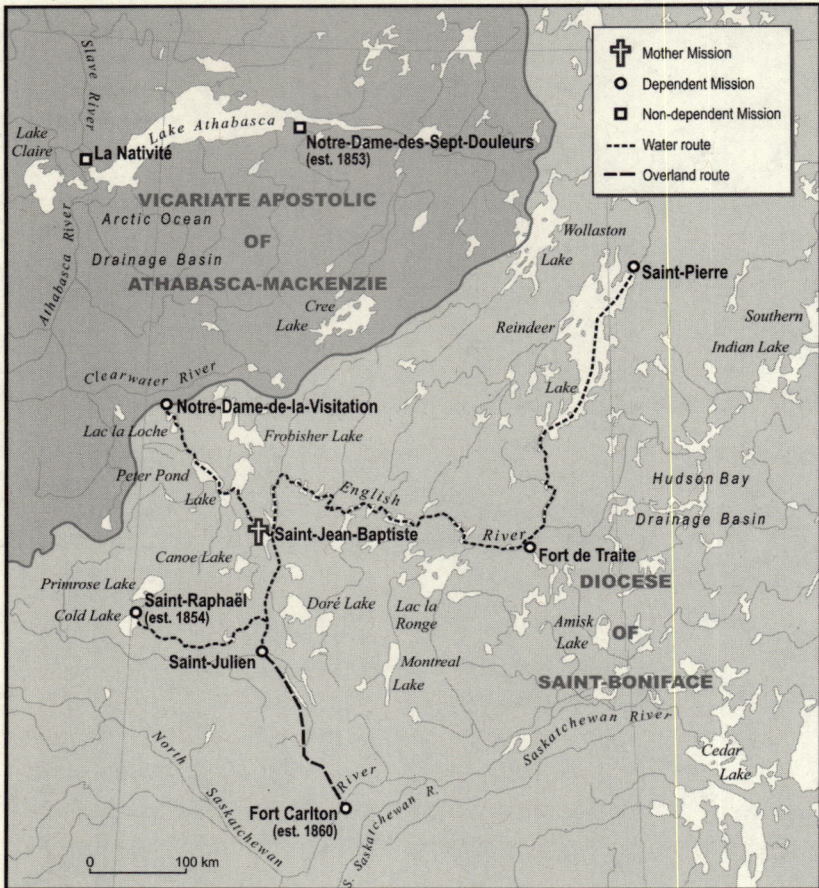

Plate 3: 1862

Over the following decade, the mission network underwent continued expansion with the deployment of additional Oblate personnel to Saint-Jean-Baptiste. These missionaries ventured beyond the original satellite posts and established new stations further afield. However, in attempting to consolidate their growing missions in the Arctic drainage basin, the Oblates encountered serious logistical problems due to the remoteness of these posts from their headquarters. These new missions were consequently detached from the network of Saint-Jean-Baptiste and entrusted to the Vicariate Apostolic of Athabasca-Mackenzie (founded in May 1862).

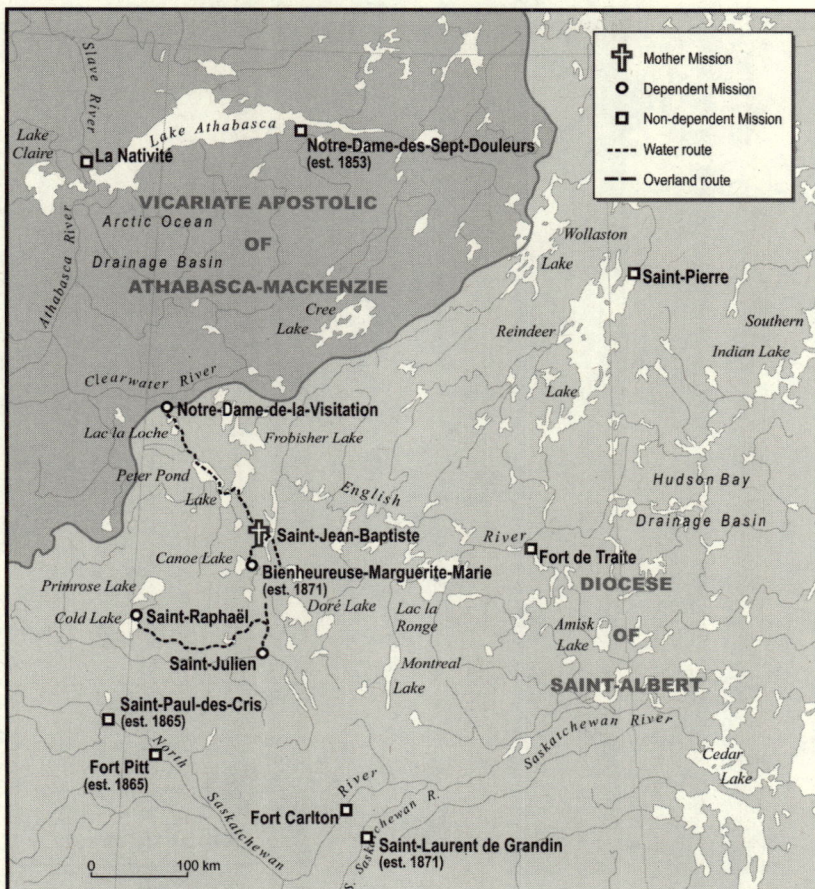

Plate 4: 1872

The mission network of Saint-Jean-Baptiste experienced contraction throughout the 1860s and early '70s as Oblates were deployed permanently to its most remote outposts. Having obtained resident missionaries, these posts no longer relied on the central mission for spiritual services or for material provisions. Meanwhile, the physical infrastructure and the administrative capacity of Saint-Jean-Baptiste were severely weakened by a fire that destroyed the mission on 1 March 1867. This event led to the transfer of the Coadjutor Bishop of Saint-Boniface from Saint-Jean-Baptiste to the more westerly mission of Saint-Albert on the Sturgeon River (a tributary of the North Saskatchewan). The latter mission subsequently became the administrative headquarters of the Diocese of Saint-Albert (carved from the northwestern portion of the former Diocese of Saint-Boniface and established in September 1871).

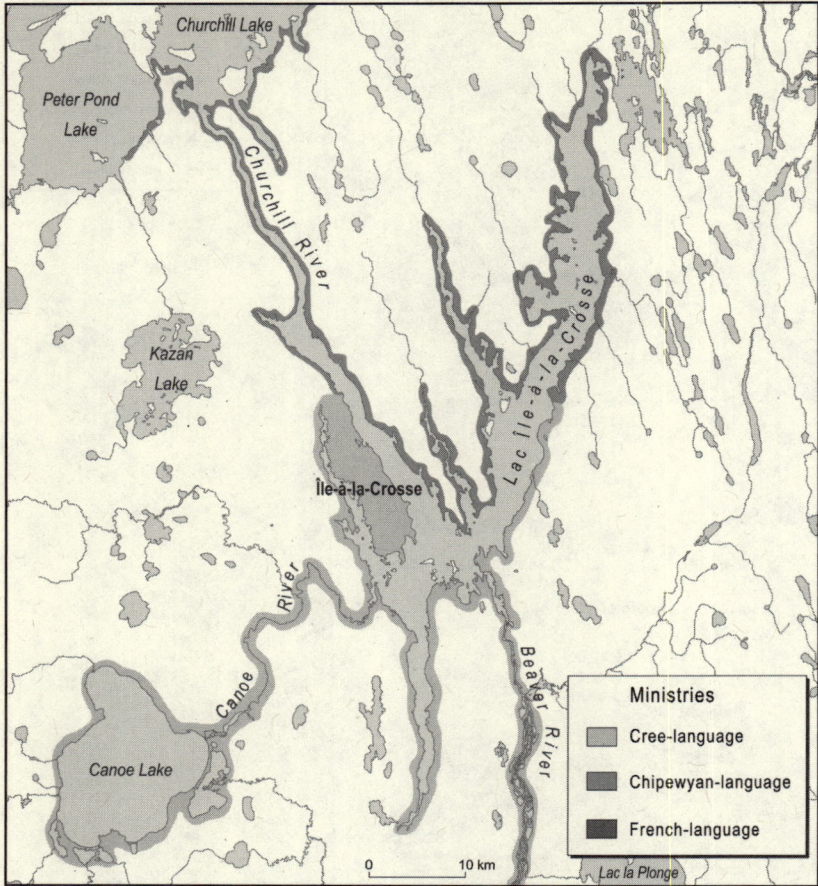

Plate 5: Pre-1862

As the mission network evolved, so too did the evangelical strategy of the Oblates. Under the terms of the congregation's constitution, Oblates were required to become proficient in the languages of their prospective converts and their regular contacts in order to preach persuasively and to guide laypeople to a genuine acceptance of Catholicism. Language was therefore the primary strategic consideration in the Oblates' identification and categorization of target audiences. In the late 1840s, '50s, and early '60s, the Oblates of Saint-Jean-Baptiste coordinated pastoral and liturgical services for two distinct language groups: "les Cris" (Cree speakers) and "les Montagnais" (Chipewyan speakers). Local families of mixed Indigenous and European ancestry were generally subsumed within either category depending on which language they spoke most frequently.

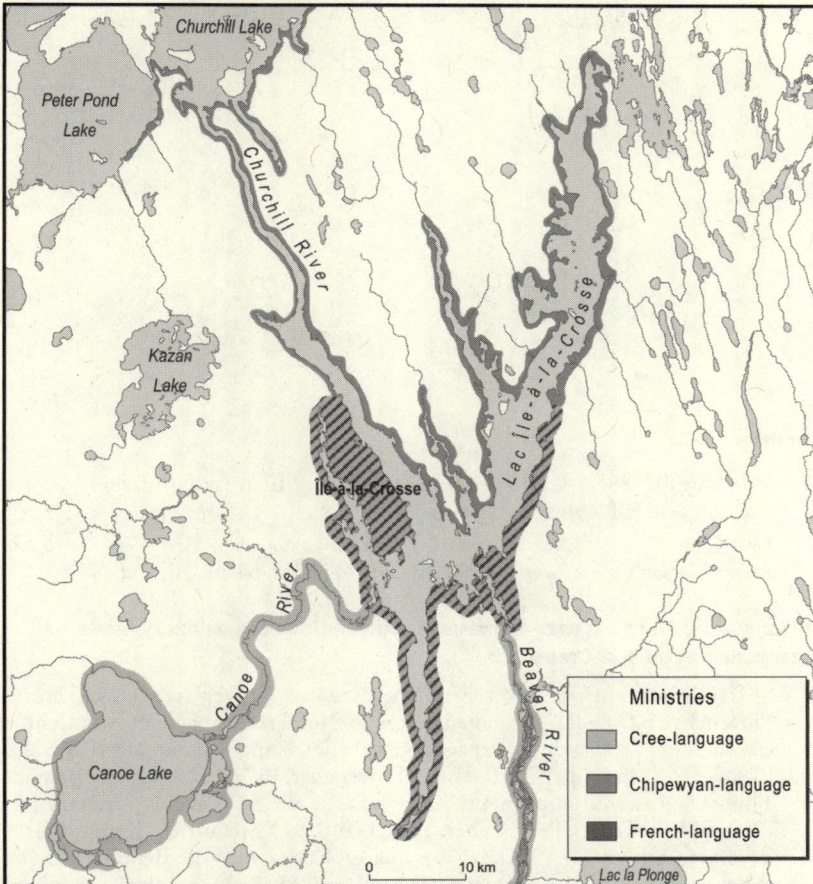

Plate 6: Post-1862

While Saint-Jean-Baptiste remained a base of operations for Oblates who travelled and who provided services in Cree and Chipewyan in the mid-1860s and '70s, the mission's local ministry became increasingly oriented toward individuals who were proficient in French. French-language homilies and pastoral services were offered with increasing regularity to laypeople who lived close enough to the mission to attend weekly Mass. The recipients of these French-language services were mostly pupils, or former pupils, of the convent boarding school, which had opened at Saint-Jean-Baptiste in 1860 and which was run by the Sisters of Charity of Montreal—known as the Grey Nuns. The school provided instruction in French exclusively until 1873, when the nuns began incorporating English into their curriculum.

NOTES

Preface

1 Macdougall, "Socio-Cultural Development and Identity Formation," 11. See also Macdougall, *One of the Family*, 3.

2 Andersen, *"Métis": Race, Recognition, and the Struggle*, 8–13, 59–74; *Truth and Reconciliation Commission of Canada*, calls to action 65, 69, 70, and 78.

Introduction: From *sauvage* to *métis*: The Evolution of Missionary-Made Categories at Île-à-la-Crosse

1 Société historique de Saint-Boniface, Archives [hereafter SHSB], Fonds Provencher, P2707–P2709, quoted in Joseph-Norbert Provencher to the Central Councils of l'Oeuvre de la Propagation de la Foi, Saint-Boniface, 1846. See also P2709–P2711 in ibid.; SHSB, Fonds Provencher, P1792–P1796, Jean-Baptiste Thibault to Archbishop Joseph Signay of Québec, St. François-Xavier, 6 July 1839; SHSB, Fonds Provencher, P1803–P1829, Thibault to Signay, Saint-Boniface, 18 June 1843; Taché, *Vingt années de missions*, 4, 13; Benoit, "Mission at Ile-à-la-Crosse," 41; Choquette, *Oblate Assault*, 35–37; Duchaussois, *Aux glaces polaires*, 134–37; Huel, *Proclaiming the Gospel*, 17, 21–22, 47; Lesage, *Capitale d'une solitude*, 23–25; Levasseur, *Les Oblats de Marie Immaculée dans l'ouest et le nord du Canada*, 12–15; McCarthy, *From the Great River to the Ends of the Earth*, 32–33, 36–37; Morice, *History of the Catholic Church in Western Canada*, 1: 200–201. All English translations of excerpts from French and Latin sources are my own.

2 SHSB, "Codex historicus, 1898–1928," 1–2, 19–20. See also SHSB, "Codex historicus, 1845–1897," 295–96; Carrière, *Dictionnaire biographique*, 3:59–60; Lesage, *Capitale d'une solitude*, 143.

3 SHSB, "Codex historicus, 1898–1928," 20.

4 Calloway, *One Vast Winter Count*, 415, 420, 423; Daschuk, *Clearing the Plains*, 51, 56, 71; Jarvenpa, "Hudson's Bay Company," 490–495, 502; Krech, "Influence of Disease and the Fur Trade"; McCarthy, *From the Great River to the Ends of the Earth*, 17, 120–24, 186, 195–209; Macdougall, "Socio-Cultural Development and Identity Formation," 41–43; Morton, *History of the Canadian West*, 35; Ray, *Indians in the Fur Trade*, 98.

5 Giraud, *Le métis canadien*, xxvi; see also xxvii–xxviii; Giraud, "Foreword," xii–xiii.

6   Giraud, *Le métis canadien*, xxvii.

7   See especially ibid., 847–59, 1040–48, 1063–79, 1092–95, 1131–33, 1145–47, 1201–7.

8   Goldring, "Religion, Missions, and Native Culture," 46–47. See also Pannekoek, *Snug Little Flock*, 9–11.

9   See for instance Payment, *"Les gens libres—Otipemisiwak,"* 19; Spry, "The Métis and Mixed-Bloods of Rupert's Land," 97.

10   Burke, *French Historical Revolution*, 53–64; Curtis, *Politics of Population*, 15–17.

11   Ens, *Homeland to Hinterland*, 7–8, 19–27, 36–40, 57–71, 93–122, 156–63, 173, 177–81; Macdougall, *One of the Family*, xvi, xvii, xviii, 11, 19; Macdougall, "Socio-Cultural Development and Identity Formation," ii, iv, 26–29, 67–76, 83–84, 96–104, 106–9, 131–38, 141, 148, 150–55, 158, 172, 212–14, 222, 228, 235–36, 246, 254, 260, 269, 289, 293, 298, 301–2, 319–20, 327, 335–47; Macdougall, "Wahkootowin," 442–43, 449; Payment, *"Les gens libres—Otipemisiwak,"* 12, 34–45, 81, 84–94, 111–43, 343–44, 363–66.

12   Prior to 1965, historical writing on Catholic evangelization in the northern and western regions of Canada was undertaken exclusively by clerics and required the ecclesiastical *imprimatur* for publication. See especially Benoît, *Vie de Mgr Taché*; Breton, *Le grand chef des prairies*; Breton, *Monseigneur Grandin vous parle*; Breton, *Vital Grandin, o.m.i.*; Champagne, *Les missions catholiques*; Le Chevallier, *Esquisse sur l'origine et les premiers développements de Calgary*; Duchaussois, *Apôtres inconnus*; Duchaussois, *Aux glaces polaires*; Jonquet, *Mgr Grandin*; Legal, *Short Sketches*; Lesage, *Capitale d'une solitude*; Lesage, *L'Evêque errant*; Morice, *History of the Catholic Church in Western Canada*; Ortolan, *Les Oblats de Marie Immaculée*; Une Sœur de la Providence, *Le Père Lacombe*; Soullier, *Vie du Révérend Père Légeard*. See also Huel, "Western Oblate History."

13   Choquette, *Oblate Assault*; Huel, "La mission Notre-Dame-des-Victoires du lac la Biche"; McCarthy, "Founding of Providence Mission"; Huel, *Proclaiming the Gospel.*

14   Huel, *Archbishop A.-A. Taché of St. Boniface*; Mulhall, *Will to Power*; Rivère, *Jean-Charles Pandosy.*

15   Champagne, *Les débuts de la mission dans le Nord-Ouest Canadien*; McCarthy, *From the Great River to the Ends of the Earth.*

16   Carney, "Native-Wilderness Equation"; Gresko, "Everyday Life at Qu'Appelle Industrial School"; Kennedy, "Qu'Appelle Industrial School"; Lundlie, "Les oblats et le Collège Mathieu"; Titley, "Dunbow Indian Industrial School."

17   Vanast, "Compassion, Cost and Competition."

18   See especially Abel, *Drum Songs*, 140; Choquette, *Oblate Assault*, 37, 138, 146, 168, 195, 199; Huel, *Proclaiming the Gospel*, xviii; McCarthy, *From the Great River to the Ends of the Earth*, 41, 46, 107–17.

19   Benoît, *Vie de Mgr Taché*, 1:96–97; Duchaussois, *Aux glaces polaires*, 137–42; Sœur de la Providence, *Le Père Lacombe*, 411–15.

20   Choquette, *Oblate Assault*, 37. See also Huel, *Archbishop A.-A. Taché of St. Boniface*, 18, 49–50, 69. On missionary encounters with the "Lower Canadian heritage" and the "folk Catholicism" of the Métis, see also Foster, *"Le missionnaire and le chef métis,"* 120.

21   McCarthy, *From the Great River to the Ends of the Earth*, 117.

22 On the colonial state's use of categories of indigeneity for governing Indigenous collectivities in the British North American and Canadian contexts, see especially Andersen, "From Nation to Population," 353–55; Andersen, *"Métis": Race, Recognition, and the Struggle*, 26–58; Andersen, "Mixed Ancestry or Metis?," 23–24, 26–27.

23 Provincial Archives of Alberta [hereafter PAA], O.M.I. Collection, Accession 84.400, Item 914, Box 32, Bishop Vital-Justin Grandin to "Mes Révérends et bien chers Pères," Saint-Albert, 6 March 1873, 7.

24 Archives Deschâtelets [hereafter AD], GLPP 2205, Prosper Légeard to Grandin, Île-à-la-Crosse, 13 January 1877; PAA, O.M.I. Collection, Accession 84.400, Item 967, Box 33, Grandin to "Mes chers pères et frères," Saint-Albert, 1885, 5–7; ibid., Grandin to "Mes Révérends et bien chers Pères et Frères," Saint-Albert, 18 November 1887, 6–7; ibid., Grandin to "Révérends et bien chers Pères," Saint-Albert, 10 August 1888, 3–4, 6.

25 PAA, O.M.I. Collection, Accession 84.400, Item 967, Box 33, Grandin to "Mes Révérends et bien chers Pères et Frères," Saint-Albert, 18 November 1887, 6–7. The "Liber animarum" and "Codex historicus" are discussed on pages 15–24. "Scrip" in this context refers to Half-breed scrip—paper vouchers redeemable for land or money.

26 On the transformation of the mission school at Île-à-la-Crosse into a federally funded boarding school, see especially SHSB, Oblats de Marie Imaculée, "Codex historicus, 1845–1897," 295; "Lettre du R.P. Pénard au T.R.P. Général," *Missions de la Congrégation des missionnaires oblats de Marie Immaculée* 151 (September 1900): 261; Abel, *Drum Songs*, 181. On boarding schools and the per capita grant system (introduced by the Department of Indian Affairs in 1893), see especially Huel, *Proclaiming the Gospel*, 148; Miller, *Shingwauk's Vision*, 102, 104, 114–20, 126–29; Miller, "The State, the Church, and Indian Residential Schools," 110, 114–15.

27 For articulations of this premise by pioneers of microhistory, see especially Ginzburg, *The Cheese and the Worms*, xii, xx–xxiv; Ginzburg, "Microhistory: Two or Three Things"; Le Roy Ladurie, *Montaillou*, xiv–xvii; Zemon Davis, *Return of Martin Guerre*, 3–5.

28 Strictly speaking, the Missionary Oblates of Mary Immaculate belong to a *congregation*, as opposed to an *order*. There is a canonical distinction: members of an order are bound by solemn, permanent vows; members of a congregation are bound by simpler, temporary ones. See especially Choquette, *Oblate Assault*, 1, 25.

29 The congregation was known as La Société des Missionnaires de Provence (The Society of Missionaries of Provence) for the first decade of its existence. Mazenod changed the name to Les Oblats de Marie Immaculée while seeking Pope Leo XII's approval for the congregation in 1826. See especially Leflon, *Eugene de Mazenod*, 2:87–152; Levasseur, *Histoire des Missionnaires Oblats de Marie Immaculée*, 1:28–67; Ortolan, *Les Oblats de Marie Immaculée*, 1:77–86, 187–97; Pielorz, "La Congrégation OMI était-elle fondée le 25 janvier 1816?."

30 "Constitutions et règles de la Société des Missionnaires de Provence, Saint-Laurent du Verdon, août–septembre 1818," *Missions de la Congrégation des missionnaires oblats de Marie Immaculée* 276 (March–June 1951): 18. On Mazenod's use of the term *les pauvres* and the meaning of this term in the Oblates' early apostolate, see especially Laframboise, "Eugène de Mazenod et les pauvres"; Lamirande, "Les pauvres et les âmes les plus abandonnées d'après Mgr de Mazenod."

31 The motto was taken from Luke 4:18, in which Jesus reads aloud from the scroll of the prophet Isaiah: "Spiritus Domini super me: propter quod unxit me, evangelizare pauperibus misit me" (The Spirit of the Lord is upon me, for he has anointed me, he has sent me to evangelize the poor). *Biblia Sacra Vulgatæ Editionis*, 681. See also Levasseur, *Histoire des Missionnaires Oblats de Marie Immaculée*, 1:28–30, 83–89; Ortolan, *Les Oblats de Marie Immaculée*, 1:41–44, 54–55, 61–67, 77.

32 Huel, *Proclaiming the Gospel*, 4, 6–7; Lamirande, "À propos des premières missions d'Eugène de Mazenod"; Leflon, *Eugene de Mazenod*, 2:90–102; Levasseur, *Histoire des Missionnaires Oblats de Marie Immaculée*, 1:79–96; McCarthy, *From the Great River to the Ends of the Earth*, 3–4; Ortolan, *Les Oblats de Marie Immaculée*, 1:78, 85, 92–104.

33 Originally from Aquinas's *Contra errores Graecorum*, pars 3, caput 38. Ortolan situated the Oblates in the vanguard of an ultramontane ecclesiology that eventually triumphed at the First Vatican Council: "They [the Oblates] vigorously denounced ... the Gallicanism that young generations were still being taught in the name of the traditions of the French Church. With unwavering conviction, they taught about the infallibility of the Sovereign Pontiff [not solemnly proclaimed until 1870] and the Immaculate Conception of the Blessed Virgin [not solemnly proclaimed until 1854] long before these two truths were dogmatically defined. As for philosophy and dogma, they followed Saint Thomas Aquinas." Ortolan, *Les Oblats de Marie Immaculée*, 1:205. See also Champagne, *Les débuts de la mission dans le Nord-Ouest Canadien*, 36–40; Champagne, "La formation des Oblats," 25–30.

34 Levasseur, *Histoire des Missionnaires Oblats de Marie Immaculée*, 1:69–70, 90; Ortolan, *Les Oblats de Marie Immaculée*, 1:310–23.

35 Levasseur, *Histoire des Missionnaires Oblats de Marie Immaculée*, 1:72–73, 74, 77, 165; Ortolan, *Les Oblats de Marie Immaculée*, 1:363–65

36 Levasseur, *Histoire des Missionnaires Oblats de Marie Immaculée*, 1:122–25; Levasseur, *Les Oblats de Marie Immaculée dans l'ouest et le nord du Canada*, 24–25; Ortolan, *Les Oblats de Marie Immaculée*, 2:7–14, 28–28.

37 Levasseur, *Histoire des Missionnaires Oblats de Marie Immaculée*, 1:109–12, 131, 133, 138–46, 149–54, 158–60; McNally, *The Lord's Distant Vineyard*, 15–28; Ortolan, *Les Oblats de Marie Immaculée*, 1:518–28; ibid., 2:160–62, 271–82, 330, 335–36, 359, 414–17, 451–55; Rivère, *Jean-Charles Pandosy*, 55, 83.

38 According to Claude Champagne, mid-nineteenth-century Oblates employed the term *missions étrangères* in reference to "territories whose populations had not yet been converted to Catholicism or, more precisely, where the church was not yet sufficiently established to govern itself locally; the term was applied to ... England, Ireland, Scotland, Canada, the United States, Ceylan, and Natal." "Instruction de Monseigneur de Mazenod relative aux missions étrangères, présentée et annotée par Claude Champagne, o.m.i.," 164n1.

39 Ibid., 166. On Mazenod's amendment of the *Constitution and Rules* in 1853, see Foran, "Transcending Language and Ethnicity," 510; Huel, *Proclaiming the Gospel*, 5–9; Levasseur, *Histoire des Missionnaires Oblats de Marie Immaculée*, 1:167.

40 Macdougall, *One of the Family*, 26, 32; Macdougall, "Socio-Cultural Development and Identity Formation," 13–16, 34.

41 See especially Brumbach, Jarvenpa, and Buell, "An Ethnoarcheological Approach to Chipewyan Adaptations"; Jarvenpa and Brumbach, *Ethnoarcheological and Cultural Frontiers*, 31–34; Jarvenpa, "Hudson's Bay Company," 489–90; Macdougall, "Socio-Cultural Development and Identity Formation," 40–42.

42 "Lettre du Rév. Père Taché à sa mère (suite)," *Les Cloches de Saint-Boniface* 32, no. 2 (February 1933): 46; Macdougall, *One of the Family*, 26; Macdougall, "Socio-Cultural Development and Identity Formation," 13.

43 Burpee, *Search for the Western Sea*, 1:vii, 317–19; Macdougall, "Socio-Cultural Development and Identity Formation," 11, 15–16, 37–40, 322; Morton, *Under Western Skies*, 172, 174–75.

44 Burpee, *Search for the Western Sea*, 1:499; Macdougall, "Socio-Cultural Development and Identity Formation," 34, 43–49, 60–61, 323–25; Morton, *Under Western Skies*, 213.

45 Innis, *Fur Trade in Canada*, 280, 283–87; Macdougall, "Socio-Cultural Development and Identity Formation," 30, 34, 46, 49, 325. The NWC and the XYC had merged under the name of the North West Company in 1804. See especially Innis, *Fur Trade in Canada*, 160, 203, 241, 245.

46 Macdougall, *One of the Family*, 2, 4, 24; Macdougall, "Socio-Cultural Development and Identity Formation," 11, 13, 34, 49; Macdougall, "Wahkootowin," 440.

47 Hargrave, *Red River*, 160–66; Ens, *Homeland to Hinterland*, 43–46; Macdougall, *One of the Family*, 24, 32, 38–39; Macdougall, "Socio-Cultural Development and Identity Formation," 34, 51–52.

48 Macdougall, *One of the Family*, 17–19; Macdougall, "Socio-Cultural Development and Identity Formation," 28–31, 35–36, 54–55, 58; Macdougall, "Wahkootowin," 442, 444–46, 449–51. The term "ethnogenesis" refers to a process by which "a people . . . seem to come into being as a definable group, aggregate, or category. . . . The concept of syncretism—the blending of distinct, even contrasting systems of culture to form a novel system—is a salient feature of ethnogenesis, when the phenomenon dealt with is a definable or stipulated people, rather than an institution or set of institutions." Quoted in Devine, "Les Desjarlais," 152n1.

49 Macdougall, "Socio-Cultural Development and Identity Formation," 11. Macdougall applies this distinction more generally to northwestern Saskatchewan in *One of the Family*, 3.

50 It should be noted, however, that Oblates stationed at Île-à-la-Crosse did occasionally acknowledge the presence of métis—principally "des métis de la Rivière Rouge"—in the 1850s and '60s, but generally as a transitory and seasonal presence rather than as a permanent subset of the local population. Most notably, in his letter to surveyor Simon James Dawson dated February 7, 1859, Oblate Bishop Alexandre-Antonin Taché of Saint-Boniface provided the following enumeration of Île-à-la-Crosse for the month of May 1856: "Montagnais, 530; Cris, 100; Métis, 78; Canadiens, 6." The contingent of "Métis" and "Canadiens" may have consisted of HBC boatmen who stopped at Île-à-la-Crosse in the freighting season. Later in the same letter, Taché referred to the permanent residents of Île-à-la-Crosse collectively as "poor sauvages." "Lettre de Mgr Taché à M. Dawson. Rivière-Rouge, le 7 février 1859," *Missions de la Congrégation des missionnaires oblats de Marie Immaculée* 6 (June 1863): 170, 174–75. For additional Oblate-authored references to métis at Île-à-la-Crosse prior to the mid-1870s, see especially SHSB, Fonds Taché, T0586–T0588, Valentin Végréville to Taché,

Île-à-la-Crosse, 12 June 1861; ibid., T1519–T1522, Émile Petitot to Taché, Portage La Loche, 22 July 1862. On the HBC boat brigades that passed through Île-à-la-Crosse every year, see especially Hargrave, *Red River*, 160–62; Ens, *Homeland to Hinterland*, 43–44.

51 Taché, *Vingt années de missions*, 7, 10–11. See also Choquette, *Oblate Assault*, 38–40; Huel, *Proclaiming the Gospel*, 16–17; Levasseur, *Les Oblats de Marie Immaculée dans l'ouest et le nord du Canada*, 28–30; Ortolan, *Les Oblats de Marie Immaculée*, 2:150–62.

52 SHSB, Fonds Provencher, P1571–P1574, Thomas Douglas, Earl of Selkirk to Bishop Joseph-Octave Plessis of Quebec, Montreal, 17 October 1818; "Lettre du R.P. Faraud, Missionnaire Oblat de Marie, à un Prêtre de la même Congrégation. Athabaskaw, 20 avril 1851," *Annales de la Propagation de la Foi* 24 (1852): 221; SHSB, Fonds Taché, T0316–T0319, Henri Grollier to Taché, Fort Good Hope, 24 February 1861. See also Joseph-Étienne Champagne, *Les missions catholiques dans l'ouest canadien*, 49–57; Dauphinais, *Histoire de Saint-Boniface*, 1:54–70.

53 Taché, *Esquisse sur le Nord-Ouest de l'Amérique*, 65. The Iroquois progenitors of these "Iroquois métis" had migrated west from the Montreal area under the auspices of the HBC, the NWC, and the XYC. They were contracted as crewmen and as skilled hunters and trappers. After the expiry of their contracts, many of the Montreal Iroquois opted to remain in the Northwest as freemen. On the Montreal Iroquois *engagés* and their role in the ethnogenesis of the western Métis, see especially Grabowski and St-Onge, "Montreal Iroquois *engagés* in the Western Fur Trade"; St-Onge, "'He Was Neither a Soldier Nor a Slave,'" 3–6, 9–26.

54 "Extrait d'une lettre de Mgr Taché, Vicaire apostolique de la Baie d'Hudson, à sa mère," *Annales de la Propagation de la Foi* 24 (1852): 332–33. See also Petitot, *Dictionnaire de la langue Dènè-Dindjié*, vii; Abel, *Drum Songs*, 11.

55 It should be noted, however, that historians have cited evidence of vernacular or "folk" Catholicism in and around Île-à-la-Crosse well before the arrival of ordained clergy. Popularized rituals and beliefs were imported by NWC and HBC servants from Lower Canada and the Red River Colony in the late eighteenth and early nineteenth century. See Jarvenpa, "Hudson's Bay Company," 491; Macdougall, *One of the Family*, 4–5; Macdougall, "Socio-Cultural Development and Identity Formation," 12, 69; Podruchny, "Baptizing Novices," 173–74, 180–81; Podruchny, *Making the Voyageur World*, 59–60, 66, 69–70.

56 "Au p. Végréville, à l'Ile à la Crosse, Marseille, le 17 avril 1860," *Bx Eugène de Mazenod . . . Lettres aux correspondants d'Amérique, 1851–1860*, 160. On Father Valentin Végréville and his tenure as local superior, see especially SHSB, Fonds Taché, T0114–T0125, Valentin Végréville to Taché, Île-à-la-Crosse, 29 July 1860; ibid., T0130–T0133, Végréville to Taché, Île-à-la-Crosse, 5 August 1860; SHSB, "Codex historicus, 1845–1897," 59–60, 68; Carrière, *Dictionnaire biographique*, 3:261–62.

57 Fernand-Michel, *Dix-huit ans chez les sauvages*, 253–55, 258. Fernand-Michel—Faraud's nephew—was the co-author and editor of this work. On the authorship of *Dix-huit ans chez les sauvages*, see especially SHSB, Fonds Taché, T3663–T3665, Marc Antoine Sardou [Oblate Treasurer General] to Taché, Paris, 30 November 1865.

58 Champagne, *Les débuts de la mission dans le Nord-Ouest Canadien*, 174, 195, 197, 199, 201, 204; Champagne, "Mission et civilisation dans l'Ouest canadien,"

341–43; McCarthy, *From the Great River to the Ends of the Earth*, xviii, 159, 160, 181.

59   Grandin reinforced this point in a letter to his benefactors in France in 1870: "Let our schools and our missions multiply, and the *sauvages* will disappear without ceasing to exist." See "Lettre de Mgr Grandin à MM. les membres des Conseils centraux de l'Œuvre de la Propagation de la Foi. Fort Pitt (mission de Saint-François Régis), 10 janvier 1870," *Annales de la Propagation de la Foi*, 44 (1872): 283.

60   "Instruction de Monseigneur de Mazenod relative aux missions étrangères," 171. Mazenod urged Oblates in *les missions étrangères* to make their letters as long and as detailed as possible so as to familiarize the addressees with the minutiae of local affairs. "Think of your letters as volumes," he instructed the Oblate superior at Red River in 1846. "Take your time on them and do not be afraid of going into minute detail." Quoted in Quéré, "La correspondance de Mgr de Mazenod avec les missionnaires," 179.

61   Taché, *Vingt années de missions*, 42, 44; *Atlas O.M.I.*, 40; Levasseur, *Les Oblats de Marie Immaculée dans l'ouest et le nord du Canada*, 46; Huel, *Proclaiming the Gospel*, 293.

62   It should be noted, however, that much of Taché's correspondence dating from before 1861 was destroyed in the fire that consumed the cathedral and the episcopal palace of Saint-Boniface on 14 December 1860. To compensate for this loss, the Archiepiscopal Corporation of St. Boniface and the Société historique de Saint-Boniface sponsored the transcription of relevant documents held at various religious and civil archives throughout Canada. See especially Dauphinais, *Histoire de Saint-Boniface*, 1:219–24; Duval, Foran, Lesage, and Bronconnier, "Des archives éloquentes," 257–59.

63   *Atlas O.M.I.*, 56; Levasseur, *Histoire des Missionnaires Oblats de Marie Immaculée*, 1:238; Levasseur, *Les Oblats de Marie Immaculée dans l'ouest et le nord du Canada*, 72.

64   PAA, O.M.I. Collection, Accession 84.400, Item 973, Box 33, "Renseignements demandés par Mgr Taché sur les missions et les Missionnaires de Mgr Grandin depuis l'érection du vicariat religieux de St. Albert 1868 jusqu'en 1872"; PAA, O.M.I. Collection, Accession 84.400, Vol. 5, Box 35, Grandin, "Notes privées sur les missions et les missionnaires du diocèse de St-Albert," 1868–84, 130–33; Carrière, *Dictionnaire biographique*, 2:106–7.

65   Research Centre for the Religious History of Canada, Écrits de Grandin [hereafter RCRHC/É.G.]. This collection was intended to facilitate canonical investigations for Grandin's beatification. The collection was completed in 1966—the very year in which Grandin was declared venerable by Pope Paul VI. See especially Bonk, "Grandin, Vital Justin"; Huel, "Vital-Justin Grandin."

66   "Lettre du Supérieur-Général à tous les membres de la congrégation. N.-D. de Montolivet, le 3 avril 1862," *Missions de la Congrégation des missionnaires oblats de Marie Immaculée* 1 (April 1862): 1–5; AD, HE 2221. T12Z 46, Joseph Fabre to Taché, Paris, 29 August 1862; Levasseur, *Histoire des Missionnaires Oblats de Marie Immaculée*, 1:173–75; Huel, *Proclaiming the Gospel*, 8, 70, 360; Ortolan, *Les Oblats de Marie Immaculée*, 3:7–31.

67   "Avertissement," *Annales de la Propagation de la Foi* 1 (1827): v–viii; Baumont, "Une source de l'histoire," 169–170; Champagne, *Les débuts de la mission dans le Nord-Ouest Canadien*, 16, 19; Huel, *Archbishop A.-A. Taché of St. Boniface*, 42, 59;

Huel, *Proclaiming the Gospel*, 23, 69–71; Kowalsy, "Mgr de Mazenod"; McCarthy, *From the Great River to the Ends of the Earth*, 9.

68 Research Centre for the Religious History of Canada, Archives de la Propagation de la Foi de Paris [hereafter RCRHC/Prop. de la Foi], "Copies sur microfilm des séries intéressant le Canada, inventaire, sommaire."

69 Beaudoin, "Le Codex historicus"; Duval, Foran, Lesage, and Bronconnier, "Des archives éloquentes," 260–63.

70 SHSB, "Codex historicus, 1845–1897," 1, 98. This fire destroyed several other important administrative records in addition to the "Codex historicus." Hence, in the personal memoirs that he commenced in 1898, Grandin noted: "Up until 1867, I had kept a journal of all my travels, and in it I made notes on all of the missions that I visited and all of the missionaries who ministered in them. After the fire at Île-à-la-Crosse destroyed these notes, I went for several years without keeping a journal. When I did resume my journal keeping, I contented myself with noting only the main facts and events." PAA, O.M.I. Collection, Accession 84.400, Item 957, Box 33, "Notes et souvenirs de Mgr Grandin (Repris à la demande de Mgr Langevin par lettre du 28 nov. 1897, rédaction commencée en mars 1898)," 26. See also ibid., 112.

71 SHSB, "Codex historicus, 1845–1897," 1, 295, and "Codex historicus, 1898–1928," 1–2; "Lettre du R.P. Pénard au T.R.P. Général," *Missions de la Congrégation des missionnaires oblats de Marie Immaculée* 151 (September 1900): 261.

72 The "Codex historicus, 1845–1897" is written entirely in the third person and contains no explicit acknowledgement of authorship. However, in his correspondence with the Oblate General Administration, Pénard did claim authorship: "Lettre du R.P. Pénard au T.R.P. Général," *Missions de la Congrégation des missionnaires oblats de Marie Immaculée* 151 (September 1900): 249. Moreover, in 1946, Oblate historian Germain Lesage noted that the document "is entirely in the hand of Father J.-M. Pénard, O.M.I., and was written around 1898." Lesage, *Capitale d'une solitude*, 187. On Pénard, see also Carrière, *Dictionnaire biographique*, 3:59–60.

73 See especially "Codex historicus, 1845–1897," 1, 6, 11, 22–23, 35, 39–40, 51, 68, 76, 83, 91, 94, 98, 105, 114, 146, 163, 165–66, 170, 183, 189–90, 203, 208, 211.

74 SHSB, "Arbre généalogique Île-à-la-Crosse" (Liber status animarum); Duval, Foran, Lesage, and Bronconnier, "Des archives éloquentes," 259–60.

75 SHSB, Acquisition record 2005-03-06; Duval, Foran, Lesage, and Bronconnier, "Des archives éloquentes," 259.

76 SHSB, "Codex historicus, 1845–1897," 229–32; Carrière, *Dictionnaire biographique*, 3:60.

77 Archives des Sœurs Grises de Montréal [hereafter ASGM], Sœur Agnès (*née* Marie-Rose Caron), "Annales de l'établissement des Sœurs Grises à l'Île à la Crosse"; ASGM, Mère (Elizabeth Forbes) McMullen, "Ancien Journal"; ASGM, Circulaire mensuelle adressée aux diverses maisons de l'Institut.

78 Library and Archives Canada, Black Series [hereafter LAC/Black Series].

79 The original documents are held at the Hudson's Bay Company Archives in Winnipeg—section B, class 89. At Library and Archives Canada, they appear on twenty four separate microfilm reels: Library and Archives Canada, Hudson's Bay Company Post Records [hereafter LAC/HBC].

Chapter 1: Saint-Jean-Baptiste in an Evolving Mission Network

1   Lesage, *Capitale d'une solitude*, 184–85. See also 7–8, 183. Lesage was an Oblate missionary and a professor at the University of Ottawa. See Carrière, "Bibliographie des professeurs oblats," 37–39.

2   Lesage, *Capitale d'une solitude*, 183–85. Lesage was not the first to refer to Saint-Jean-Baptiste as "capitale d'une solitude." The designation was coined by Paul Coze—celebrated French writer, artist, ethnologist, and co-founder of the Scouts de France—during his visit to Île-à-la-Crosse in 1931. See Martin Lajeunesse's preface in ibid., 7–8.

3   Matthew 28:18–20; Mark 16:15–18; Luke 24:44–49; John 20:19–23; Acts 1:6–8.

4   In the estimation of Jean-Marie Pénard, the founding of the mission accelerated the evangelization of the region by at least fifty years. See SHSB, "Codex historicus, 1845–1897," 5.

5   Dauphinais, *Histoire de Saint-Boniface*, 1:70–125; Morice, *History of the Catholic Church in Western Canada*, 1:116–50.

6   Boon, *Anglican Church from the Bay to the Rockies*, 49–51; Grant, *Moon of Wintertime*, 100–109; Hutchinson, "British Methodists and the Hudson's Bay Company"; Maclean, *James Evans*, 146–49, 191–92; Tucker, *Rainbow in the North*, 203–7; Semple, *The Lord's Dominion*, 174–76.

7   Provencher had planned to send Thibault onto the western plain several years earlier—since at least 1837—but it was not until the onset of the Protestant challenge that he managed to put his plan into action. SHSB, Fonds Provencher, P1792–P1796, Thibault to Signay, St. François-Xavier, 6 July 1839. See also Choquette, *Oblate Assault*, 35–37; Levasseur, *Les Oblats de Marie Immaculée dans l'ouest et le nord du Canada*, 12–13.

8   SHSB, Fonds Provencher, P1803–P1829, Thibault to Signay, Red River (?), 18 June 1843; ibid., P1841–P1854, Thibault to Provencher, Fort Pitt, 26 December 1843; Levasseur, *Les Oblats de Marie Immaculée dans l'ouest et le nord du Canada*, 13.

9   RCRHC/Prop. de la Foi, microfilm X, 10954, Provencher to the Central Councils of l'Œuvre de la Propagation de la Foi, Saint-Boniface, 26 July 1845; RCRHC/Prop. de la Foi, microfilm X, 10955, Provencher to the Central Councils of l'Œuvre de la Propagation de la Foi, Saint-Boniface, 4 August 1844; SHSB, Fonds Provencher, P2696–P2731, Provencher to the Central Councils of l'Œuvre de la Propagation de la Foi, Saint-Boniface, 1846.

10 SHSB, Fonds Provencher, P1841–P1854, Thibault to Provencher, Fort Pitt, 26 December 1843. See especially the postscript, P1854.

11 Thibault to Provencher, Lac Sainte-Anne, 23 December 1844 [P2701–P2707], quoted in SHSB, Fonds Provencher, P2696–P2731, Provencher to the Central Councils of l'Œuvre de la Propagation de la Foi, Saint-Boniface, 1846.

12 Thibault to Provencher, Île-à-la-Crosse, 24 May 1845 [P2707–P2709], quoted in ibid. See also Benoit, "Mission at Ile-à-la-Crosse," 41.

13 Thibault to Provencher, Île-à-la-Crosse, 24 May 1845 [P2707–P2709].

14 Ibid.

15 Ibid. Thibault reiterated this appeal one month later. See Thibault to Provencher, Portage de [*sic*] La Loche, 24 June 1845 [P2709–P2711], quoted in SHSB, Fonds

Provencher, P2696–P2731, Provencher to the Central Councils of l'Œuvre de la Propagation de la Foi, Saint-Boniface, 1846.

16 LAC/HBC, microfilm HBC 1M64, B.89/a/23, Île à la Crosse Post Journal (1843–1845), Monday, 26 May 1845, 58.

17 Taché, *Vingt années de missions*, 4, 12–14. See also Benoît, *Vie de Mgr Taché*, 1:101–2; Choquette, *Oblate Assault*, 41–42; Huel, *Archbishop A.-A. Taché of St. Boniface*, 24–26; Huel, *Proclaiming the Gospel*, 17–18, 21–22.

18 Taché, *Vingt années de missions*, 3–6. The Roman Catholic clergy consists of two canonically distinct bodies: regular clergy and secular clergy. Regular clerics belong to religious orders or—in the case of the Oblates—congregations. They live communally under a rule (*regula*) and are bound by vows of poverty, chastity, and obedience. Their administration is distinct from diocesan structures. Secular—or "diocesan"—clerics owe canonical obedience directly to a bishop. Levasseur, *Histoire des Missionnaires Oblats de Marie Immaculée*, 1:50–52, 59–67. See also Aston, *Christianity and Revolutionary Europe*, 30–34, 38–40; Mullet, *Catholic Reformation*, 69–110, 142–45; Hsia, *World of Catholic Renewal*, 106–21.

19 RCRHC/Prop. de la Foi, microfilm X, 10955, Provencher to the Central Councils of l'Œuvre de la Propagation de la Foi, Saint-Boniface, 4 August 1844; SHSB, Fonds Provencher, P2754–P2758, Provencher to Signay, Saint-Boniface, 20 June 1845. This belief was informed by an ongoing disagreement between Provencher and secular clerics at Red River—principally Georges-Antoine Bellecourt (1803–74). At issue was the mission to the local Saulteaux population. Whereas Provencher advocated a "mission ambulante," in which a priest would follow the itinerant Saulteaux, Bellecourt advocated—and attempted to implement—a program of supervised agricultural settlements and intensive schooling. See Huel, *Proclaiming the Gospel*, 13–16; St-Onge, "Uncertain Margins."

20 Levasseur, *Histoire des Missionnaires Oblats de Marie Immaculée*, 1:132–34; Levasseur, *Les Oblats de Marie Immaculée dans l'ouest et le nord du Canada*, 26–30; Levasseur, "La venue des Oblats de Marie Immaculée en Amérique"; Ortolan, *Les Oblats de Marie Immaculée*, 2:28–139.

21 SHSB, Fonds Provencher, P2736–P2747, Provencher to Pierre-Flavien Turgeon (Bishop of Sidyme *in partibus infidelium*), Saint-Boniface, 14 June 1847. See also Huel, *Proclaiming the Gospel*, 16–17. It should be noted, however, that Guigues did not endorse the Oblate General Administration's decision to dispatch missionaries to the Red River Colony and beyond. He wrote to Mazenod on 14 February 1845: "I consider this venture imprudent and therefore contrary to the will of God. Eight hundred leagues lie between us and Red River . . . , communications are extremely difficult. This posting will mean a life of isolation and all manner of danger for our missionaries." Mazenod responded to Guigues on 24 March 1845, asserting that the decision was non-negotiable: "I was not submitting a proposal for your consideration and review; I was informing you of a resolution that I expect you to implement." Quoted in Joseph-Étienne Champagne, *Les missions catholiques dans l'ouest canadien*, 70–71.

22 Benoît, *Vie de Mgr Taché*, 1:15–29, 53–56; Huel, *Archbishop A.-A. Taché of St. Boniface*, 12–16. Both biographers have suggested that Taché felt destined to serve in the *pays d'en haut* and thus to follow in the footsteps of his paternal ancestor, Louis Jolliet ("discoverer" and explorer of the Mississippi), and his maternal ancestor, Pierre Gaultier de Varennes, Sieur de la Vérendrye.

23 Taché, *Vingt années de missions*, 10–12. See also Levasseur, *Histoire des Missionnaires Oblats de Marie Immaculée*, 1:133; Levasseur, *Les Oblats de Marie Immaculée dans l'ouest et le nord du Canada*, 30. Upon his arrival at Saint-Boniface, Taché was barely twenty-two years old and had yet to be ordained. He was elevated to the deaconate on 1 September 1845 and ordained a priest eleven days later. Provencher officiated at both ceremonies.

24 "Lettre du Rév. Père Taché à sa mère, Île-à-la-Crosse, 5 janvier 1847," *Les Cloches de Saint-Boniface* 32, no. 1 (January 1933): 13; Taché, *Vingt années de missions*, 12. See also Ens, *Homeland to Hinterland*, 43–46; Macdougall, *One of the Family*, 38–39; Macdougall, "Socio-Cultural Development and Identity Formation," 51–52.

25 SHSB, Fonds Taché, T0001, Simpson to Donald Ross, Red River, 8 July 1846; Taché, *Vingt années de missions*, 13. For more details on their voyage, see Benoit, "Mission at Ile-à-la-Crosse," 42–44; Benoît, *Vie de Mgr Taché*, 1:107–22; Choquette, *Oblate Assault*, 41. See also Hargrave, *Red River*, 160–66; Marchildon and Robinson, *Canoeing the Churchill River*, 23–65, 141–43.

26 Taché, *Vingt années de missions*, 14. See also Benoît, *Vie de Mgr Taché*, 1:125–30.

27 According to Pénard, the dedication to John the Baptist reflected the Lower Canadian origins of Taché and Laflèche: "The establishment was placed under the protection of Saint John the Baptist, no doubt because of the profound devotion of these two Canadian missionaries for that great saint, the patron of Canada." See SHSB, Oblats de Marie Immaculée, "Codex historicus, 1845–1897," 9. It is also possible that Taché and Laflèche sought to pay tribute to their predecessor, Jean-Baptiste Thibault, by invoking his patron saint. In 1861, Taché would pay similar tribute to Oblate Father Albert Lacombe by dedicating a new mission to Saint Albert (Albertus Magnus). See Sœur de la Providence, *Le Père Lacombe*, 137–38.

28 "Lettre du R.P. Taché, OMI, à un Père de sa Compagnie. Lac Caribou, 16 avril 1848," *Les Cloches de Saint-Boniface* 32, no. 4 (April 1933): 93; Taché, *Vingt années de missions*, 18. See also SHSB, "Codex historicus, 1845–1897," 8–9; Benoit, "Mission at Ile-à-la-Crosse," 46–47; Benoît, *Vie de Mgr Taché*, 1:147–48.

29 Benoît, *Vie de Mgr Taché*, 1:147.

30 Quoted in ibid., 153.

31 Ibid., 138, 151, 161–62. In his letters from Île-à-la-Crosse (1846–54), Taché made repeated references to abundant potato harvests and to the centrality of potatoes in the local missionary diet. Writing to his mother in 1853, he commented: "Our gardens yield generously in proportion to their size. We have harvested nearly 200 bushels of potatoes, so if we don't find ourselves turning Irish soon, it will be for lack of faith rather than for lack of potatoes." HE 2221. T12L 25, Alexandre Taché to Louise-Henriette Taché, Île-à-la-Crosse, 5 January 1853. On the soil conditions around the mission site, see especially "Lettre du Rév. Père Taché à sa mère (suite)," *Les Cloches de Saint-Boniface* 32, no. 2 (February 1933): 45.

32 Quoted in Benoît, *Vie de Mgr Taché*, 1:138 (from Taché's letter to his mother, Île-à-la-Crosse, 23 July 1847). See also Lesage, *Capitale d'une solitude*, 37.

33 SHSB, Fonds Provencher, P2732–P2735, Provencher to Signay, Saint-Boniface, 24 November 1846; Fernand-Michel, *Dix-huit ans chez les sauvages*, 12–18, 23–76, 87; Taché, *Vingt années de missions*, 25.

34 SHSB, "Codex historicus, 1845–1897," 17; Fernand-Michel, *Dix-huit ans chez les sauvages*, 79–81.

35 SHSB, Fonds Provencher, P2760–P2765, Provencher to Turgeon, Saint-Boniface, 14 June 1848; ibid., P2766–P2770, Provencher to Turgeon, Saint-Boniface, July 1848; Taché, *Vingt années de missions*, 17, 22–23.

36 AD, Microfilm W 404.M62 F86 (Missions indiennes, St-Albert), Taché, "Notice sur la Mission du lac Caribou"; Taché, *Vingt années de missions*, 17. See also SHSB, "Codex historicus, 1845–1897," 7; Benoît, *Vie de Mgr Taché*, 1:130–31. The journey from Île-à-la-Crosse to the HBC post at Reindeer Lake was approximately 330 kilometres longer by summer route (i.e., by canoe along circuitous waterways).

37 AD, Microfilm W 404.M62 F86 (Missions indiennes, St-Albert), Taché, "Notice sur la Mission du lac Caribou"; Taché, *Vingt années de missions*, 18. See also SHSB, "Codex historicus, 1845–1897," 8; Benoît, *Vie de Mgr Taché*, 1:131–37. Taché's mission to Cree- and Chipewyan-speakers of Reindeer Lake was severely hindered by his lack of fluency in either Cree or Chipewyan. In his report on the founding of the mission, Taché recalled his dependence on an ad hoc team of translators (which included Charles Thomas): "Father Taché spoke in French to Mr. Thomas, who in turn translated his words into Cree, while a Montagnais translated Mr. Thomas's translation. Needless to say, this multitude of interpreters posed tremendous difficulties, and even annoyances, for the missionary." Quoted in Benoît, *Vie de Mgr Taché*, 1:135–36.

38 Taché, *Vingt années de missions*, 20–21. See also SHSB, "Codex historicus, 1845–1897," 9–10; Benoît, *Vie de Mgr Taché*, 1:138–41; McCarthy, "Founding of Providence Mission," 37.

39 Benoit, "Mission at Ile-à-la-Crosse," 47; Benoît, *Vie de Mgr Taché*, 1:141, 144–45. Barbara Benoit erroneously dates Taché's arrival at Fort Chipewyan to 5 September 1847. This date corresponds to his celebration of the first Mass at the fort, not to his arrival there.

40 Taché, *Vingt années de missions*, 21.

41 Benoît, *Vie de Mgr Taché*, 1:146, 148.

42 SHSB, "Codex historicus, 1845–1897," 1, 10–11, 15, 20.

43 Taché, *Vingt années de missions*, 23–28. See also SHSB, "Codex historicus, 1845–1897," 12–15; Benoit, "Mission at Ile-à-la-Crosse," 48–49; Benoît, *Vie de Mgr Taché*, 1:156–60, 162; Huel, *Archbishop A.-A. Taché of St. Boniface*, 28–30.

44 Taché, *Vingt années de missions*, 28–29; Benoît, *Vie de Mgr Taché*, 1:163–69.

45 "Lettre du R.P. Faraud, Missionnaire Oblat de Marie Immaculée, à un Prêtre de la même Congrégation, Athabaskaw, 20 avril, 1851," *Annales de la Propagation de la Foi* 24 (1852): 220–23. See also Fernand-Michel, *Dix-huit ans chez les sauvages*, 95–125; McCarthy, "Founding of Providence Mission," 37–38.

46 Taché, *Vingt années de missions*, 34–36, 45. See also SHSB, "Codex historicus, 1845–1897," 20–28; Carrière, *Dictionnaire biographique*, 2:355–56, and 3:233; Huel, "Life Cycle of an Early Oblate Establishment," 239–40.

47 SHSB, Fonds Provencher, P2805–P2809, Provencher to Turgeon, Saint-Boniface, 28 August 1849; Taché, *Vingt années de missions*, 31; SHSB, "Codex historicus, 1845–1897," 18–19.

48 "Coup-d'œil sur l'Œuvre de la Propagation de la Foi," *Annales de la Propagation de la Foi* 18 (1846): 1–44; *Oeuvre de la Propagation de la Foi,* 1–4. See also Baumont, "Une source de l'histoire," 165–70.

49 "Lettre de Mgr Provencher," *Annales de la Propagation de la Foi* 4 (1830): 719; SHSB, Fonds Provencher, P2696–P2697, Provencher to the Central Councils of l'Œuvre de la Propagation de la Foi, Saint-Boniface, 1846; ibid., P1876–P1883, Provencher to Turgeon, Saint-Boniface, 5 August 1850.

50 RCRHC/Prop. de la Foi, microfilm X, 10955, Provencher to the Central Councils of l'Œuvre de la Propagation de la Foi, Saint-Boniface, 4 August 1844; RCRHC/Prop. de la Foi, microfilm X, 10954, Provencher to the Central Councils of l'Œuvre de la Propagation de la Foi, Saint-Boniface, 26 July 1845; SHSB, Fonds Provencher, P2810–P2813, Provencher to Turgeon, Saint-Boniface, 30 November 1849.

51 "Compte-rendu de 1847," *Annales de la Propagation de la Foi* 20 (1848): I, 145–52; "Compte-rendu de 1848," ibid., I–IV. See also Langlois, "Politique et religion"; Huel, *Archbishop A.-A. Taché of St. Boniface,* 59; Huel, *Proclaiming the Gospel,* 70.

52 These orders were issued by Pierre Aubert, Oblate superior at Red River. They reached Île-à-la-Crosse in January 1849. Aubert's orders are quoted in Faraud's report to the Central Councils of l'Œuvre de la Propagation de la Foi (1863): "Confine your ministrations to the mission at Île-à-la-Crosse. The recent revolution in France [February and June 1848] will exhaust the resources of the Propagation de la Foi; we may even be obliged to abandon the new mission field altogether. Do not, therefore, expand beyond your present state." "De Mgr Faraud, Vicaire apostolique d'Atthabaska et de Mackensie, à MM. les Directeurs de l'Œuvre de la Propagation de la Foi," *Annales de la Propagation de la Foi* 36 (1864): 382. See also ibid., 378–95; "Compte-rendu de 1846," *Annales de la Propagation de la Foi* 19 (1847): 208; "Compte-rendu de 1848," *Annales de la Propagation de la Foi* 21 (1849): XXIX; "Compte-rendu de 1849," *Annales de la Propagation de la Foi* 22 (1850): 194; Taché, *Vingt années de missions,* 30; SHSB, "Codex historicus, 1845–1897," 18–19.

53 The Oblate General Administration was originally located in Aix-en-Provence (Carmel d'Aix, 1815–21) and was later moved to Marseilles (Maison du Calvaire, 1821–62). It was transferred to Paris (rue Saint-Pétersbourg) in 1862. *Atlas O.M.I.,* 3–5; Levasseur, *Histoire des Missionnaires Oblats de Marie Immaculée,* 1:36–38, 68–69; Ortolan, *Les Oblats de Marie Immaculée,* 1:105–6, 150–53.

54 Taché, *Vingt années de missions,* 140–41; SHSB, "Codex historicus, 1845–1897," 18.

55 PAA, O.M.I. Collection, Accession 71.200, Item 6, Box 1, Mazenod to the Central Councils of l'Œuvre de la Propagation de la Foi, Marseilles, February 1850. See also "Mgr l'Evêque de Marseille aux Conseils centraux, Février 1850," *Annales de la Propagation de la Foi* 22 (1850): 315–16; Huel, *Proclaiming the Gospel,* 23; McCarthy, *To Evangelize the Nations,* 31.

56 "Compte-rendu," *Annales de la Propagation de la Foi* 23 (1851): 194; "À Messieurs les Membres du Conseil central du Midi, pour l'Œuvre de la Propagation de la foi, à Lyon. Marseille, le 15 janvier 1855," *Bx de Mazenod: Lettres . . . 1832–1861,* 166; RCRHC/Prop. de la Foi, microfilm X, 10956, Taché to Central Council of l'Œuvre de la Propagation de la Foi (Paris), Paris, 6 February 1855; AD, H 3209. P76R5, Mazenod to the Central Council of l'Œuvre de la Propagation

de la Foi (Paris), Marseilles, 7 May 1859. Saint-Jean-Baptiste and its satellite posts—staffed by Taché, Faraud, Tissot, Maisonneuve, and Dubé—were the only Oblate missions in Rupert's Land and the North-Western Territory in 1850. Only one Oblate—François-Xavier Bermond—was posted at Saint-Boniface at this time. He resided in Provencher's episcopal palace and was not actively involved in the mission field. See Taché, *Vingt années de missions*, 34–36.

57 Baumont, "Une source de l'histoire," 169–70; Champagne, *Les débuts de la mission dans le Nord-Ouest Canadien*, 16, 19; Huel, *Archbishop A.-A. Taché of St. Boniface*, 42, 59, 187; Huel, *Proclaiming the Gospel*, 23, 70; Kowalsy, "Mgr de Mazenod"; McCarthy, *From the Great River to the Ends of the Earth*, 9.

58 SHSB, Fonds Provencher, P1884–P1886, Provencher to Signay, Saint-Boniface, 29 November 1849; Levasseur, *Les Oblats de Marie Immaculée dans l'ouest et le nord du Canada*, 41–43. Provencher had initially favoured Laflèche as his successor, but the latter declined the nomination on account of his rheumatism. Provencher subsequently chose Taché because of his physical vigour, his competence in Cree and Chipewyan, and his status as a British subject. See SHSB, Fonds Provencher, P1876–P1883, Provencher to Turgeon, Saint-Boniface, 5 August 1850; ibid., P2805–P2809, Provencher to Turgeon, Saint-Boniface, 28 August 1849; ibid., P2814–2819, Provencher to Signay, Saint-Boniface, 21 July 1851.

59 "À Messieurs les Membres du Conseil central de la Propagation de la foi, à Lyon. Marseille, le 17 avril 1852," *Bx de Mazenod: Lettres . . . 1832–1861*, 152; Huel, *Archbishop A.-A. Taché of St. Boniface*, 32–34; Huel, *Proclaiming the Gospel*, 25; Levasseur, *Les Oblats de Marie Immaculée dans l'ouest et le nord du Canada*, 45–46.

60 SHSB, Fonds Taché, T0005–T0006, Pierre Aubert to Louise-Henriette Taché, Saint-Boniface (?), 29 May 1850; Taché, *Vingt années de missions*, 38–43; SHSB, "Codex historicus, 1845–1897," 23–25.

61 Taché, *Vingt années de missions*, 42, 44; *Atlas O.M.I.*, 40; Levasseur, *Les Oblats de Marie Immaculée dans l'ouest et le nord du Canada*, 46.

62 Taché, *Vingt années de missions*, 49–51; SHSB, "Codex historicus, 1845–1897," 29–31.

63 PAA, O.M.I. Collection, Accession 71.200, Item 6, Box 1, Taché to Mazenod, Île-à-la-Crosse, 7 July 1854; Taché, *Vingt années de missions*, 53, 56–59, 65–66, 68–70; SHSB, "Codex historicus, 1845–1897," 32–38; Benoît, *Vie de Mgr Taché*, 1:258–63, 297.

64 RCRHC/Prop. de la Foi, microfilm X, 10961a, Taché to Étienne Paul Hippolyte Bérard des Glajeux (President of the Paris Council of l'Œuvre de la Propagation de la Foi), Île-à-la-Crosse, 26 March 1856; Taché, *Vingt années de missions*, 72–73, 129, 139–43, 208–12; SHSB, "Codex historicus, 1845–1897," 38–39, 68–71, 83–85. On Bérard des Glajeux and his tenure as President of the Paris Council (1847–65), see Verhelst, *La Congrégation du Cœur Immaculé de Marie (Scheut)*, 69 (n129).

65 SHSB, Fonds Provencher, P2826–P2829, Prelates of Quebec to Pope Pius IX, Quebec, November 1856. See especially article 7: "The Coadjutor [of the Bishop of Saint-Boniface] should reside in a place called Île-à-la-Crosse, which is the central station among the *missions sauvages.*" See also Taché, *Vingt années de missions*, 89–90; Carrière, "L'élévation du P. Vital-J. Grandin"; Huel, *Archbishop A.-A. Taché of St. Boniface*, 53–54.

66   SHSB, Fonds Provencher, P2820–P2825, Provencher to Turgeon, Saint-Boniface, 6 July 1852; Carrière, *Dictionnaire biographique*, 2:115.

67   Taché, *Vingt années de missions*, 46, 49, 51–52, 57–59; SHSB, "Codex historicus, 1845–1897," 27, 29, 32; Choquette, *Oblate Assault*, 55–56.

68   Taché, *Vingt années de missions*, 46, 52–53, 57, 73; SHSB, "Codex historicus, 1845–1897," 32–33, 36–40; Carrière, *Dictionnaire biographique*, 3:261–62.

69   PAA, O.M.I. Collection, Accession 71.200, Item 6, Box 1, Taché to Mazenod, Île-à-la-Crosse, 7 July 1854; Taché, *Vingt années de missions*, 57–58; Carrière, *Dictionnaire biographique*, 3:119; Choquette, *Oblate Assault*, 55.

70   "Lettre du R.P. Grandin, missionnaire Oblat de Marie Immaculée, à sa famille," *Annales de la Propagation de la Foi* 30 (1858): 468–75; Carrière, *Dictionnaire biographique*, 2:106; Champagne, *Les débuts de la mission dans le Nord-Ouest Canadien*, 11–50, 56; Jonquet, *Mgr Grandin*, 2–19, 63–66.

71   Taché, *Vingt années de missions*, 89–91.

72   "Messieurs les Membres du Conseil central du Midi pour l'Œuvre de la Propagation de la Foi, à Lyon. Marseille, le 10 mai 1859," *Bx de Mazenod: Lettres . . . 1832–1861*, 182; AD, H 3209. P76R5, Mazenod to the Central Council of l'Œuvre de la Propagation de la Foi (Paris), Marseilles, 7 May 1859; RCRHC/É.G., vol. 6, Grandin, "Notice sur le diocèse de S. Albert," 31; RCRHC/É.G., vol. 6, Grandin, "Notes de Monseigneur Grandin sur l'Église du Nord-Ouest," 151–55. On Grandin's speech impediment, see Jonquet, *Mgr Grandin*, 23.

73   Duchaussois, *Apôtres inconnus*, 15–17, 19–20; Huel, "Western Oblate History," 30–36. Huel describes Oblate lay brothers as the underappreciated and understudied "proletariat of the missions, the very foundations of the missionary edifice. . . . [T]hey built the residences and missions, cultivated fields, hunted and fished to provide food for mission personnel, prepared meals, participated in religious services and rendered '*une foule de services inappréciables.*'" See ibid., 30. See also Gresko, "The 'Serfs of the System'?"

74   SHSB, "Codex historicus, 1845–1897," 19–20; Carrière, *Dictionnaire biographique*, 1:302; Duchaussois, *Apôtres inconnus*, p. 243.

75   Taché, *Vingt années de missions*, 31–32.

76   AD, HE 2221. T12L 25, Alexandre Taché to Louise-Henriette Taché, Île-à-la-Crosse, 5 January 1853. In addition to this ample yield, the mission garden produced 200 barrels of potatoes in 1852. No wheat was sown at the mission until the following year.

77   Ibid.

78   RCRHC/É.G., vol. 6, Grandin, "Notes de Monseigneur Grandin sur l'Église du Nord-Ouest," 149; SHSB, "Codex historicus, 1845–1897," 31, 38; Carrière, *Dictionnaire biographique*, 1:129.

79   SHSB, "Codex historicus, 1845–1897," 31, 38–39; Duchaussois, *Apôtres inconnus*, 85; Lesage, *Capitale d'une solitude*, 59–60. According to Pénard and Lesage, this edifice was acclaimed as a masterpiece throughout Rupert's Land and the North-Western Territory. At the time of its completion in 1856, it was reportedly the largest and most impressive church outside of Red River. By 1861, however, Faraud had overseen the construction of a larger and more impressive church at la Nativité (Fort Chipewyan). See PAA, O.M.I. Collection, Accession 84.400, Item 911, Box 32, Grandin to Taché, Mission de la Nativité d'Athabaskaw, 24 June 1861.

80   SHSB, Fonds Taché, T0483–T0486, Moulin to Taché, Île-à-la-Crosse, 8 May 1861; SHSB, "Codex historicus, 1845–1897," 40, 47; Lesage, *Capitale d'une solitude*, 61, 68.

81   SHSB, Fonds Taché, T0568–T0571, Boisramé [as transcribed by Grandin] to Taché, Portage La Loche, 5 June 1861; PAA, O.M.I. Collection, Accession 84.400, Item 911, Box 32, Grandin to Taché, Île-à-la-Crosse, 9 January 1861; ibid., Accession 84.400, Item 911, Box 32, Grandin to Taché, Île-à-la-Crosse, 1 April 1861; Taché, *Vingt années de missions*, 129–30; Carrière, *Dictionnaire biographique*, 1:110.

82   SHSB, Fonds Taché, T0492–T0499, Grandin to Taché, Île-à-la-Crosse, 15 May 1861.

83   SHSB, Fonds Taché, T0411–T0422, Végréville to Taché, Île-à-la-Crosse, 15 April 1861.

84   PAA, O.M.I. Collection, Accession 84.400, Item 911, Box 32, Grandin to Taché, Île-à-la-Crosse, 15 May 1861.

85   "Extrait d'une lettre de Mgr Vital Grandin, évêque de Satala et coadjuteur de Mgr l'évêque de Saint-Boniface, à MM. les Directeurs de l'Œuvre de la Propagation de la Foi. Mission de Saint-Jean-Baptiste de l'Île-à-la-Crosse, 3 décembre, 1861," *Annales de la Propagation de la Foi* 35 (1863): 350. See also RCRHC/Prop. de la Foi, microfilm X, 10986, Grandin to Glajeux, Île-à-la-Crosse, 19 December 1860: "I implore you to make known my plea for more lay brothers and to point out the good that we could accomplish if only we were stronger in number. Perhaps in reading this, some generous young men will . . . join our ranks and eventually share in our work, our suffering, and our reward."

86   ASGM, Agnès, "Annales de l'établissement des Sœurs Grises à l'Île à la Crosse," 1:196–98; ASGM, Mère McMullen, "Ancien Journal," 1:26, 45. See also SHSB, "Codex historicus, 1845–1897," 67–68; Duchaussois, *Aventures canadiennes des Sœurs Grises*, 15–18.

87   SHSB, "Codex historicus, 1845–1897," 43; Dauphinais, *Histoire de Saint-Boniface*, 1:125, 130–31; Duchaussois, *Aventures canadiennes des Sœurs Grises*, 1–11; Huel, *Proclaiming the Gospel*, 49, 65; Levasseur, *Les Oblats de Marie Immaculée dans l'ouest et le nord du Canada*, 57–58, 66–67.

88   RCRHC/É.G., vol. 6, "Convention entre Mgr Grandin, Evêque de Satala . . . Et la Révérende Sœur Charlesbois, Assistante Générale de la Congrégation des Sœurs de la Charité," Saint-Albert, 4 March 1872, 234–36; PAA, O.M.I. Collection, Accession 84.400, Item 915, Box 32, Grandin to Marc Antoine Sardou (Oblate Treasurer General), Saint-Albert, 12 December 1874; Levasseur, *Les Oblats de Marie Immaculée dans l'ouest et le nord du Canada*, 57–58.

89   ASGM, Agnès, "Annales de l'établissement des Sœurs Grises à l'Île à la Crosse," 1:167–69; ASGM, McMullen, "Ancien Journal," 1:45. See also ASGM, L018, Île à la Crosse, "Historique," 1; Lesage, *Capitale d'une solitude*, 75–76. It should be noted that neither woman had volunteered for this posting. Bound by vows of obedience, Sisters Agnès and Boucher were appointed by their Mother Superior—Julie Hainault Deschamps—and were dispatched without discussion or consultation. See SHSB, Fonds Taché, T0137–T0139, Agnès to Taché, "sur le rivage du Lac Winipig," 6 August 1860.

90   ASGM, Agnès, "Annales de l'établissement des Sœurs Grises à l'Île à la Crosse," 1:174–76; ASGM, L018, Île à la Crosse, "Historique," 1–2; Lesage, *Capitale d'une solitude*, 75–76.

91   SHSB, Fonds Taché, T0149–T0152, Grandin to Taché, "sur le lac Winipeg," 12 August 1860; ASGM, Agnès, "Annales de l'établissement des Sœurs Grises à l'Île à la Crosse," 1:175; Carrière, *Dictionnaire biographique*, 3:179–80.

92   Their journey from Saint-Boniface to Saint-Jean-Baptiste was fraught with complications: Grandin fell violently ill; there were no available HBC servants to conduct the travellers beyond Lac la Ronge; and the barge ran aground near Frog Portage. See Séguin's account of the journey quoted in SHSB, "Codex historicus, 1845–1897," 62–68. See also ASGM, Agnès, "Annales de l'établissement des Sœurs Grises à l'Île à la Crosse," 1:175–97.

93   ASGM, Agnès, "Annales de l'établissement des Sœurs Grises à l'Île à la Crosse," 1:198–99; ASGM, L018, Île à la Crosse, "Historique," 2, 4–5.

94   SHSB, "Codex historicus, 1845–1897," 43.

95   SHSB, Fonds Taché, T1085–T1087, Grandin, Inventory of Supplies at Saint-Jean-Baptiste, Île-à-la-Crosse, 1861; ASGM, Agnès, "Annales de l'établissement des Sœurs Grises à l'Île à la Crosse," 1:199.

96   SHSB, Fonds Taché, T1921–T1924, Julien Moulin to Taché, Île-à-la-Crosse, 9 January 1863; ibid., T2017–T2022, Faraud to Taché, Île-à-la-Crosse, 6 April 1863. "Homeopathic medicine," according to McCarthy, "involves treating the patient with minute doses of drugs that would incite similar symptoms in a healthy person (i.e., treating like with like [homeopathic] rather than with contraries [allopathic])." Oblates in the mission field adopted a variety of homeopathy that was popular as self-help medicine in nineteenth-century France. Developed by the German physician Christian Friedrich Samuel Hahnemann (1755–1843), this medicine was made available in kits that were sold with instruction manuals on appropriate remedies and dosages. See McCarthy, *From the Great River to the Ends of the Earth*, 124–25, 130, 231 (n28). See also McCarthy, "The Missions of the Oblates of Mary Immaculate to the Athapaskans," 271–74.

97   SHSB, Fonds Taché, T0332–T0335, Isidore Clut to Taché, Mission de la Nativité (Fort Chipewyan), 10 March 1861; ibid., T1523–T1526, Faraud to Taché, Île-à-la-Crosse, 22 July 1862; ibid., T1721–T1724, Moulin to Taché, Île-à-la-Crosse, 16 November 1862; ibid., T1921–T1924, Moulin to Taché, Île-à-la-Crosse, 9 January 1863; ibid., T1932–T1935, Agnès to Taché, Île-à-la-Crosse, 16 January 1863; ibid., T1936–T1939, Faraud to Taché, Île-à-la-Crosse, 17 January 1863; ibid., T2017–T2022, Faraud to Taché, Île-à-la-Crosse, 6 April 1863.

98   ASGM, Agnès, "Annales de l'établissement des Sœurs Grises à l'Île à la Crosse," 1:202–6; SHSB, "Codex historicus, 1845–1897," 71.

99   SHSB, Fonds Taché, T0582–T0585, Végréville to Taché, Île-à-la-Crosse, 12 June 1861. The distinction between *pensionnats* reflected the divided responsibility for the feeding of schoolchildren. In principle, children in the *pensionnat supérieur* were fed at the expense of the mission and ate their meals at the Oblates' table. Children in the *pensionnat inférieur* were fed at the expense of their parents and ate their meals in the classroom. Yet this distinction was by no means clear-cut, as the mission was frequently compelled to feed both cohorts at its own expense. See SHSB, Fonds Taché, T3099–T3102, Grandin to Taché, Île-à-la-Crosse, 18 January 1865.

100 SHSB, Fonds Taché, T0291–T0294, Grandin to Taché, Île-à-la-Crosse, 7 January 1861; ibid., T0350–T0353, Agnès to Taché, Île-à-la-Crosse, 1 April 1861; ibid., T0391–T0393, Moulin to Taché, Île-à-la-Crosse, 6 April 1861; ibid.,

T0688–T0690, Agnès to Taché, Île-à-la-Crosse, 24 July 1861; ibid., T1401–1404, Faraud to Taché, Île-à-la-Crosse, 19 May 1862; ibid., T1721–T1724, Moulin to Taché, Île-à-la-Crosse, 16 November 1862; AD, HPF 4191. C75R 183, Pepin to "Ma Très Chère Sœur," Île-à-la-Crosse, 14 June 1863; SHSB, Fonds Taché, T2302–T2305, Pepin to Taché, Île-à-la-Crosse, 15 July 1863; ibid., T3079–T3082, Agnès to Taché, Île-à-la-Crosse, 13 January 1865; ibid., T3772–T3773, Agnès to Taché, Île-à-la-Crosse, 9 January 1866.

101 SHSB, Fonds Taché, T1215–T1217, Dubé to Taché, Île-à-la-Crosse, February 1862; ibid., T2302–T2305, Pepin to Taché, Île-à-la-Crosse, 15 July, 1863; ibid., T2680–T2683, Moulin to Taché, Île-à-la-Crosse, 10 March 1864; ibid., T3112–T3115, Pepin to Taché, Île-à-la-Crosse, 20 February 1865; PAA, O.M.I. Collection, Accession 84.400, Item 911, Box 32, Grandin to Taché, Saint-Boniface, 12–13 June 1866; ASGM, Agnès, "Annales de l'établissement des Sœurs Grises à l'Île à la Crosse," 1:203, 205–6.

102 SHSB, Fonds Taché, T1401–1404, Faraud to Taché, Île-à-la-Crosse, 19 May 1862; ibid., T2680–T2683, Moulin to Taché, Île-à-la-Crosse, 10 March 1864; ASGM, Agnès, "Annales de l'établissement des Sœurs Grises à l'Île à la Crosse," 1:206.

103 SHSB, Fonds Taché, T3282–T3283, Samuel McKenzie to Grandin, Île-à-la-Crosse, 20 May 1865; ibid., T3284–T3285, Samuel McKenzie to Agnès, Île-à-la-Crosse, 20 May 1865; ASGM, Agnès, "Annales de l'établissement des Sœurs Grises à l'Île à la Crosse," 1:206, 221, 231.

104 SHSB, Fonds Taché, T1108–T1111, Moulin to Taché, Île-à-la-Crosse, 14 January 1862; PAA, O.M.I. Collection, Accession 84.400, Item 911, Box 32, Grandin, "Mission de St J.Bte de l'Ile à la Crosse, recettes et dépenses du mois de juin 1864 au mois de janvier 1866"; PAA, O.M.I. Collection, Accession 84.400, Item 912, Box 32, Grandin to Végréville, Saint-Albert, 31 December 1868.

105 SHSB, Fonds Taché, T0492–T0499, Grandin to Taché, Île-à-la-Crosse, 15 May 1861; ibid., T1116–T1119, Faraud to Joseph Lestanc [Taché's Oblate counsellor at Saint-Boniface], Île-à-la-Crosse, 13 January 1862; AD, HE 2221. T12Z 60, Faraud to Taché, Île-à-la-Crosse, 16 November 1862; AD, HE 2221. T12Z, 183, Moulin to Taché, Île-à-la-Crosse, 16 November 1862; SHSB, Fonds Taché, T1921–T1924, Moulin to Taché, Île-à-la-Crosse, 9 January 1863; ibid., T2023–T2029, Moulin to Taché, Île-à-la-Crosse, 8 April 1863; PAA, O.M.I. Collection, Accession 84.400, Item 911, Box 32, Grandin to Taché, Île-à-la-Crosse, 5 January 1866.

106 SHSB, Fonds Taché, T1719–T1720, Joseph Salasse to Taché, Île-à-la-Crosse, 16 November 1862; ibid., T1925–T1928, Salasse to Taché, Île-à-la-Crosse, 10 January 1863; SHSB, "Codex historicus, 1845–1897," 77; Carrière, *Dictionnaire biographique*, 3:157. The hand-powered mill fell into disrepair after three years of faithful service. Taché consequently purchased a state-of-the-art mill for the mission. See SHSB, Fonds Taché, T3765–T3768, Grandin, "Mission de Saint-Jean-Baptiste," Île-à-la-Crosse, 9 January 1866. See also ibid., T3778–T3781, Patrick Bowes to Taché, Île-à-la-Crosse, 14 January, 1866; AD, HPF 4191. C75R 204, Taché to "Ma très Honorée Sœur," Saint-Boniface, 28 December 1866.

107 SHSB, Fonds Taché, T2680–T2683, Moulin to Taché, Île-à-la-Crosse, 10 March 1864; ibid., T2931–T2934, Grandin to Taché, Île-à-la-Crosse, 31 August 1864; PAA, O.M.I. Collection, Accession 84.400, Item 911, Box 32, Grandin to Taché,

Île-à-la-Crosse, 5 January 1866; PAA, O.M.I. Collection, Accession 84.400, Item 923, Box 32, Grandin to Clut, Île-à-la-Crosse, 2 February 1866.

108 PAA, O.M.I. Collection, Accession 84.400, Item 911, Box 32, Grandin to Taché, Île-à-la-Crosse, 5 April 1861; SHSB, Fonds Taché, T0385–T0388, Grandin to Taché, Île-à-la-Crosse, 15 April 1861; ibid., T0391–T0393, Moulin to Taché, Île-à-la-Crosse, 6 April 1861; PAA, O.M.I. Collection, Accession 84.400, Item 911, Box 32, Grandin to Taché, Île-à-la-Crosse, 15 May 1861; SHSB, Fonds Taché, T1108–T1111, Moulin to Taché, Fort Carlton, 14 January 1862; AD, HE 2221. T12Z 60, Faraud to Taché, Île-à-la-Crosse, 16 November 1862; SHSB, Fonds Taché, T3765–T3768, Grandin, "Mission de Saint-Jean-Baptiste," Île-à-la-Crosse, 9 January 1866; SHSB, "Codex historicus, 1845–1897," 70, 72–73, 75, 85, 88, 107, 111–13; Carrière, *Dictionnaire biographique*, 2:409–10.

109 SHSB, Fonds Taché, T1601–T1602, Végréville to Taché, Reindeer Lake, 22 August 1862; ibid., T2023–T2029, Moulin to Taché, Île-à-la-Crosse, 8 April 1863; PAA, O.M.I. Collection, Accession 84.400, Item 912, Box 32, Grandin to Végréville, Saint-Albert, 31 December 1868; SHSB, "Codex historicus, 1845–1897," 71–72, 75; Carrière, *Dictionnaire biographique*, 2:64–65; Carrière, *Dictionnaire biographique*, 3:64–65. Végréville's recurrent requisitioning of supplies caused much consternation at Saint-Jean-Baptiste, especially as the 1860s witnessed a sharp increase in the number of residents at the mission (Oblates, Grey Nuns, schoolchildren, and hired workers). In April 1863, Moulin urged Taché to release Saint-Jean-Baptiste from the duty of provisioning Saint-Pierre: "Ideally, the mission at Reindeer Lake would be completely detached from the mission at Île-à-la-Crosse . . . I realize that they do not have all of the resources that we have here, but they have far fewer mouths to feed." See SHSB, Fonds Taché, T2023–T2029, Moulin to Taché, Île-à-la-Crosse, 8 April 1863.

110 SHSB, Fonds Taché, T1745–T1748, Végréville to Taché, Reindeer Lake, 27 November 1862; ibid., T2011–T2016, Gasté to Taché, Île-à-la-Crosse, 6 April 1863; ibid., T2017–T2022, Faraud to Taché, Île-à-la-Crosse, 6 April 1863; ibid., T2229–T2237, Faraud to Taché, Île-à-la-Crosse, 1 June 1863; ibid., T2746–T2750, Gasté to Taché, Reindeer Lake, 10 April 1864; ibid., T3765–T3768, Grandin, "Mission de Saint-Jean-Baptiste," Île-à-la-Crosse, 9 January 1866.

111 SHSB, "Codex historicus, 1845–1897," 78–79; Choquette, *Oblate Assault*, 58–59; Levasseur, *Histoire des Missionnaires Oblats de Marie Immaculée*, 1:232–34.

112 SHSB, Fonds Taché, T1503–T1506, Émile Grouard to Taché, Portage La Loche, 20 July 1862; ibid., T1519–T1522, Émile Petitot to Taché, Portage La Loche, 22 July 1862; ibid., T1523–1526, Faraud to Taché, Île-à-la-Crosse, 22 July 1861; Carrière, *Dictionnaire biographique*, 2:116; Carrière, *Dictionnaire biographique*, 3:69. On Petitot and Grouard's journey from Saint-Boniface to la Nativité (May–August 1862), see Grouard, *Souvenir de mes soixante ans d'apostolat*, 21–27.

113 Choquette, *Oblate Assault on Canada's Northwest*, 41; Ens, *Homeland to Hinterland*, 44–46; McCarthy, *From the Great River to the Ends of the Earth*, 68–69; Macdougall, *One of the Family*, 38–39; Macdougall, "Socio-Cultural Development and Identity Formation," 51–52.

114 SHSB, Fonds Taché, T0010–T0013, Simpson to Taché, Fort Garry, 30 June 1853. On the extension of this agreement—the so-called *entente cordiale*—into the 1860s, see ibid., T0949–T0951, Bernard Rogan Ross to Taché, Fort Simpson, 20 November 1861; ibid., T1792–1793, Alexander Grant Dallas to Robert Campbell, Fort Garry, 11 December 1862 (copy).

115 SHSB, Fonds Taché, T1108–T1111, Moulin to Taché, Carlton, 14 January 1862; ibid., T1116–T1119, Faraud to Taché, Île-à-la-Crosse, 13 January 1862; ibid., T2575–T2577, Moulin to Lestanc, Île-à-la-Crosse, 9 January 1864; ibid., T2768–T2773, Gasté to Taché, Reindeer Lake, 22 April 1864; ibid., T3759–T3761, Jean-Marie Caër to Taché, Portage La Loche, 8 January 1866; ibid., T3769–T3771, Grandin to Taché, "Demandes pour la mission S.-J. Bte (Île à la Crosse)," Île-à-la-Crosse, 11 January 1866; Huel, *Archbishop A.-A. Taché of St. Boniface*, 78–79, 81–82, 333; Huel, *Proclaiming the Gospel*, 55–56.

116 SHSB, Fonds Taché, T1116–T1119, Faraud to Taché, Île-à-la-Crosse, 13 January 1862; McCarthy, *From the Great River to the Ends of the Earth*, 68.

117 SHSB, Fonds Taché, T1601–T1602, Végréville to Taché, Reindeer Lake, 22 August 1862; PAA, O.M.I. Collection, Accession 84.400, Item 911, Box 32, Grandin to Taché, Île-à-la-Crosse, 22 November 1864; SHSB, Fonds Taché, T3765–T3768, Grandin, "Mission de Saint-Jean-Baptiste," Île-à-la-Crosse, 9 January 1866; PAA, O.M.I. Collection, Accession 84.400, Item 911, Box 32, Grandin to Taché, Reindeer Lake, 27 October 1866.

118 SHSB, Fonds Taché, T3765–T3768, Grandin, "Mission de Saint-Jean-Baptiste," Île-à-la-Crosse, 9 January 1866; ibid., T3759–T3761, Caër to Taché, Portage La Loche, 8 January 1866.

119 SHSB, Fonds Taché, T0379–T0382, Végréville to Taché, Île-à-la-Crosse, 2 April 1861; ibid., T3068–T3078, Grandin to Taché and Florent Vandenberghe, Île-à-la-Crosse, 12 January 1865; ibid., T3116–T3119, Grandin to Taché, Île-à-la-Crosse, 23 February 1865; PAA, O.M.I. Collection, Accession 84.400, Item 911, Box 32, Grandin to Taché and Vandenberghe, Île-à-la-Crosse, 3 March 1865; SHSB, Fonds Taché, T3189–T3191, Grandin to Vandenberghe, Île-à-la-Crosse, 9 April 1865; PAA, O.M.I. Collection, Accession 84.400, Item 923, Box 32, Grandin to Clut, Île-à-la-Crosse, 2 February 1866.

120 Grandin was away from Saint-Jean-Baptiste between June 1861 and August 1864 on an extensive tour of Catholic missions in the Athabasca and Mackenzie River basins. During his absence, he was replaced as resident superior of Saint-Jean-Baptiste by Faraud (June 1861–December 1862) and Moulin (December 1862–August 1864). SHSB, Fonds Taché, T0614–T0617, Grandin to Taché, Mission de la Nativité d'Athabaska, 24 June 1861; ibid., T1693–T1702, Grandin to Taché, Mission de la Providence, 10 November 1862; ibid., T2117–T2128, Grandin to Taché, Mission de la Providence, 3 May 1863; ibid., T2575–T2577, Moulin to Lestanc, Île-à-la-Crosse, 9 January 1864. See also McCarthy, "Founding of Providence Mission," 44–49.

121 See for instance: RCRHC/Prop. de la Foi, microfilm X, 10986, Grandin to Glajeux, Île-à-la-Crosse, 19 December 1860; SHSB, Fonds Taché, T0291–T0294, Grandin to Taché, Île-à-la-Crosse, 7 January 1861; ibid., T0298–T0301, Grandin to Taché, Île-à-la-Crosse, 17 January 1861; ibid., T0362–T0368, Grandin to Taché, Île-à-la-Crosse, 1 April 1861; AD, HE 2221. T12Z 64, Faraud to Taché, Île-à-la-Crosse, 1 June 1863; SHSB, Fonds Taché, T3068–T3078, Grandin to Taché and Vandenberghe, Île-à-la-Crosse, 12 January 1865; ibid., T3189–T3191, Grandin to Vandenberghe, Île-à-la-Crosse, 9 April 1865.

122 AD, HE 2221. T12Z 251, Végréville to Taché, Île-à-la-Crosse, 5 April 1861; SHSB, Fonds Taché, T1725–T1728, Faraud to Taché, Île-à-la-Crosse, 16 November 1862; ibid., T2575–T2577, Moulin to Lestanc, Île-à-la-Crosse, 9 January 1864; ibid., T3548–T3551, Grandin to Taché, Île-à-la-Crosse, 25 August 1865.

123 Lestanc served as Taché's counsellor from 1860 to 1870. Concurrently, Lestanc served as director of Saint-Boniface College. Carrière, *Dictionnaire biographique*, 2:321–22; Huel, *Archbishop A.-A. Taché of St. Boniface*, 90–91.

124 SHSB, Fonds Taché, T0937–T0939, Superior General Joseph Fabre to Taché, Marseilles, 13 November 1861; ibid., T2793–T2796, Sardou to Taché, Paris, 10 May 1864; ibid., T2953–T2955, Sardou to Taché, Paris, 7 November 1864; ibid., T3091–T3093, Glajeux to Taché, Paris, 11 January 1865; ibid., T2793–T2796, Sardou to Taché, Paris, 10 May 1864; ibid., T3253–T3256, Sardou to Taché, Paris, 12 May 1865.

125 "À Son Éminence Monsieur le cardinal Barnabò. Marseille, le 20 décembre 1857," *Bx de Mazenod: Lettres . . . 1832–1861*, 72; AD, HE 2221. T12Z 251, Végréville to Taché, Île-à-la-Crosse, 5 April 1861; SHSB, Fonds Taché, T0492–T0499, Grandin to Taché, Île-à-la-Crosse, 15 May 1861; ibid., T2793–T2796, Sardou to Taché, Paris, 10 May 1864; ibid., T2953–T2955, Sardou to Taché, Paris, 7 November 1864.

126 Grandin's preferred medium of communication with Oblates in outlying posts was the "lettre commune," or circular, carried from mission to mission by an Oblate lay brother or by an HBC courier. Grandin stated frequently that this medium saved him time, paper, and ink while fostering an *esprit de corps* among his personnel. Each circular followed a set formula whereby general information—news affecting all Oblates—was presented in the first half of the letter. Information relevant to particular Oblates was presented in the second. See for instance PAA, O.M.I. Collection, Accession 84.400, Item 911, Box 32, Grandin to "[Les] Rds Missionnaires d'Athabaskaw, de l'Ile à la Crosse et de la Rivière Rouge," Mission du Sacré-Coeur (Fort Simpson), 27 September 1861; PAA, O.M.I. Collection, Accession 84.400, Item 912, Box 32, Grandin to "[Les] missionnaires oblats d'Attabaskaw, de l'Ile à la Crosse, de St. Boniface et des autres missions s'il est possible," Mission de la Providence, 23 April 1863; PAA, O.M.I. Collection, Accession 84.400, Item 912, Box 32, Grandin to "Mes bien chers pères et frères," Île-à-la-Crosse, 21 January 1865.

127 Taché, *Vingt années de missions*, 141; SHSB, "Codex historicus, 1845–1897," 68. From 1871 onward, the retreat was held in the second week of February. See SHSB, "Codex historicus, 1845–1897," 115.

128 Taché, *Vingt années de missions*, 139–43, 164; SHSB, "Codex historicus, 1845–1897," 68–71. The term *évêque-roi* was coined by Grollier in 1859 after several prominent HBC officers petitioned Simpson and the CMS to authorize a permanent Anglican mission at Fort Simpson (headquarters of the Mackenzie District). According to Grollier, this request portended a church-state alliance that could only be counterbalanced by a locally based Catholic prelate wielding quasi-feudal political, religious, and social authority. See SHSB, Fonds Taché, T0316–T0319, Grollier to Taché, Fort Good Hope, 24 February, 1861. See also ibid., T0130–T0133, Végréville to Taché, Île-à-la-Crosse, 5 August 1860; McCarthy, "Founding of Providence Mission," 40–44; McCarthy, *From the Great River to the Ends of the Earth*, 47, 63.

129 Carrière, *Dictionnaire biographique*, 3:257–58; Huel, *Proclaiming the Gospel*, 40.

130 PAA, O.M.I. Collection, Accession 84.400, Item 923, Box 32, Grandin to Clut, Île-à-la-Crosse, 14 August 1864; SHSB, Fonds Taché, T2931–T2934, Grandin to Taché, Île-à-la-Crosse, 31 August 1864; PAA, O.M.I. Collection, Accession 84.400, Item 912, Box 32, Grandin to "Mes bien chers pères et frères," Île-à-

la-Crosse, 21 January, 1865; Taché, *Vingt années de missions*, 194–198, 202, 207, 211–212; SHSB, "Codex historicus, 1845–1897," 68–71.

131 SHSB, "Codex historicus, 1845–1897," 18; Benoît, *Vie de Mgr Taché*, 1:123–95; Duchaussois, *Aux glaces polaires*, 151–95; Fernand-Michel, *Dix-huit ans chez les sauvages*, 79–81; Jonquet, *Mgr Grandin*, 89–109; Morice, *History of the Catholic Church in Western Canada*, 1:203–8.

132 Taché, *Vingt années de missions*, 209–11. Taché's study was also published serially in the March, June, September, and December 1866 issues of *Missions de la Congrégation des missionnaires oblats de Marie Immaculée*.

133 Ibid., 140–41. The phrase "ad propria" was likely taken from a prayer in the *Breviarium Romanum* (Roman Breviary) recited by travelling priests: " . . . & Angelus Raphael comitetur nobiscum in via, ut cum pace, salute & gaudio revertamur ad propria" (" . . . and may the [Arch]Angel Raphael accompany us on our travels, that we may return once again to our home in peace, health, and joy"). See *Breviarium Romanum*, cxcviii.

134 SHSB, Fonds Taché, T1503–T1506, Grouard to Taché, Portage La Loche, 20 July 1862; ibid., T1519–T1522, Petitot to Taché, Portage La Loche, 22 July 1862.

135 "Lettre du R.P. Caër au Très-Révérend Père Supérieur Général. Mission de Saint-Jean-Baptiste, Ile à la Crosse, 1er janvier 1866," *Missions de la Congrégation des missionnaires oblats de Marie Immaculée* 27 (September 1868): 275–76. See also Carrière, *Dictionnaire biographique*, 1:155.

136 Two eyewitness accounts of the fire were published. The first was Grandin's letter to the central councils of l'Œuvre de la Propagation de la Foi (dated 4 January 1868). The second appeared in Sœur Agnès's "Annales" (written in 1883). Here I draw principally from Grandin's account because it was written fifteen years earlier than Agnès's, and because it offers a more exclusively "Oblate" perspective on the event. See ASGM, Agnès, "Annales de l'établissement des Sœurs Grises à l'Île à la Crosse," 1:222–28; "Lettre de Mgr Grandin, évêque de Satala, à MM. les Membres des Conseils centraux de l'Œuvre de la Propagation de la Foi. 4 janvier 1868," *Annales de la Propagation de la Foi* 40 (1868): 246–52. For an unpublished primary account of the fire, see RCRHC/É.G., vol. 26, Grandin to Maisonneuve and Végréville, Île-à-la-Crosse, 7 March 1867, 201–3. For a detailed secondary account, see SHSB, "Codex historicus, 1845–1897," 98–102.

137 "Lettre de Mgr Grandin, évêque de Satala, à MM. les Membres des Conseils centraux de l'Œuvre de la Propagation de la Foi. 4 janvier 1868," *Annales de la Propagation de la Foi* 40 (1868): 247–48.

138 Ibid., 248–52. Grandin provided l'Œuvre de la Propagation de la Foi with detailed lists of destroyed items and their estimated value. See RCRHC/Prop. de la Foi, microfilm X, 10822, Grandin to "Monsieur le Président et à Messieurs les conseillers de la Propagation de la Foi à Paris," Paris, 28 December 1867; RCRHC/Prop. de la Foi, microfilm X, 10823, Grandin to "M. le Président et à Messieurs les conseillers de la Propagation de la Foi à Paris," Paris, 13 April 1868; RCRHC/Prop. de la Foi, microfilm X, 10824, "État des recettes et dépenses présumées pour l'année 1868."

139 RCRHC/Prop. de la Foi, microfilm X, 10822, Grandin to "Monsieur le Président et à Messieurs les conseillers de la Propagation de la Foi à Paris," Paris, 28 December 1867; "Missions d'Amérique: Nouvelle Bretagne," *Annales de la*

Propagation de la Foi 40 (1868): 239; PAA, O.M.I. Collection, Accession 84.400, Item 973, Box 33, "Renseignements demandés par Mgr Taché sur les missions et les Missionnaires de Mgr Grandin depuis l'érection du vicariat religieux de St Albert 1868 jusqu'en 1872," 2–3.

140 PAA, O.M.I. Collection, Accession 84.400, Item 912, Box 32, Grandin to Gasté, Saint-Boniface, 27 April 1867. See also "Lettre de Mgr Grandin, évêque de Satala, à MM. les Membres des Conseils centraux de l'Œuvre de la Propagation de la Foi. 4 janvier 1868," *Annales de la Propagation de la Foi* 40 (1868): 248–49.

141 RCRHC/Prop. de la Foi, microfilm X, 10822, Grandin to "Monsieur le Président et à Messieurs les conseillers de la Propagation de la Foi à Paris," Paris, 28 December 1867; "Missions d'Amérique: Nouvelle Bretagne," *Annales de la Propagation de la Foi* 40 (1868): 239.

142 PAA, O.M.I. Collection, Accession 84.400, Item 911, Box 32, Grandin to Taché, Grazai, 31 October 1867; ibid., Grandin to Taché, Paris, 15 January 1868; RCRHC/Prop. de la Foi, microfilm X, 10823, Grandin to "M. le Président et à Messieurs les conseillers de la Propagation de la Foi à Paris," Paris, 13 April 1868; "Compte-rendu," *Annales de la Propagation de la Foi* 41 (1869): 201.

143 *Atlas O.M.I.*, 5; Levasseur, *Histoire des Missionnaires Oblats de Marie Immaculée*, 1:177–78.

144 PAA, O.M.I. Collection, Accession 84.400, Vol. 5, Box 35, Grandin, "Notes privées sur les missions et les missionnaires du diocèse de St-Albert," 1868–1884, 134–35, 160–61, 171–72; Carrière, *Dictionnaire biographique*, 2:126, 300–301, 317; Carrière, *Dictionnaire biographique*, 3:14–15; Duchaussois, *Apôtres inconnus*, 104–14; 236–40; Jonquet, *Mgr Grandin*, 187.

145 PAA, O.M.I. Collection, Accession 84.400, Item 956, Box 33, Taché to Fabre, Saint-Albert, 20 December 1868; PAA, O.M.I. Collection, Accession 84.400, Vol. 5, Box 35, Grandin, "Notes privées sur les missions et les missionnaires du diocèse de St-Albert," 1868–1884, 12.

146 PAA, O.M.I. Collection, Accession 84.400, Item 911, Box 32, Grandin to Taché, Marseilles, 10 September 1867; PAA, O.M.I. Collection, Accession 84.400, Item 957, Box 33, "Mgr Grandin, Notes Intimes sur le Diocèse de St Albert, rédigées en 1884," 21–22.

147 PAA, O.M.I. Collection, Accession 84.400, Item 956, Box 33, Grandin to Fabre, Carlton, 12 August 1868; AD, G LPP 2199, Prosper Légeard to Grandin, Île-à-la-Crosse, 11 January 1869; PAA, O.M.I. Collection, Accession 84.400, Vol. 5, Box 35, Grandin, "Notes privées sur les missions et les missionnaires du diocèse de St-Albert," 1868–1884, 171.

148 PAA, O.M.I. Collection, Accession 84.400, Item 956, Box 33, Taché to Fabre, Saint-Albert, 20 December 1868; PAA, O.M.I. Collection, Accession 84.400, Vol. 5, Box 35, Grandin, "Notes privées sur les missions et les missionnaires du diocèse de St-Albert," 1868–1884, 13, 134, 147, 160; PAA, O.M.I. Collection, Accession 84.400, Item 957, Box 33, "Mgr Grandin, Notes Intimes sur le Diocèse de St Albert, rédigées en 1884," 21.

149 AD, G LPP 2199, Prosper Légeard to Grandin, Île-à-la-Crosse, 11 January 1869; PAA, O.M.I. Collection, Accession 84.400, Item 973, Box 33, "Renseignements demandés par Mgr Taché sur les missions et les Missionnaires de Mgr Grandin depuis l'érection du vicariat religieux de St Albert 1868 jusqu'en 1872," 15, 17–18.

150 PAA, O.M.I. Collection, Accession 84.400, Item 911, Box 32, Grandin to Taché, Mission de Saint-Joachim (Fort Edmonton), 13 February 1869; PAA, O.M.I. Collection, Accession 84.400, Item 973, Box 33, "Renseignements demandés par Mgr Taché sur les missions et les Missionnaires de Mgr Grandin depuis l'érection du vicariat religieux de St Albert 1868 jusqu'en 1872," 2–3. Grandin contemplated moving the Grey Nuns of Saint-Bruno closer to Fort Edmonton—either to join the existing community of Grey Nuns at Saint-Albert or to establish a new convent at Saint-Joachim (within the palisades of the HBC fort). PAA, O.M.I. Collection, Accession 84.400, Item 911, Box 32, Grandin to Taché, Mission de Saint-Joachim (Fort Edmonton), 13 February 1869.

151 PAA, O.M.I. Collection, Accession 84.400, Vol. 5, Box 35, Grandin, "Notes privées sur les missions et les missionnaires du diocèse de St-Albert," 1868–1884, 12–13.

152 RCRHC/Prop. de la Foi, microfilm X, 10904, Grandin to "M.M., les Présidents et Conseillers de la Propagation de la Foi à Lyon et à Paris," Saint-Albert, 20 December 1868; "Lettre de Mgr Grandin, évêque de Satala, à MM. les Membres des Conseils centraux de l'Œuvre de la Propagation de la Foi," *Annales de la Propagation de la Foi* 41 (1869): 286, 292–93.

153 Carrière, *Dictionnaire biographique*, 2:219; Hughes, *Father Lacombe*, 82–91; Legal, *Short Sketches*, 14–19; MacGregor, *Father Lacombe*, 113–32; Smith, "History of French-Speaking Albertans," 87; Sœur de la Providence, *Le Père Lacombe*, 137–41.

154 "Missions d'Amérique: Nouvelle Bretagne," *Annales de la Propagation de la Foi*, 40 (1868): 243–45; "Renseignements demandés par Mgr Taché sur les missions et les Missionnaires de Mgr Grandin depuis l'érection du vicariat religieux de St Albert 1868 jusqu'en 1872," 6–9; PAA, O.M.I. Collection, Accession 84.400, Item 986, Box 34, Grandin, "Missions et Résidences du diocèse de St. Albert." See also Venini Byrne, *From the Buffalo to the Cross*, 17–30.

155 PAA, O.M.I. Collection, Accession 84.400, Vol. 5, Box 35, Grandin, "Notes privées sur les missions et les missionnaires du diocèse de St-Albert," 1868–1884, 2–11; Duchaussois, *Aventures canadiennes des Sœurs Grises*, 15; Legal, *Short Sketches*, 16–17; Levasseur, *Les Oblats de Marie Immaculée dans l'ouest et le nord du Canada*, 61.

156 PAA, O.M.I. Collection, Accession 84.400, Item 957, Box 33, "Mgr Grandin, Notes Intimes sur le Diocèse de St Albert, rédigées en 1884," 15–25; PAA, O.M.I. Collection, Accession 84.400, Item 959, Box 33, "Notes et souvenirs de Mgr Grandin (Repris à la demande de Mgr Langevin par lettre du 28 nov. 1897, rédaction commencée en mars 1898)," 190. See also *Atlas O.M.I.*, 56; Levasseur, *Histoire des Missionnaires Oblats de Marie Immaculée*, 1:238; Levasseur, *Les Oblats de Marie Immaculée dans l'ouest et le nord du Canada*, 72; Morice, *History of the Catholic Church in Western Canada*, 2:76, 86–88.

157 AD, G LPP 2201, Légeard to Aubert, Île-à-la-Crosse, 29 August 1873; AD, HEC 2500. P96C 23, Légeard to Maisonneuve, Île-à-la-Crosse, 8 October 1878; McCarthy, *From the Great River to the Ends of the Earth*, 69.

158 PAA, O.M.I. Collection, Accession 84.400, Item 911, Box 32, "CONVENTION entre Monseigneur GRANDIN, évêque de Satala in partibus infidelium nommé oralement vicaire apostolique des districts unis de la Kisiskajiwan et de la Rivière aux Anglais d'une part et Monseigneur FARAUD, évêque d'Anemour in partibus in fidelium, vicaire apostolique des Districts unis d'Athabaskaw et du fleuve McKenzie," Île-à-la-Crosse, 1 July 1869. This agreement eventually

became a source of acrimony between Grandin and Faraud. In 1872, Grandin began pressing his claim on Lac La Biche and accused Faraud of neglecting the spiritual welfare of its inhabitants. Faraud refused to relinquish the mission citing its overriding strategic importance to his vicariate. Notre-Dame-des-Victoires did not revert to the Diocese of Saint-Albert until 20 May 1889. See PAA, O.M.I. Collection, Accession 84.400, Item 911, Box 32, Grandin and Faraud to Taché, Saint-Albert, 14 April 1877. See also Choquette, *Oblate Assault*, 74, 89; Fay, *History of Canadian Catholics*, 94; Huel, "La mission Notre-Dame-des-Victoires du lac la Biche," 23–36.

159 PAA, O.M.I. Collection, Accession 84.400, Item 987, Box 34, Grandin, "Liste des missions du diocèse catholique de St. Albert," Saint-Albert, 1883; Choquette, *Oblate Assault*, 55, 74; Huel, *Proclaiming the Gospel*, 58; Levasseur, *Les Oblats de Marie Immaculée dans l'ouest et le nord du Canada*, 59.

160 Freight destined for Saint-Pierre (Reindeer Lake) was not transshipped through Fort Carlton and Saint-Julien but sent north by way of Cumberland House. Freight destined for Saint-Albert was sent by way of Fort Edmonton. AD, HEC 2500. P96C 8, Légeard to Maisonneuve, Île-à-la-Crosse, 12 January 1874; AD, HEC 2500. P96C 9, Légeard to Maisonneuve, Île-à-la-Crosse, 11 March 1874.

161 AD, HEC 2500. P96C 15, Légeard to Maisonneuve, Île-à-la-Crosse, 16 January 1871; AD, G LPP 2201, Légeard to Maisonneuve, Île-à-la-Crosse, 29 August 1873; AD, HEC 2500. P96C 23, Légeard to Maisonneuve, Île-à-la-Crosse, 8 October 1878. In 1875, Légeard estimated that it took twelve to fifteen days to transport freight from Fort Carlton to Saint-Jean-Baptiste via Saint-Julien. AD, G LPP 2203, Légeard to "Ma très honorée Sœur," Île-à-la-Crosse, 27 July 1875.

162 AD, G LPP 2202, Légeard to Aubert, Île-à-la-Crosse, 3 January 1875. Aubert had been appointed Oblate Assitant General in 1867. See Carrière, *Dictionnaire biographique*, 1:34.

163 AD, LC 6301. K26R 7, Légeard, "Allocation demandée pour la mission de l'Ile à la Crosse," Île-à-la-Crosse, June 1876; PAA, O.M.I. Collection, Accession 84.400, Vol. 5, Box 35, Grandin, "Notes privées sur les missions et les missionnaires du diocèse de St-Albert," 1868–1884, 13–14, 115, 134; Soullier, *Vie du Révérend Père Légeard*, 62–63, 125. This sum represented an increasingly marginal proportion of the total allocation from l'Œuvre de la Propagation de la Foi to the Diocese of Saint-Albert, from 38.5% in 1870 to 18.8% in 1879. See "Compte-rendu," *Annales de la Propagation de la Foi* 43–52 (1871–80).

164 Barnoud and Maviel, "Paray religieux," 71–75, 79; Boutry, "Religions «populaires» et religions dissidentes," 492–94; Jonas, *France and the Cult of the Sacred Heart*, 4, 9–32, 144; Julia, "La pesée d'un phénomène," 192; Langlois, "Une France duelle?," 323.

165 AD, G LPP 2203, Légeard to "Ma très honorée Sœur," Île-à-la-Crosse, 27 July 1875; AD, HPF 4191. C75R 177, Légeard to "Ma très honorée et Vénérée Mère" [Superior of the Visitation Convent at Paray-le-Monial], Île-à-la-Crosse, 20 December 1877; "Missions d'Amérique: Nouvelle Bretagne, Diocèse de Saint-Albert," *Annales de la Propagation de la Foi* 49 (1877): 443, 448, 453; Soullier, *Vie du Révérend Père*, 69, 125–26; SHSB, "Codex historicus, 1845–1897," 161–62.

166 LAC/Black Series, microfilm C-10113, file no. 7780, "Privy Council's Report on Grants to Schools at Lac La Biche, Isle a la Crosse and St. Albert," 1877; LAC/Black Series, microfilm C-10117, file no. 10125, "Ile-a-la-Crosse Agency—Reverend

Mr. Legard's [*sic*] Report on the School at Ile-a-la-Crosse," 1878; PAA, O.M.I. Collection, Accession 84.400, Item 928, Box 33, Grandin to Lawrence Clarke (MLA), St. Laurent de Grandin, 15 October 1887 (copy), 66–68; PAA, O.M.I. Collection, Accession 84.400, Item 928, Box 33, Grandin to Joseph Wrigley (HBC Chief Commissioner for British North America), Ottawa, 19 November 1887 (copy), 98–102.

167 AD, G LPP 2200, Légeard to Fabre, Île-à-la-Crosse, 13 January 1870; AD, HPF 4191. C75R 177, Légeard to "Ma très honorée et Vénérée Mère," Île-à-la-Crosse, 20 December 1877; PAA, O.M.I. Collection, Accession 84.400, Vol. 5, Box 35, Grandin, "Notes privées sur les missions et les missionnaires du diocèse de St-Albert," 1868–1884, 147; Carrière, *Dictionnaire biographique*, 1:129.

168 PAA, O.M.I. Collection, Accession 84.400, Vol. 5, Box 35, Grandin, "Notes privées sur les missions et les missionnaires du diocèse de St-Albert," 1868–1884, 147; SHSB, "Codex historicus, 1845–1897," 121; Carrière, *Dictionnaire biographique*, 1:115.

169 AD, HEC 2500. P96C 8, Légeard to Maisonneuve, Île-à-la-Crosse, 12 January 1874; AD, G LPP 2202, Légeard to Aubert, Île-à-la-Crosse, 3 January 1875; AD, HEC 2500. P96C 11, Légeard to Maisonneuve, Île-à-la-Crosse, 19 January 1875; ASGM, Agnès, "Annales de l'établissement des Sœurs Grises à l'Île à la Crosse," 2:201–3; SHSB, "Codex historicus, 1845–1897," 123, 134–35, 142, 167.

170 AD, HEC 2500. P96C 8, Légeard to Maisonneuve, Île-à-la-Crosse, 13 February 1877; AD, HEC 2500. P96C 18, Légeard to Maisonneuve, Île-à-la-Crosse, 25 November 1877; AD, HEC 2500. P96C 19, Légeard to Maisonneuve, Île-à-la-Crosse, 14 January 1878; AD, HEC 2500. P96C 22, Légeard to Maisonneuve, Île-à-la-Crosse, 24 June 1878.

171 ASGM, Agnès, "Annales de l'établissement des Sœurs Grises à l'Île à la Crosse," 2:225–27; SHSB, "Codex historicus, 1845–1897," 168–70. According to Pénard, the cause of death was neuralgia compounded by tuberculosis. Légeard's neuralgia appears to have been chronic throughout his tenure as local superior. See for instance PAA, O.M.I. Collection, Accession 84.400, Item 911, Box 32, Grandin to Taché, Saint-Albert, 29 August 1872; ibid., Grandin to Taché, Fort Carlton, 30 July 1874; ibid., Grandin to Taché, Fort Cumberland, 30 July 1875; PAA, O.M.I. Collection, Accession 84.400, Vol. 5, Box 35, Grandin, "Notes privées sur les missions et les missionnaires du diocèse de St-Albert," 1868–1884, 14–16, 134–35.

172 Soullier, *Vie du Révérend Père Légeard*, 1–4. On Soullier, see *Atlas O.M.I.*, 4; Levasseur, *Histoire des Missionnaires Oblats de Marie Immaculée*, 1:175.

173 Soullier, *Vie du Révérend Père Légeard*, 146.

174 See for instance "Lettre de Mgr Grandin à MM. les membres des Conseils centraux de l'Œuvre de la Propagation de la Foi. Fort Pitt (mission de Saint-François Régis), 10 janvier 1870," *Annales de la Propagation de la Foi* 44 (1872): 272–73: "Having lately been ceded to the Canadian government, our country will surely draw many strangers, in all likelihood the dregs of Canada and the United States."

175 "Copy of Treaty and Supplementary Treaty No. 7, Made 22nd Sept., and 4th Dec., 1877," 4; PAA, O.M.I. Collection, Accession 84.400, Item 986, Box 34, Grandin, "Missions et Résidences du diocèse de St. Albert," Saint-Albert, 1882; Le Chevallier, *Esquisse*, 17–21; Dempsey, *Indian Tribes of Alberta*, 7, 14–15, 22–23, 28–29, 31; Kerbiriou, *Les Indiens de l'ouest canadien*, 112–22; Levasseur, *Histoire*

des Missionnaires Oblats, 1:242; Huel, *Proclaiming the Gospel*, 52; Knowles, *Winds of Change*, 179; Venini Byrne, *From the Buffalo to the Cross*, 23–40.

176   PAA, O.M.I. Collection, Accession 84.400, Item 987, Box 34, Grandin, "Liste des missions du diocèse catholique de St. Albert," Saint-Albert, 1883; M.L. Foran, "Urban Calgary 1884–1895," 61–69, 75–76; Smith and Klassen, "Onward! Calgary in the 1890s," 1–4.

177   PAA, O.M.I. Collection, Accession 84.400, Item 967, Box 33, "Lettre de Mgr Vital Justin Grandin, O.M.I., Vicaire de la Congrégation des Missionnaires O.M.I. dans le Diocèse de S. Albert et Évêque de ce même diocèse, aux RR. PP. Oblats missionnaires dans le diocèse," Ottawa, 18 November 1887, 2. Although none had been incorporated as a city, the "eight cities" in question were most likely Regina, Battleford, Swift Current, Medicine Hat, Lethbridge, Fort Macleod, Calgary, and Pincher Creek. For information on the Oblate ministry to these settler communities, see *"Prairie Grass to Mountain Pass,"* 195–97, 219, 235–36, 239–42, 794–95; Le Chevallier, *Esquisse*, 43–68; Ortolan, *Les Oblats de Marie Immaculée*, 4:164–91; Venini Byrne, *From the Buffalo to the Cross*, 61–81, 143–48, 205–15, 232–39, 283–86, 373–76.

178   PAA, O.M.I. Collection, Accession 71.220, Item 76, Box 2, "Extrait du rapport sur le Vicariat de St. Albert au chapitre général de la congrégation des O.M.I.," Rome, 28 April 1887; SHSB, "Codex historicus, 1845–1897," 172, 279.

179   PAA, O.M.I. Collection, Accession 84.800, Item 930, Box 33, Grandin to Hippolyte Leduc (Vicar General of Saint-Albert), St. Antoine de Batoche, 16 October 1887; PAA, O.M.I. Collection, Accession 84.400, Item 967, Box 33, "Lettre de Mgr Vital Justin Grandin, O.M.I., Vicaire de la Congrégation des Missionnaires O.M.I. dans le Diocèse de S. Albert et Évêque de ce même diocèse, aux RR. PP. Oblats missionnaires dans le diocèse," Ottawa, 18 November 1887, 6; Carrière, *Dictionnaire biographique*, 2:288–89.

180   "Mission de Saint-Albert. Lettre du R.P. Rapet, supérieur de l'Ile-à-la-Crosse. Mission de Saint-Jean-Baptiste, Ile-à-la-Crosse, le 1er janvier 1889," *Missions de la Congrégation des missionnaires oblats de Marie Immaculée*, 106 (June 1889): 171; SHSB, "Codex historicus, 1845–1897," 173, 181, 202. A notable exception was Dubé, who had died at Saint-Jean-Baptiste on 29 April 1872 (during Légeard's tenure as local superior). See PAA, O.M.I. Collection, Accession 84.400, Vol. 5, Box 35, Grandin, "Notes privées sur les missions et les missionnaires du diocèse de St-Albert," 1868–1884, 145–46; ASGM, Agnès, "Annales de l'établissement des Sœurs Grises à l'Île à la Crosse," 2:240.

181   PAA, O.M.I. Collection, Accession 84.400, Vol. 5, Box 35, Grandin, "Notes privées sur les missions et les missionnaires du diocèse de St-Albert," 1868–1884, 200; SHSB, "Codex historicus, 1845–1897," 173; Carrière, *Dictionnaire biographique*, 2:363.

182   PAA, O.M.I. Collection, Accession 84.800, Item 922, Box 32, Grandin to Gasté, Île-à-la-Crosse, 11 September 1881; SHSB, "Codex historicus, 1845–1897," 182; Carrière, *Dictionnaire biographique*, 2:212–13.

183   PAA, O.M.I. Collection, Accession 84.800, Item 922, Box 32, Grandin to Lestanc, Saint-Albert, 5 November 1881; SHSB, "Codex historicus, 1845–1897," 182; Carrière, *Dictionnaire biographique*, 3:115–16.

184   SHBH, "Codex historicus, 1845–1897," 183, 191; Carrière, *Dictionnaire biographique*, 1:255, 3:220–21.

185 PAA, O.M.I. Collection, Accession 84.400, Item 986, Box 34, Grandin, "Missions et Résidences du diocèse de St. Albert," Saint-Albert, 1882; PAA, O.M.I. Collection, Accession 84.400, Item 987, Box 34, Grandin, "Liste des missions du diocèse catholique de St. Albert," Saint-Albert, 1883.

186 PAA, O.M.I. Collection, Accession 84.800, Item 926, Box 33, Grandin to Lacombe, Saint-Albert, 26 February 1884.

187 PAA, O.M.I. Collection, Accession 84.800, Item 911, Box 32, Grandin to Taché, Lac des Maskeys [Muskeg Lake?], 16 September 1886; SHSB, "Codex historicus, 1845–1897," 206–7.

188 "Mission de Saint-Albert. Lettre du R.P. Rapet, supérieur de l'Ile-à-la-Crosse, le 1ᵉʳ janvier 1889," *Missions de la Congrégation des missionnaires oblats de Marie Immaculée* 106 (June 1889): 166–68; PAA, O.M.I. Collection, Accession 84.800, Item 932, Box 33, Grandin to Leduc, Battleford, 16 September 1889; SHSB, "Codex historicus, 1845–1897," 207, 210–11, 213–16.

189 SHSB, "Codex historicus, 1845–1897," 207–8, 216–17. See also ASGM, L018, Île à la Crosse, "Historique," 10. According to Pénard, the shortage of ordained clergy at Saint-Jean-Baptiste was especially problematic during the epidemic outbreaks of the late 1880s. On the outbreak of 1887, he noted: "The two priests [Rapet and Teston] struggled to visit all of the afflicted. While they were off visiting sick people in one area, people from three or four other areas would send for them. Seeing no abatement in the intensity of the scourge, the priests held public prayers—which were well attended—to implore God's mercy."

190 Furet, *La Révolution de Turgot à Jules Ferry*, 533–37, 564; Mellor, *Histoire de l'anticléricalisme français*, 317–25; Rémond, *L'anti-cléricalisme en France*, 176–197; Rémond, *La droite en France*, 154–56. On the category "unauthorized congregations" and the legal recognition of select orders/congregations, see Langlois, "Politique et religion," 134–43.

191 "Maisons de France. Consummatum est!," *Missions de la Congrégation des missionnaires oblats de Marie Immaculée* 73 (March 1881): 5–111; Levasseur, *Histoire des Missionnaires Oblats de Marie Immaculée*, 1:187; Ortolan, *Les Oblats de Marie Immaculée*, 3:226–55.

192 PAA, O.M.I. Collection, Accession 84.800, Item 966, Box 33, Grandin to the Oblates of the Diocese of Saint-Albert, Battleford, 31 August 1880; PAA, O.M.I. Collection, Accession 84.800, Item 966, Box 33, Grandin to Gasté, Bonald, Pasquette and Lecoq, Saint-Albert, 19 November 1880; PAA, O.M.I. Collection, Accession 84.800, Item 911, Box 32, Grandin to Taché, Saint-Albert, February 1881. See also "Compte-rendu de 1880," *Annales de la Propagation de la Foi* 53 (1881): 141–42.

193 PAA, O.M.I. Collection, Accession 84.800, Item 911, Box 32, Grandin to Taché, Saint-Albert, 19 December 1880. See also Grandin's letter from the following month, ibid., Grandin to Taché, Saint-Albert, 12 January 1881.

194 PAA, O.M.I. Collection, Accession 84.400, Item 923, Box 32, Grandin to Clut, Île-à-la-Crosse, 7 September 1881; RCRHC/É.G., vol. 6, "Procès verbal de la Conférence tenue le 12 septembre '83 à l'Evêché de Saint-Albert sous la Présidence de Monseigneur l'Evêque de St-Albert: 1ᵉ Division du Diocèse," 214.

195 Quoted in PAA, O.M.I. Collection, Accession 84.400, Item 911, Box 32, Grandin to Taché, Saint-Albert, February 1881.

196 PAA, O.M.I. Collection, Accession 71.220, Item 76, Box 2, "Extrait du rapport sur le Vicariat de St. Albert au chapitre général de la congrégation des O.M.I.," Rome, 28 April 1887; PAA, O.M.I. Collection, Accession 84.400, Item 967, Box 33, "Lettre de Mgr Vital Justin Grandin, O.M.I., Vicaire de la Congrégation des Missionnaires O.M.I. dans le Diocèse de S. Albert et Évêque de ce même diocèse, aux RR. PP. Oblats missionnaires dans le diocèse," Ottawa, 18 November 1887, 9; Levasseur, *Histoire des Missionnaires Oblats de Marie Immaculée*, 1:187. On the republicans' formulation and application of a more moderate policy toward the clergy after 1880, see Bertocci, *Jules Simon*, 192–211; Chevalier, "Jules Ferry et le Saint-Siège"; Mayeur, "Jules Ferry et la laïcité."

197 *Atlas O.M.I.*, 56; Choquette, *Oblate Assault*, 90–93; Lesage, *Capitale d'une solitude*, 137; Levasseur, *Histoire des Missionnaires Oblats de Marie Immaculée*, 1:246.

198 PAA, O.M.I. Collection, Accession 71.220, Item 77, Box 2, "Rapport du Vicariat de Saskatchewan," Prince Albert, February 1898; "Compte-rendu," *Annales de la Propagation de la Foi* 64–71 (1892–99). Oblates in the new vicariate considered both benefactions totally insufficient. They received only three recruits from the Oblate General Administration between 1891 and 1898, and their annual allocation from l'Œuvre de la Propagation de la Foi declined incrementally from 33,500 francs in 1891 to 27,000 francs in 1898.

199 RCRHC/Prop. de la Foi, microfilm X, 10846, Albert Pascal to the Central Councils of l'Œuvre de la Propagation de la Foi, Prince Albert, 3 December 1895; RCRHC/Prop. de la Foi, microfilm X, 10845, Pascal to "Monsieur le Directeur de l'Œuvre de la Propagation de la Foi, Bureau de Paris [Charles Hamel]," Prince Albert, 7 December 1895; AD, G LPP 2201, Albert Pascal to Oblate Superior General Louis Soullier, Prince Albert, 15 April 1896; Carrière, *Dictionnaire biographique*, 3:47–48; Ouellet, "Mgr Albert Pascal, o.m.i."

200 PAA, O.M.I. Collection, Accession 71.220, Item 77, Box 2, "Rapport du Vicariat de Saskatchewan," Prince Albert, February 1898.

201 "Vicariat de la Saskatchewan. Mission de la Visitation au Portage-La-Loche. Lettre du R.P. Pénard au T.R.P. Supérieur Général. Mission Saint-Jean-Baptiste, Ile-à-la-Crosse, 11 avril 1895," *Missions de la Congrégation des missionnaires oblats de Marie Immaculée* 131 (September 1895); 290–92; SHSB, "Codex historicus, 1845–1897," 247; Carrière, *Dictionnaire biographique*, 3:59–60. Before his ministry at Notre-Dame-de-la-Visitation, Pénard had served at Saint-Raphaël mission, Cold Lake (1888–1890). He was transferred to Saint-Jean-Baptiste in May 1890 and undertook several pastoral visits to Notre-Dame-de-la-Visitation before becoming resident missionary there. See SHSB, "Codex historicus, 1845–1897," 229–36, 239–41, 244.

202 SHSB, "Codex historicus, 1845–1897," 248–50, 252–66. Rapet's workload was especially onerous at harvest time, when the Oblate lay brothers and their male charges spent weeks on end mowing and reaping near Canoe Lake and Waterhen Lake. In their absence, Rapet was the only adult male at Saint-Jean-Baptiste. See Pénard's account of the harvest in ibid., 252–53.

203 "Vicariat de la Saskatchewan. Rapport de Mgr Pascal, vicaire apostolique," *Missions de la Congrégation des missionnaires oblats de Marie Immaculée* 121 (March 1893): 18, 21; "Vicariat de la Saskatchewan. Lettre de R.P. Rapet a Mgr Pascal," *Missions de la Congrégation des missionnaires oblats de Marie Immaculée* 132 (December 1895): 428–29; SHSB, "Codex historicus, 1845–1897," 257.

204 SHSB, "Codex historicus, 1845–1897," 253, 256–57, 259–62. Rapet and Pénard began making their appeals in August 1893: "During this time, Father Rapet and Father Pénard wrote letter upon letter to Monseigneur Pascal (who was then attending the meeting of the Oblate General Chapter in France [held once every six years]), requesting that he obtain a new missionary for the district of Île-à-la-Crosse. But he was unable to grant their request, and so they had to make do with the status quo." Ibid., 253.

205 "Vicariat de la Saskatchewan. Mission de la Visitation au Portage-La-Loche. Lettre du R.P. Pénard au T.R.P. Supérieur Général. Mission Saint-Jean-Baptiste, Ile-à-la-Crosse, 11 avril 1895," *Missions de la Congrégation des missionnaires oblats de Marie Immaculée* 131 (September 1895): 285, 291; SHSB, "Codex historicus, 1845–1897," 266; Carrière, *Dictionnaire biographique*, 2:178.

206 SHSB, "Codex historicus, 1845–1897," 270–71, 275–77.

207 ASGM, Circulaire mensuelle adressée aux diverses maisons de l'Institut 8 (May and June 1897): 425–426; SHSB, "Codex historicus, 1845–1897," 271–72, 275–77.

208 ASGM, Circulaire mensuelle adressée aux diverses maisons de l'Institut 11 (November and December 1897): 534; SHSB, "Codex historicus, 1845–1897," 283–84, 288–89, 293–94.

209 PAA, O.M.I. Collection, Accession 71.220, Item 77, Box 2, "Rapport du Vicariat de Saskatchewan," Prince Albert, February 1898.

210 Ibid.; SHSB, "Codex historicus, 1845–1897," 295–96, and "Codex historicus, 1898–1928," 1–2.

211 "Lettre du R.P. Pénard au T.R.P. Général," *Missions de la Congrégation des missionnaires oblats de Marie Immaculée* 151 (September 1900): 257–58; SHSB, "Codex historicus, 1845–1897," 296, and "Codex historicus, 1898–1928," 1–2.

212 "Lettre du R.P. Pénard au T.R.P. Général," *Missions de la Congrégation des missionnaires oblats de Marie Immaculée* 151 (September 1900): 258.

Chapter 2: Oblate Perceptions of the Hudson's Bay Company

1 Grant, *Moon of Wintertime*, 106. See generally 106–9.

2 See especially Champagne, *Les débuts de la mission dans le Nord-Ouest Canadien*, 95–97; Choquette, *Oblate Assault*, 127, 130–31, 165–68; Huel, *Archbishop A.-A. Taché of St. Boniface*, 27, 63–64; Huel, "The Oblates of Mary Immaculate and the Hudson's Bay Company"; Huel, *Proclaiming the Gospel*, 35–37, 56, 79, 102–3; Huel, "Western Oblate History," 28–30; McCarthy, *From the Great River to the Ends of the Earth*, 27–43.

3 Huel, "Western Oblate History," 28. See also Huel, "The Oblates of Mary Immaculate and the Hudson's Bay Company," 446.

4 For expressions of friendship between individual Oblates and HBC officers, see especially Choquette, *Oblate Assault*, 165–68; Huel, *Archbishop A.-A. Taché of St. Boniface*, 63–64; Huel, *Proclaiming the Gospel*, 35, 37; Huel, "Western Oblate History," 28–30.

5 Choquette, *Oblate Assault*, 165.

6 Ibid, 130–31, 165–69; Choquette, "Les rapports entre catholiques et protestants," 138–40. According to Choquette, the HBC consistently preferred Catholic to Protestant missionaries. It considered Catholics better suited to the rigours of

frontier life and more supportive of company interests because of their material abnegation, their accommodation of local customs (including marriage *à la façon du pays* and Sunday work) and their strict policy of non-interference in company affairs. By contrast, HBC officers expressed hostility toward Protestants missionaries, particularly the Anglican contingent. These clergymen drew copiously on HBC resources to support their families and to maintain a lifestyle that they deemed commensurate with their elevated social status. Moreover, Anglican missionaries sowed social disharmony through their propagation of elitist, racist, and sectarian attitudes.

7   Neither Huel nor Choquette pursued an investigation of HBC-missionary relations beyond the early 1870s. For her part, McCarthy ended her investigation with the expiry of HBC's Licence for Exclusive Trade in the Athabasca and Mackenzie Districts (1859). See Choquette, *Oblate Assault*, 168–69; Huel, *Proclaiming the Gospel*, 177–78; Huel, "Western Oblate History," 28–30; McCarthy, *From the Great River to the Ends of the Earth*, 43.

8   Joseph-Norbert Provencher and Sévère Dumoulin (secular priests from the Archdiocese of Quebec) were the first Catholic clergy assigned to the Red River Colony. Their arrival in 1818 prompted the HBC to articulate its position on missionaries and to establish regulations on evangelization. Missionaries were instructed to remain within the boundaries of the colony, to refrain from indulging in sectarian polemics, and above all to avoid meddling with the Company's trade. SHSB, Fonds Provencher, P1592–P1600, Thomas Douglas, Earl of Selkirk to Archbishop Joseph-Octave Plessis of Quebec, Pau (department of Pyrénées-Atlantiques, France), 30 December 1819; ibid., P1627–P1631, John (Wedderburn) Halkett to Plessis, York Factory, 26 August 1822. See also Choquette, *Oblate Assault*, 30, 36; McCarthy, *From the Great River to the Ends of the Earth*, 30–31.

9   "The Red River Settlement and the Hudson's Bay Company," *The Colonial Intelligencer, or, Aborigines' Friend* 2, no. 3–4 (July and August 1848): 39. See also ibid., 35–47; Tweedie, *Canada West and the Hudson's Bay Company*, 7, 17–19; Grant, *Moon of Wintertime*, 106; Semple, *The Lord's Dominion*, 174.

10 Champagne, *Les débuts de la mission dans le Nord-Ouest Canadien*, 94; Giraud, *Le métis canadien*, 1063. Over the following decade, Catholic missionaries came to regard Rowand as a trusted friend and an invaluable ally. He became renowned for his generosity in providing them room, board, and travel provisions. Ironically, Sylvia Van Kirk has noted that Rowand was harshly critical of missionaries—Catholic and Protestant alike—as they placed an excessive burden on the Company's supplies and its transport system. See especially de Smet, *Missions de l'Orégon*, 148–49; SHSB, Fonds Provencher, P1803–P1829, Thibault to Signay, Red River (?), 18 June 1843; ibid., P1841–P1854, Thibault to Provencher, Fort Pitt, 26 December 1843; Van Kirk, "John Rowand," *Dictionary of Canadian Biography Online*, vol. 8 (1851–1860).

11 Abel, *Drum Songs*, 114–15; Grant, *Moon of Wintertime*, 101, 107; Maclean, *James Evans*, 146–49, 191–92; Semple, *The Lord's Dominion*, 174–75.

12 McCarthy, *From the Great River to the Ends of the Earth*, 30, 32–33; Tucker, *The Rainbow in the North*, 203–207.

13 SHSB, Fonds Taché, T0010–T0013, Simpson to Taché, Fort Garry, 30 June 1853. See also Grant, *Moon of Wintertime*, 105; McCarthy, *From the Great River to the Ends of the Earth*, 31.

14 LAC/HBC, microfilm HBC 1M270, B.89/c/1, Ile-a-Lacrosse [*sic*] Correspondence Inward, 1810–1862, Simpson to Taché, Norway House, 1 June 1854. See also Benoit, "Mission at Ile-à-la-Crosse," 42; McCarthy, *From the Great River to the Ends of the Earth*, 35. The rationale for the last rule was two-fold. First, the HBC sought to reduce the financial and ecological burden of missionary activity in each district. Second, it sought to isolate the separate denominations so as to avoid sectarian conflict. Despite Simpson's efforts, the 1850s and '60s witnessed intense rivalry between Catholic and Anglican missionaries, especially in the Athabasca and Mackenzie Districts. See especially Choquette, *Oblate Assault on Canada's Northwest*, 141–63, 169–78; McCarthy, *From the Great River to the Ends of the Earth*, 45–56.

15 SHSB, Fonds Provencher, P2754–P2758, Provencher to Signay, Saint-Boniface, 20 June 1845; ibid., P2696–P2731, Provencher to the Central Councils of l'Œuvre de la Propagation de la Foi, Saint-Boniface, 1846; Benoît, *Vie de Mgr Taché*, 1:102, 125. Contrary to Provencher's assertion, Thibault was not the first missionary to visit Île-à-la-Crosse. James Evans—General Superintendent of Wesleyan Missions—had sojourned at the post in 1842. Evans attempted a second visit to Île-à-la-Crosse in 1844. En route, however, he accidentally shot and killed his Chipewyan interpreter—Thomas Hassall (also Hassel)—and was obliged to return to his headquarters at Norway House. Evans's withdrawal enabled Thibault to travel unchecked to Île-à-la-Crosse, where he baptized 218 people in May 1845. See especially Maclean, *James Evans*, 194–96; Taché, *Vingt années de missions*, 13; Young, *Apostle of the North*, 198–99, 243–48.

16 SHSB, Fonds Taché, T0001, Simpson to Donald Ross, Red River, 8 July 1846; Benoît, *Vie de Mgr Taché*, 1:104, 108; McCarthy, *From the Great River to the Ends of the Earth*, 33. Simpson may have been swayed by Chief Factor Roderick McKenzie's insistence on the commercial value of missionaries. In July 1845, McKenzie reported that Thibault had attracted Chipewyan- and Cree-speaking hunters to Île-à-la-Crosse and had thus stemmed their ongoing migration to the prairies. "[E]very Indian at Île à la Crosse would have been in the Plains, had he [Thibault] not come," insisted McKenzie. Quoted in McCarthy, *From the Great River to the Ends of the Earth*, 32. See also Benoit, "Mission at Ile-à-la-Crosse," 42.

17 Benoit, "Mission at Ile-à-la-Crosse," 42; Benoît, *Vie de Mgr Taché*, 1:108, 125; McCarthy, *From the Great River to the Ends of the Earth*, 33.

18 Taché, *Vingt années de missions*, 14.

19 Ibid., 18; PAA, O.M.I. Collection, Accession 84.400, Item 957, Box 33, "Mgr Grandin, Notes Intimes sur le Diocèse de St Albert, rédigées en 1884," 51. See also Benoit, "Mission at Ile-à-la-Crosse," 45; Benoît, *Vie de Mgr Taché*, 1:126–27, 129; Duchaussois, *Aux glaces polaires*, 152; Huel, *Archbishop A.-A. Taché of St. Boniface*, 26.

20 Quoted in Benoit, "Mission at Ile-à-la-Crosse," 43. See also "Lettre écrite par le Père Taché à sa mère pendant son troisième voyage au lac Caribou. Lac Serpent, 6 juin 1850," *Les Cloches de Saint-Boniface*, 32, no. 7 (July 1933): 165. According to Dom Benoît, "Mr. MacKenzie [*sic*] rejoiced in the company and conversation of such distinguished men." McKenzie claimed an enormous amount of their time and attention. His visits to their room became so frequent that the missionaries' language studies began to suffer. Taché and Laflèche consequently resorted to "an innocent little strategy to keep him away without hurting his feelings" Afflicted

by chronic rheumatic pain, the seventy-two-year-old McKenzie walked with the support of two canes. Whenever the missionaries heard the distinctive *thud* of these canes on the floor outside their room, they would drop to their knees and cast their eyes heavenward. Loath to disrupt the missionaries' devotions, McKenzie would withdraw from their doorway without uttering a word. Benoît, *Vie de Mgr Taché*, 1:129.

21   Quoted in Benoit, "Mission at Ile-à-la-Crosse," 46. See also: Benoît, *Vie de Mgr Taché*, 1:147; Huel, *Archbishop A.-A. Taché of St. Boniface*, 26.

22   SHSB, "Codex historicus, 1845–1897," 7; Benoît, *Vie de Mgr Taché*, 1:130–31.

23   AD, Microfilm W 404.M62 F86 (Missions indiennes, St-Albert), Taché, "Notice sur la Mission du lac Caribou"; Taché, *Vingt années de missions*, 17–18. See also SHSB, "Codex historicus, 1845–1897," 7–8; Benoit, "Mission at Ile-à-la-Crosse," 46; Benoît, *Vie de Mgr Taché*, 1:131–34.

24   AD, Microfilm W 404.M62 F86 (Missions indiennes, St-Albert), Taché, "Notice sur la Mission du lac Caribou"; Benoît, *Vie de Mgr Taché*, 1:134–37; Huel, *Archbishop A.-A. Taché of St. Boniface*, 27–28; Huel, "Life Cycle of an Early Oblate Establishment," 236–37.

25   Taché, *Vingt années de missions*, 28; Benoît, *Vie de Mgr Taché*, 1:141, 144–46.

26   Taché, *Vingt années de missions*, 28–29.

27   Benoit, "Mission at Ile-à-la-Crosse," 48; Benoît, *Vie de Mgr Taché*, 1:156–58. Taché marvelled at Thomas's hospitality and affability while making light of his Protestantism; see Benoît, *Vie de Mgr Taché*, 1:158.

28   "Lettre du R.P. Faraud, Missionnaire Oblat de Marie Immaculée, à un Prêtre de la même Congrégation, Athabaskaw, 20 avril, 1851," *Annales de la Propagation de la Foi* 24 (1852): 223; Fernand-Michel, *Dix-huit ans chez les sauvages*, 101; Benoît, *Vie de Mgr Taché*, 1:162–64.

29   "Extrait d'une lettre de Mgr Taché, évêque de Saint-Boniface, à Mgr l'Évêque de Marseille, Supérieur-Général des Oblats de Marie Immaculée," *Annales de la Propagation de la Foi* 27 (1855): 211; PAA, O.M.I. Collection, Accession 84.400, Item 911, Box 32, Grandin to Taché, Île-à-la-Crosse, 9 January 1861; ibid., Grandin to Taché, Île-à-la-Crosse, 1 April 1861; ibid., Grandin to Taché, Île-à-la-Crosse, 5 April 1861; ibid., Grandin to Taché, Île-à-la-Crosse, 15 May 1861. See also Benoît, *Vie de Mgr Taché*, 1:178–79, 181, 247.

30   AD, HE 2221. T12L 25, Alexandre Taché to Louise-Henriette Taché, Île-à-la-Crosse, 5 January 1853. See also Benoît, *Vie de Mgr Taché*, 1:247; Huel, *Archbishop A.-A. Taché of St. Boniface*, 61.

31   SHSB, Fonds Taché, T0010–T0013, Simpson to Taché, Fort Garry, 30 June 1853. This arrangement was one of Taché's first initiatives as Bishop of Saint-Boniface. He brokered it less than a month after Provencher's death (7 June 1853).

32   LAC/HBC, microfilm HBC 1M270, B.89/c/1, Ile-a-Lacrosse [*sic*] Correspondence Inward, 1810–1862, Simpson to Taché, Norway House, 1 June 1854; SHSB, Fonds Taché, T1116–T1119, Faraud to Taché, Île-à-la-Crosse, 13 January 1862; ibid., T2575–T2577, Moulin to Lestanc, Île-à-la-Crosse, January 9, 1864; ibid., T3769–T3771, Grandin to Taché, "Demandes pour la mission S.-J. Bte (Île à la Crosse)," Île-à-la-Crosse, 11 January 1866.

33   AD, HE 2221. T12Z 251, Végréville to Taché, Île-à-la-Crosse, 5 April 1861; PAA, O.M.I. Collection, Accession 84.400, Item 911, Box 32, Grandin to Taché, Great

Slave Lake, 12 April 1862. The brigade's effectiveness at relaying information by
word of mouth was clearly demonstrated in July 1858 when it notified Grandin
(then superior at Saint-Jean-Baptiste) that he had been appointed Coadjutor
Bishop of Saint-Boniface. Grandin would not receive written notice of his
appointment until the following January (delivered by winter express). See
SHSB, "Codex historicus, 1845–1897," 46–47, 49–50.

34 AD, HE 2221. T12L 25, Alexandre Taché to Louise-Henriette Taché, Île-à-
la-Crosse, 5 January 1853; "À Son Éminence Monsieur le cardinal Barnabò.
Marseille, le 20 décembre 1857," *Bx de Mazenod: Lettres . . . 1832–1861*, 72; AD,
HE 2221. T12Z 251, Végréville to Taché, Île-à-la-Crosse, 5 April 1861; ASGM,
Agnès, "Annales de l'établissement des Sœurs Grises à l'Île à la Crosse," 1:207,
213; ibid., 2:196–97, 222; SHSB, "Codex historicus, 1845–1897," 23, 49, 76, 115.

35 LAC/HBC, microfilm HBC 1M493, B.89/d/70, Isle a la Crosse Account Book,
1849–1850, 7; LAC/HBC, microfilm HBC 1M64, B.89/a, Isle a la Crosse Post
Journal (1850), Tuesday, 10 September 1850, 39.

36 SHSB, Fonds Taché, T0140–T0146, "Rom: Cath: Mission D[ts] to the Honble
Hudson's Bay Comp[y] For the following Supplies at Sundry Districts, Outfit
1859"; ibid., T1401–1404, Faraud to Taché, Île-à-la-Crosse, 19 May 1862; ibid.,
T1741–T1743, Faraud to Taché, Île-à-la-Crosse, 26 November 1862; SHSB,
"Codex historicus, 1845–1897," 31. See also Huel, *Proclaiming the Gospel*, 62–63.

37 LAC/HBC, microfilm HBC 1M494, B.89/d/85, Isle a la Crosse Account Book,
1854–55, 22; LAC/HBC, microfilm HBC 1M64, B.89/a, Isle a la Crosse Post
Journal (1856), Thursday, 24 January 1856, 15.

38 SHSB, Fonds Taché, T0492–T0499, Grandin to Taché, Île-à-la-Crosse, 15 May
1861; RCRHC/É.G., vol. 16, "Lettre de Mgr Vital J. Grandin, évêque de Satala
à M. le Directeur et a MM. les Conseillers de la Propagation de la Foi à Paris,
15 novembre 1865," 585–94.

39 For inventories of *butin* at Saint-Jean-Baptiste, see SHSB, Fonds Taché, T2023–
T2029, Moulin to Taché, Île-à-la-Crosse, 8 April 1863; ibid., T3765–T3771,
"Mission de Saint-Jean-Baptiste de l'Île-à-la-Crosse, recettes et dépenses du
mois de juin 1864 au mois de janvier 1866," 8–9 January 1866.

40 AD, HE 2221. T12Z 183, Moulin to Taché, Île-à-la-Crosse, 16 November 1862;
AD, HE 2221. T12Z 184, Moulin to Taché, Île-à-la-Crosse, 9 January 1863;
AD, HE 2221. T12Z 188, Moulin to Taché, Île-à-la-Crosse, 29 May 1864; PAA,
O.M.I. Collection, Accession 84.400, Item 923, Box 32, Grandin to Clut, Île-
à-la-Crosse, 26 January 1865; SHSB, Fonds Taché, T3160–T3163, Grandin to
Taché, Île-à-la-Crosse, 22 March 1865.

41 LAC/HBC, microfilm HBC 1M493, B.89/d/68, Isle a la Crosse Account Book,
1848–1849, 3–4; PAA, O.M.I. Collection, Accession 84.400, Item 911, Box 32,
Grandin to Taché, Île-à-la-Crosse, 1 April 1861; SHSB, "Arbre généalogique
Île-à-la-Crosse" (Liber animarum), "Famille Malbœuf," 15.

42 SHSB, "Codex historicus, 1845–1897," 116, 131, 136, 140, 146–47. See also Huel,
Proclaiming the Gospel, 78–79; Jarvenpa, "Hudson's Bay Company," 491–92;
Jarvenpa and Brumbach, "The Microeconomics of Southern Chipewyan Fur-
Trade History," 156–58.

43 SHSB, "Codex historicus, 1845–1897," 22, 35–36, 44, 166–67, 183. It is difficult
to assign a precise year to the first *mission de l'automne* or *mission du printemps*
at Île-à-la-Crosse, as there is no primary record of the event. In his Codex

entry for 1850, however, Pénard noted the following: "It was around this time . . . that the *sauvages* began gathering around the mission in the spring and autumn in order to attend the exercises of the mission and to fulfill some of their religious duties." The corresponding marginalia reads: "Établissement de missions au printemps et à l'automne pour les sauvages." See ibid., 22.

44 LAC/HBC, microfilm HBC 1M65, B.89/a/35, Isle a la Crosse Post Journal (1865), Sunday, 24 September 1865, 35; PAA, O.M.I. Collection, Accession 84.400, Item 957, Box 33, "Mgr Grandin, Notes Intimes sur le Diocèse de Sᵗ Albert, rédigées en 1884," 52, 60–61; ASGM, Agnès, "Annales de l'établissement des Sœurs Grises à l'Île à la Crosse," 1:208, and 2:200–201, 211–12. See also Huel, *Proclaiming the Gospel*, 78.

45 AD, HE 2221. T12Z 178, Moulin to Taché, Portage La Loche, 31 July 1860; SHSB, Fonds Taché, T0586–T0588, Végréville to Taché, Île-à-la-Crosse, 12 June 1861; ibid., T2814–T2816, Moulin to Taché, Île-à-la-Crosse, 29 May 1864; ibid., T3303–T3305, Grandin to Taché, Île-à-la-Crosse, 30 May 1865. See also SHSB, "Codex historicus, 1845–1897," 73–74, 77, 79, 90, 92–93, 96, 116, 129, 131.

46 SHSB, Fonds Taché, T0586–T0588, Végréville to Taché, Île-à-la-Crosse, 12 June 1861. See also Taché, *Vingt années de missions*, 155; SHSB, "Codex historicus, 1845–1897," 72.

47 Benoît, *Vie de Mgr Taché*, 1:127; Macdougall, *One of the Family*, 183–85; Macdougall, "Socio-Cultural Development and Identity Formation," 277–79, 282–83.

48 SHSB, Fonds Taché, T0010–T0013, Simpson to Taché, Fort Garry, 30 June 1853. In his response to Taché's entreaty, Simpson expressed his desire to "encourage habits of temperance throughout the country" but insisted that an outright ban on alcohol would not produce the desired result. It would instead "induce greater evils than at present exist, as the Red River Settlers would engage in illicit distillation while spirits would likewise be imported from the States—and by these means, an increased supply, & consequent consumption would follow from the change." Ibid., T0011–T0012.

49 SHSB, Fonds Taché, T4255–T4259, Grandin to Taché, Île-à-la-Crosse, 25 September 1866. See also Goossen, "William Mactavish."

50 ASGM, Agnès, "Annales de l'établissement des Sœurs Grises à l'Île à la Crosse," 1:216–17, 218, 231, 237, 243–44; Soullier, *Vie du Révérend Père Légeard*, 56–57, 85–87, 107–8; SHSB, "Codex historicus, 1845–1897," 127–28, 159–60.

51 SHSB, Fonds Taché, T3282–T3283, Samuel McKenzie to Grandin, Île-à-la-Crosse, 20 May 1865; ibid., T3284–T3285, Samuel McKenzie to Agnès, Île-à-la-Crosse, 20 May 1865; SHSB, "Codex historicus, 1845–1897," 127–28. In 1865, Christie was in charge of the Saskatchewan District and visited Île-à-la-Crosse en route to the annual meeting of the HBC's Council of the Northern Department at Norway House. He returned in 1873 during his official inspection of northern posts. See also Spry, "William Joseph Christie."

52 Quoted in Soullier, *Vie du Révérend Père Légeard*, 86–87. This quotation is drawn from "la correspondance du P. Légeard avec la Congrégation" (1873). See ibid., 92.

53 SHSB, Fonds Taché, T0582–T0585, Végréville to Taché, Île-à-la-Crosse, 12 June 1861; ibid., T1721–T1724, Moulin to Taché, Île-à-la-Crosse, 16 November 1862.

54 SHSB, Fonds Taché, T0291–T0294, Grandin to Taché, Île-à-la-Crosse, 7 January 1861; ibid., T0362–T0368, Grandin to Taché, Île-à-la-Crosse, 1 April 1861 (postscript); AD, HPF 4191. C75R 183, Pepin to "Ma Très Chère Sœur," Île-à-la-Crosse, 14 June 1863. Deschambault's son was identified simply as "le petit Déchambault [*sic*]" ("little Déchambault"). Laliberté's son was identified as Antoine. Ross's son was identified as Edouard (possibly Edward). On Pierriche Laliberté and his immediate family, see LAC/HBC, microfilm HBC 1M1066, B.89/b/4, Ile-a-la-Crosse Correspondence Book (1872–1875), "Memoranda regarding Officers in Upper English River Dis᷇," 38–39; SHSB, "Arbre généalogique Île-à-la-Crosse" (Liber animarum), "Famille La Liberté [*sic*]," 109. On Bernard Rogan Ross, see Bowsfield, "Bernard Rogan Ross,"; Lindsay, "The Hudson's Bay Company-Smithsonian Connection"; Lindsay, *Modern Beginnings of Subarctic Ornithology*, xviii.

55 AD, HPF 4191. C75R 187, Pepin to "Ma Très Chère Sœur," Île-à-la-Crosse, 1 January 1870. On William Spencer's career in the English River District, see LAC/HBC, microfilm HBC 1M1066, B.89/b/4, Ile-a-la-Crosse Correspondence Book (1872–1875), "Memoranda regarding Officers in Upper English River Dis᷇," 38. Aware that the Spencer family was avowedly Protestant, the Oblates did not insist on Catholicizing the Spencer children in their charge. In 1870, Légeard reported to the Oblate General Administration: "We do not have much hope of bringing them to our holy religion, but at least their parents have entrusted ... them to our care and the instruction that they are now receiving will influence them for the rest of their lives." AD, G LPP 2200, Légeard to Fabre, Île-à-la-Crosse, 13 January 1870.

56 AD, HE 2221. T12Z 233, Simpson to Deschambault, Lachine, 15 August 1859; Grant, *Moon of Wintertime*, 108; Huel, *Proclaiming the Gospel*, 35–36; McCarthy, *From the Great River to the Ends of the Earth*, 43.

57 LAC/HBC, microfilm HBC 778, B.89/e/4, Isle-à-la-Crosse, Report on District (1862), "Memorandum regarding the English River District," 1. See also Macdougall, "Socio-Cultural Development and Identity Formation," 198.

58 SHSB, Fonds Taché, T1401–T1404, Faraud to Taché, Île-à-la-Crosse, 19 May 1862 and 2 June 1862 (Faraud wrote the letter on two separate days).

59 SHSB, Fonds Taché, T1428–T1431, Moulin to Taché, Île-à-la-Crosse, 29 May 1862.

60 SHSB, Fonds Taché, T1097–T1100, Faraud, to Taché, Île-à-la-Crosse, 4 January 1862. On the Oblates' conceptual correlation of free traders with alcohol (and alcoholism), see Huel, *Proclaiming the Gospel*, 36.

61 SHSB, Fonds Taché, T2229–T2237, Faraud to Taché, Île-à-la-Crosse, 1 June 1863; ibid., T3083–T3085, Lawrence Clarke (resident clerk at Fort-à-la-Corne) to Grandin, Fort-à-la-Corne, 14 January 1865; AD, G LPP 2202, Légeard to Aubert, Île-à-la-Crosse, 3 January 1875; SHSB, "Codex historicus, 1845–1897," 134, 235, 267–68.

62 LAC/HBC, microfilm HBC 1M64, B.89/a/30, Isle a la Crosse Post Journal (1860), Wednesday, 14 November 1860, 4; SHSB, Fonds Taché, T0362–T0368, Grandin to Taché, Île-à-la-Crosse, 1 April, 1861; LAC/HBC, microfilm HBC 1M64, B.89/a/31, Isle a la Crosse Post Journal (1861), Saturday, 20 April 1861, 4; LAC/HBC, microfilm HBC 1M65, B.89/a/33, Isle a la Crosse Post Journal (1863), Friday, 2 January 1863, 7. See also "Cinquième lettre de Mgr Taché à sa

mère, pendant son second séjour à l'Ile-à-la-Crosse. Mission de Sr-Jean-Baptiste, 26 mai 1854," *Les Cloches de Saint-Boniface* 34, no. 5 (May 1935): 126. Information on Deschambault's employment history and residence at Île-à-la-Crosse is available online through the Hudson's Bay Company Archives: http://www.gov.mb.ca/chc/archives/hbca/biographical/d/deschambeault_george-sr1818-1870.pdf (accessed 18 May 2016).

63   SHSB, Fonds Taché, T1097–T1100, Faraud, to Taché, Île-à-la-Crosse, 4 January 1862; ibid., T1116–T1119, Faraud, to Lestanc, Île-à-la-Crosse, 13 January 1862. On the foundering of the local fishery, see ASGM, Agnès, "Annales de l'établissement des Sœurs Grises à l'Île à la Crosse," 1:210; SHSB, "Codex historicus, 1845–1897," 75. This phenomenon may have been caused by the accumulation of algae and/or bacteria in Lake Île-à-la-Crosse. Agnès noted the following in her entry for 1861: "Strangely, there was very little wind this summer and the surface of our immense lake remained very still. Weeds grew to a considerable height on the surface and were covered in a green moss that detached easily and gave the water an unpleasant taste, rendering it . . . thick, undrinkable, and awful." See ASGM, Agnès, "Annales de l'établissement des Sœurs Grises à l'Île à la Crosse," 1:209–10.

64   LAC/HBC, microfilm HBC 1M64, B.89/a/26, Isle a la Crosse Post Journal (1849), Monday, 16 July 1849, 5; LAC/HBC, microfilm HBC 1M494, B.89/d/85, Isle a la Crosse Account Book, 1854–1855, 26; LAC/HBC, microfilm HBC 1M65, B.89/a/35, Isle a la Crosse Post Journal (1865), Saturday, 6 May 1865, 24; SHSB, Fonds Taché, T3282–T3283, Samuel McKenzie to Grandin, Île-à-la-Crosse, 20 May 1865; PAA, O.M.I. Collection, Accession 84.400, Item 913, Box 32, Grandin to Gasté, Saint-Albert, 24 August 1872.

65   SHSB., Fonds Taché, T0379–T0382, Végréville to Taché, Île-à-la-Crosse, 2 April 1861; ibid., T0492–T0499, Grandin to Taché, Île-à-la-Crosse, 15 May 1861; ibid., T1725–T1728, Faraud to Taché, Île-à-la-Crosse, 16 November 1862; ibid., T1741–T1743, Faraud to Taché, Île-à-la-Crosse, 26 November 1862; ibid., T3160–T3163, Grandin to Taché, Île-à-la-Crosse, 22 March 1865; AD, HEC 2500. P96C 15, Légeard to Maisonneuve, Île-à-la-Crosse, 16 January 1871.

66   AD, HE 2221. T12Z 233, Simpson to Deschambeault, Lachine, 15 August 1859; SHSB, Fonds Taché, T0134–T0136, Bernard Rogan Ross to Taché, Portage La Loche, 6 August 1860; McCarthy, *From the Great River to the Ends of the Earth*, 43.

67   SHSB, Fonds Taché, T0952–T0959, Germain Eynard, "Histoire de la Mission de St Joseph, Grand lac des Esclaves," Fort Resolution, 21 November 1861. According to this account, Faraud began construction of Saint-Joseph mission in 1854. It did not become a permanent mission until late July 1858, when it received its first resident Oblate—thirty-two-year-old Henri Grollier (an ordained Oblate from the department of Hérault). Joining Grollier two weeks later were thirty-seven-year-old Germain Eynard (an ordained Oblate from Piedmont-Sardinia) and thirty-year-old Jean Pérréard (an Oblate lay brother from the department of the Rhône). See ibid., T0952–T0953. See also Carrière, *Dictionnaire biographique*, 1:342, 2:114–15, and 3:64–65.

68   Choquette, *Oblate Assault*, 55–58, 141–63; McCarthy, "Founding of Providence Mission," 40–43; McCarthy, *From the Great River to the Ends of the Earth*, 45–56.

69   SHSB, Fonds Taché, T0316–T0319, Grollier to Taché, Fort Good Hope, 24 February 1861; ibid., T0564–T0567, Grollier to Lestanc, Fort Good Hope, 9

June 1861; ibid., T1555–T1559, Grollier to Taché, Fort Good Hope, 2 August 1862.

70 SHSB, Fonds Taché, T0852–T0856, Grandin to Mactavish, Fort Simpson, 20 September 1861 (Taché's copy).

71 SHSB, Fonds Taché, T0949–T0951, Ross to Taché, Fort Simpson, 20 November 1861. There was likely some validity to Ross's suggestion, as Grollier was known to make enemies wherever he went. Even his fellow Oblates considered him extraordinarily abrasive and cantankerous. "I have no idea how to cope with this dear priest," lamented Grandin in 1863. "He is supremely hated by everyone, especially by the *bourgeois* [HBC officers] and is not better liked by the métis or the *sauvages*." Ibid., T2272–T2274, Grandin to Taché, Providence Mission, 29 June 1863. See also Choquette, *Oblate Assault*, 56–57.

72 SHSB, Fonds Taché, T1313–T1315, Grandin to Taché, Fort Resolution (Saint-Joseph), 12 April 1862. Grandin undertook this three-year tour to make preparations for the establishment of the Vicariate Apostolic of Athabasca-Mackenzie (canonically erected on 13 May 1862). He also chose the site and laid the foundations of Providence Mission during the tour. See RCRHC/É.G., vol. 6, Grandin, "Notes de Monseigneur Grandin sur l'Église du Nord-Ouest," 162–78; SHSB, "Codex historicus 1845–1897," 73–74, 82–83.

73 Taché, *Vingt années de missions*, 17–18. Information on Samuel McKenzie's employment history and residence at Rapid River is available online through the Hudson's Bay Company Archives: http://www.gov.mb.ca/chc/archives/hbca/biographical/mc/mckenzie_samuel1827-1874.pdf (accessed 18 May 2016). On cooperation between Samuel McKenzie and Robert Hunt (1850–60), see especially Goossen, "The Relationship between the Church Missionary Society and the Hudson's Bay Company," 2–48.

74 SHSB, Fonds Taché, T0291–T0294, Grandin to Taché, Île-à-la-Crosse, 7 January 1861; ibid., T0298–T0301, Grandin to Taché, Île-à-la-Crosse, 17 January 1861. On the establishment of the Oblate presence at Reindeer Lake (1847), see AD, Microfilm W 404.M62 F86 (Missions indiennes, St-Albert), Taché, "Notice sur la Mission du lac Caribou"; Taché, *Vingt années de missions*, 18, 23–24; SHSB, "Codex historicus, 1845–1897," 7–8.

75 SHSB, Fonds Taché, T0411–T0422, Végréville to Taché, Île-à-la-Crosse, 15 April 1861; ibid., T0492–T0499, Grandin to Taché, Île-à-la-Crosse, 15 May 1861. See also Huel, *Archbishop A.-A. Taché of St. Boniface*, 61; Rodgers, "Lac du Brochet."

76 SHSB, Fonds Taché, T0362–T0370, Grandin to Taché, Île-à-la-Crosse, April 1–2, 1861. Grandin appears to have based these comments on information obtained from Végréville, who had lately travelled from Reindeer Lake to Île-à-la-Crosse by way of Rapid River. See ibid., T0379–T0382, Végréville to Taché, Île-à-la-Crosse, 2 April 1861; SHSB, "Codex historicus, 1845–1897," 72. On Chief Trader Campbell, see Coates, "Robert Campbell."

77 SHSB, Fonds Taché, T1057–T080, Gasté to Taché, Lac-du-Brochet House, spring 1862. This letter is undated, but contains a brief account of "la mission du printemps" (T1079). See also ibid., T1551–T1554, Végréville to Taché, Portage du Fort de Traite, 1 August 1862; "Chronique historique de la mission Saint-Pierre du lac Caribou, depuis 1846 jusqu'à nos jours, 1912. Par le R.P. Turquetil, O.M.I.," *Missions de la Congrégation des missionnaires oblats de Marie Immaculée* 198 (June 1912): 184, 188–89. On the voyage of Végréville, Gasté, and Pérréard

from Île-à-la-Crosse to Lac-du-Brochet House (3 August–4 October 1861) and their early ministry on the northern shore of Reindeer Lake, see Taché, *Vingt années de missions*, 158, 172–73; SHSB, "Codex historicus, 1845–1897," 75, 78.

78   SHSB, Fonds Taché, T1745–T1748, Végréville to Taché, Lac-du-Brochet House, 27 November 1862. Végréville had made a similar—though somewhat less emphatic—declaration three months earlier. See ibid., T1601–T1602, Végréville to Taché, Reindeer Lake, 22 August 1862.

79   LAC/HBC, microfilm HBC 1M784, B.89/f/1, Ile-à-la-Crosse List of Servants, 1865–1882, 2. See also the online biographical sheets of Georges Deschambeault [*sic*] Sr. and Samuel McKenzie: http://www.gov.mb.ca/chc/archives/hbca/biographical/d/deschambeault_george-sr1818-1870.pdf; http://www.gov.mb.ca/chc/archives/hbca/biographical/mc/mckenzie_samuel1827-1874.pdf (accessed 18 May 2016).

80   Grandin outlined his policy toward "bourgeois protestants" while dispensing administrative advice to thirty-three-year-old Isidore Clut (an ordained Oblate from the department of Drôme) in February 1866. Clut had been nominated Bishop of Arindela *in partibus infidelium* (Coadjutor of Athabasca-Mackenzie) one month earlier: "As you know, we are very often in need of assistance from Protestant *bourgeois* who delegate tasks to ther co-religionist subordinates. For instance, six years ago when I was returning to Île-à-la-Crosse with the Grey Nuns, our fanatical *bourgeois* [MacKenzie, who was then postmaster at Rapid River] transported us in the barge of the minister [Hunt], along with some provisions that he had lent us and even a steersman. I think, therefore, that it is always best in these cases to conceal one's displeasure and to admit it only to oneself." PAA, O.M.I. Collection, Accession 84.400, Item 923, Box 32, Grandin to Isidore Clut, Île-à-la-Crosse, 2 February 1866. On McKenzie's conveyance of Grandin and the Grey Nuns by barge (September 1860), see SHSB, "Codex historicus, 1845–1897," 65–66. On Isidore Clut, see Carrière, *Dictionnaire biographique*, 1: 210–11; Choquette, *Oblate Assault on Canada's Northwest*, 67–73.

81   SHSB, Fonds Taché, T2939–T2942, Grandin to Taché, Île-à-la-Crosse, 22 September 1864; ibid., T3116–T3119, Grandin to Taché, Île-à-la-Crosse, 23 February 1865; AD, G LPP 2199, Légeard to Grandin, Île-à-la-Crosse, 11 January 1869. On Protestant services at McKenzie's home, see LAC/HBC, microfilm HBC 1M65, B.89/a/35, Isle a la Crosse Post Journal (1865), Sunday, 30 April 1865, 23; Sunday, 15 October 1865, 37; Sunday, 22 October 1865, 38. See also Macdougall, *One of the Family*, 155; Macdougall, "Socio-Cultural Development and Identity Formation," 116.

82   SHSB, Fonds Taché, T3116–T3119, Grandin to Taché, Île-à-la-Crosse, 23 February 1865.

83   SHSB, Fonds Taché, T3099–T3102, Grandin to Taché, Île-à-la-Crosse, 18 January 1865. Grandin reported that there were altogether twelve "children of the fort" at Saint-Bruno: three in the *pensionnat supérieur*; nine in the *pensionnat inférieur*. He noted also that the latter *pensionnat* included eight children of HBC servants from other posts. Thus, of the twenty-eight pupils attending Saint-Bruno, twenty were children of HBC officers and servants.

84   Ibid. Grandin may have overstated the extent and frequency of Deschambault's assistance. Between 1860 and 1864, Oblates and Grey Nuns occasionally complained that the HBC was not sufficiently forthcoming with food and/or fuel for schoolchildren. See especially SHSB, Fonds Taché, T2814–T2816,

Moulin to Taché, Île-à-la-Crosse, 29 May 1864; ASGM, Agnès, "Annales de l'établissement des Sœurs Grises à l'Île à la Crosse," 1:205; SHSB, "Codex historicus de l'Île-à-la-Crosse, 1845–1897," 71.

85   SHSB, Fonds Taché, T3134–T3137, Grandin to Taché, Île-à-la-Crosse, 13 March 1865.

86   SHSB, Fonds Taché, T3751–T3754, Grandin to Taché, 5 January 1866. The two bishops drafted this plan at Saint-Jean-Baptiste during the visit of Florent Vandenberghe (delegate of the Oblate Superior General). It is likely that Vandenberghe was consulted on the matter.

87   Ibid. According to this letter, McKenzie was vehemently opposed to the project. He consented grudgingly after Laliberté threatened to become a free trader and to use the projected road to sustain a private enterprise. Information on Laliberté's employment history and residence at Portage La Loche and Green Lake (1857–91) is available online through the Hudson's Bay Company Archives: http://www.gov.mb.ca/chc/archives/hbca/biographical/l/laliberte_pierre.pdf (accessed 18 May 2016).

88   SHSB, "Codex historicus, 1845–1897," 95.

89   "Lettre de Mgr Grandin, évêque de Satala, à MM. les Membres des Conseils centraux de l'Œuvre de la Propagation de la Foi. 4 janvier 1868," *Annales de la Propagation de la Foi* 40 (1868): 249–52.

90   PAA, O.M.I. Collection, Accession 84.400, Vol. 5, Box 35, Grandin, "Notes privées sur les missions et les missionnaires du diocèse de St-Albert," 1868–1884, 13–14. When work resumed in the spring of 1869, Oblate lay brother Patrick Bowes and some *engagés* attempted to extend the ox-cart road northward from Green Lake to Île-à-la-Crosse so that Saint-Jean-Baptiste could be provisioned entirely by land. They do not appear to have completed the extension as the waterway remained the main route of transportation between Green Lake and Île-à-la-Crosse during the period under study. See PAA, O.M.I. Collection, Accession 84.400, Item 912, Box 32, Grandin to Leduc, Fort Carlton, 26 January 1870; SHSB, "Codex historicus, 1845–1897," 109.

91   AD, G LPP 2201, Légeard to Aubert, Île-à-la-Crosse, 29 August 1873; AD, HPF 4191. C75R 177, Légeard to "Ma très honorée et Vénérée Mère," Île-à-la-Crosse, 20 December 1877. Duration of travel varied according to weather conditions. The road could be extremely difficult to navigate when awash with rainwater and mud. Hence, after a particularly rainy summer in 1872, Grandin experienced "a continual series of accidents and setbacks of all kinds" while travelling from Fort Carlton to Green Lake. SHSB, "Codex historicus, 1845–1897," 124. See also ibid., 173–74, 184–85.

92   PAA, O.M.I. Collection, Accession 84.400, Item 973, Box 33, "Renseignements demandés par Mgr Taché sur les missions et les Missionnaires de Mgr Grandin depuis l'érection du vicariat religieux de St Albert 1868 jusqu'en 1872," 3, 16; AD, HEC 2500. P96C 8, Légeard to Maisonneuve, Île-à-la-Crosse, 12 January 1874.

93   LAC/HBC, microfilm HBC 1M1066, B.89/b/4, Ile-a-la-Crosse Correspondence Book (1872–1875), Samuel McKenzie to Lawrence Clarke, Green Lake, 27 March 1872, 18–19; ibid., William McMurray to James A. Grahame (HBC Chief Commissioner), Île-à-la-Crosse, 5 December 1874.

94   AD, HEC 2500. P96C 9, Légeard to Maisonneuve, Île-à-la-Crosse, 11 March 1874; LAC/HBC, microfilm HBC 1M1066, B.89/b/4, Ile-a-la-Crosse Correspondence

Book (1872–1875), McMurray to Laliberté, Île-à-la-Crosse, 16 March 1874, 60; AD, HEC 2500. P96C 23, Légeard to Maisonneuve, Île-à-la-Crosse, 8 October 1878; SHSB, "Codex historicus, 1845–1897," 130, 185–86.

95 This strategy was at least partly a response to strikes—"mutinous conduct" according to Hargrave—by the crewmen of the Portage La Loche Brigade after 1866. See Hargrave, *Red River*, 160, 165, 167, 168; McCarthy, *From the Great River to the Ends of the Earth*, 69; Tough, *"As Their Natural Resources Fail,"* 52–57.

96 LAC/HBC, microfilm HBC 1M1066, B.89/b/4, Ile-a-la-Crosse Correspondence Book (1872–1875), McMurray to Donald A. Smith (HBC Chief Commissioner), South End of Green Lake, 30 May 1873, 31–34.

97 Quoted in SHSB, "Codex historicus, 1845–1897," 146–47. Légeard repeated this observation in subsequent years. See ibid., 155, 167; AD, HPF 4191. C75R 177, Légeard to "Ma très honorée et Vénérée Mère," Île-à-la-Crosse, 20 December 1877.

98 AD, HEC 2500. P96C 8, Légeard to Maisonneuve, Île-à-la-Crosse, 12 January 1874; "Missions d'Amérique: Nouvelle Bretagne, Diocèse de Saint-Albert," *Annales de la Propagation de la Foi*. 49 (1877): 443–44; SHSB, "Codex historicus, 1845–1897," 117–18, 126–29, 132, 136–37, 139, 144, 147, 151–53, 167.

99 "Missions d'Amérique: Nouvelle Bretagne, Diocèse de Saint-Albert," *Annales de la Propagation de la Foi* 49 (1877): 440–43, 445–46; AD, HEC 2500. P96C 21, Légeard to Maisonneuve, Île-à-la-Crosse, 5 May 1878; SHSB, "Codex historicus, 1845–1897," 130–31, 135, 137–41, 144, 147–50, 153–54, 164, 166.

100 LAC/HBC, microfilm HBC 1M1066, B.89/b/4, Ile-a-la-Crosse Correspondence Book (1872–1875), McKenzie to Smith, Île-à-la-Crosse, 2 January 1872, 1–2; ibid., McKenzie to Smith, Île-à-la-Crosse, 1 June 1872, 21–25; ibid., McMurray, "Remarks regarding the HBCo's Posts in Upper English River Dis᷎," Île-à-la-Crosse, 10 January 1873, 35–37; SHSB, "Codex historicus, 1845–1897," 131.

101 SHSB, "Codex historicus, 1845–1897," 133–34. Légeard made this prediction in his report to the Oblate General Administration in 1873. The report is quoted in its entirety in ibid., 127–38. See also AD, LC 6301. K26R 7, Légeard, "Allocation demandée pour la mission de l'Ile à la Crosse," Île-à-la-Crosse, June 1876.

102 Despite having been appointed Junior Chief Trader in Charge of the English River District in 1875, McDonald did not assume direction of the district until after Chief Factor McMurray's retirement two years later. Information on McMurray's and McDonald's employment history and residence at Île-à-la-Crosse is available online through the Hudson's Bay Company Archives: http://www.gov.mb.ca/chc/archives/hbca/biographical/mc/mcmurray_william.pdf; http://www.gov.mb.ca/chc/archives/hbca/biographical/mc/mcdonald_ewen.pdf (accessed 18 May 2016).

103 LAC/HBC, microfilm HBC 1M1066, B.89/b/6, Ile-a-la-Crosse Correspondence Book (1877–1881), McDonald to Grahame, Fort Carlton, 30 January 1879, 104–6. On McDonald's treatment of Cree- and Chipewyan-speaking hunters, see especially Macdougall, *One of the Family*, 236–37; Macdougall, "Socio-Cultural Development and Identity Formation," 206.

104 AD, HEC 2500. P96C 23, Légeard to Maisonneuve, Île-à-la-Crosse, 8 October 1878. See also ASGM, Agnès, "Annales de l'établissement des Sœurs Grises à l'Île à la Crosse," 2:224. On Maisonneuve as commissary, see Carrière, *Dictionnaire biographique*, 2:356; Huel, *Archbishop A.-A. Taché of St. Boniface*, 336.

105 PAA, O.M.I. Collection, Accession 84.400, Item 911, Box 32, Grandin to Taché, "sur une île du lac l'Île d'ours," 9 July 1880. On Grandin's visit to Saint-Jean-Baptiste in June 1880, see PAA, O.M.I. Collection, Accession 84.400, Vol. 5, Box 35, Grandin, "Notes privées sur les missions et les missionnaires du diocèse de St-Albert," 1868–1884, 16–19.

106 PAA, O.M.I. Collection, Accession 84.400, Item 911, Box 32, Grandin to Taché, "sur une île du lac l'Île d'ours," 9 July 1880.

107 Information on Fortescue's employment history and residence at Île-à-la-Crosse (1885–89) is available online through the Hudson's Bay Company Archives: http://www.gov.mb.ca/chc/archives/hbca/biographical/f/fortescue_joseph.pdf (accessed 18 May 2016).

108 LAC/HBC, microfilm HBC 1M1067, B.89/b/10, Ile-a-la-Crosse Correspondence Book (1885–1886), Fortescue to Joseph Wrigley, Île-à-la-Crosse, 6 June 1886, 207–10; ibid., Fortescue to Wrigley, Île-à-la-Crosse, 19 June 1886, 232–35. Information on Wrigley's tenure as Trade Commissioner for the HBC in Canada (1884–91) is available online through the Hudson's Bay Company Archives: http://www.gov.mb.ca/chc/archives/hbca/biographical/w/wrigley_joseph.pdf (accessed 18 May 2016).

109 For a published primary account of this episode, see Weekes, *Trader King as Told to Mary Weekes*, 170–71. See also Jarvenpa, "Hudson's Bay Company," 496; Macdougall, *One of the Family*, 197, 200–203; Macdougall, "Socio-Cultural Development and Identity Formation," 271–74.

110 LAC/HBC, microfilm HBC 1M1067, B.89/b/15, Ile-a-la-Crosse Correspondence Book (1888–1891), Fortescue to Wrigley, Île-à-la-Crosse, 10 May 1888, 1a–1c; ibid., Fortescue to Rapet, Île-à-la-Crosse, 30 May 1888, 17–20; ibid., Fortescue to Rapet, Île-à-la-Crosse, 2 June 1888, 22–25; SHSB, "Codex historicus, 1845–1897," 218.

111 LAC/HBC, microfilm HBC 1M1067, B.89/b/15, Ile-a-la-Crosse Correspondence Book (1888–1891), Fortescue to Wrigley, Île-à-la-Crosse, 10 May 1888, 1a–1c. Jarvenpa and Macdougall have described Fortescue's "protestation" as an expression of profound frustration rather than a genuine policy proposal. According to both authors, the chief factor must have known that the labour pool in his district was overwhelmingly Roman Catholic. See Jarvenpa, "Hudson's Bay Company," 496n19; Macdougall, *One of the Family*, 201–2; Macdougall, "Socio-Cultural Development and Identity Formation," 274.

112 LAC/HBC, microfilm HBC 1M1067, B.89/b/15, Ile-a-la-Crosse Correspondence Book (1888–1891), Fortescue to Wrigley, Île-à-la-Crosse, 18 June 1888; ibid., Fortescue to Wrigley, Île-à-la-Crosse, 20 July 1888. See also Macdougall, "Socio-Cultural Development and Identity Formation," 275.

113 Moberly, *When Fur Was King*, 175–77. The promotion was never granted: Wrigley resigned as trade commissioner in 1891 and his successor—Clarence Campbell Chipman—refused to honour Wrigley's verbal promise. See ibid., 176–77. Information on Moberly's employment history and residence at Île-à-la-Crosse (1888–94) is available online through the Hudson's Bay Company Archives: http://www.gov.mb.ca/chc/archives/hbca/biographical/m/moberly_henry-john.pdf (accessed 18 May 2016). See also Jarvenpa, "Hudson's Bay Company," 497, 504.

114 LAC/HBC, microfilm HBC 1M1068, B.89/b/18, Ile-a-la-Crosse Correspondence Book (1891–1893), Moberly to Chipman, Île-à-la-Crosse, 19 August 1891, 104,

117–20. See also Moberly, *When Fur Was King*, 176. Information on Chipman's tenure as Commissioner of the HBC in Canada (1891–1911) is available online through the Hudson's Bay Company Archives: http://www.gov.mb.ca/chc/archives/hbca/biographical/c/chipman_clarence_campbell.pdf (accessed 18 May 2016).

115 SHSB, "Codex historicus, 1845–1897," 238, 241, 242, 244. See also Jarvenpa, "Hudson's Bay Company," 503.

116 SHSB, "Codex historicus, 1845–1897," 210. According to Pénard, this practice was initiated during Grandin's episcopal visit to Saint-Jean-Baptiste in September 1887.

117 LAC/HBC, microfilm HBC 1M1068, B.89/b/18, Ile-a-la-Crosse Correspondence Book (1891–1893), Moberly to Rapet, Île-à-la-Crosse, 8 June 1891, 25–26; ibid., Moberly to Rapet, Île-à-la-Crosse, 10 June 1891, 28–30 (contains an English translation of Rapet's letter to Moberly); ibid., Moberly to Chipman, Île-à-la-Crosse, 4 September 1891, 135–37.

118 SHSB, "Codex historicus, 1845–1897," 242. It is not clear from Pénard's account whether the furs were sold to a free trader or to an agent of the HBC in Prince Albert.

119 Ibid., 234.

120 Ibid., 236. See also ibid., 237–39, 241–42, 256.

121 Ibid., 242–43. Information on McDougall's tenure as Inspecting Chief Factor in the HBC's Northern Department is available online through the Hudson's Bay Company Archives: http://www.gov.mb.ca/chc/archives/hbca/biographical/mc/mcdougall_james.pdf (accessed 18 May 2016). On Moberly's response to the Oblates' allegations, see Jarvenpa, "Hudson's Bay Company," 500–502; Macdougall, *One of the Family*, 183–85; Macdougall, "Socio-Cultural Development and Identity Formation," 281–83.

122 SHSB, "Codex historicus, 1845–1897," 244. See also LAC/HBC, microfilm HBC 1M1068, B.89/b/18, Ile-a-la-Crosse Correspondence Book (1891–1893), Moberly to James Macdougal [*sic*], Île-à-la-Crosse, 2 March 1892.

123 SHSB, "Codex historicus, 1845–1897," 247. See also LAC/HBC, microfilm HBC 1M1007, B.89/a/37, Île-à-la Crosse Journal (1891–1896), Friday, 10 June and Monday, 13 June 1892, 15; "Vicariat de la Saskatchewan. Rapport de Mgr Pascal, vicaire apostolique," *Missions de la Congrégation des missionnaires oblats de Marie Immaculée* 121 (March 1893): 17–19.

124 SHSB, "Codex historicus, 1845–1897," 247. See also LAC/HBC, microfilm HBC 1M1068, B.89/b/18, Ile-a-la-Crosse Correspondence Book (1891–1893), Moberly to Chipman, Île-à-la-Crosse, 18 June 1892; ibid., Moberly to Chipman, Île-à-la-Crosse, 30 June 1892.

125 According to Pénard, the Vicar Apostolic achieved only a qualified improvement in relations between Oblates and the HBC; see SHSB, "Codex historicus, 1845–1897," 247.

126 LAC/HBC, microfilm HBC 1M1007, B.89/a/37, Île-à-la Crosse Journal (1891–1896), Monday, 3 September 1894, 51; Moberly, *When Fur Was King*, 177. William Cornwallis King had previously served at Île-à-la Crosse as a junior chief trader from 1885 to 1886. See Weekes, *Trader King as Told to Mary Weekes*, 9, 168. Information on King's employment history and residence at Île-à-la-Crosse (1885–86, 1894–99) is available online through the Hudson's Bay

Company Archives: http://www.gov.mb.ca/chc/archives/hbca/biographical/k/king_william-cornwallis.pdf (accessed 18 May 2016).

127 SHSB, "Codex historicus, 1845–1897," 265. See also Pénard's account of New Year's Day 1896, in ibid., 272.

128 Ibid., 281–82, 290–92, 294.

129 Ibid., 265.

130 Ibid., 267–68, 271–73.

131 Ibid., 267. See also 272.

132 Ibid., 272.

133 Ibid., 282. Pénard provided no specific examples of these "impairs" but referred to them broadly as inadvertent expressions of antipathy toward Oblates and/or their congregants. For instance, he noted the following of King's voyage to Prince Albert in the company of Vicar Apostolic Pascal (August 1896): "During this voyage, Mr. King tried yet again to pass himself off before Monseigneur Pascal as a devoted friend to the missionaires. But his want of tact made him commit numerous *impairs*, which showed His Excellency the worth of such declarations of devotion and friendship. Mr. King nevertheless persisted in trying to conceal his true feelings." Ibid., 281–82.

134 Ibid., 291.

135 Ibid., 278–79, 281–82.

136 Ibid., 282, 290–92.

137 Ibid., 292, 294; "Lettre du Révérend Père Pénard au Très Révérend Père Général," *Missions de la Congrégation des missionnaires oblats de Marie Immaculée* 151 (September 1900): 259.

138 AD, GLPP 2582, Pascal to Sardou, Prince Albert, 9 February 1898. Pénard also described King's implementation of the new policy as tantamount to a declaration of war; see SHSB, "Codex historicus, 1845–1897," 291–92.

139 "Mort de M. Ant. Marcelin, un pionnier de l'ouest canadien," *Le Patriote de l'ouest*, Thursday, 15 July 1915, 4; Lapointe, *100 noms*, 260.

140 LAC/HBC, microfilm HBC 1M1007, B.89/a/38, Isle a la Crosse Post Journal (1897), Wednesday, 24 February 1897, 30; SHSB, "Codex historicus, 1845–1897," 287–88, 295.

141 Pénard noted the following of Marcelin's first visit: "A new trader came down to Île-à-la-Crosse. It was Mr. Marcelin. This good man is a Catholic, and more importantly, a practising Catholic. He therefore deserves the sympathies of the mission, given that all of the HBC officers and all of the other free traders are Protestants." See SHSB, "Codex historicus, 1845–1897," 287.

142 ASGM, Circulaire mensuelle adressée aux diverses maisons de l'Institut 13 (March–April 1898): 622; SHSB, "Codex historicus, 1845–1897," 295; Lesage, *Capitale d'une solitude*, 143.

143 SHSB, "Codex historicus, 1898–1928," 8.

144 "Lettre du Révérend Père Pénard au Très Révérend Père Général," *Missions de la Congrégation des missionnaires oblats de Marie Immaculée* 151 (September 1900): 259–60; SHSB, "Codex historicus, 1898–1928," 1, 8, 10, 15–16, 19.

145 SHSB, "Codex historicus, 1845–1897," 295; "Lettre du Révérend Père Pénard au Très Révérend Père Général," *Missions de la Congrégation des missionnaires*

oblats de Marie Immaculée 151 (September 1900): 259; SHSB, "Codex historicus, 1898–1928," 4, 15.

146 SHSB, "Codex historicus, 1898–1928," 15–16, 21.

Chapter 3: Oblates and the Beginnings of Residential Education

1   See especially Carney, "Native-Wilderness Equation"; Carney, "Residential Schooling at Fort Chipewyan and Fort Resolution"; Gresko, "Creating Little Dominions Within the Dominion"; Gresko, "Everyday Life at Qu'Appelle Industrial School"; Huel, *Proclaiming the Gospel*, 99–175; McCarthy, *From the Great River to the Ends of the Earth*, 159–69; Miller, "Denominational Rivalry in Indian Residential Education"; Miller, *Shingwauk's Vision*, 125, 177, 191, 201–2, 241–45, 274, 310, 312, 320, 346, 361, 366, 381, 394, 428; Miller, *Skyscrapers Hide the Heavens*, 265, 298; Miller, "The State, the Church, and Indian Residential Schools," 109, 118, 120–24; Persson, "The Changing Experience of Indian Residential Schooling"; Smith, "The 'Policy of Aggressive Civilization' and Projects of Governance"; Titley, "Dunbow Indian Industrial School." The term "joint venture" was incorporated into the "Statement of Apology to Former Students of Residential Schools" delivered by Conservative Prime Minister Stephen Harper on 11 June 2008. The full text of the statement is available online through the Parliament of Canada website: http://www.parl.gc.ca/HousePublications/Publication.aspx?DocId=3568890 (accessed 18 May 2016).

2   Quoted in Smith, "The 'Policy of Aggressive Civilization' and Projects of Governance," 259. There was more than a passing resemblance between the assimilative projects of the United States and Canada in the late nineteenth century. In January 1879, the Canadian government appointed Nicholas Flood Davin to travel to Washington, DC, to investigate "the policy of aggressive civilization" that had been implemented under the administration of President Ulysses S. Grant (1869–77). In his report to the Minister of the Interior (submitted 14 March 1879), Davin identified "industrial schools"—missionary-run boarding schools in which pupils learned industrial skills and trades—as the principal feature of the American policy and recommended that the Canadian government establish similar institutions. Davin's report was appended to the order-in-council (1883) that created the first industrial schools in Canada. According to Derek G. Smith, Davin's report "is the de facto founding document, in effect the charter document, which specified the terms within which industrial schools functioned for almost a century." Ibid., 254. See also ibid., 255, 259–60; Koester, *Mr. Davin, M.P.*, 40; Miller, *Shingwauk's Vision*, 101–3; Miller, *Skyscrapers Hide the Heavens*, 264; Thompson, "Nicholas Flood Davin"; *Honouring the Truth, Reconciling for the Future*, 59–60.

3   McCarthy, *From the Great River to the Ends of the Earth*, 166.

4   Miller, *Shingwauk's Vision*, 391, 414–16. See also Miller, "The State, the Church, and Indian Residential Schools in Canada," 113, 118, 120–22, 125.

5   Miller, *Shingwauk's Vision*, 391, 416, 471n94; Miller, "The State, the Church, and Indian Residential Schools in Canada," 120–22.

6   It bears mention that the Congregation of Oblates of Mary Immaculate has not attempted to distance itself from responsibility in the residential schooling experiment. On 24 July 1991, the Oblate Conference of Canada issued "An Apology to the First Nations of Canada" acknowledging that the congregation had played "a key role" in formulating, implementing, and sustaining residential

schools. The apology makes no reference to co-option or coercion by federal authorities, but rather affirms that Oblate involvement in the system reflected "the cultural, ethnic, linguistic, and religious imperialism that was part of the mentality with which the peoples of Europe first met the Indigenous peoples and which consistently has lurked behind the way the Native peoples of Canada have been treated by civil governments and by churches. We [i.e., Oblates] were, naively, part of this mentality." "An Apology to the First Nations of Canada," 259–60.

7   "Instruction de Monseigneur de Mazenod relative aux missions étrangères," 175.

8   Taché, *Vingt années de missions*, 91–93. In January 1857, Taché visited Marseilles to consult personally with Mazenod on two pressing matters: the nomination of the Coadjutor Bishop of Saint-Boniface *cum future successione*, and the establishment of communities of Grey Nuns at various missions west of the Red River Colony. Mazenod consented willingly to the latter proposal and left the details of its implementation to Taché. Ibid., 93. See also Benoît, *Vie de Mgr Taché*, 1:344–49.

9   Taché, *Vingt années de missions*, 92, 109–11. Taché's episcopal predecessor—Bishop Joseph-Norbert Provencher—had invited the Sisters of Charity of Montreal to establish a convent in the Red River Colony in October 1843. Mother Superior Elizabeth Forbes McMullen accepted the invitation and despatched four nuns to "l'Hôpital Général de Saint-Boniface" the following April. The Grey Nuns opened a school for fifty-three children at Saint-Boniface in July 1844. See especially ASGM, McMullen, "Ancien Journal," 1:19, 26, 44; Dauphinais, *Histoire de Saint-Boniface*, 130–31; Duchaussois, *Aventures canadiennes des Sœurs Grises*, 4–12; Duchaussois, *Grey Nuns in the Far North*, 29–40.

10 Taché, *Vingt années de missions*, 110–11. The Grey Nuns established a convent at Lac Sainte-Anne in 1859, another at Île-à-la-Crosse in 1860, and another at Lac La Biche in 1862. The convent at Lac Sainte-Anne was relocated to Saint-Albert in 1863. See especially ASGM, McMullen, "Ancien Journal," 1:20–23, 45–46; Duchaussois, *Aventures canadiennes des Sœurs Grises*, 14–18, 21; Duchaussois, *Grey Nuns in the Far North*, 46–52, 54; Levasseur, *Les Oblats de Marie Immaculée dans l'ouest et le nord du Canada*, 57–59.

11 Taché, *Vingt années de missions*, 91–92. See also SHSB, "Codex historicus, 1845–1897," 43.

12 SHSB, Fonds Taché, T0137–T0139, Agnès to Taché, "sur le rivage du Lac Winipig," 6 August 1860. For primary accounts of Agnès's voyage to Île-à-la-Crosse (4 June–4 October 4 1860), see "Extrait d'une lettre de Mgr Vital Grandin, évêque de Satala et coadjuteur de Mgr l'évêque de Saint-Boniface, à MM. les Directeurs de l'Œuvre de la Propagation de la Foi. Mission de Saint-Jean-Baptiste de l'Île-à-la-Crosse, 3 décembre, 1861," *Annales de la Propagation de la Foi* 35 (1863): 345–49; ASGM, Agnès, "Annales de l'établissement des Sœurs Grises à l'Île à la Crosse," 1:175–87, 195–97; SHSB, "Codex historicus, 1845–1897," 62–68.

13 ASGM, McMullen, "Ancien Journal," 1:45, 163; ASGM, L018, Île à la Crosse, "Historique," 1, 5.

14 ASGM, Agnès, "Annales de l'établissement des Sœurs Grises à l'Île à la Crosse," 1:206.

15 On the ascription of maternal qualities to non-cloistered nuns—especially
teaching nuns—in nineteenth-century French Catholic discourse, see especially
Mills, "Negotiating the Divide"; Rogers, "Retrograde or Modern?," 146–49.

16 McCarthy, *From the Great River to the Ends of the Earth*, 159.

17 "Extrait d'une lettre de Mgr Vital Grandin, évêque de Satala et coadjuteur
de Mgr l'évêque de Saint-Boniface, à MM. les Directeurs de l'Œuvre de la
Propagation de la Foi. Mission de Saint-Jean-Baptiste de l'Île-à-la-Crosse, 3
décembre, 1861," *Annales de la Propagation de la Foi* 35 (1863): 349.

18 SHSB, Fonds Taché, T0291–T0294, Grandin to Taché, Île-à-la-Crosse, 7 January
1861; ASGM, Agnès, "Annales de l'établissement des Sœurs Grises à l'Île à la
Crosse," 1:202–3, 205.

19 SHSB, Fonds Taché, T0354–T0357, Pepin to Taché, Île-à-la-Crosse, 1 April 1861;
AD, HPF 4191. C75R 183, Pepin to "Ma Très Chère Sœur," Île-à-la-Crosse,
14 June 1863; SHSB, "Arbre généalogique Île-à-la-Crosse" (Liber animarum),
"Famille La Fleur [*sic*]," 41, and "Famille La Liberté [*sic*]," 109; ASGM, Agnès,
"Annales de l'établissement des Sœurs Grises à l'Île à la Crosse," 1:200, 203.
Information on the employment histories of Lafleur, Morin, and Laliberté is
available online through the Hudson's Bay Company Archives: http://www.gov.
mb.ca/chc/archives/hbca/biographical/l/lafleur_charles-b.pdf ; http://www.gov.
mb.ca/chc/archives/hbca/biographical/m/morin_antoine-b.pdf ; http://www.
gov.mb.ca/chc/archives/hbca/biographical/l/laliberte_pierre.pdf (all accessed
18 May 2016).

20 ASGM, Agnès, "Annales de l'établissement des Sœurs Grises à l'Île à la Crosse,"
1:205–6; see also 1:203. The Grey Nuns of Saint-Bruno appear to have pursued
the same objective as their *consœurs* in Saint-Boniface. The latter nuns, according
to Lesley Erickson, "sought ultimately to prepare their boarding school students
to become ideal Catholic wives and mothers." Erickson, "'Bury Our Sorrows in
the Sacred Heart,'" 26; See also ibid., 23–24; Mitchell, *Grey Nuns of Montreal
and the Red River Settlement*, 75.

21 See especially PAA, O.M.I. Collection, Accession 84.400, Item 957, Box 33,
"Notes et souvenirs de Mgr Grandin (Repris à la demande de Mgr Langevin
par lettre du 28 nov. 1897, rédaction commencée en mars 1898)," 71. See also
Abel, *Drum Songs*, 135; Huel, *Proclaiming the Gospel*, 22; McCarthy, *From the
Great River to the Ends of the Earth*, 90–91.

22 "Extrait d'une lettre de Mgr Taché, Vicaire apostolique de la Baie d'Hudson,
à sa mère. Mission de St-Jean-Baptiste, Île à la Crosse, 4 janvier 1851," *Annales
de la Propagation de la Foi* 24 (1852): 343.

23 Ibid., 352. See generally ibid., 350–53.

24 Taché's assumption reflected a common Victorian discursive practice wherein
"the status of women" served as an index of civilization. "Advanced" societies were
characterized by respect and care for their womenfolk; "primitive" societies by
contempt and cruelty toward them. See especially Hall, "Of Gender and Empire,"
50–51; Levine, "Introduction: Why Gender and Empire?," 6–7; McGrath and
Stevenson, "Gender, Race and Policy," 53.

25 "Extrait d'une lettre de Mgr Vital Grandin, évêque de Satala et coadjuteur
de Mgr l'évêque de Saint-Boniface, à MM. les Directeurs de l'Œuvre de la
Propagation de la Foi. Mission de Saint-Jean-Baptiste de l'Île-à-la-Crosse, 3
décembre, 1861," *Annales de la Propagation de la Foi* 35 (1863): 349.

26 AD, HPF 4191. C75R 183, Pepin to "Ma Très Chère Sœur," Île-à-la-Crosse, 14 June 1863; SHSB, "Arbre généalogique Île-à-la-Crosse" (Liber animarum), "Famille La Fleur [*sic*]," 41, and "Famille La Liberté [*sic*]," 109; ASGM, Agnès, "Annales de l'établissement des Sœurs Grises à l'Île à la Crosse," 1:199. Information on James Bruce's employment history (1860–67) is available online through the Hudson's Bay Company Archives: http://www.gov.mb.ca/chc/archives/hbca/biographical/b/bruce_james.pdf (accessed 18 May 2016).

27 ASGM, Agnès, "Annales de l'établissement des Sœurs Grises à l'Île à la Crosse," 1:204–6. According to Agnès, the first cohort of schoolboys had no knowledge of French whatsoever; ibid., 1:203–4. See also SHSB, Fonds Taché, T0582–T0585, Végréville to Taché, Île-à-la-Crosse, 12 June 1861; SHSB, "Codex historicus, 1845–1897," 71.

28 ASGM, Agnès, "Annales de l'établissement des Sœurs Grises à l'Île à la Crosse," 1:204–5.

29 SHSB, Fonds Taché, T1215–T1217, Dubé to Taché, Île-à-la-Crosse, February 1862; ibid., T1401–1404, Faraud to Taché, Île-à-la-Crosse, 19 May 1862; ibid., T1719–T1720, Salasse to Taché, Île-à-la-Crosse, 16 November 1862; ibid., T1721–T1724, Moulin to Taché, Île-à-la-Crosse, 16 November 1862; ibid., T1925–T1928, Salasse to Taché, Île-à-la-Crosse, 10 January 1863; ibid., T2680–T2683, Moulin to Taché, Île-à-la-Crosse, 10 March 1864.

30 SHSB, Fonds Taché, T1401–1404, Faraud to Taché, Île-à-la-Crosse, 19 May 1862.

31 SHSB, Fonds Taché, T0582–T0585, Végréville to Taché, Île-à-la-Crosse, 12 June 1861.

32 SHSB, Fonds Taché, T1721–T1724, Moulin to Taché, Île-à-la-Crosse, 16 November 1862.

33 SHSB, Fonds Taché, T1921–T1924, Moulin to Taché, Île-à-la-Crosse, 9 January 1863.

34 AD, HE 2221. T12Z 57, Faraud to Taché, Île-à-la-Crosse, 19 March 1862; SHSB, Fonds Taché, T1725–T1728, Faraud to Taché, Île-à-la-Crosse, 16 November 1862; ibid., T1936–T1939, Faraud to Taché, Île-à-la-Crosse, 17 January 1863; ibid., T2017–T2022, Faraud to Taché, Île-à-la-Crosse, 6 April 1863; ibid., T2229–T2237, Faraud to Taché, Île-à-la-Crosse, 1 June 1863. On Faraud's tenure as principal, see SHSB, "Codex historicus, 1845–1897," 75, 79.

35 SHSB, Fonds Taché, T0350–T0353, Agnès to Taché, Île-à-la-Crosse, 1 April 1861; ASGM, Agnès, "Annales de l'établissement des Sœurs Grises à l'Île à la Crosse," 1:205; SHSB, "Codex historicus, 1845–1897," 71.

36 SHSB, Fonds Taché, T0391–T0393, Moulin to Taché, Île-à-la-Crosse, 6 April 1861; ibid., T0483–T0486, Moulin to Taché, Île-à-la-Crosse, 8 May 1861; ibid., T0582–T0585, Végréville to Taché, Île-à-la-Crosse, 12 June 1861.

37 ASGM, Agnès, "Annales de l'établissement des Sœurs Grises à l'Île à la Crosse," 1:220–21; SHSB, "Codex historicus, 1845–1897," 95–96. The failure of the local fishery may have resulted from the accumulation of algae and/or bacteria in Lake Île-à-la-Crosse. Agnès recorded that the lake water became "green and undrinkable" in spring 1866, prompting Oblates to dig a well and install a pump in the basement of the Grey Nuns' residence. See ASGM, Agnès, "Annales de l'établissement des Sœurs Grises à l'Île à la Crosse," 1:222.

38   RCRHC/Prop. de la Foi, microfilm X, 10822, Grandin to "Monsieur le Président et à Messieurs les conseillers de la Propagation de la Foi à Paris," Paris, 28 December 1867; ASGM, Agnès, "Annales de l'établissement des Sœurs Grises à l'Île à la Crosse," 1:227; SHSB, "Codex historicus, 1845–1897," 101.

39   PAA, O.M.I. Collection, Accession 84.400, Vol. 5, Box 35, Grandin, "Notes privées sur les missions et les missionnaires du diocèse de St-Albert," 1868–1884, 145; SHSB, "Codex historicus, 1845–1897," 107–8, 120.

40   AD, HPF 4191. C75R 187, Pepin to "Ma Très Chère Sœur," Île-à-la-Crosse, 1 January 1870; AD, G LPP 2200, Légeard to Fabre, Île-à-la-Crosse, 13 January 1870; AD, HEC 2500. P96C4, Légeard to Maisonneuve, Île-à-la-Crosse, 9 April 1871; ASGM, Agnès, "Annales de l'établissement des Sœurs Grises à l'Île à la Crosse," 1:231, 241; Soullier, *Vie du Révérend Père Légeard*, 56, 82.

41   According to Agnès, the original fee for each student was £1 per year. Pénard noted, however, that this fee could be substituted by the provision of foodstuffs. ASGM, Agnès, "Annales de l'établissement des Sœurs Grises à l'Île à la Crosse," 1:205; SHSB, "Codex historicus, 1845–1897," 71.

42   SHSB, Fonds Taché, T1721–T1724, Moulin to Taché, Île-à-la-Crosse, 16 November 1862; ibid., T1741–T1743, Faraud to Taché, Île-à-la-Crosse, 26 November 1862; ibid., T1921–T1924, Moulin to Taché, Île-à-la-Crosse, 9 January 1863; ibid., T2023–T2029, Moulin to Taché, Île-à-la-Crosse, 8 April 1863.

43   SHSB/Arch., Fonds Taché, T1741–T1743, Faraud to Taché, Île-à-la-Crosse, 26 November 1862.

44   SHSB, Fonds Taché, T2575–T2577, Moulin to Lestanc, Île-à-la-Crosse, 9 January 1864; ibid., T2680–T2683, Moulin to Taché, Île-à-la-Crosse, 10 March 1864; ibid., T3099–T3102, Grandin to Taché, Île-à-la-Crosse, 18 January 1865; ASGM, Agnès, "Annales de l'établissement des Sœurs Grises à l'Île à la Crosse," 1:234; SHSB, "Codex historicus, 1845–1897," 80, 163.

45   SHSB, Fonds Taché, T3134–T3137, Grandin to Taché, Île-à-la-Crosse, 13 March 1865; ASGM, Agnès, "Annales de l'établissement des Sœurs Grises à l'Île à la Crosse," 1:205, 234; SHSB, "Codex historicus, 1845–1897," 122, 128, 159. There was at least one instance in the early 1860s in which a pupil was actually withdrawn from Saint-Bruno by a family member. In spring 1862, a young girl identified as Marguerite Sasté was removed from the Grey Nuns' custody by her aunt—a local Chipewyan-speaking woman whom Pepin had nicknamed "the Seven Deadly Sins." SHSB, Fonds Taché, T1413–T1415, Agnès to Taché, Île-à-la-Crosse, 26 May 1862.

46   See pp. 50–51. See also ASGM, Agnès, "Annales de l'établissement des Sœurs Grises à l'Île à la Crosse," 1:216–17, 218, 231, 237, 243–44; Soullier, *Vie du Révérend Père Légeard*, 56–57, 86–87, 107–8; SHSB, "Codex historicus, 1845–1897," 127–28, 159–60.

47   ASGM, Agnès, "Annales de l'établissement des Sœurs Grises à l'Île à la Crosse," 1:234. Légeard noted thirty-six—rather than thirty-five—"pensionnaires" at Saint-Bruno in 1871. See AD, HEC 2500. P96C4, Légeard to Maisonneuve, Île-à-la-Crosse, 9 April 1871.

48   ASGM, Agnès, "Annales de l'établissement des Sœurs Grises à l'Île à la Crosse," 1:216, 218–19, and 2:207, 209–10. François Beaulieu was a grandson of the well-known "patriarche Beaulieu"—François Beaulieu, salt trader at Salt River (Athabasca District) and long-time supporter of Oblates. The "patriarche

Beaulieu" had confided his grandson to Grandin's care during the latter's three-year tour of the northern missions (1861–64) so that the boy could receive a mission education. See ibid., 1:216; SHSB, Fonds Taché, T3079–T3082, Agnès to Taché, Île-à-la-Crosse, 13 January 1865; PAA, O.M.I. Collection, Accession 84.400, Item 912, Box 32, Grandin to "Mes bien chers pères et frères," Île-à-la-Crosse, 21 January, 1865; PAA, O.M.I. Collection, Accession 84.400, Item 923, Box 32, Grandin to Clut, Île-à-la-Crosse, 26 January 1865; RCRHC/É.G., vol. 6, Grandin, "Notes de Monseigneur Grandin sur l'Église du Nord-Ouest," 162–78. On the relationship between the "patriarche Beaulieu" and the Oblates, see especially PAA, O.M.I. Collection, Accession 84.400, Item 957, Box 33, "Mgr Grandin, Notes Intimes sur le Diocèse de St Albert, rédigées en 1884," 63; McCarthy, *From the Great River to the Ends of the Earth*, 109–14; Neatby, "François Beaulieu." Patrice Stevenson may have been a member of the family identified as "Famille Stewenson" in the *liber status animarum* of Saint-Jean-Baptiste. However, this document contains no mention of his baptism or burial. See SHSB, "Arbre généalogique Île-à-la-Crosse" (Liber animarum), "Famille Stewenson," 65.

49 ASGM, Agnès, "Annales de l'établissement des Sœurs Grises à l'Île à la Crosse," 2:210.

50 Some of the most fulsome of these descriptions appeared in Taché's memoir, *Vingt années de mission* (1866). For instance, Taché likened the cooperation between Oblates and Grey Nuns to that between Paul the Apostle and "the women who worked with him in spreading the Gospel" (presumably a reference to Phoebe, Julia, and the other female disciples mentioned in Romans 16:1–16). See Taché, *Vingt années de missions*, 92, 111–12.

51 The Oblate General Administration did not issue regulations concerning interaction between Oblates and nuns (or secular women for that matter) until after the canonical visit of Oblate Assistant General Louis Soullier to Canada in 1883: Huel, *Proclaiming the Gospel*, 66. On Soullier's canonical visit to Canada, see *Acte de visite du R.P. Soullier*.

52 Moulin assumed the temporary direction of Saint-Bruno (and of Saint-Jean-Baptiste in general) in the winter of 1862–63 when Faraud was consigned to the Grey Nun's infirmary because of his crippling rheumatism. Moulin's second principalship began in July 1863 after Faraud left Île-à-la-Crosse to be consecrated in France. Moulin was relieved by Grandin in autumn 1864. Moulin's third principalship began immediately after the fire of 1 March 1867 and ended when Légeard took charge in October 1870. See SHSB, Fonds Taché, T1721–T1724, Moulin to Taché, Île-à-la-Crosse, 16 November 1862; ibid., T1936–T1939, Faraud to Taché, Île-à-la-Crosse, 17 January 1863; PAA, O.M.I. Collection, Accession 84.400, Item 973, Box 33, "Renseignements demandés par Mgr Taché sur les missions et les Missionnaires de Mgr Grandin depuis l'érection du vicariat religieux de St Albert 1868 jusqu'en 1872," 11; SHSB, "Codex historicus, 1845–1897," 78, 79, 85, 102, 112–13; Carrière, *Dictionnaire biographique*, 2:410.

53 AD, HE 2221. T12Z 189, Moulin to Taché, Île-à-la-Crosse, 8 May 1867. Taché and Grandin subsequently rejected this recommendation. Throughout the 1870s, Oblates retained responsibility for procuring and delivering supplies to the Grey Nuns' schools and infirmaries in western and northern Canada. See RCRHC/É.G., vol. 6, "Convention entre Mgr Grandin, Evêque de Satala ... Et la Révérende Sœur Charlebois, Assistante Générale de la Congrégation

des Sœurs de la Charité," Saint-Albert, 4 March 1872, 234–36; PAA, O.M.I. Collection, Accession 84.400, Vol. 5, Box 35, Grandin, "Notes privées sur les missions et les missionnaires du diocèse de St-Albert," "Les Sœurs grises," March 1880, 232. For examples of earlier lists compiled through consultation with the Grey Nuns of Saint-Bruno, see SHSB, Fonds Taché, T1085–T1087, Grandin, "Pour la mission de St Jean Baptiste, l'île à la Crosse," 1861; ibid., T1120–T1121, Faraud, "Articles demandées à YF [York Factory] pour l'automne 1862," 15 January 1862; ibid., T3765–T3768, Grandin, "Mission de St. J. Bte de l'Ile à la Crosse, Du mois de juin 1864 au mois de janvier 1866," 9 January 1866.

54   SHSB, Fonds Taché, T1925–T1928, Salasse to Taché, Île-à-la-Crosse, 10 January 1863; ibid., T3079–T3082, Agnès to Taché, Île-à-la-Crosse, 13 January 1865.

55   On Grandin's three-year tour of the northern missions and his return to Île-à-la-Crosse, see SHSB, Fonds Taché, T2931–T2934, Grandin to Taché, Île-à-la-Crosse, 31 August 1864; RCRHC/É.G., vol. 6, Grandin, "Notes de Monseigneur Grandin sur l'Église du Nord-Ouest," 162–78; SHSB, "Codex historicus, 1845–1897," 73–74, 82–83.

56   SHSB, Fonds Taché, T3068–T3078, Grandin to Taché and Florent Vandenberghe, Île-à-la-Crosse, 12 January 1865. On Vandenberghe and his canonical visit of Oblate missions in Rupert's Land and the North-Western Territory (1864–67), see Taché, *Vingt années de missions*, 194–98, 202, 207, 211–16, 218–23, 229–32; Carrière, *Dictionnaire biographique*, 3:257–58.

57   "Lettre de Mgr Grandin, évêque de Satala, à MM. les Membres des Conseils centraux de l'Œuvre de la Propagation de la Foi," *Annales de la Propagation de la Foi* 41 (1869): 289; RCRHC/É.G., vol. 6, "Notes sur les origines des missions du N.O." 110–13; Jonquet, *Mgr Grandin*, 173–88.

58   PAA, O.M.I. Collection, Accession 84.400, vol. 5, Box 35, Grandin, "Notes privées sur les missions et les missionnaires du diocèse de St-Albert," 1868–1884, 12.

59   Ibid., 115. In November 1868, Grandin recorded the following assessment of Moulin and his performance as an administrator: "An excellent religious and of sound virture, but of tiresome severity and unpleasant bearing; he simply cannot get along with others. He cannot be entrusted with temporal authority over a large mission in this country as he is totally inflexible."

60   SHSB, Fonds Taché, T2023–T2029, Moulin to Taché, Île-à-la-Crosse, 8 April 1863. In giving the nuns daily lessons in Cree and Chipewyan, Faraud may have sought to alleviate what he perceived as their sense of despondency and disengagement. A year earlier, he had reported that the nuns were effectively isolated by their inability to communicate in the local Indigenous languages: "The sisters find themselves very much alone: they have no communication with the world outside the mission and cannot interact with local people because they do not know the language." SHSB, Fonds Taché, T1401–1404, Faraud to Taché, Île-à-la-Crosse, 19 May 1862.

61   SHSB, Fonds Taché, T4255–T4259, Grandin to Taché, Île-à-la-Crosse, 25 September 1866. On Grandin's absence from Île-à-la-Crosse and Caër's interim administration, see especially ibid., T4043–T4046, Jean-Marie Caër to Taché, Île-à-la-Crosse, 15 June 1866; ibid., T4072–T4075, Caër to Taché, Île-à-la-Crosse, 1 July 1866; ibid., T4123–T4126, Caër to Taché, Île-à-la-Crosse, 24 July 1866; ibid., T4127–T4130, Caër to Taché, Île-à-la-Crosse, 24 July 1866; ibid., T4150–T4151, Caër to Taché, Île-à-la-Crosse, 1 August 1866; SHSB, "Codex historicus, 1845–1897," 95–96.

62   SHSB, Fonds Taché, T6286–T6292, Grandin to Taché, Mission de Saint-Joachim (Fort Edmonton), 13 February 1869. Grandin did indeed suffer from "lazy ears" and grew steadily deaf in the late 1860s and '70s. He experienced chronic pain and frequent abscesses in both ears, forcing him to undergo intensive medical treatment in Paris and to make a healing pilgrimage to Lourdes in 1878. Neither undertaking was effective and in 1892, Grandin's condition was deemed untreatable. See PAA, O.M.I. Collection, Accession 84.400, Item 916, Box 32, Grandin to Leduc, Saint-Albert, 10 December 1875; PAA, O.M.I. Collection, Accession 84.400, Item 911, Box 32, Grandin to Taché, Saint-Albert, 29 December 1875; PAA, O.M.I. Collection, Accession 84.400, Item 919, Box 32, Grandin "aux R^d Pères du Lac Caribou" [i.e., Gasté and Moulin], Paris, 3 February 1878; ibid., Grandin to "Mes Révérends pères et bien chers frères," Paris, 22 April 1878; ibid., Grandin to "Mes bien chers pères et frères," Cauterets (department of Hautes-Pyrénées, thirty-two kilometres south-west of Lourdes), 11 August 1878; PAA, O.M.I. Collection, Accession 84.400, Item 936, Box 33, Dr. P. Royal to Grandin, Edmonton, 27 April 1892 (and appended note [from Royal's secretary?]).

63   PAA, O.M.I. Collection, Accession 84.400, Vol. 5, Box 35, Grandin, "Notes privées sur les missions et les missionnaires du diocèse de St-Albert," 1868–1884, 118. Caër had informed the Oblate General Administration of his desire to join the Carthusian Order in 1866, but decided against leaving Saint-Jean-Baptiste short-staffed after the fire of 1 March 1867. He entered the Carthusian charterhouse of Le Reposoir (department of Haute-Savoie) in 1870 and left ten years later, prompting Grandin to remark: "It would seem that a bad Oblate does not make a good Carthusian; he has abandoned that order." Ibid.; SHSB, Fonds Taché, T4555–T4558, Caër to Taché, Île-à-la-Crosse, 13 March 1867; Carrière, *Dictionnaire biographique*, 1:155.

64   PAA, O.M.I. Collection, Accession 84.400, Vol. 5, Box 35, Grandin, "Notes privées sur les missions et les missionnaires du diocèse de St-Albert," 1868–1884, 14; PAA, O.M.I. Collection, Accession 84.400, Item 973, Box 33, "Renseignements demandés par Mgr Taché sur les missions et les Missionnaires de Mgr Grandin depuis l'érection du vicariat religieux de St Albert 1868 jusqu'en 1872," 3. On Sister Charlebois's visit to the missions of northern and western Canada in 1871, see *Notes and Sketches Collected from a Voyage*; ASGM, Agnès, "Annales de l'établissement des Sœurs Grises à l'Île à la Crosse," 1:236–38; Erickson, "At the Cultural and Religious Crossroads," 62, 100–101, 111–13, 118.

65   PAA, O.M.I. Collection, Accession 84.400, Item 973, Box 33, "Renseignements demandés par Mgr Taché sur les missions et les Missionnaires de Mgr Grandin depuis l'érection du vicariat religieux de St Albert 1868 jusqu'en 1872," 13. See also PAA, O.M.I. Collection, Accession 84.400, Vol. 5, Box 35, Grandin, "Notes privées sur les missions et les missionnaires du diocèse de St-Albert," 1868–1884, 14, 134; SHSB, "Codex historicus, 1845–1897," 113, 118–19.

66   Légeard provided descriptions of these buildings in his report to David Laird (Lieutenant Governor of the North-West Territories) dated 25 March 1878: LAC/Black Series, microfilm C-10117, file no. 10125, "Ile-a-la-Crosse Agency—Reverend Mr. Legard's [*sic*] Report on the School at Ile-a-la-Crosse," 1878. See also SHSB, "Codex historicus, 1845–1897," 123, 134–35, 142.

67   ASGM, Agnès, "Annales de l'établissement des Sœurs Grises à l'Île à la Crosse," 2:202.

68 Raymond Jonas has used the term "interlocutor"—rather than simply "visionary"—in reference to Marguerite-Marie Alacoque because she reported having a dialogic/interactive relationship with the Sacred Heart. During her visions, Marguerite-Marie spoke to and interacted with the divine organ. Jonas, *France and the Cult of the Sacred Heart*, 17–24, 143.

69 Soullier, *Vie du Révérend Père Légeard*, 17–26; Carrière, *Dictionnaire biographique*, 2:30. In France, the devotion to the Sacred Heart underwent dramatic renewal and popularization after 1864 when Marguerite-Marie Alacoque was beatified by Pope Pius IX. According to Jonas, this process of renewal and popularization was accelerated by "l'année terrible" (1870–1871) when France was invaded by Prussia and riven by domestic strife during the Paris Commune. Thereafter, the Sacred Heart was increasingly invoked in pursuit of religious, moral, and political regeneration. See especially Jonas, *France and the Cult of the Sacred Heart*, 4, 9–13, 17–33, 147–96. On the Oblate scholasticate of Sacré-Cœur and its relationship with Paray-le-Monial in the 1860s, see Ortolan, *Les Oblats de Marie Immaculée*, 3:32–37.

70 Quoted in Soullier, *Vie du Révérend Père Légeard*, 19–20. Hortense Légeard—like her elder brother—was a member of a religious community. She belonged to the Sisters of Providence at Ruillé-sur-Loire (department of Sarthe). Ibid., 16.

71 AD, G LPP 2199, Légeard to Grandin, Île-à-la-Crosse, 11 January 1869; AD, G LPP 2200, Légeard to Fabre, Île-à-la-Crosse, 13 January 1870; AD, HPF 4191. C75R 188, Pepin to "Ma très chère Sœur," Île-à-la-Crosse, 7 August 1872; ASGM, Agnès, "Annales de l'établissement des Sœurs Grises à l'Île à la Crosse," 1:230, 235; Soullier, *Vie du Révérend Père Légeard*, 77–79; SHSB, "Codex historicus, 1845–1897," 117–19, 126.

72 There are several primary accounts of Sara Riel's healing. The present account is based on the following: SHSB/Arch., Fonds Taché, T11500–T11507, Légeard to Taché, Île-à-la-Crosse, 9 January 1873; PAA, O.M.I. Collection, Accession 84.400, Item 914, Box 32, Grandin to "Mes Révérends et bien chers Pères," Saint-Albert, 6 March 1873; AD, G LPP 2201, Légeard to Aubert, Île-à-la-Crosse, 29 August 1873; ASGM, Agnès, "Annales de l'établissement des Sœurs Grises à l'Île à la Crosse," 1:243; Soullier, *Vie du Révérend Père Légeard*, 84–85. For secondary accounts, see especially Erickson, "'Bury Our Sorrows in the Sacred Heart,'" 33–34; Erickson, "At the Cultural and Religious Crossroads," 3, 122–23; Flanagan, *Louis "David" Riel*, 40; Jordan, *To Louis from Your Sister Who Loves You*, 70–86.

73 ASGM, Agnès, "Annales de l'établissement des Sœurs Grises à l'Île à la Crosse," 1:246–47; SHSB, "Codex historicus, 1845–1897," 134.

74 AD, G LPP 2203, Légeard to "Ma très honorée Sœur," Île-à-la-Crosse, 27 July 1875; SHSB, "Codex historicus, 1845–1897," 52, 154.

75 AD, HPF 4191. C75R 177, Légeard to "Ma très honorée et Vénérée Mère," Île-à-la-Crosse, 20 December 1877; "Missions d'Amérique: Nouvelle Bretagne, Diocèse de Saint-Albert," *Annales de la Propagation de la Foi* 49 (1877): 453.

76 AD, G LPP 2202, Légeard to Aubert, Île-à-la-Crosse, 3 January 1875; ASGM, Agnès, "Annales de l'établissement des Sœurs Grises à l'Île à la Crosse," 2:201, 204; SHSB, "Codex historicus, 1845–1897," 143, 145, 159, 162.

77 AD, G LPP 2203, Légeard to "Ma très honorée Sœur," Île-à-la-Crosse, 27 July 1875; SHSB, "Codex historicus, 1845–1897," 154.

78   AD, G LPP 2201, Légeard to Aubert, Île-à-la-Crosse, 29 August 1873.

79   PAA, O.M.I. Collection, Accession 84.400, Item 965, Box 33, Grandin "aux Rᵈˢ Missionnaires O.M.I. de St. Albert et des environs et à communiquer aux Rᵈᵉˢ sœurs," Marseilles, 24 Mars 1875.

80   Champagne, *Les débuts de la mission dans le Nord-Ouest Canadien*, 186, 194–95; Champagne, "Mission et civilisation dans l'Ouest canadien," 342–43, 348–53.

81   PAA, O.M.I. Collection, Accession 84.400, Item 914, Box 32, Grandin to "Monsieur le Secrétaire" (secretary of the Lyons council of l'Œuvre de la Propagation de la Foi), Rome, 26 November 1873. It should be noted, however, that another French society—l'Œuvre de la Sainte-Enfance—had begun supporting Oblate missions in the Northwest by the early 1870s. Established in 1843 by Charles-Auguste de Forbin-Janson, Bishop of Nancy (1823–1844), l'Œuvre de la Sainte-Enfance provided funds to promote the baptism and education of children in foreign mission fields. Grandin does not appear to have received regular assistance from this society before 1869 or 1870. In 1868 he declared that he had no revenue other than his annual allocation from l'Œuvre de la Propagation de la Foi, but added: "I hope to receive assistance from the Sainte-Enfance." By the mid-1870s, he was receiving an annual allocation from l'Œuvre de la Sainte-Enfance, but this amount was significantly less than his annual allocation from l'Œuvre de la Propagation de la Foi. See RCRHC/Prop. de la Foi, microfilm X, 10824, "État des recettes et dépenses présumées pour l'année 1868"; PAA, O.M.I. Collection, Accession 84.400, Item 915, Box 32, "État des recettes et dépenses présumées pour l'année 1876–77"; "Compte-rendu," *Annales de la Propagation de la Foi* 49 (1877): 328; Huel, *Archbishop A.-A. Taché of St. Boniface*, 41, 59, 98; Huel, *Proclaiming the Gospel*, 69–71. On Bishop Forbin-Janson and the establishment of l'Œuvre de la Sainte-Enfance, see Sylvain, "Charles-Auguste-Marie-Joseph de Forbin-Janson."

82   Between August 1873 and February 1874, Grandin lectured in favour of l'Œuvre de la Propagation de la Foi in the (arch)dioceses of Dijon, Laval, Poitiers, Bordeaux, Nevers, Autun, Tours, Lyons, Grenoble, Marseilles, Montpellier, Bourges, Mende, Rodez, Clermont-Ferrand, Besançon, Nancy, Saint-Dié, and possibly Limoges. As a beneficiary of l'Œuvre, Grandin was forbidden to elicit private donations for his diocese. Instead, he was required to elicit support for l'Œuvre and then to content himself with an annual allocation disbursed by the central councils in Paris and Lyons. See PAA, O.M.I. Collection, Accession 84.400, Item 914, Box 32, Grandin to "M.M. les Présidents et M.M. les Conseillers de la Propagation de la foi à Lyons et à Paris," Autun, 10 August 1873; ibid., Grandin to "Monsieur le Président," Paris, 1 September 1873; ibid., Grandin to Leduc, Saint-Andelain (Diocese of Nevers), 23 September 1873; PAA, O.M.I. Collection, Accession 84.400, Item 965, Box 33, Grandin to "Mes Révérends Pères et bien chers Frères," Saint-Andelain, 24 September 1873; PAA, O.M.I. Collection, Accession 84.400, Item 914, Box 32, Grandin to "Monsieur le Président," Autun, 25 February 1874; Jonquet, *Mgr Grandin*, 260–67.

83   "Lettre de Mgr Grandin à MM. les membres des Conseils centraux de l'Œuvre de la Propagation de la Foi. Fort Pitt (mission de Saint-François Régis), 10 janvier 1870," *Annales de la Propagation de la Foi* 44 (1872): 282–83.

84   See "Compte-rendu," *Annales de la Propagation de la Foi* 42–52 (1870–80). Grandin was allocated the following sums between 1869 and 1879: 38,150 francs in 1869; 26,000 francs in 1870; 39,500 francs in 1871; 43,160 francs in 1872; 46,315 francs

in 1873; 45,135 francs in 1874; 47,000 francs in 1875; 49,000 francs in 1876; 48,000 francs in 1877; 49,000 francs in 1878; and 50,611 francs in 1879. The decrease in his allocation in 1870 resulted from the Franco-Prussian War and subsequent civil unrest during the Paris Commune. These episodes strained l'Œuvre de la Propagation de la Foi to its limits by destroying its communications network and halting its flow of finances. See especially "À nos associés," *Annales de la Propagation de la Foi* 43 (1871): 157–69; "Compte-rendu," ibid., 391–93.

85 Grandin made this observation repeatedly, especially in the second half of the 1870s. See for instance PAA, O.M.I. Collection, Accession 84.400, Item 965, Box 33, Grandin "aux R^ds Missionnaires O.M.I. de St. Albert et des environs et à communiquer aux R^des sœurs," Marseilles, 24 March 1875; PAA, O.M.I. Collection, Accession 84.400, Item 919, Box 32, Grandin to Leduc, Paris, 21 October 1878; PAA, O.M.I. Collection, Accession 84.400, Item 911, Box 32, Grandin to Taché, Laval, 16 April 1879.

86 PAA, O.M.I. Collection, Accession 84.400, Vol. 5, Box 35, Grandin, "Notes privées sur les missions et les missionnaires du diocèse de St-Albert," 1868–1884, 135; PAA, O.M.I. Collection, Accession 84.400, Item 973, Box 33, "Renseignements demandés par Mgr Taché sur les missions et les Missionnaires de Mgr Grandin depuis l'érection du vicariat religieux de St Albert 1868 jusqu'en 1872," 13.

87 AD, G LPP 2203, Légeard to "Ma très honorée Sœur," Île-à-la-Crosse, 27 July 1875 (my italics). See also Soullier, *Vie du Révérend Père Légeard*, 69, 80, 126–27.

88 AD, G LPP 2203, Légeard to "Ma très honorée Sœur," Île-à-la-Crosse, 27 July 1875; ASGM, Agnès, "Annales de l'établissement des Sœurs Grises à l'Île à la Crosse," 2:212; Jonquet, *Mgr Grandin*, 5–6. There is fragmentary evidence that a member of Légeard's family also sponsored an orphan or foundling at Notre-Dame du Sacré-Cœur. In the table of contents of the *liber status animarum* of Île-à-la-Crosse, the geneology of a "famille Légeard" is listed as beginning on page 178. Unfortunately, this page has been removed from the document. SHSB, "Arbre généalogique Île-à-la-Crosse" (Liber animarum), 2.

89 PAA, O.M.I. Collection, Accession 84.400, Item 911, Box 32, "Circulaire de Mgr Grandin à ses missionnaires," March–April 1878. In a letter to a potential benefactor written two months earlier, Grandin had referred to this charitable association as l'Œuvre de la civilisation des sauvages par les petits enfants. See RCRHC/Prop. de la Foi, microfilm X, 10905, Grandin to "Madame," Pontmain (department of Mayenne), 17 January 1878.

90 PAA, O.M.I. Collection, Accession 84.400, Item 919, Box 32, Grandin to Robert Cooke, N.D. de Sion (Paris), 5 July 1878; PAA, O.M.I. Collection, Accession 84.400, Item 974, Box 33, Grandin, "Remarques importantes sur le plan d'association en faveur des écoles du Nord-Ouest," 1878; PAA, O.M.I. Collection, Accession 84.400, Item 959, Box 33, "Notes et souvenirs de Mgr Grandin (Repris à la demande de Mgr Langevin par lettre du 28 nov. 1897, rédaction commencée en mars 1898)," 199, 275. On Father Robert Cooke and the Oblates' Anglo-Irish Province, see especially Ortolan, *Les Oblats de Marie Immaculée*, 3:326–45. On Cardinal Archbishop Manning, see especially Gray, *Cardinal Manning*; Pereiro, *Cardinal Manning*.

91 RCRHC/Prop. de la Foi, microfilm X, 10911-a, François-Adolphe Certes (treasurer of the Paris council), "Lettre de M. Marquis" and "Réponse," 1 June 1878; PAA, O.M.I. Collection, Accession 84.400, Item 911, Box 32, Grandin

to Taché, Paris, 17 June 1878. On François-Adolphe Certes and his tenure as treasurer of the Paris council (1857–87), see especially "Nécrologie," *Annales de la Propagation de la Foi* 59 (1887): 200.

92 RCRHC/Prop. de la Foi, microfilm X, 10911-b, Léon Colin de Verdière to Grandin, Paris, 7 June 1878. See also PAA, O.M.I. Collection, Accession 84.400, Item 911, Box 32, Colin de Verdière to Grandin, Paris, 7 June 1878. On Colin de Verdière and his tenure as president of the Paris council (1873–15), see especially "Nécrologie," *Annales de la Propagation de la Foi* 58 (1886): 120.

93 RCRHC/Prop. de la Foi, microfilm X, 10906, Grandin to Colin de Verdière, Paris, 7 June 1878.

94 RCRHC/Prop. de la Foi, microfilm X, 10907, Grandin to Certes, Paris, 22 June 1878; PAA, O.M.I. Collection, Accession 84.400, Item 911, Box 32, Grandin to Taché, N.D. de Sion (Paris), 30 June 1878.

95 RCRHC/Prop. de la Foi, microfilm X, 10908, Grandin to "Monsieur le Président et Messieurs," Paris, 24 June 1878.

96 SHSB, Fonds Taché, T20652–T20655, Grandin to Taché, Angoulême (department of Charente), 21 July 1878. Grandin was profoundly humiliated and embittered by his conflict with the Paris council of l'Œuvre de la Propagation de la Foi. In his personal memoirs—written a full twenty years after this incident—he expressed resentment that a council consisting chiefly of laymen had had the audacity to overturn the initiative of a bishop. In his estimation, these Parisian laymen had been motivated more by commercial interests than by the glory of God: "It is appalling that the directors of this beautiful charity should choose to reject the good that we might have done under another's sponsorship. . . . Most of these pious laymen approach the affairs of God like commercial affairs . . . and for this reason I would very much like to see the administration of this important charity transferred to clerics or religious, under the direct authority of the Propaganda Fide [the congregation of the Roman Curia responsible for coordinating missionary activity and for promoting the interests of Catholics living in predominantly non-Catholic countries]." PAA, O.M.I. Collection, Accession 84.400, Item 959, Box 33, "Notes et souvenirs de Mgr Grandin (Repris à la demande de Mgr Langevin par lettre du 28 nov. 1897, rédaction commencée en mars 1898)," 200. Grandin's wish was fulfilled two decades later. In 1922, the headquarters of l'Œuvre de la Propagation de la Foi were transferred to Rome and the organization was placed under the administrative control of the Propaganda Fide. See Baumont, "Une Source de l'Histoire," 165; Perin, *Rome in Canada*, 40–42.

97 PAA, O.M.I. Collection, Accession 84.400, Item 915, Box 32, Grandin to "son excellence, le Lieutenant Gouverneur de Manitoba," Saint-Albert, 4 January 1875. On Alexander Morris and his tenure as Lieutenant Governor of Manitoba and the Northwest Territories (1872–76), see especially Friesen, "Alexander Morris"; Talbot, *Negotiating the Numbered Treaties*.

98 PAA, O.M.I. Collection, Accession 84.400, Item 915, Box 32, Grandin to "Colonel McLeod [*sic*], Magistrat stipendiaire du Nord-Ouest," Saint-Albert, 3 January 1876. Underlined passages ("des moines ou des dévots de notre Religion" and "faire des hommes") appear in the original document. On James Farquharson Macleod and his judicial career in the Northwest Territories (1876–94), see especially Macleod, "James Farquharson Macleod."

99 LAC/Black Series, microfilm C-10113, file no. 7780, "Privy Council's Report on Grants to Schools at Lac La Biche, Isle a la Crosse and St. Albert," 1877; LAC/Black Series, microfilm C-10117, file no. 10125, "Ile-a-la-Crosse Agency—Reverend Mr. Legard's [*sic*] Report on the School at Ile-a-la-Crosse," 1878; SHSB, "Codex historicus, 1845–1897," 168; Huel, *Proclaiming the Gospel*, 117.

100 "Copy of Treaty No. 6"; Morris, *Treaties of Canada with the Indians of Manitoba and the North-West Territories*, 168–244.

101 "Copy of Treaty No. 6"; Morris, *Treaties of Canada*, 353. On David Laird and his tenure as first resident Lieutenant Governor of the Northwest Territories (1876–81), see especially Robb, "David Laird."

102 LAC/Black Series, microfilm C-10117, file no. 10125, "Ile-a-la-Crosse Agency—Reverend Mr. Legard's [*sic*] Report on the School at Ile-a-la-Crosse," 25 March 1878.

103 Ibid. In his report to the Oblate General Administration for 1873, Légeard noted that the Grey Nuns began teaching English at the request of HBC Chief Factor William Joseph Christie. During his sojourn in Montreal the previous winter (1872–73), Christie had visited the Grey Nuns' motherhouse and met the Mother Superior: "[Christie] told her how impressed he was with his visit to our school. At the same time, however, he admitted disappointment that we did not teach English there; this language is, after all, becoming increasingly necessary. The order was given immediately from Montreal to start teaching English. This will give our school greater importance." Quoted in SHSB, "Codex historicus, 1845–1897," 134. On 20 June 1876, Notre-Dame du Sacré-Cœur held its first public exam in both French and English. "Missions d'Amérique: Nouvelle Bretagne, Diocèse de Saint-Albert," *Annales de la Propagation de la Foi* 49 (1877): 449. See also ASGM, Agnès, "Annales de l'établissement des Sœurs Grises à l'Île à la Crosse," 1:247.

104 LAC/Black Series, microfilm C-10117, file no. 10125, "Ile-a-la-Crosse Agency—Reverend Mr. Legard's [*sic*] Report on the School at Ile-a-la-Crosse," 25 March 1878.

105 PAA, O.M.I. Collection, Accession 84.400, Item 915, Box 32, Grandin to "son Honneur le Ministre de l'Intérieur à Ottawa," 5 April 1875. Champagne quotes a similar passage from Grandin's writings on convent boarding schools: "Métis children mix with *sauvage* children in our schools, and the latter benefit a great deal from this contact. . . . Almost all of the *sauvage* children who were raised in our establishments have merged with the métis and cannot be distinguised from them. Admittedly, this is not full civilization, but at least it is a good start." Champagne, "Mission et civilisation dans l'Ouest canadien," 353. On Laird's tenure as federal Minister of the Interior (1873–76) during the Liberal administration of Alexander Mackenzie, see especially Robb, "David Laird."

106 Champagne, *Les débuts de la mission dans le Nord-Ouest Canadien*, 190; Huel, *Proclaiming the Gospel*, 104. It is worth noting that Nicholas Flood Davin—author of the "Report on Industrial Schools for Indians and Half-Breeds" (1879)—expounded similar views on the role of "mixed bloods" in the education of Indigenous children. See Miller, *Shingwauk's Vision*, 101.

107 PAA, O.M.I. Collection, Accession 84.400, Item 932, Box 33, Grandin to Leduc, Battleford, 16 September 1889; PAA, O.M.I. Collection, Accession 84.400, Item 928, Box 33, Grandin "to the Most Honorable Sir John A. Macdonald,"

c. 1887 (postscript); RCRHC/É.G., vol. 6, Grandin, "Mémoire de l'Evêque de Saint-Albert sur ses difficultés avec le Département Indien," 1890, 369–71; PAA, O.M.I. Collection, Accession 84.400, Item 976, Box 33, Grandin, "Diocèse de St. Albert, missions sauvages avant le traité," c. 1890, 12. There is fragmentary evidence of an exception to this rule. Sister Langelier's correspondence with Vankoughnet's office indicates that Notre-Dame du Sacré-Cœur was awarded four federal grants of $75 for teachers' honoraria and for renovation work in 1879, but that only one of these grants was received. See LAC/Black Series, microfilm C-10125, file no. 20505, "Northwest Territories—A Request from Bishop Grandin Regarding Money Sent to the Mission of Ile a la Crosse," 19 March 1880 (Langelier to Vankoughnet, Île-à-la-Crosse, 19 March 1880). On Lawrence Vankoughnet and his tenure as Deputy Superintendent General of Indian affairs (1874–93), see especially Carter, *Lost Harvests*, 50–51, 66, 81–82, 108, 138, 142, 196; Leighton, "A Victorian Civil Servant at Work."

108 PAA, O.M.I. Collection, Accession 84.400, Item 976, Box 33, Grandin, "Diocèse de St. Albert, missions sauvages avant le traité," c. 1890, p. 12. The Protestant schools in question were likely the Anglican day school at St. Peter's Mission on Lesser Slave Lake (established in 1886) and the Irene Training School and Industrial Farm at Vermillion Mission on the Peace River (established in 1879). On these two establishments, see especially *Missionary Diocese of Athabasca*, 13–15, 17–20; Abel, *Drum Songs*, 180.

109 PAA, O.M.I. Collection, Accession 84.400, Item 911, Box 32, Grandin to Taché, Ottawa, 8 November 1887 (featuring a copy of Grandin's letter to Thomas White—Minister of the Interior and Superintendent General of Indian Affairs—dated 8 November 1887). See also Huel, *Proclaiming the Gospel*, 126–27, 178–86; Huel, "Western Oblate History," 24–28; Miller, "Denominational Rivalry in Indian Residential Education," 139, 143, 155; Miller, "The State, the Church, and Indian Residential Schools," 113–14, 123–24. On Thomas White and his tenure as Minister of the Interior (1885–88) and Superintendent General of Indian Affairs (1887–88) in the Macdonald administration, see especially Waite, "Thomas White."

110 PAA, O.M.I. Collection, Accession 71.220, Item 76, Box 2, Grandin, "Extrait du Rapport sur le Vicariat de St. Albert au Chapitre Général de la Congrégation des O.M.I. à Rome," 28 April 1887, 3.

111 PAA, O.M.I. Collection, Accession 84.400, Item 967, Box 33, "Lettre de Mgr Vital Justin Grandin, O.M.I., Vicaire de la Congrégation des Missionnaires O.M.I. dans le Diocèse de S. Albert et Évêque de ce même diocèse, aux RR. PP. Oblats missionnaires dans le diocèse," Ottawa, 18 November 1887, 3. Grandin was not alone in his conviction that the Department of Indian Affairs discriminated against Catholics. This conviction was expressed by each of the bishops of the Ecclesiastical Province of Saint-Boniface—Taché, Faraud, Clut, and of course, Grandin. On behalf of these prelates, Taché presented a formal complaint against the Department of Indian Affairs to Lord Stanley of Preston—Governor General of Canada—in 1889. Taché alleged that the department did not treat Catholics "with the degree of impartiality that the law of the country guarantees." He noted in particular that Catholics were so grossly underrepresented in the department itself "that it is impossible not to be surprised and astonished at it." In response, Vankoughnet offered assurances that department personnel observed a policy of strict religious neutrality and that they respected the freedom of conscience of Treaty Indians. PAA, O.M.I.

Collection, Accession 84.400, Item 911, Box 32, Taché to "His Excellency the Governor General in Council," 1889; Huel, *Proclaiming the Gospel*, 182–85; Huel, "Western Oblate History," 25, 28. On Frederick Arthur Stanley and his gubernatorial career, see especially Waite, "Frederick Arthur Stanley."

112 While there is historiographical consensus on the cause of Riel's death (tuberculosis), there is a discrepancy on the date. According to Agnès and Pénard, she died on 27 December 1883. According to Erickson, she died on 25 December 1883. ASGM, Circulaire mensuelle adressée aux diverses maisons de l'Institut 18 (August 1879): 400–402; ASGM, Circulaire mensuelle adressée aux diverses maisons de l'Institut 1 (March 1884): 21–23; ASGM, Agnès, "Annales de l'établissement des Sœurs Grises à l'Île à la Crosse," 2:226, 251–52; SHSB, "Codex historicus, 1845–1897," 169–71, 190; Erickson, "'Bury Our Sorrows in the Sacred Heart,'" 36; Soullier, *Vie du Révérend Père Légeard*, 85, 142–43.

113 PAA, O.M.I. Collection, Accession 84.400, Vol. 5, Box 35, Grandin, "Notes privées sur les missions et les missionnaires du diocèse de St-Albert," 1868–1884, 19, 135; Soullier, *Vie du Révérend Père Légeard*, 80, 126.

114 Agnès and Pénard both commented on this transformation of the landscape. Agnès noted the following in her chronicle of mission life in January–February 1874: "It is very difficult to gather wood these days. By camping as close as possible to the mission, our good *sauvages* destroy all of the trees, and those who settle permanently near the mission are clearing the land in order to farm. Thus, on the part of the peninsula occupied by the mission, there are only willows left." Writing fifteen years later, Pénard noted that Île-à-la-Crosse had experienced drastic ecological erosion since 1846: "At that time it was all dark forest. Today, alas, the forest is nearly gone and all that is left is a bare, desolate, sunburnt beach with its sterile sand hills that the wind scatters across the entire peninsula." ASGM, Agnès, "Annales de l'établissement des Sœurs Grises à l'Île à la Crosse," 2:195–96; SHSB, "Codex historicus, 1845–1897," 9.

115 PAA, O.M.I. Collection, Accession 84.400, Item 928, Box 33, Grandin to Lawrence Clarke, Saint-Laurent de Grandin, October 14, 1884. Grandin had been concerned about this depletion of natural resources for at least four years before writing to Clarke. In 1880, for instance, the bishop observed that "this entire peninsula is now cleared and . . . one can no longer find firewood; farm animals can barely survive here during the winter months." PAA, O.M.I. Collection, Accession 84.400, Vol. 5, Box 35, Grandin, "Notes privées sur les missions et les missionnaires du diocèse de St-Albert," 1868–1884, 18. Information on Lawrence Clarke and his employment history with the HBC (1851–90) is available online through the Hudson's Bay Company Archives: http://www. gov.mb.ca/chc/archives/hbca/biographical/c/clarke_lawrence.pdf (accessed 18 May 2016).

116 The most detailed eyewitness account of the evacuation was written by Sister Langelier and appears in ASGM, "Sur le bord de la Rivière aux Anglais, 19 Mai 1885," Circulaire mensuelle adressée aux diverses maisons de l'Institut 12 (July 1885): 251–58. Pénard also produced a detailed account of the evacuation based on the recollections of Father Joseph Rapet, Father Louis Dauphin, Brother Félix-Victor Marcilly, Brother Fabien Labelle, and Brother Auguste Némoz. Pénard's account appears in SHSB, "Codex historicus, 1845–1897," 192–202.

117 Information on Roderick Ross's employment history and residence at Île-à-la-Crosse (as Factor in charge of the English River District, 1884–85) is available

online through the Hudson's Bay Company Archives: http://www.gov.mb.ca/
chc/archives/hbca/biographical/r/ross_roderick1857-1889.pdf (accessed 18 May
2016).

118 Writing in 1898, Pénard asserted that the origins of the "day-student system"
at Notre-Dame du Sacré-Cœur could be traced directly to the "Hegira to Île
Sainte-Croix" in April–May 1885: "This escapade wasted many of the mission's
resources. After returning from Île Sainte-Croix, the missionaries realized that
it would be absolutely impossible to feed and board all of the children whom
they had returned to their families before the departure.... The school therefore
continued operating [primarily as a day school], but the mission's expenses were
reduced by more than half." SHSB, "Codex historicus, 1845–1897," 201.

119 "Lettre du R.P. Rapet, supérieur de l'Ile-à-la-Crosse. Mission Saint-Jean-
Baptiste, l'Ile-à-la-Crosse, le 1ᵉʳ janvier 1889," *Missions de la Congrégation des
missionnaires oblats de Marie Immaculée* 106 (June 1889): 172.

120 ASGM, updates from various daughter houses, Circulaire mensuelle adressée
aux diverses maisons de l'Institut 11 (September 1888): 161–62; ASGM, untitled
excerpt from Agnès's letter, Circulaire mensuelle adressée aux diverses maisons
de l'Institut 14 (January and February 1889): 232; SHSB, "Codex historicus,
1845–1897," 214.

121 SHSB, "Codex historicus, 1845–1897," 214.

122 "Vicariat de la Saskatchewan. Rapport de Mᵍʳ Pascal, vicaire apostolique,"
Missions de la Congrégation des missionnaires oblats de Marie Immaculée 121 (March
1893): 18, 21; RCRHC/Prop. de la Foi, microfilm X, 10846, Albert Pascal to
the Central Councils of l'Œuvre de la Propagation de la Foi, Prince Albert,
3 December 1895; PAA, O.M.I. Collection, Accession 71.220, Item 77, Box 2,
"Rapport du Vicariat de Saskatchewan," Prince Albert, February 1898; "Lettre
du R.P. Pénard au T.R.P. Général," *Missions de la Congrégation des missionnaires
oblats de Marie Immaculée* 151 (September 1900): 261.

123 It should be noted, however, that Île-à-la-Crosse was not included in Treaty Eight
negotiations. Treaty Eight was intended to cover areas disrupted by the Klondike
gold rush (1896–98). Because of its location east of the principal thoroughfares
to the Yukon, Île-à-la-Crosse was excluded from the Treaty Commissioner's
itinerary. Not until the signing of Treaty Ten in 1906 was the Île-à-la-Crosse
area brought under treaty. See especially SHSB, "Codex historicus, 1898–1928,"
4; Abel, *Drum Songs*, 181; Coates and Morrison, "Treaty Research Report: Treaty
No. 10 (1906)," 12–13, 17, 21, 24; Madill, "Treaty Research Report: Treaty Eight
(1899)," 6, 29, 38, 50.

124 ASGM, "Ile à la Crosse," Circulaire mensuelle adressée aux diverses maisons de
l'Institut 13 (March and April 1898): 621–22; SHSB, "Codex historicus, 1845–1897,"
295; "Lettre du R.P. Pénard au T.R.P. Général," *Missions de la Congrégation des
missionnaires oblats de Marie Immaculée* 151 (September 1900): 261. Beginning
in 1883, the Department of Indian Affairs sponsored two distinct categories of
residential institutions—industrial schools and boarding schools. The former
were large establishments providing training in industrial skills and trades. They
were generally located away from reserves. Boarding schools were smaller, more
modest institutions that served as feeders for industrial schools. Boarding schools
were generally located in closer proximity to reserves and were operated under
the auspices of the Catholic, Anglican, Presbyterian, and Methodist Churches.
In 1923, the Department of Indian Affairs fused industrial schools and boarding

schools into a single administrative category—residential schools. See especially Huel, *Proclaiming the Gospel*, 123–45, 148; Miller, *Shingwauk's Vision*, 104, 114–41; Miller, "The State, the Church, and Indian Residential Schools in Canada," 110–11, 114.

125 "Lettre du R.P. Pénard au T.R.P. Général," *Missions de la Congrégation des missionnaires oblats de Marie Immaculée* 151 (September 1900): 261. See also SHSB, "Codex historicus, 1845–1897," 295.

Chapter 4: Oblates and the Categorization of Indigeneity

1   On the collaborative relationship between missionaries and practitioners of the human sciences in the second half of the nineteenth century, see especially Cinnamon, "Missionary Expertise, Social Science, and the Uses of Ethnographic Knowledge in Colonial Gabon"; Cole, "The Origins of Canadian Anthropology, 1850–1910"; Harries, "Anthropology"; Porter, "Religion, Missionary Enthusiasm, and Empire," 240–41; Staum, "Nature and Nurture in French Ethnography and Anthropology," 475; Stocking, *Victorian Anthropology*, 79–109.

2   Smithsonian Institution Archives [hereafter SIA], Record Unit 7215, Box 13, Fort Simpson, Robert Kennicott [Smithsonian naturalist] to Spencer Fullerton Baird [Assistant Secretary of the Smithsonian], 23 March 1860; "Report of the Secretary," *Annual Report of the Board of Regents of the Smithsonian Institution* (1861), 41; SHSB, Fonds Taché, T1572–T1577, George Gibbs [Smithsonian ethnologist and philologist] to Taché, Washington, DC, 9 August 1862; "Proceedings of the Regents," *Annual Report of the Board of Regents of the Smithsonian Institution* (1863), 87–89; George Gibbs, "The Intermixture of Races," *Annual Report of the Board of Regents of the Smithsonian Institution* (1865), 373–77; SIA, Record Unit 7002, Box 57, Folder 5, Baird, "List of Correspondents in Hudson Bay Region," 2 February 1872. This collaborative relationship was forged as a consequence of Robert Kennicott's three-year expedition through the subarctic boreal forest region (1859–62)—an expedition sponsored in part by the Smithsonian Institution, the University of Michigan, and the HBC. With special permission from Governor George Simpson, Kennicott enlisted the assistance of several HBC officers as well as Catholic and Protestant missionaries in collecting specimens of natural history and in accumulating ethnographic data on Indigenous peoples. In the process, he established an expansive network of collectors and correspondents for the Smithsonian in Rupert's Land and the North-Western Territory. See especially SIA, Record Unit 561, Box 1, George Simpson Folder (unnumbered), Simpson to "Gentlemen," Lachine, 30 April 1860; SIA, Record Unit 7221, Box 1, Folders 1 and 2, Bernard Rogan Ross's notebooks, 1860–1861; Lindsay, "The Hudson's Bay Company-Smithsonian Connection"; Lindsay, *Modern Beginnings of Subarctic Ornithology*, ix–xxii.

3   See for instance Émile Petitot, "De la prétendue origine orientale des Algonquins," *Bulletins de la Société d'anthropologie de Paris* (1884), 248–56; "Discussion sur des contes analogues répandus en diverses contrées," ibid., 265–71; Pilling, *Bibliography of the Athapascan Languages*, 77–83. There is a profound irony in the fact that the Société d'anthropologie de Paris drew on Oblate knowledge. As Martin Staum and Jean-Claude Wartelle have noted, the Société became increasingly dominated by militant atheists and philosophical materialists after the death of its founder, Paul Broca (1824–80). Many of these anthropologists rejected the notion that *sauvages* were adaptable and civilizable—a notion at the very core

of the Oblate apostolate. Staum, "Nature and Nurture in French Ethnography and Anthropology," 477–78, 492–93; Wartelle, "La Société d'anthropologie de Paris de 1859 à 1920," 143–44, 161–62, 164.

4 Dawson, *Report on the Exploration of the Country between Lake Superior and the Red River Settlement*, 10. On Dawson and the Canadian Exploring Expedition, see also ibid., passim; Arthur, "Simon James Dawson"; Huel, *Archbishop A.-A. Taché of St. Boniface*, 52, 69–71. A French-language version of Taché's report to Dawson was published in the Oblates' periodical: "Lettre de Mgr Taché à M. Dawson. Rivière-Rouge, le 7 février 1859," *Missions de la Congrégation des missionnaires oblats de Marie Immaculée* 6 (June 1863): 146–81.

5 Taché, *Esquisse sur le Nord-Ouest de l'Amérique*, 3–5. This publication also appeared serially in the Oblates' periodical: "Esquisse sur le Nord-Ouest de l'Amérique, par Mgr Taché, Évêque de Saint-Boniface," *Missions de la Congrégation des missionnaires oblats de Marie Immaculée* 29–32 (March, June, September, and December 1869); Huel, *Archbishop A.-A. Taché of St. Boniface*, 99–101, 363n 138.

6 "Esquisse sur le Nord-Ouest de l'Amérique, par Mgr Taché, Évêque de Saint-Boniface," *Missions de la Congrégation des missionnaires oblats de Marie Immaculée* 31 (September 1869): 217–85.

7 Carrière, "Contributions des missionnaires à la sauvegarde de la culture indienne." Among other works inventoried in this article, Carrière lists eleven published dictionaries, 181 unpublished dictionaries, twelve published grammars and seventy-six unpublished grammars involving twenty-six Indigenous languages in present-day northern and western Canada. For subsequent acknowledgements of the Oblates' role as purveyors of knowledge of Indigenous peoples, see especially Choquette, *Oblate Assault*, 59, 65; Huel, *Proclaiming the Gospel*, 30–31, 96, 272; McCarthy, *From the Great River to the Ends of the Earth*, 20, 22, 79, 170–71.

8 McCarthy, *From the Great River to the Ends of the Earth*, 20. It should be noted that Petitot also saw vestiges of Judaism in Dene birthing, marriage, and burial practices as well as in certain seasonal ceremonies. Moreover, he suggested that there were a number of linguistic analogies between Hebrew and Chipewyan. See especially Émile Petitot, "Étude sur la nation montagnaise," *Annales de la Propagation de la Foi des Provinces de Québec et Montréal* (1871), 41–47. If—as McCarthy claims—some of Petitot's *confrères* rejected his theory about the Jewish origins of the Dene, other Oblates endorsed it. For instance, in his personal memoirs (1898), Bishop Grandin asserted that the Chipewyan descended either from "the Hebrews" or from "a people closely associated with them." The bishop noted that Chipewyan oral tradition contained vague traces of stories of the Flood and Noah's Ark, the sale of Esau's birthright to Jacob, and the epic journey of Tobias and Raphael. PAA, O.M.I. Collection, Accession 84.400, Item 957, Box 33, "Notes et souvenirs de Mgr Grandin (Repris à la demande de Mgr Langevin par lettre du 28 nov. 1897, rédaction commencée en mars 1898)," 107–10.

9 On the "Lost Tribes of Israel" and their conceptual role in modern Christian mission projects, see especially Goldman, *God's Sacred Tongue*, 15–18, 93; Kirsch, "Lost Tribes," 59–60.

10 Taché, *Vingt années de missions*, 13–14. For his part, Oblate Superior General Eugène de Mazenod had also described the inhabitants of Île-à-la-Crosse as *des sauvages* in his account of Taché's early ministry there: "The ever-happy Father Taché . . . has departed with another priest [Laflèche] to proclaim Jesus Christ

on an island inhabited by *sauvages* about 300 leagues from Saint-Boniface. The island is called La Crosse." "À Mgr I. Bourget, évêque de Montréal. Marseille, le 20 janvier 1847," *Bx Eugène de Mazenod . . . Lettres aux correspondants d'Amérique, 1841–1850*, 117.

11   "Cinquième lettre de Mgr Taché à sa mère, pendant son second séjour à l'Ile-à-la-Crosse. Mission de Sᵗ-Jean-Baptiste, 26 mai 1854," *Les Cloches de Saint-Boniface* 34, no. 5 (May 1935): 126. Henri Faraud had produced a very similar assessment of the inhabitants of Île-à-la-Crosse three years earlier: "Lettre du R.P. Faraud, Missionnaire Oblat de Marie Immaculée, à un Prêtre de la même Congrégation, Athabaskaw, 20 avril, 1851," *Annales de la Propagation de la Foi* 24 (1852): 221–23.

12   Champagne, *Les débuts de la mission dans le Nord-Ouest Canadien*, 174, 195, 197, 199, 201, 204; Champagne, "Mission et civilisation dans l'Ouest canadien," 341–43; McCarthy, *From the Great River to the Ends of the Earth*, xviii, 159, 181; Plongeron, "Affirmation et transformations d'une 'civilisation chrétienne,'" 10–11.

13   These baptisms are recorded in the "Registre des Forts-des-Prairies"—the sacramental register in which Thibault documented his ministrations at Lac-Sainte-Anne, Fort Edmonton, Fort Pitt, Fort Carlton, Rocky Mountain House, Dog Pound Creek, and several other locations along the North Saskatchewan River and in the foothills from 1842 to 1851. The list of baptisms administered at Île-à-la-Crosse in May 1845 begins with baptism #849 (Julie Charbon) and ends with baptism #1066 (Michel l'Homatsho). PAA, O.M.I. Collection, Accession 71.220, Item 5214, Box 255, "Forts des Prairies—Registre des baptêmes, mariages et sépultures, 1842–1851," 83–99.

14   The original sacramental register of Saint-Jean-Baptiste was destroyed by fire on 1 March 1867. These figures were quoted in Taché's letter to S.J. Dawson (1859) and were prefaced with the following assurance: "I copied these figures personally from the abovementioned registers during my last visit [to the interior missions] in the summer of 1856." "Lettre de Mᵍʳ Taché à M. Dawson. Rivière-Rouge, le 7 février 1859," *Missions de la Congrégation des missionnaires oblats de Marie Immaculée* 6 (June 1863): 173. Of the estimated 617 baptisms administered at Île-à-la-Crosse between 1845 and 1856, one merits particular attention because it reflects the sense of urgency with which Oblates dispensed the sacrament. In the winter of 1852–53, Taché administered extreme unction to a dying *sauvagesse* who was six months pregnant. Immediately after she expired, Taché asked another woman in attendance to remove the foetus from its dead mother's womb so that he could baptize it. The woman—although initially resistant—ultimately obliged for "motives of religion." Taché administered the sacrament to the exposed foetus, which died shortly thereafter. "Deuxième lettre de Mgr Taché à sa mère pendant son second séjour à l'Ile-à-la-Crosse. Mission Sᵗ-Jean-Baptiste, Ile à le [*sic*] Crosse, 2 mai 1853," *Les Cloches de Saint-Boniface* 34, no. 8 (August 1935): 205–6.

15   In his personal memoirs—written forty-four years after his arrival at Île-à-la-Crosse—Grandin identified baptism as the first step in a long-term Christianizing process: "I see a major difference between a Christian *sauvage* and a Christianized *sauvage*. Baptism makes him a Christian, but he will continue to feel the effects of his pagan education for a long time afterwards." PAA, O.M.I. Collection, Accession 84.400, Item 957, Box 33, "Notes et souvenirs de Mgr Grandin (Repris à la demande de Mgr Langevin par lettre du 28 nov.

1897, rédaction commencée en mars 1898)," 61. The seven sacraments of the
Catholic Church are baptism, confirmation, the eucharist, penance, anointing
of the sick (or extreme unction), matrimony, and holy orders. See *Catechism of
the Catholic Church*, 239, 311–420.

16 According to Acts 2:1–6, the Apostles were enabled to evangelize the world
through the Gift of Tongues (dispensed by the Holy Spirit at Pentecost).

17 "Le sermon provençal," *Missions de la Congrégation des missionnaires oblats de
Marie Immaculée* 254 (June–September 1935): 421; Lamirande, "À propos des
premières missions d'Eugène de Mazenod," 7–8; Lamirande, "Les pauvres et
les âmes les plus abandonnées d'après Mgr de Mazenod," 6; Ortolan, *Les Oblats
de Marie Immaculée*, 1:77; Quéré, "Monseigneur de Mazenod et le missionnaire
oblat," 247–48. Mazenod had been convinced of the need for a vernacular-
based ministry in Provence since at least 1814. See "Lettres choisies de Mgr de
Mazenod," *Missions de la Congrégation des missionnaires oblats de Marie Immaculée*
305 (June 1962): 202. For his part, Mazenod was renowned for his mastery of
Provençal and for his eloquent preaching in that dialect. See especially "Oraison
funèbre de Monseigneur Charles-Joseph-Eugène de Mazenod, Évêque de
Marseille, prononcée le 4 juillet 1861 dans l'Église de Saint-Martin (Cathédrale
provisoire), à Marseille, par Mgr Jeancard, Évêque de Cérame," *Missions de
la Congrégation des missionnaires oblats de Marie Immaculée* 65 (March 1879):
119; "Témoignage de Frédéric Mistral sur Mgr de Mazenod," *Missions de la
Congrégation des missionnaires oblats de Marie Immaculée* 241 (December 1930):
502; Leflon, *Eugène de Mazenod*, 2:100–101, 121, 123.

18 "Instruction de Monseigneur de Mazenod relative aux missions étrangères,"
174. See also "Aux pères Végréville et Moulin, et au f. Dubé, à l'Île à la Crosse.
Marseille, le 13 décembre 1859," *Bx Eugène de Mazenod...Lettres aux correspondants
d'Amérique, 1851–1860*, 156.

19 Benoit, "Mission at Ile-à-la-Crosse," 44; Benoît, *Vie de Mgr Taché*, 1:113. In a
letter to his mother dated 31 July 1846, Taché identified these oarsmen-tutors as
"three Montagnais" from Île-à-la-Crosse. He also recorded his first impression
of their language: "It is a veritable jargon which, in terms of pronunciation,
presents difficulties that can barely be comprehended before hearing it.... Father
Laflèche has recently told me that he fears uprooting his uvula on account of
the contortions of the tongue that this language demands." Quoted in Benoît,
Vie de Mgr Taché, 1:113.

20 PAA, O.M.I. Collection, Accession 84.400, Item 957, Box 33, "Notes et souvenirs
de Mgr Grandin (Repris à la demande de Mgr Langevin par lettre du 28 nov.
1897, rédaction commencée en mars 1898)," 51–52; Benoît, *Vie de Mgr Taché*,
1:126–27; Huel, *Archbishop A.-A. Taché of St. Boniface*, 26; Huel, *Proclaiming the
Gospel*, 30.

21 "Extrait d'une lettre de Mgr Taché, Vicaire apostolique de la Baie d'Hudson,
à sa mère. Mission de St-Jean-Baptiste, Ile à la Crosse, 4 janvier 1851," *Annales
de la Propagation de la Foi* 24 (1852): 340. See also Benoît, *Vie de Mgr Taché*,
1:126–27.

22 "Extrait d'une lettre de Mgr Taché, Vicaire apostolique de la Baie d'Hudson,
à sa mère. Mission de St-Jean-Baptiste, Ile à la Crosse, 4 janvier 1851," *Annales
de la Propagation de la Foi* 24 (1852): 340–41.

23 It should be noted, however, that Faraud's reputation as a linguist was a source of
acrimony among Oblates. Fuelling this acrimony was the brazen self-promotion

evident in Faraud's autobiography, *Dix-huit ans chez les sauvages* (1866)—co-written with his nephew, Fortuné-François Fernand-Michel. This work contains several passages trumpeting Faraud's "mastery" of Indigenous languages. In one such passage, a Chipewyan is quoted as saying of Faraud: "He speaks better than we do, so he is more of a man than we are." Fernand-Michel, *Dix-huit ans chez les sauvages*, 111. The Oblate General Administration expressed dismay at the egotistical tone of the work. SHSB, Fonds Taché, T3663–T3665, Sardou to Taché, Paris, 30 November 1865. For his part, Bishop Grandin attempted to keep the work hidden from the Oblates in his jurisdiction for fear that they should be scandalized by its many inflated claims. SHSB, Fonds Taché, T4255–T4259, Grandin to Taché, Île-à-la-Crosse, 25 September 1866.

24 "Lettre du R.P. Faraud, Missionnaire Oblat de Marie Immaculée, à un Prêtre de la même Congrégation, Athabaskaw, 20 avril, 1851," *Annales de la Propagation de la Foi* 24 (1852): 222–23; Fernand-Michel, *Dix-huit ans chez les sauvages*, 81, 86, 119–22; Benoît, *Vie de Mgr Taché*, 1:154, 359; Huel, *Archbishop A.-A. Taché of St. Boniface*, 28, 41, 61–62; Huel, *Proclaiming the Gospel*, 30–31. Faraud's dictionaries, grammars, and vocabularies were continually circulated through the Oblate mission network in the 1850s, '60s and '70s. See especially AD, HEC 2500. P96C 3, Prosper Légeard to Augustin Maisonneuve, Île-à-la-Crosse, 16 January 1871; AD, HEC 2500. P96C 4, Légeard to Maisonneuve, Île-à-la-Crosse, 9 April 1871; AD, HEC 2500. P96C 15, Légeard to Maisonneuve, Île-à-la-Crosse, 16 January 1877; AD, HEC 2500. P96C 17, Légeard to Maisonneuve, Île-à-la-Crosse, 1 May 1877.

25 SHSB, Fonds Taché, T0295–T0296, Jean Séguin to Taché, Île-à-la-Crosse, 9 January 1861; ibid., T1492–T1495, Julien Moulin to Taché, Île-à-la-Crosse, 17 June 1862; ibid., T1721–T1724, Moulin to Taché, Île-à-la-Crosse, 16 November 1862; ibid., T1921–T1924, Moulin to Taché, Île-à-la-Crosse, 9 January 1863; ibid., T2023–T2029, Moulin to Taché, Île-à-la-Crosse, 8 April 1863.

26 SHSB, Fonds Taché, T1721–T1724, Moulin to Taché, Île-à-la-Crosse, 16 November 1862.

27 SHSB, Fonds Taché, T2229–T2237, Faraud to Taché, Île-à-la-Crosse, 1 June 1863. Grandin and Faraud had both issued pessimistic appraisals of Moulin's progress over the previous two years. See especially ibid., T0492–T0499, Grandin to Taché, Île-à-la-Crosse, 15 May 1861; ibid., T1097–T1100, Faraud to Taché, Île-à-la-Crosse, 4 January 1862; ibid., T1401–T1404, Faraud to Taché, Île-à-la-Crosse, 19 May 1862; ibid., T1523–T1526, Faraud to Taché, Île-à-la-Crosse, 22 July 1862; ibid., T1725–T1728, Faraud to Taché, Île-à-la-Crosse, 16 November 1862.

28 This situation appears to have remained relatively consistent for the first five years of Moulin's active ministry at Saint-Jean-Baptiste and its satellite missions (1859–64). See especially AD, HE 2221. T12Z 178, Moulin to Taché, Portage La Loche, 31 July 1860; SHSB, Fonds Taché, T1428–T1431, Moulin to Taché, Île-à-la-Crosse, 29 May 1862; ibid., T1492–T1495, Moulin to Taché, Île-à-la-Crosse, 17 July 1862; ibid., T2575–T2577, Moulin to Joseph Lestanc, Île-à-la-Crosse, 9 January 1864; ibid., T2814–T2816, Moulin to Taché, Île-à-la-Crosse, 29 May 1864. See also Carrière, *Dictionnaire biographique*, 2:410.

29 PAA, O.M.I. Collection, Accession 84.400, Item 957, Box 33, "Notes et souvenirs de Mgr Grandin (Repris à la demande de Mgr Langevin par lettre du 28 nov. 1897, rédaction commencée en mars 1898)," 54. See also RCRHC/É.G., vol.

6, Grandin, "Notice sur le diocèse de S. Albert," 31. Grandin's difficulties were likely exacerbated by his pronounced speech impediment—an affliction that had already hampered his missionary ambitions at least once before. Upon leaving the Grand séminaire du Mans in 1851, Grandin had sought admission to the Séminaire des missions étrangères in Paris in hopes of becoming a missionary in Asia. However, his application was rejected because the directors of the Séminaire des missions étrangères considered his speech impediment too great an obstacle to acquiring Asian languages. Grandin subsequently turned to the Oblates of Mary Immaculate and was accepted into the congregation on 28 December 1851. See Jonquet, *Mgr Grandin*, 21–25.

30   SHSB, Fonds Taché, T3068–T3078, Grandin to Taché and Florent Vandenberghe, Île-à-la-Crosse, 12 January 1865; PAA, O.M.I. Collection, Accession 84.400, Item 923, Box 32, Grandin to Isidore Clut, Île-à-la-Crosse, 7 July 1865; ibid., Grandin to Clut, Île-à-la-Crosse, 21 August 1865; PAA, O.M.I. Collection, Accession 84.400, Item 912, Box 32, Grandin to Alphonse Gasté, Saint-Boniface, 27 April 1867; SHSB, "Codex historicus, 1845–1897," 180. Other Oblates made similar admissions. In 1872, for instance, Father Prosper Légeard reported to the Oblate General Administration that he and his *confrères* devoted the winter months to studying local languages, adding: "We normally take advantage of this quiet time to apply ourselves to the study of the *sauvage* languages spoken in his region, *languages that we rarely master even through long and difficult study*" (my italics). Quoted in SHSB, "Codex historicus, 1845–1897," 113.

31   AD, G LPP 2199, Légeard to Grandin, Île-à-la-Crosse, 11 January 1869. See also Soullier, *Vie du Révérend Père Légeard*, 53–54, 57; SHSB, "Codex historicus, 1845–1897," 129, 140, 205. See also Erickson, "At the Cultural and Religious Crossroads," 132; Lesage, *Capitale d'une solitude*, 123.

32   AD, HEC 2500. P96C 8, Légeard to Maisonneuve, Île-à-la-Crosse, 12 January 1874; PAA, O.M.I. Collection, Accession 84.400, Vol. 5, Box 35, Grandin, "Notes privées sur les missions et les missionnaires du diocèse de St-Albert," 1868–1884, 130–33; PAA, O.M.I. Collection, Accession 84.400, Item 916, Box 32, Grandin to Albert Lacombe, "sur le lac Castor," 28 July 1875; SHSB, "Codex historicus, 1845–1897," 181, 204–5, 208; Carrière, *Dictionnaire biographique*, 2:302.

33   Quoted in Lesage, *Capitale d'une solitude*, 123. According to Pénard, this collaboration produced mixed results, as Catherine imparted words and turns of phrase that were becoming obsolete by the late nineteenth century. Le Goff's hymns and sermons were therefore of little use in the local ministry by the time of Pénard's arrival (1890): "This aged Catherine was of great service to Father Legoff [*sic*] in the composition of all his Montaignais works. She can only be criticized for one thing: this elderly woman loved using the language of her childhood, that is to say the <u>old</u> Montagnais, and her favourite expressions were no longer used in conversation and so were no longer understood by the majority of Montagnais. She made Father Legoff fill his books with these expressions that, though often beautiful, are now completely outdated and almost incomprehensible." SHSB, "Codex historicus, 1845–1897," 205. The underlined word ["le <u>vieux</u> Montagnais"] appears in the original document.

34   According to the *liber status animarum* of Saint-Jean-Baptiste, Marie-Rose and members of her family were known variously by the Cree surname Piwapiskus (or Piwabiskus), by its French translation (Petit-Fer), and by its English translation (Iron). SHSB, "Arbre généalogique Île-à-la-Crosse" (Liber animarum), "Famille Piwabiskus," 150–58.

35 AD, G LPP 2200, Légeard to Joseph Fabre, Île-à-la-Crosse, 13 January 1870; AD, HPF 4191. C75R 177, Légeard to "Ma très honorée et Vénérée Mère," Île-à-la-Crosse, 20 December 1877; Soullier, *Vie du Révérend Père Légeard*, 59, 66; SHSB, "Arbre généalogique Île-à-la-Crosse" (Liber animarum), "Famille Piwabiskus," 150; SHSB, "Codex historicus, 1845–1897," 228–29. Marie-Rose Piwapiskus lived into her nineties and died in the Grey Nuns' hospital at Île-à-la-Crosse on 5 June 1931. See Lesage, *Capitale d'une solitude*, 106.

36 PAA, O.M.I. Collection, Accession 84.400, Item 986, Box 34, Grandin, "Missions et Résidences du diocèse de St. Albert, décembre 1872"; AD, G LPP 2203, Légeard to "Ma très honorée Sœur," Île-à-la-Crosse, 27 July 1875; Soullier, *Vie du Révérend Père Légeard*, 66; SHSB, "Codex historicus, 1845–1897," 118, 136–37.

37 "Missions d'Amérique: Nouvelle Bretagne, Diocèse de Saint-Albert," *Annales de la Propagation de la Foi* 49 (1877): 444. Légeard's report on the day school at Canoe Lake is quoted in SHSB, "Codex historicus, 1845–1897," 152–53.

38 The canonical term "Ordinary Time" refers to all parts of the Roman Catholic liturgical calendar that do not fall under the seasons of Advent, Christmas, Lent, or Easter. See especially *Catechism of the Catholic Church*, 285, 301–4.

39 SHSB, Fonds Taché, T2680–T2683, Moulin to Taché, Île-à-la-Crosse, 10 March 1864; ibid., T3068–T3078, Grandin to Taché and Vandenberghe, Île-à-la-Crosse, 12 January 1865; SHSB, "Codex historicus, 1845–1897," 113–14, 122, 133. Moulin's letter reveals that Oblates taught catechism both at the mission and at the fort: "I am extremely busy here. I teach catechism three times nearly every day: once for the schoolchildren, once in Cree for the people of the mission, and once in Montagnais. I am far from being fluent in the montagnais language. . . . I go twice a week to the fort to teach catechism there."

40 Soullier, *Vie du Révérend Père Légeard*, 91; SHSB, "Codex historicus, 1845–1897," 133. On the timing and duration of Lent, see especially *Catechism of the Catholic Church*, 138, 361.

41 It should be noted, however, that *missions* were occasionally disrupted by unforeseen circumstances. In September 1862, for instance, the usual exercises of the *mission de l'automne* were all but cancelled because of the outbreak of illness among Cree- and Chipewyan-speaking neophytes camped at Île-à-la-Crosse. SHSB, Fonds Taché, T1725–T1728, Faraud to Taché, Île-à-la-Crosse, 16 November 1862. In 1873, some devotional exercises of the *mission du printemps* were cancelled because of dangerously high water levels and flooding at the mission site. SHSB, "Codex historicus de l'Île-à-la-Crosse, 1845–1897," 129.

42 ASGM, Agnès, "Annales de l'établissement des Sœurs Grises à l'Île à la Crosse," 2:246. Agnès's account features a lively, first-hand description of the transformation that Île-à-la-Crosse typically underwent at the time of the *mission*: "Gathered on the shore, they [Cree and Chipewyan families] all greet each other with the customary embrace. . . . After these friendly exchanges, the women begin unloading the baggage from the canoes. A baby sleeps soundly in one of these light craft, snuggled in among two, three, or four dogs. . . . In less than an hour, the tents are all up and covered with pine branches to make them waterproof. . . . Then a good fire is lit. Our Island—ordinarily so empty, so still—acquires an altogether different appearance. It reverberates with sounds of laughter and play late into the night. Our rest is disrupted by the sounds of women singing, children crying, boys and men calling. Suddenly, from far away, a fusillade announces new arrivals. Family members and old friends come ashore and are greeted with joyful embracing." Ibid., 2:245–46.

43 SHSB, Fonds Taché, T0586–T0588, Végréville to Taché, Île-à-la-Crosse, 12 June 1861. The title *Pange Lingua* refers to "Pange Lingua Gloriosi Corporis Mysterium" ("Sing, my tongue, the mystery of His glorious Body")—a Latin hymn written by Saint Thomas Aquinas for the Feast of Corpus Christi. See especially *Breviarium Romanum*, 73–74. Grandin's account of this particular *mission du printemps* was transcribed by Pénard in SHSB, "Codex historicus, 1845–1897," 73–74. For other discussions of the schedule employed during the biannual *mission* at Saint-Jean-Baptiste, see especially AD, HE 2221.T12Z 178, Moulin to Taché, Île-à-la-Crosse, 31 July 1860; SHSB, Fonds Taché, T2814–T2816, Moulin to Taché, Île-à-la-Crosse, 29 May 1864; ibid., T3303–T3305, Moulin to Taché, Île-à-la-Crosse, 30 May 1865; AD, HPF 4191. C75R 177, Légeard to "Ma très honorée et Vénérée Mère," Île-à-la-Crosse, 20 December 1877; SHSB, "Codex historicus, 1845–1897," 92, 116, 129–30, 145, 155–56.

44 PAA, O.M.I. Collection, Accession 84.400, Item 957, Box 33, "Notes et souvenirs de Mgr Grandin (Repris à la demande de Mgr Langevin par lettre du 28 nov. 1897, rédaction commencée en mars 1898)," 61–62; Abel, *Drum Songs*, 117–18; Huel, *Proclaiming the Gospel*, 30, 33, 44; McCarthy, *From the Great River to the Ends of the Earth*, 80. On James Evans and his invention of the Cree syllabic system in the early 1840s, see especially Maclean, *James Evans*, 160–74; Young, *Apostle of the North*, 181–96.

45 PAA, O.M.I. Collection, Accession 84.400, Item 957, Box 33, "Notes et souvenirs de Mgr Grandin (Repris à la demande de Mgr Langevin par lettre du 28 nov. 1897, rédaction commencée en mars 1898)," 62. See also ibid., 63–65; SHSB, "Codex historicus, 1845–1897," 116.

46 AD, HEC 2500. P96C 3, Légeard to Maisonneuve, Île-à-la-Crosse, 16 January 1871; AD, HEC 2500. P96C 4, Légeard to Maisonneuve, Île-à-la-Crosse, 9 April 1871; AD, HEC 2500. P96C 5, Légeard to Maisonneuve, Île-à-la-Crosse, 8 January 1872; AD, HEC 2500. P96C 8, Légeard to Maisonneuve, Île-à-la-Crosse, 12 January 1874. The earliest of these works were printed in France and in Québec under Oblate supervision. By October 1878, however, Légeard had acquired a hand press from French benefactors and was printing devotional literature at Saint-Jean-Baptiste. See especially Lacombe, *Le catéchisme en images pour l'instruction des sauvages*; Lacombe, *Catéchisme en image à l'usage des Indiens*; AD, HEC 2500. P96C 23, Légeard to Maisonneuve, Île-à-la-Crosse, 8 October 1878.

47 "Lettre de Mgr Grandin à MM. les membres des Conseils centraux de l'Œuvre de la Propagation de la Foi. Fort Pitt (mission de Saint-François Régis), 10 janvier 1870," Annales de la Propagation de la Foi 44 (1872): 280, 281.

48 PAA, O.M.I. Collection, Accession 84.400, Vol. 5, Box 35, Grandin, "Notes privées sur les missions et les missionnaires du diocèse de St-Albert," 1868–1884, 18.

49 Between 1868 and 1883, Grandin recognized at least seven different language groups in his ecclesiastical jurisdiction: speakers of Cree, Chipewyan, Blackfoot (subdivided into the dialects of the Blackfoot proper [Siksika], the Blood [Kainai] and the Peigan [Piikani]), French, and English. See especially PAA, O.M.I. Collection, Accession 84.400, Item 973, Box 33, "Renseignements demandés par Mgr Taché sur les missions et les Missionnaires de Mgr Grandin depuis l'érection du vicariat religieux de St Albert 1868 jusqu'en 1872," 1–18; PAA, O.M.I. Collection, Accession 84.400, Item 986, Box 34, Grandin, "Missions et

Résidences du diocèse de St. Albert," Saint-Albert, 1882; PAA, O.M.I. Collection, Accession 84.400, Item 987, Box 34, Grandin, "Liste des missions du diocèse catholique de St. Albert," Saint-Albert, 1883, 3–16. See also Dempsey, *Indian Tribes of Alberta*, 14–15, 22–23, 28–29, 31.

50 PPAA, O.M.I. Collection, Accession 84.400, Item 973, Box 33, "Renseignements demandés par Mgr Taché sur les missions et les Missionnaires de Mgr Grandin depuis l'érection du vicariat religieux de St Albert 1868 jusqu'en 1872," 2–4; PAA, O.M.I. Collection, Accession 84.400, Item 911, Box 32, Grandin to Taché, Fort Cumberland, 30 July 1875; ibid., Grandin to Taché, "sur une île du lac l'Île d'ours," 9 July 1880; PAA, O.M.I. Collection, Accession 84.400, Item 977, Box 33, "Notes sur le commencement du Diocèse de St. Albert," 1884, 6–8.

51 PAA, O.M.I. Collection, Accession 84.400, Vol. 5, Box 35, Grandin, "Notes privées sur les missions et les missionnaires du diocèse de St-Albert," 1868–1884, 14–19, 113, 130–33, 134–35, 220, 229; PAA, O.M.I. Collection, Accession 84.400, Item 922, Box 32, Grandin to Lacombe, Saint-Albert, 26 March 1881; SHSB, "Codex historicus, 1845–1897," 78, 114, 120, 131–32, 140, 153.

52 These initiatives are discussed in Chapter 2. See especially pp. 57–61. See also Tough, *"As Their Natural Resources Fail,"* 17, 52–58, 253, 273–76.

53 AD, G LPP 2202, Légeard to Pierre Aubert [Oblate Assitant General], Île-à-la-Crosse, 3 January 1875; AD, G LPP 2203, Légeard to "Ma très honorée Sœur," Île-à-la-Crosse, 27 July 1875; AD, G LPP 2205, Légeard to Grandin, Île-à-la-Crosse, 13 January 1877; AD, HPF 4191. C75R 177, Légeard to "Ma très honorée et Vénérée Mère," Île-à-la-Crosse, 20 December 1877; SHSB, "Codex historicus, 1845–1897," 131, 146–47, 155, 167, 183–84.

54 SHSB, "Codex historicus, 1845–1897," 147. Légeard's report for 1875 is quoted in ibid., 146–47. See also ibid., 158; AD, G LPP 2202, Légeard to Aubert, Île-à-la-Crosse, 3 January 1875.

55 AD, G LPP 2202, Légeard to Aubert, Île-à-la-Crosse, January 3, 1875. See also AD, HEC 2500. P96C11, Légeard to Maisonneuve, Île-à-la-Crosse, 19 January 1875. In insisting on the nefarious effects of free trade on Cree- and Chipewyan-speaking hunters and their families, Légeard echoed an observation made twelve years earlier by Faraud when free traders had first arrived in the English River District: "Because these free traders are inflating the price of everything, the *sauvages* will eventually believe that their furs are of immense value. Senseless pride is bound to cloud their minds and corrupt them." SHSB, Fonds Taché, T2229–T2237, Faraud to Taché, Île-à-la-Crosse, 1 June 1863.

56 This phrase is quoted from canon 1247 of the Code of Canon Law: "Die dominica aliisque diebus festis de praecepto fideles obligatione tenentur Missam participandi" ("On Sundays and other Holy Days of Obligation, the faithful are obliged to participate in the Mass"). The preceding canon—canon 1246 *§1*— lists the following ten days as Holy Days of Obligation (apart from Sundays): Christmas; Epiphany; the Ascension; Corpus Christi; the Solemnity of Mary, Mother of God; the Feast of the Immaculate Conception; the Assumption of the Blessed Virgin Mary; the Solemnity of Saint Joseph; the Solemnity of Saint Peter and Saint Paul the Apostles; and All Saints Day. See *Code of Canon Law, Latin-English Edition*, 384.

57 See especially AD, HEC 2500. P96C 11, Légeard to Maisonneuve, Île-à-la-Crosse, 19 January 1875; AD, G LPP 2205, Légeard to Grandin, Île-à-la-Crosse, 13 January 1877; AD, HEC 2500. P96C 11, Légeard to Maisonneuve,

Île-à-la-Crosse, 16 January 1877; PAA, O.M.I. Collection, Accession 84.400, Vol. 5, Box 35, Grandin, "Notes privées sur les missions et les missionnaires du diocèse de St-Albert," 1868–1884, 14–15.

58 It should be noted that the term "free people" (*les gens libres*) (as applied by Oblates) was not entirely synonymous with the term "freemen" (as applied by HBC officers in the English River District). According to Macdougall, the term "freemen" was generally applied to former HBC servants who continued to live in the English River District after the completion of their contracts. Although free of contractual obligations to the HBC, freemen performed occasional services for the Company as hunters, trappers, fishermen, and freighters. In contradistinction, the term "free people" was applied to men who lived permanently in the vicinity of Saint-Jean-Baptiste and whose labour was not—and may never have been—claimed by the HBC. In July 1880, Grandin referred to "free people" as the local labour pool from which the Oblates of Saint-Jean-Baptiste could hire short-term workers. PAA, O.M.I. Collection, Accession 84.400, Item 911, Box 32, Grandin to Taché, "sur une île du lac l'Île d'ours," 9 July 1880. See also PAA, O.M.I. Collection, Accession 84.400, Vol. 5, Box 35, Grandin, "Notes privées sur les missions et les missionnaires du diocèse de St-Albert," 1868–1884, 18; Macdougall, "'The Comforts of Married Life,'" 31–34; Macdougall, *One of the Family*, 260; Macdougall, "Socio–Cultural Development and Identity Formation," 167–68; Macdougall, "Wahkootowin," 440, 458.

59 AD, G LPP 2205, Légeard to Grandin, Île-à-la-Crosse, 13 January 1877. Légeard conducted the enumeration in late November and early December 1876. On the geographic distribution of "people of the fort" and "free people" at and around Île-à-la-Crosse, see also AD, HEC 2500. P96C11, Légeard to Maisonneuve, Île-à-la-Crosse, 19 January 1875; PAA, O.M.I. Collection, Accession 84.400, Item 911, Box 32, Grandin to Taché, "sur une île du lac l'Île d'ours," 9 July 1880; PAA, O.M.I. Collection, Accession 84.400, Vol. 5, Box 35, Grandin, "Notes privées sur les missions et les missionnaires du diocèse de St-Albert," 1868–1884, 18.

60 AD, G LPP 2205, Légeard to Grandin, Île-à-la-Crosse, 13 January 1877; AD, HEC 2500. P96C 15, Légeard to Maisonneuve, Île-à-la-Crosse, 16 January 1877; "Missions d'Amérique: Nouvelle Bretagne, Diocèse de Saint-Albert," *Annales de la Propagation de la Foi* 49 (1877): 446–47; SHSB, "Codex historicus, 1845–1897," 122, 131, 133, 174.

61 Quoted in SHSB, "Codex historicus, 1845–1897," 122. On the role of the cemetery at Île-à-la-Crosse in the elaboration and expression of local community identity, see especially Gambell, "Cemetery Spaces of Shxwōwhámel Stó:lō and the Île-à-la-Crosse Métis," 25–50.

62 "Ile à la Crosse. Extrait d'une lettre du Révérend Père Légeard au R.P. Martinet," *Missions de la Congrégation des missionnaires oblats de Marie Immaculée* 59 (September 1877): 314. Légeard's report is also quoted in SHSB, "Codex historicus, 1845–1897," 151–63. The addressee of Légeard's report—Father Aimé Martinet—was Oblate Assistant General and Secretary General. On Martinet and his career in the Oblate General Administration (1867–94), see especially "R.P. Aimé Martinet, assistant général o.m.i.," *Missions de la Congrégation des missionnaires oblats de Marie Immaculée* (1914), 489–92; Huel, *Archbishop A.-A. Taché of St. Boniface*, 280–81.

63 AD, G LPP 2203, Légeard to "Ma très honorée Sœur," Île-à-la-Crosse, 27 July 1875. On the veneration of the Sacred Heart as a local and *métis* devotion, see also "Missions d'Amérique: Nouvelle Bretagne, Diocèse de Saint-Albert," *Annales de la Propagation de la Foi* 49 (1877): 446; SHSB, "Codex historicus, 1845–1897," 155, 159.

64 AD, G LPP 2205, Légeard to Grandin, Île-à-la-Crosse, 13 January 1877; AD, HEC 2500. P96C 15, Légeard to Maisonneuve, Île-à-la-Crosse, 16 January 1877; SHSB, "Codex historicus, 1845–1897," 133, 174.

65 See especially PAA, O.M.I. Collection, Accession 84.400, Item 967, Box 33, "Lettre de Mgr Vital Justin Grandin, O.M.I., Vicaire de la Congrégation des Missionnaires O.M.I. dans le Diocèse de S. Albert et Évêque de ce même diocèse, aux RR. PP. Oblats missionnaires dans le diocèse," Ottawa, 18 November 1887, 2–3; PAA, O.M.I. Collection, Accession 84.400, Item 960, Box 33, "Notes et souvenirs de Mgr Grandin (Repris à la demande de Mgr Langevin par lettre du 28 nov. 1897, rédaction commencée en mars 1898)," 216–18. See also Champagne, *Les débuts de la mission dans le Nord-Ouest Canadien*, 177–79, 181, 184; Champagne, "Mission et civilisation dans l'Ouest canadien," 346–47; Huel, "The Oblates, the Métis, and 1885," 11.

66 PAA, O.M.I. Collection, Accession 84.400, Item 966, Box 33, Grandin "À Sa Grâce Mgr l'Archevêque de Québec et à leurs Grandeurs, Messeigneurs les Évêques de la Provinces de Québec," Ottawa, 29 January 1883, 4–6, 9; PAA, O.M.I. Collection, Accession 84.400, Item 923, Box 32, Grandin to Clut, Prince Albert, 7 August 1884; SHSB, Fonds Taché, T29966–T29973, Grandin to Taché, Grande Prairie, 8 September 1884. See also Huel, *Proclaiming the Gospel*, 209–10.

67 AD, HE 2223 TI 2Z 3, Grandin to Taché, Saint-Laurent-de-Grandin, 14 July 1885; PAA, O.M.I. Collection, Accession 84.400, Item 960, Box 33, "Notes et souvenirs de Mgr Grandin (Repris à la demande de Mgr Langevin par lettre du 28 nov. 1897, rédaction commencée en mars 1898)," 216–17. On the foundation and early history of these three missions—each of which was located on the South Saskatchewan River—see especially PAA, O.M.I. Collection, Accession 84.400, Item 986, Box 34, Grandin, "Missions et Résidences du diocèse de St. Albert," 1882 (numbers 26, 27 and 28); Payment, *"Les gens libres—Otipemisiwak,"* 114–15, 117. On Riel's prophetic leadership and his inauguration of a messianic movement, see especially Bélisle and St-Onge, "Between García Moreno and Chan Santa Cruz," 105–06, 109–112; Flanagan, *Louis "David" Riel*, 57–104, 133–65; Martel, *Le messianisme de Louis Riel*, 211–88. For an account of the conversion to "Riel-ism" of William Henry Jackson (a.k.a. Honoré Jaxon), see Smith, *Honoré Jaxon*, 49, 58, 61–62, 64.

68 "Lettre de Mgr Grandin. Saint-Albert, district d'Alberta, Canada, 12 mai 1885," *Missions de la Congrégation des missionnaires oblats de Marie Immaculée* 91 (September 1885): 310–14; "Vicariat de Saint-Albert. Les martyrs du Nord-Ouest. Lettre de Mgr Grandin au père et à la mère du R.P. Fafard, martyrisé au Lac la Grenouille," *Missions de la Congrégation des missionnaires oblats de Marie Immaculée* 2 (December 1885): 417–30. See also Carrière, *Dictionnaire biographique*, 2:13, 361–62; Carter, *Capturing Women* 58; Le Chevallier, *Batoche*, 99–112.

69 In offering his condolences to the family of Marchand, Grandin attributed the Frog Lake massacre to the same irreligious current that underlay the general persecution of Catholicism in France: "You live, dear sir, in a milieu in which

religion is no doubt represented as contemptible supersition and the priest as the wretched enemy of science and progress.... Such ideas are now widespread in our poor France, and now they have reached us here. They have caused the *sauvages* to steep their hands in human blood, in the blood of priests. Because this way of thinking has come from abroad—from Paris—they believed their actions justified." PAA, O.M.I. Collection, Accession 84.400, Item 927, Box 33, Grandin to "Mr Amb. Marchand" (brother of the slain Oblate), Battleford, 17 July 1885. See also PAA, O.M.I. Collection, Accession 84.400, Item 927, Box 33, Grandin to "la famille Marchand," Saint-Albert, 27 August 1885.

70   PAA, O.M.I. Collection, Accession 71.220, Item 76, Box 2, Grandin, "Extrait du Rapport sur le Vicariat de St. Albert au Chapitre Général de la Congrégation des O.M.I. à Rome," 28 April 1887, 2–3, 8. An edited and abridged version of this report was published later in 1887: "Extrait d'un rapport de Mgr Grandin, Evêque de Saint-Albert, au Supérieur général de la Congrégation des Oblats. Rome, mai 1887." *Annales de la Propagation de la Foi* 60 (1888): 112–23.

71   Huel, "The Oblates, the Métis, and 1885," 20–21, 29; Huel, *Proclaiming the Gospel*, 211–12, 215.

72   In his secondary account of the evacuation of the fort and the mission at Île-à-la-Crosse (published in 1941), Le Chevallier referred to a rumour that Louis Riel was determined to exact revenge on the Grey Nuns for having allowed his sister—Sara Riel (Sister Marguerite-Marie)—to die without proper care a year and a half earlier. See Le Chevallier, *Batoche*, 129. However, neither of the older accounts contains any mention of this rumour: ASGM, Langelier, "Sur le bord de la Rivière aux Anglais, 19 Mai 1885," Circulaire mensuelle adressée aux diverses maisons de l'Institut 12 (July 1885): 251–58; SHSB, "Codex historicus, 1845–1897," 192–202.

73   ASGM, Langelier, "Sur le bord de la Rivière aux Anglais, 19 Mai 1885," 252–55, 259; SHSB, "Codex historicus, 1845–1897," 193–95, 197–98; Lesage, *Capitale d'une solitude*, 131. Paquette was the founder and resident Oblate superior of Notre-Dame-de-Pontmain mission on Muskeg Lake. See Carrière, *Dictionnaire biographique*, 3:42–43.

74   ASGM, Langelier, "Sur le bord de la Rivière aux Anglais, 19 Mai 1885," 252, 255–56; SHSB, "Codex historicus, 1845–1897," 196, 198–200.

75   Quoted in ASGM, Langelier, "Sur le bord de la Rivière aux Anglais, 19 Mai 1885," 257. According to Pénard, the island refuge was dubbed "Île Sainte-Croix" in reference to this large wooden cross. The island was still known by this name when Pénard wrote his account thirteen years later. See SHSB, "Codex historicus, 1845–1897," 200.

76   SHSB, "Codex historicus, 1845–1897," 193. The crossed-out words ["~~les représailles~~"] appear in the original document.

77   Ibid., 194, 196–98, 201.

78   Ibid., 201. See also ASGM, Langelier, "Sur le bord de la Rivière aux Anglais, 19 Mai 1885," 258.

79   See, for instance, Pénard's assessment of "the post-1885 generation": "The new generation taking root on the point [i.e., the peninsula of Île-à-la-Crosse] did not count for much and was not very inclined to listen to the priests.... A new attitude infused the members of this generation, whose sole ambition can be summed up in a phrase coined by Father Rapet: 'to saunter about in a coat of

fine cloth, with a bit of ribbon in one's cap.' He might also have added 'always being up to no good.'" SHSB, "Codex historicus, 1845–1897," 211–12.

80   These developments are discussed at length in Chapter 1.

81   SHSB, "Codex historicus, 1845–1897," 174, 202–7.

82   PAA, O.M.I. Collection, Accession 84.800, Item 911, Box 32, Grandin to Taché, Lac des Maskeys [Muskeg Lake?], 16 September 1886; "Vicariat de Saint-Albert. Journal de voyage de Mgr Grandin," *Missions de la Congrégation des missionnaires oblats de Marie Immaculée* 101 (March 1888): 35; SHSB, "Codex historicus, 1845–1897," 206; Carrière, *Dictionnaire biographique*, 1:255. For information on Saint-Louis mission at Onion Lake, see especially PAA, O.M.I. Collection, Accession 84.400, Item 986, Box 34, Grandin, "Missions et Résidences du diocèse de St. Albert," 1882 (number 21).

83   SHSB, "Codex historicus, 1845–1897," 206–7.

84   Ibid., 205–8, 210–11, 213, 215–29, 233; ASGM, L018, Île à la Crosse, "Historique," 10; Lesage, *Capitale d'une solitude*, 132–34.

85   "Mission de Saint-Albert. Lettre du R.P. Rapet, supérieur de l'Ile-à-la-Crosse. Mission de Saint-Jean-Baptiste, Ile-à-la-Crosse, le 1er janvier 1889," *Missions de la Congrégation des missionnaires oblats de Marie Immaculée* 106 (June 1889): 168; "Vicariat de la Saskatchewan. Rapport de Mgr Pascal, vicaire apostolique," *Missions de la Congrégation des missionnaires oblats de Marie Immaculée* 121 (March 1893): 19; "Vicariat de la Saskatchewan. Mission de la Visitation au Portage-La-Loche. Lettre du R.P. Pénard au T.R.P. Supérieur Général. Mission Saint-Jean-Baptiste, Ile-à-la-Crosse, 11 avril 1895," *Missions de la Congrégation des missionnaires oblats de Marie Immaculée* 131 (September 1895): 285, 288–92; SHSB, "Codex historicus, 1845–1897," 221–22, 229–30, 236–37, 253, 256–57, 259–62, 266, 274; Lesage, *Capitale d'une solitude*, 137–39.

86   SHSB, "Codex historicus, 1845–1897," 257, 263, 266, 267, 270–71, 276, and "Codex historicus, 1898–1928," 3, 13.

87   ASGM, Circulaire mensuelle adressée aux diverses maisons de l'Institut 8 (May and June 1897): 425–26; ASGM, Circulaire mensuelle adressée aux diverses maisons de l'Institut 11 (November and December 1897): 534; SHSB, "Codex historicus, 1845–1897," 271–72, 275–77, 283–84, 288–89, 293–94.

88   SHSB, "Codex historicus, 1898–1928," 2.

89   Ibid., 211–12, 223, 229, 239, 241, 267–68. It should be noted, however, that the Oblates of Saint-Jean-Baptiste held one particular free trader—William Venne—in reasonably high regard. Venne operated outposts at Île-à-la-Crosse, Green Lake, and Canoe Lake for the fur-trading enterprise founded by his father—Salomon Venne from Saint-Norbert, Manitoba. A practising Catholic, William Venne was attending Mass on a regular basis at Saint-Jean-Baptiste by 1891. See especially ibid., 229, 239, 241; Payment, *"Les gens libres—Otipemisiwak,"* 219, 249n68 and 69.

90   SHSB, "Codex historicus, 1845–1897," 234, 236, 237–39. The corollary of this perception was the notion that Indigenous Catholics stood to benefit morally and spiritually from the HBC's withdrawal from their communities. Hence, in his report to the Oblate General Administration in 1895, Pénard noted that the *sauvages* of Portage La Loche had been undergoing moral improvement and spiritual renewal since the late 1880s, when the HBC had abandoned this portage in favour of the Athabasca Landing Trail (between Edmonton and

Athabasca Landing). According to Pénard, the Christianization of "les sauvages du Portage-la-Loche" had been virtually impossible in the heyday of the Portage La Loche Brigade: "At that time, Portage-la-Loche took on the atmosphere of a veritable Babel. It was the major transport link through which the Hudson's Bay Company shipped merchandise into the North and furs out of it. The boats would arrive in large flotillas on either end of the portage. There they would unload, along with crates and bales of all kinds, the most mixed groups of people imaginable: whites from all nations of Europe, métis from everywhere, *sauvages* from all tribes, all would rub shoulders.... One could not expect much [interest in moral or spiritual] edification from this mélange of people from so many different religious backgrounds—and indeed most of them had no religion at all. Our *sauvages* suffered as a result of their regular contact with this motley pack.... This contact was especially harmful to our newly converted *sauvages*, who as yet had no resident priest to counterbalance the influence of protestants and corrupt people." "Vicariat de la Saskatchewan. Mission de la Visitation au Portage-La-Loche. Lettre du R.P. Pénard au T.R.P. Supérieur Général. Mission Saint-Jean-Baptiste, Ile-à-la-Crosse, 11 avril 1895," *Missions de la Congrégation des missionnaires oblats de Marie Immaculée* 131 (September 1895): 287–88. On the displacement of Portage La Loche by Athabasca Landing, see especially SHSB, "Codex historicus, 1845–1897," 220; Innis, *Fur Trade in Canada*, 344–45.

91 Relations between Moberly and the Oblates of Saint-Jean-Baptiste are discussed in Chapter 2. See also SHSB, "Codex historicus, 1845–1897," 233, 234, 236, 237–39, 241, 242–44, 256.

92 SHSB, "Codex historicus, 1845–1897," 256. For Pénard's account of the New Year's celebration hosted by Moberly two years earlier, see ibid., 41.

93 Choquette, "Problèmes de mœurs et de discipline ecclésiastique," 108–9, 118. On Oblate hostility to social dance in the nineteenth and early twentieth centuries, see especially Choquette, *Oblate Assault*, 5; Huel, *Proclaiming the Gospel*, 86.

94 SHSB, "Codex historicus, 1845–1897," 211. According to Pénard, the métis of Île-à-la-Crosse had scrupulously heeded this prohibition over the previous four decades. As Brenda Macdougall has ascertained, however, Chief Trader Moberly took a very different view of this issue. In response to the Oblates' allegations that he had encouraged disturbances at Île-à-la-Crosse, Moberly riposted: "What has been said about Drinking and dancing is almost unworthy of notice, as it shews plainly that it is only a trumped up charge for the sake of doing me harm. The evidence shews that whether I was here or not, the HalfBreeds of this place always did and always will dance in spite of the Priests orders." LAC/ HBC, microfilm HBC 1M1068, B.89/b/18, Ile-a-la-Crosse Correspondence Book (1891–1893), Moberly to Inspecting Chief Factor James McDougall, Île-à-la-Crosse, 2 March 1892. See also Macdougall, *One of the Family*, 183; Macdougall, "Socio-Cultural Development and Identity Formation," 282.

95 SHSB, "Codex historicus, 1845–1897," 212.

96 Ibid., 236.

97 Ibid., 237–38.

98 Ibid., 238–39.

99 Ibid., 239–40. In the late 1850s and '60s, however, Grandin had barred certain neophytes from taking communion if they were known to have been habitual drinkers, dancers, or gamblers, or if they cohabitated with individuals other than

their lawfully wedded spouses (i.e., spouses recognized as such by the Catholic Church). Offenders could only be readmitted to the sacrament after mending their ways and undergoing penance. PAA, O.M.I. Collection, Accession 84.800, Item 912, Box 32, Grandin to Father Ambroise Tamburini (Procurator to the Holy See), Île-à-la-Crosse, June 1869. On Tamburini, see especially Champagne, *Les débuts de la mission dans le Nord–Ouest Canadien*, 131, 134, 155.

100 SHSB, "Codex historicus, 1845–1897," 239–40, 242.

101 Ibid., 240, 241, 242, 254, 256, 262, 266; SHSB, "Codex historicus, 1898–1928," 19–20.

102 SHSB, "Codex historicus, 1845–1897," 274.

103 Ibid., 184. See also ibid., 183, 240, 295–96; SHSB, "Codex historicus, 1898–1928," 1–2, 9.

104 SHSB, "Codex historicus, 1845–1897," 240, 241, 252; "Lettre du Révérend Père Pénard au Très Révérend Père Général," *Missions de la Congrégation des missionnaires oblats de Marie Immaculée* 151 (September 1900): 247–48.

105 "Lettre du Révérend Père Pénard au Très Révérend Père Général," *Missions de la Congrégation des missionnaires oblats de Marie Immaculée* 151 (September 1900): 247–48, 250, 251, 255; SHSB, "Codex historicus, 1898–1928," 3, 5, 11, 14–15, 16–17.

106 "Lettre du Révérend Père Pénard au Très Révérend Père Général," *Missions de la Congrégation des missionnaires oblats de Marie Immaculée* 151 (September 1900): 249. This passage was quoted directly from SHSB, "Codex historicus, 1898–1928," 9. See also "Codex historicus, 1898–1928," 4–5.

107 SHSB, "Codex historicus, 1845–1897," 211, 214–15, and "Codex historicus, 1898–1928," 2, 19–21.

108 SHSB, "Codex historicus, 1845–1897," 214–215.

109 SHSB, "Codex historicus, 1898–1928," 19. Pénard provided no information on the procedure according to which he conducted this "inquisition." Nor did he cite any of the questions that he posed.

110 Ibid., 20.

111 Genesis 19:24–25. See also Deuteronomy 29:23.

Conclusion: *La civilisation moderne*: The World Came Seeping In

1 PAA, O.M.I. Collection, Accession 71.220, Item 6533, Box 156, Albert Lacombe to Oblate Superior General Cassien Augier, 12 November 1896; PAA, O.M.I. Collection, Accession 71.220, Item 6522, Box 156, Lacombe to Augier, December 1896. Historians have commonly acknowledged Lacombe as the sole architect of the project, but in fact he and Thérien designed it together between 1893 and 1895. See especially PAA, O.M.I. Collection, Accession 71.220, Item 6555, Box 157, Adéodat Thérien to Lacombe, Calgary, 22 November 1893; PAA, O.M.I. Collection, Accession 71.220, Item 6533, Box 156, Lacombe to "Père Antoine," Prince Albert, 22 November 1895; PAA, O.M.I. Collection, Accession 71.220, Item 6555, Box 157, Thérien to Lacombe, Onion Lake, 14 January 1896; Drouin, "La colonie Saint-Paul-des-Métis, Alberta," 2–16; Hughes, *Father Lacombe*, 351–58; Legal, *Short Sketches*, 71; MacGregor, *Father Lacombe*, 304–8; Sœur de la Providence, *Le Père Lacombe*, 423–40; 137–41; Stanley, "Alberta's Half-breed Reserve Saint-Paul-des-Métis," 78–81. On Adéodat Thérien, see especially Carrière, *Dictionnaire biographique*, 3:224.

2   PAA, O.M.I. Collection, Accession 71.220, Item 6555, Box 157, Thérien to Lacombe, Calgary, 22 November 1893. In his history of Saint-Paul-des-Métis, Émile Legal (Grandin's successor as Bishop of Saint-Albert) suggested that the inspiration behind this vision came from the seventeenth- and eighteenth-century Jesuit *reducciones* in Paraguay: "[Lacombe] had conceived the plan of withdrawing his beloved Half-breed population from the pernicious influences of vice, not indeed by force, but solely by persuasion, of gathering them together, far away from the White men and of placing them under the paternal direction of their priests, and in a colony of their own; to train them to regular work and industry by means of which there could come . . . some good and consoling results, such as had been brought about in the reductions of Paraguay, under the direction of the Jesuits." See Legal, *Short Sketches*, 71.

3   PAA, O.M.I. Collection, Accession 71.220, Item 6555, Box 157, "Extract from a Report of the Committee of the Honourable the Privy Council, approved by His Excellency on the 28th December, 1895," Ottawa; PAA, O.M.I. Collection, Accession 71.220, Item 6542, Box 156, "Mémoire et pétition à l'Honorable Laurier, premier ministre et aux autres membres du ministère, en faveur de la nation métisse du Manitoba et du Nord-Ouest," submitted by Lacombe on behalf of Archbishop Adélard Langevin of Saint-Boniface, Bishop Vital-Justin Grandin of Saint-Albert and Vicar Apostolic Albert Pascal of Saskatchewan; Legal, *Short Sketches*, 71; Sawchuk, Sawchuk, and Ferguson, *Metis Land Rights in Alberta*, 166–67; Smith, "History of French-Speaking Albertans," 87–88; Stanley, "Alberta's Half-breed Reserve Saint-Paul-des-Métis," 81–83.

4   AD, HEC 2142 A33C 21, Ex. 2, Lacombe, "À mes chers enfants et amis, les métis du Manitoba et du Nord-Ouest," Saint-Albert, 1896; PAA, O.M.I. Collection, Accession 71.220, Item 6555, Box 157, Johnny Chartrand to Lacombe, Willow Bunch (Northwest Territories), February 1896; "Lacombe's Land of Grub," *Saskatchewan Herald*, Friday, 6 March 1896; PAA, O.M.I. Collection, Accession 71.220, Item 6556, Box 157, Thérien to Théodule Népreu, curé, Saint-Paul-des-Métis, 19 March 1897; Legal, *Short Sketches*, 71–72; Devine, *People Who Own Themselves*, 183–84.

5   PAA, O.M.I. Collection, Accession 84.400, Item 970, Box 33, Grandin to "Nos Seigneurs les Archevêques et Evêques du Canada qui pourront voir ces lignes," Saint-Albert, 22 August 1898. See also PAA, O.M.I. Collection, Accession 84.400, Item 960, Box 33, "Notes et souvenirs de Mgr Grandin (Repris à la demande de Mgr Langevin par lettre du 28 nov. 1897, rédaction commencée en mars 1898)," 216, 218; Champagne, *Les débuts de la mission dans le Nord-Ouest Canadien*, 184–85; Champagne, "Mission et civilisation dans l'Ouest canadien," 347–48; Huel, "The Oblates, the Métis, and 1885," 23–25, 29; Huel, *Proclaiming the Gospel*, 213–14.

6   PAA, O.M.I. Collection, Accession 71.220, Item 76, Box 2, Grandin, "Extrait du Rapport sur le Vicariat de St. Albert au Chapitre Général de la Congrégation des O.M.I. à Rome," 28 April 1887, 1–3, 11; PAA, O.M.I. Collection, Accession 84.400, Item 960, Box 33, "Notes et souvenirs de Mgr Grandin (Repris à la demande de Mgr Langevin par lettre du 28 nov. 1897, rédaction commencée en mars 1898)," 218; Champagne, *Les débuts de la mission dans le Nord-Ouest Canadien*, 181, 184, 194, 197, 199, 204; Champagne, "Mission et civilisation dans l'Ouest canadien," 347.

7	AD, HEC 2142. A33C 21 Ex. 2, Lacombe, "À mes chers enfants et amis"; AD, Microfilm W 404.M62 F10 (Calgary Mission Ste. Marie, Saint Paul des Metis [codex et notes du P. Thérien]), Thérien, "St. Paul des Métis, Alberta. Origines de cette paroisse," 1909.

8	PAA, O.M.I. Collection, Accession 71.220, Item 6527, Box 156, Albert Lacombe to Oblate Superior General Cassien Augier, 1 February 1903; Drouin, "La colonie Saint-Paul-des-Métis," 289–305.

9	AD, Microfilm W 404.M62 F76 (Edmonton, Archives Oblates, Codex historicus de plusieurs missions du diocèse de Saint-Albert), "Notes historiques sur la colonie St Paul des Métis (Alberta) par le Rév. Père Adéodat Thérien OMI," 1930, 11–15; Drouin, "La colonie Saint-Paul-des-Métis," 275–88, 364–405; Sawchuk, Sawchuk, and Ferguson, *Metis Land Rights in Alberta*, 168–70; Stanley, "Alberta's Half-breed Reserve Saint-Paul-des-Métis," 84–94.

10	AD, Microfilm W 404.M62 F76 (Edmonton, Archives Oblates, Codex historicus de plusieurs missions du diocèse de Saint-Albert), "Notes historiques sur la colonie St Paul des Métis (Alberta) par le Rév. Père Adéodat Thérien OMI," 1930, 15–20. See also AD, Microfilm W 404.M62 F9 (Long Lake, St-Laurent, &c), "Incendie de Saint Paul des Métis (notes)," written by an eyewitness to the fire, Oblate lay brother Louis Guillaume; Drouin, "La colonie Saint-Paul-des-Métis," 494–529.

11	AD, Microfilm W 404.M62 F76 (Edmonton, Archives Oblates, Codex historicus de plusieurs missions du diocèse de Saint-Albert), "Notes historiques sur la colonie St Paul des Métis (Alberta) par le Rév. Père Adéodat Thérien OMI," 1930, 20, 22–27; Sawchuk, Sawchuk, and Ferguson, *Metis Land Rights in Alberta*, 176. On *missionnaires-colonisateurs*, see especially Painchaud, *Un rêve français dans le peuplement de la Prairie*, 1–44; Pariseau, *Les Oblats de Marie-Immaculée*, 47–68; Trottier, "Les Oblats et la colonisation en Alberta."

BIBLIOGRAPHY

Primary Sources

Archival collections

Société historique de Saint-Boniface (Centre du patrimoine), Winnipeg

Corporation archiépiscopale catholique romaine de St-Boniface, Fonds Taché.

Lettres de la Cie d'Hudson et des missionnaires de la Riv. Rouge, Cahiers D, 7 novembre 1815–20 août 1823, P1528–P1911, Fonds Provencher.

Lettres de Mgr J.N. Provencher, Cahiers G, 27 mars 1818–6 juillet 1852, P2526–P2881, Fonds Provencher.

Oblats de Marie Immaculée Keewatin-Le Pas, PA 1492, "Arbre généalogique (Liber status animarum) Île-à-la-Crosse, 1845–1897."

Oblats de Marie Immaculée Keewatin-Le Pas, "Codex historicus de l'Île-à-la-Crosse, 1845–1897."

Oblats de Marie Immaculée Keewatin-Le Pas, "Codex historicus de l'Île-à-la-Crosse, 1898–1928."

Provincial Archives of Alberta (Grandin Archives), Edmonton

O.M.I. Collection, Oblate General Administration Documents, Accession 71.220, Boxes 1–2.

O.M.I., Lacombe Papers, Accession 71.220, Boxes 156–57.

O.M.I., Leduc Papers, Accession 71.220, Box 166.

O.M.I., Grandin Papers, Accession 84.400, Boxes 32–35.

O.M.I., "Forts des Prairies—Registre des baptêmes, mariages et sépultures, 1842–1851," Accession 71.220, Item 5214, Box 255

Research Centre for the Religious History of Canada (Saint Paul University), Ottawa

Archives de la Propagation de la Foi de Paris, Copies sur microfilm des séries intéressant le Canada, films II, X, and XI.

Écrits de Grandin, 26 vols.

Archives Deschâtelets (Oblats de Marie Immaculée), Richelieu

Lettres du R.P. Prosper Légeard, G LPP 2199–G LPP 2205.

Lettres de Mgr Albert Pascal, G LPP 2581–G LPP 2595.

Lettres de Mgr Eugène de Mazenod, H 3209. P76R.

Correspondance de Mgr Albert Pascal, HE 2121. P7C.

Correspondance de Mgr Alexandre Taché, HE 2221. T12.

Lettres de Mgr Vital-Justin Grandin, HE 2223. T12Z.

Lettres du R.P. Albert Lacombe, HEC 2142. A33.

Correspondance principalement relative à l'approvisionnement de la mission de Prosper Légeard, o.m.i., HEC 2500. P96C 3–P96C 26.

Lettres du R.P. Joseph Lestanc, HEC 3926. J94C.

Lettres du R.P. Prosper Légeard, HPF 4191. C75R.

Correspondance des Sœurs Grises, Île-à-Crosse, HPF 4191. C75R.

Mission de Saint-Jean-Baptiste, LC 6301. K26R.

Microfilm W 404.M62 F9 (Long Lake, St-Laurent, &c).

Microfilm W 404.M62 F10 (Calgary Mission Ste. Marie, Saint Paul des Metis [codex et notes du P. Thérien]).

Microfilm W 404.M62 F76 (Edmonton, Archives Oblates, Codex historicus de plusieurs missions du diocèse de Saint-Albert).

Microfilm W 404.M62 F86 (Missions indiennes, St-Albert).

Archives des Sœurs Grises de Montréal

"Ancien Journal," vols. 1–3, F103-26/5 G5/11C48.

"Annales de l'établissement des Sœurs Grises à l'Île à la Crosse." 2 vols. Hôpital St-Bruno, Île-à-la-Crosse, 1883.

Circulaire mensuelle adressée aux diverses maisons de l'Institut.

Library and Archives Canada

Black Series: microfilm C-10113, file no. 7780; microfilm C-10117, file no. 10125; microfilm C-10125, file no. 20505.

Hudson's Bay Company. Post Records, Ile-à-la-Crosse, microfilm reels: HBC 1M63–HBC 1M65; HBC 1M183; HBC 1M270; HBC 1M490–HBC 1M499; HBC 1M778; HBC 1M784; HBC 1M877; HBC 1M1007; HBC 1M1066–HBC 1M1070.

Smithsonian Institution Archives

Assistant Secretary in Charge of the United States National Museum. Correspondence and Memoranda 1858–1869 and undated. Record Unit 561, Box 1.

Spencer F. Baird Papers, 1833–1889. Record Unit 7002, Box 57.

Caleb Burwell Rowan Kennerly Papers, 1855–1860. Record Unit 7202, Box 1.

Collected Notes, Lists and Catalogues on Birds. Record Unit 7215, Boxes 1 and 13.

Bernard Rogan Ross Notebook, c. 1860–1861. Record Unit 7221, Box 1.

Published Documents

Acte de visite du R.P. Soullier, premier assistant général pour le vicariat de Saint-Albert. Octobre 1883. Saint-Albert: Typographie privée O.M.I., 1885.

Biblia Sacra Vulgatæ Editionis, Sixti V et Clementis VIII. Romæ: Typis S. Congregationis de Propaganda Fide, 1861.

Breviarium Romanum ex decreto sacrosancti concilii tridentini restitutum. Venetiis: Ex typographia Balleoniana, 1799.

Bx de Mazenod: Lettres à la S. Congrégation et à l'Œuvre de la Propagation de la Foi, 1832–1861. Rome: Postulation générale O.M.I., Via Aurelia 290, 1977.

Bx Eugène de Mazenod (1782–1861): Lettres aux correspondants d'Amérique, 1841–1850. Rome: Postulation générale O.M.I., Via Aurelia 290, 1977.

Bx Eugène de Mazenod (1782–1861): Lettres aux correspondants d'Amérique, 1851–1860. Rome: Postulation générale O.M.I., Via Aurelia 290, 1977.

"Copy of Treaty No. 6 between Her Majesty the Queen and the Plain and Wood Cree Indians and other Tribes of Indians at Fort Carlton, Fort Pitt and Battle River with Adhesions." Ottawa: Roger Duhamel, F.R.S.C., Queen's Printer and Controller of Stationary, 1964.

"Copy of Treaty and Supplementary Treaty No. 7, Made 22nd Sept., and 4th Dec., 1877, Between Her Majesty the Queen and the Blackfeet and Other Indian Tribes." Ottawa: Roger Duhamel, F.R.S.C., Queen's Printer and Controller of Stationary, 1966.

Dawson, Simon James. *Report on the Exploration of the Country between Lake Superior and the Red River Settlement and between the Latter Place and the Assiniboine and Saskatchewan.* Toronto: John Lovell, 1859.

De Aquino, Sancti Thomae. *Opera Omnia. Tomus XL. Contra Errores Graecorum.* Romae: Ad Sanctae Sabinae, 1967.

De Smet, Pierre-Jean. *Missions de l'Orégon et voyages dans les montagnes Rocheuses en 1845 et 1846.* Paris: Poussielgue-Rusand, 1848.

Fernand-Michel, Fortuné-François. *Dix-huit ans chez les sauvages: Voyages et missions de Mgr Henry Faraud, évêque d'Anemour, vicaire apostolique de Mackensie, dans l'extrême nord de l'Amérique britannique.* Paris: Régis Ruffet & Cie, 1866.

Grouard, Émile. *Souvenir de mes soixante ans d'apostolat dans l'Athabaska-Mackensie.* Lyon: Œuvre Apostolique de Marie Immaculée, 1923.

Hargrave, Joseph James. *Red River.* Montreal: John Lovell, 1871.

"Instruction de Monseigneur de Mazenod relative aux missions étrangères, présentée et annotée par Claude Champagne, o.m.i." *Kerygma* 24 (1975): 164–77.

Lacombe, Albert. *Catéchisme en image à l'usage des Indiens.* Paris: O.M.I., Imprimerie Bouasse Lebel, 1874.

———. *Le catéchisme en images pour l'instruction des sauvages.* Montréal: Imprimerie de l'Asile de la Providence, 1874.

Moberly, Henry John. *When Fur Was King.* Toronto: J.M. Dent and Sons, 1929.

Morris, Alexander. *The Treaties of Canada with the Indians of Manitoba and the North-West Territories: Including the Negotiations on Which They Were Based, and Other Information Relating Thereto.* Toronto: Bedfords, Clarke and Co., 1880.

Notes and Sketches Collected from a Voyage in the North-West by a Sister of Charity of Montreal for the Furtherance of a Charitable Object. Montreal: Callahan, Book and Job Printer, 1875.

Oeuvre de la Propagation de la Foi. Québec: P.G. Delisle, 1857.

Petitot, Émile. *Dictionnaire de la langue Dènè-Dindjié, dialectes montagnais ou chippewayan, peaux de lièvre et loucheux, renfermant en outre un grand nombre de termes propres à sept autres dialectes de la même langue.* Paris: E. Leroux, 1876.

Pilling, James Constantine. *Bibliography of the Athapascan Languages.* Washington, DC: Government Printing Office, 1892.

Soullier, Louis. *Vie du Révérend Père Légeard.* Paris: 1886.

Taché, Alexandre-Antonin. *Esquisse sur le Nord-Ouest de l'Amérique par Mgr. Taché, Évêque de St. Boniface, 1868.* Montréal: Typographie du Nouveau monde, 1869.

———. *Vingt années de missions dans le Nord-Ouest de l'Amérique.* Montréal: Eusèbe Senécal, 1866.

Tucker, Sarah. *The Rainbow in the North: A Short Account of the First Establishment of Christianity in Rupert's Land by the Church Missionary Society.* New York: Robert Carter and Brothers, 1852.

Tweedie, William. *Canada West and the Hudson's Bay Company: A Political and Humane Question of Vital Importance to the Honour of Great Britain, to the Prosperity of Canada, and to the Existence of the Native Tribes: Being an Address to the Right Honorable Henry Labouchere, Her Majesty's Principal Secretary of State for the Colonies: With an Appendix.* London: Aborigines' Protection Society, 1856.

Periodicals

Les Annales de la Propagation de la Foi (Lyons).

Les Annales de la Propagation de la Foi pour les Provinces de Québec et Montréal (Montreal).

The Annual Report of the Board of Regents of the Smithsonian Institution (Washington, DC).

Bulletins de la Société d'anthropologie de Paris (Paris).

Les Cloches de Saint-Boniface (Saint-Boniface, Manitoba).

The Colonial Intelligencer, or, Aborigines' Friend (London).

Missions de la Congrégation des missionnaires oblats de Marie Immaculée (Paris).

Le Patriote de l'ouest (Prince Albert, Saskatchewan).

Saskatchewan Herald (Battleford, Saskatchewan).

Secondary Sources

Abel, Kerry. *Drum Songs: Glimpses of Dene History.* Montreal and Kingston: McGill-Queen's University Press, 1993.

"An Apology Statement: An Apology to the First Nations of Canada by the Oblate Conference of Canada." In *Western Oblate Studies 2—Études oblates de l'ouest 2*, edited by Raymond Huel, 259–62. Edmonton: Edwin Mellen Press, 1992.

Andersen, Chris. "From Nation to Population: The Racialisation of 'Métis' in the Canadian Census." *Nations and Nationalisms* 12, no. 2 (2008): 347–68.

————. *"Métis": Race, Recognition, and the Struggle for Indigenous Peoplehood*. Vancouver: University of British Columbia Press, 2014.

————. "Mixed Ancestry or Metis?" In *Indigenous Identity and Resistance: Researching the Diversity of Knowledge*, edited by Brendan Hokowhitu et al., 23–36. Dunedin, New Zealand: Otago University Press, 2010.

Anderson, N.R. *Oblate Fathers in Calgary: Roman Catholic Church, 1875–1889*. Calgary: Century Calgary Publications, 1975.

Archives of Manitoba. Hudson's Bay Company Archives, HBCA biographical sheets. http://www.gov.mb.ca/chc/archives/hbca/biographical/index.html (accessed 18 May 2016).

Arthur, Elizabeth. "Simon James Dawson." *Dictionary of Canadian Biography Online*, vol. 13 (1901–1910). http://www.biographi.ca/en/index.php.

Aston, Nigel. *Christianity and Revolutionary Europe, 1750–1830*. New York: Cambridge University Press, 2002.

Atlas O.M.I. Rome: Curia Generalizia, 1990.

Bakker, Peter. "Ethnogenesis, Language, and Identity: The Genesis of Michif and Other Mixed Languages." In *Contours of a People: Metis Family, Mobility, and History*, edited by Nicole St-Onge, Carolyn Podruchny, and Brenda Macdougall, 169–93. Norman: University of Oklahoma Press, 2012.

————. *A Language of Our Own: The Genesis of Michif, the Mixed Cree-French Language of the Canadian Métis*. New York: Oxford University Press, 1997.

Bank, Andrew. "Losing Faith in the Civilizing Mission: The Premature Decline of Humanitarian Liberalism at the Cape, 1840–60." In *Empire and Others: British Encounters with Indigenous Peoples, 1600–1850*, edited by Martin Daunton and Rick Halpern, 364–83. Philadelphia: University of Pennsylvania Press, 1999.

Barnoud, Jean-Noël, and Bernard Maviel. "Paray religieux." In *Histoire de ma commune: Paray-le-Monial*, 71–92. Paray: Association "Histoire de Paray-le-Monial", 1986.

Baumont, Jean-Claude. "Une source de l'histoire du XIXe et du début du XXe siècle: archives et publications de l'œuvre de la propagation de la foi." *History in Africa* 3 (1976): 165–70.

Baumont, Jean-Claude, Jacques Gadille, and Xavier de Montclos. "L'exportation des modèles de christianisme français à l'époque contemporaine. Pour une nouvelle problématique de l'histoire missionnaire." *Revue d'histoire de l'Église de France* 63, no. 170 (1977): 5–23.

Bayly, C.A. "The British and Indigenous Peoples, 1760–1860: Power, Perception and Identity." In *Empire and Others: British Encounters with Indigenous Peoples, 1600–1850*, edited by Martin Daunton and Rick Halpern, 19–41. Philadelphia: University of Pennsylvania Press, 1999.

Beaudoin, Yvon. "Le Codex historicus." *Vie Oblate Life* 67, no. 1 (2008): 67–75.

Bélisle, Jean-François and Nicole St-Onge. "Between García Moreno and Chan Santa Cruz: Riel and the Métis Rebellions." In *Mixed Blessings: Indigenous Encounters with Christianity in Canada*, edited by Tolly Bradford and Chelsea Horton, 102–16. Vancouver and Toronto: University of British Columbia Press, 2016.

Benoit, Barbara. "The Mission at Ile-à-la-Crosse." *The Beaver* (Winter 1980): 40–50.

Benoît, Dom Paul. *Vie de Mgr Taché, Archevêque de St-Boniface*. 2 vols. Montréal: Librairie Beauchemin, 1904.

Bertocci, Philip A. *Jules Simon: Republican Anticlericalism and Cultural Politics in France, 1848–1886*. Columbia and London: University of Missouri Press, 1978.

Bolt, Christine. *Victorian Attitudes to Race*. Toronto: University of Toronto Press, 1971.

Bonk, Jonathan J. "Grandin, Vital Justin." In *Biographical Dictionary of Christian Missions*, edited by G.H. Anderson, 255. New York: Macmillan Reference, 1998.

Boon, T.C. *The Anglican Church from the Bay to the Rockies: A History of the Ecclesiastical Province of Rupert's Land and Its Diocese from 1820 to 1950*. Toronto: Ryerson Press, 1962.

Boutry, Philippe. "Religions «populaires» et religions dissidentes: les mutations des croyances." In *Histoire de la France religieuse: Du roi Très Chrétien à la laïcité républicaine*, edited by Jacques Le Goff and René Rémond, 3:490–500. Paris: Éditions du Seuil, 1991.

Bowsfield, Hartwell. "Bernard Rogan Ross," *Dictionary of Canadian Biography Online*, vol. 10 (1871–1880). http://www.biographi.ca/en/index.php.

Breton, Paul-Émile. *Le grand chef des prairies: Le père Albert Lacombe, 1827–1916*. Edmonton: Éditions de l'ermitage, 1954.

———. *Monseigneur Grandin vous parle*. Edmonton: Éditions de l'ermitage, 1958.

———. *Vital Grandin, o.m.i.: La merveilleuse aventure de "l'Evêque sauvage" des prairies et du grand nord*. Montréal: Librairie Arthème Fayard, 1960.

Brown, Jennifer S.H. *Strangers in Blood: Fur Trade Company Families in Indian Country*. Norman: University of Oklahoma Press, 1980.

Brown, Robert Craig, and Ramsay Cook. *Canada 1896–1921: A Nation Transformed*. Toronto: McClelland and Stewart, 1974.

Brumbach, Hetty Jo, Robert Jarvenpa, and Clifford Buell. "An Ethnoarcheological Approach to Chipewyan Adaptations in the Late Fur Trade Period." *Arctic Anthropology* 19 (1982): 1–49.

Burke, Peter. *The French Historical Revolution: The Annales School, 1929–89*. Stanford, CA: Stanford University Press, 1990.

Burpee, Lawrence J. *The Search for the Western Sea: The Story of the Exploration of North Western America*. Toronto: Macmillan Company of Canada, 1935.

Calloway, Colin G. *One Vast Winter Count: The Native American West before Lewis and Clark*. Lincoln and London: University of Nebraska Press, 2003.

Carney, Robert. "The Native-Wilderness Equation: Catholic and Other School Orientations in the Western Arctic." *Study Sessions, Canadian Catholic Historical Association* 48 (1981): 61–78.

———. "Residential Schooling at Fort Chipewyan and Fort Resolution 1874–1974." In *Western Oblate Studies 2—Études oblates de l'ouest 2*, edited by Raymond Huel, 115–38. Edmonton: Edwin Mellen Press, 1992.

Carrière, Gaston. "Bibliographie des professeurs oblats des facultés ecclésiastiques de l'Université d'Ottawa (1932–1961)." *Revue de l'université d'Ottawa* (1962): 1–39.

———. "Contributions des missionnaires à la sauvegarde de la culture indienne." *Études Oblates* 31, no. 3 (juillet–septembre 1972): 165–204.

———. *Dictionnaire biographique des Oblats de Marie Immaculée au Canada*. 4 vols. Ottawa: Éditions de l'Université d'Ottawa, 1976–89.

———. "L'élévation du P. Vital-J. Grandin, O.M.I., à l'épiscopat, 11 décembre, 1857." *Études Oblates* 32, no. 2 (avril–juin 1973): 100–34.

Carter, Sarah. *Capturing Women: The Manipulation of Cultural Imagery in Canada's Prairie West.* Montreal and Kingston: McGill-Queen's University Press, 1997.

———. *Lost Harvests: Prairie Indian Reserve Farmers and Government Policy.* Montreal and Kingston: McGill-Queen's University Press, 1990.

Catechism of the Catholic Church, Second Edition. Rome: Libreria Editrice Vaticana, 2000.

Champagne, Claude. "La formation des Oblats, missionnaires dans le Nord-Ouest canadien." *Study Sessions of the Canadian Catholic Historical Association/Sessions d'études de la Société canadienne d'histoire de l'Église catholique* 56 (1989): 21–33.

———. *Les débuts de la mission dans le Nord-Ouest canadien: Mission et Église chez Mgr Vital Grandin, o.m.i. (1829–1902).* Ottawa: Éditions de l'Université St-Paul, Éditions de l'Université d'Ottawa, 1983.

———. "Mission et civilisation dans l'Ouest canadien: Vital Grandin, 1829–1902." *La Société canadienne d'histoire de l'église catholique, Sessions d'études* 50 (1983): 341–58.

Champagne, Joseph-Étienne. *Les missions catholiques dans l'ouest canadien (1818–1875).* Ottawa: Éditions des études oblates et éditions de l'université, 1949.

Chevalier, Pierre. "Jules Ferry et le Saint-Siège." In *Jules Ferry, fondateur de la République*, edited by François Furet, 171–89. Paris: Éditions de l'École des Hautes Études en Sciences Sociales, 1985.

Choquette, Robert. "English-French Relations in the Canadian Catholic Community." In *Creed and Culture: The Place of English-Speaking Catholics in Canadian Society, 1750–1930*, edited by T. Murphy and G. Stortz, 3–24. Montreal and Kingston: McGill-Queen's University Press, 1993.

———. "Les rapports entre catholiques et protestants dans le Nord-Ouest du Canada avant 1840." In *Western Oblate Studies 1—Études oblates de l'ouest 1*, edited by Raymond Huel, 129–40. Edmonton: Western Canadian Publishers et l'Institut de recherche de la Faculté Saint-Jean, 1990.

———. *The Oblate Assault on Canada's Northwest.* Ottawa: University of Ottawa Press, 1995.

———. "Problèmes de moeurs et de discipline ecclésiastique: les catholiques des Prairies canadiennes de 1900 à 1930." *Histoire sociale—Social History* 8, no. 15 (May 1975): 102–19.

Cinnamon, John M. "Missionary Expertise, Social Science, and the Uses of Ethnographic Knowledge in Colonial Gabon." *History in Africa* 33 (2006): 413–32.

Coates, Kenneth Stephen. "Robert Campbell." *Dictionary of Canadian Biography Online*, vol. 12 (1891–1900). http://www.biographi.ca/en/index.php.

Coates, Kenneth S., and William R. Morrison. "Treaty Research Report, Treaty No. 10 (1906)." Ottawa: Treaties and Historical Research Centre, Indian and Northern Affairs Canada, 1986.

Code of Canon Law, Latin-English Edition: New English Translation. Washington, DC: Canon Law Society of America, 1999.

Cole, Douglas. "The Origins of Canadian Anthropology, 1850–1910." *Journal of Canadian Studies* 8, no. 1 (1973): 33–45.

Costigan, Richard F. *The Consensus of the Church and Papal Infallibility: A Study in the Background of Vatican I.* Washington, DC: Catholic University of America Press, 2005.

Courvoisier, Michel. "Une amitié difficile et décisive aux sources de l'existence oblate: Eugène de Mazenod et Charles de Forbin-Janson." *Vie Oblate Life* 66, no. 2 (2007): 1–24.

Coze, Paul. *Wakanda: Croquis de l'auteur.* Paris: Librairie de la Revue française, c1929.

Crosby, Douglas. "Homily Presented at Lac Ste. Anne, Alberta, 24 July 1991." In *Western Oblate Studies 2—Études oblates de l'ouest 2*, edited by Raymond Huel, 253–58. Edmonton: Edwin Mellen Press, 1992.

Curtis, Bruce. *The Politics of Population: State Formation, Statistics, and the Census of Canada, 1840–1875.* Toronto: University of Toronto Press, 2001.

Danylewycz, Marta. *Taking the Veil: An Alternative to Marriage, Motherhood, and Spinsterhood in Quebec, 1840–1920.* Toronto: McClelland and Stewart, 1987.

Daschuk, James. *Clearing the Plains: Disease, Politics of Starvation, and the Loss of Aboriginal Life.* Regina: University of Regina Press, 2013.

Daum Shanks, Signa A.K. "Searching for Sakitawak: Place and People in Northern Saskatchewan's Île-à-la-Crosse." PhD diss., University of Western Ontario, 2015.

Dauphinais, Luc. *Histoire de Saint-Boniface.* Vol. 1, *À l'ombre des cathédrales, des origines de la colonie jusqu'en 1870.* Saint-Boniface: Les Éditions du Blé, 1991.

Dempsey, Hugh A. *Indian Tribes of Alberta.* Calgary: Glenbow-Alberta Institute, 1978.

Deschâtelets, Léo. "Notes sur l'histoire de nos saintes Règles, l'élaboration du texte définitif." *Études oblates* 1 (1942): 11–27.

———. "Qui a traduit les saintes Règles?" *Études oblates* 1 (1942): 172–74.

Devine, Heather. "Les Desjarlais: The Development and Dispersion of a Proto-Métis Hunting Band, 1785–1870." In *From Rupert's Land to Canada*, edited by Theodore Binnema et al., 129–58. Edmonton: University of Alberta Press, 2001.

———. *The People Who Own Themselves: Aboriginal Ethnogenesis in a Canadian Family, 1660–1900.* Calgary: University of Calgary, 2004.

Drouin, Eméric O. "La colonie Saint-Paul-des-Métis, Alberta, 1896–1909." PhD diss., University of Ottawa, 1962.

Dubois, Daniel. "Indianism in France." *Native American Studies* 7, no. 1 (1993): 27–36.

Duchaussois, Pierre. *Apôtres inconnus.* Paris: Éditions Spes, 1924.

———. *Aux glaces polaires: Indiens et Esquimaux.* Lyon: Stephanus Faugier, 1921.

———. *Aventures canadiennes des Sœurs Grises.* Paris: Flammarion, 1934.

———. *The Grey Nuns in the Far North.* Toronto: McClelland and Stewart, 1919.

Duval, Jacinthe. "The Catholic Church and the Formation of Métis Identity." *Past Imperfect* 9 (2001): 65–87.

Duval, Jacinthe, Timothy Foran, Gilles Lesage, and Les Bronconnier. "Des archives éloquentes: Construction nationale, mémoire collective et la Société historique de Saint-Boniface." In *De Pierre-Esprit Radisson à Louis Riel: Voyageurs et Métis/From Pierre-Esprit Radisson to Louis Riel: Voyageurs and Métis*, edited by D. Combet et al., 251–75. Winnipeg: Presses universitaires de Saint-Boniface, 2014.

Ens, Gerhard J. *Homeland to Hinterland: The Changing Worlds of the Red River Metis in the Nineteenth Century.* Toronto: University of Toronto Press, 1996.

Erickson, Lesley. "At the Cultural and Religious Crossroads: Sara Riel and the Grey Nuns in the Canadian Northwest, 1848–1883." MA thesis, University of Calgary, 1997.

———. "'Bury Our Sorrows in the Sacred Heart': Gender and the Métis Response to Colonialism—The Case Study of Sara and Louis Riel, 1848–83." In *Unsettled Pasts: Reconceiving the West through Women's History*, edited by Sarah Carter et al., 17–46. Calgary: University of Calgary Press, 2005.

Fay, Terence J. *A History of Canadian Catholics: Gallicanism, Romanism, and Canadianism.* Montreal and Kingston: McGill-Queen's University Press, 2002.

Flanagan, Thomas. *Louis "David" Riel: Prophet of the New World.* Toronto: University of Toronto Press, 1996.

Foran, M.L. "Urban Calgary 1884–1895." *Histoire sociale/Social History* 5, no. 9 (April 1972): 61–76.

Foran, Max. *Calgary: An Illustrated History.* Toronto: James Lorimer, 1978.

Foran, Timothy P. "The Oblate Apostolate to the Métis: A Reconnaissance of Scholarship and Research." In *Un passé à découvrir ou redécouvrir/A Past to Be Visited or Revisited. Actes du Premier symposium consacré à l'histoire des missions oblates auprès des Premières Nations/Proceedings of the First Symposium Dedicated to the History of the Oblate Missions to the First Nations*, edited by Pierre Hurtubise, o.m.i., 171–86. Ottawa: Saint Paul University, 2015.

———. "Transcending Language and Ethnicity: Oblates of Mary Immaculate and the Canonical Erection of the Diocese of Calgary, 1912–1916." *Histoire sociale/Social History* 41, no. 82 (November 2008): 506–34.

Foster, John E. "*Le Missionnaire* and *le Chef Métis*." In *Western Oblate Studies 1—Études oblates de l'ouest 1*, edited by Raymond Huel, 117–27. Edmonton: Western Canadian Publishers et l'Institut de recherche de la Faculté Saint-Jean, 1990.

———. "The Origins of the Mixed Bloods in the Canadian West." In *The Prairie West: Historical Readings*, edited by R. Douglas Francis and Howard Palmer, 86–99. Edmonton: Pica Pica Press, 1985.

———. "Wintering, the Outsider Adult Male and the Ethnogenesis of the Western Plains Métis." In *From Rupert's Land to Canada*, edited by Theodore Binnema et al., 179–93. Edmonton: University of Alberta Press, 2001.

Fowler, Rodney. "The Contribution of Adrien-Gabriel Morice to Linguistic Ethnology: A Contextual Evaluation." In *Western Oblate Studies 2—Études oblates de l'ouest 2*, edited by Raymond Huel, 39–50. Edmonton: Edwin Mellen Press, 1992.

Friesen, Jean. "Alexander Morris." *Dictionary of Canadian Biography Online*, vol. 11 (1881–1890). http://www.biographi.ca/en/index.php.

Furet, François. *La Révolution de Turgot à Jules Ferry, 1770–1880.* Paris: Hachette, 1988.

Gadille, Jacques. "Le concept de civilisation chrétienne dans la pensée romantique." In *Civilisation chrétienne: Approche historique d'une idéologie. XVIIIe–XXe siècle*, edited by Jean-René Derré et al., 183–210. Paris: Beauchesne, 1975.

Gambell, Kevin. "Cemetery Spaces of Shxwõwhámel Stó:lō and the Île-à-la-Crosse Métis." MA thesis, University of Saskatchewan, 2009.

Giguère, Mario. "*Les missionnaires sauvages*: Roman Catholic Missionaries and *la mission ambulante* with the Métis, Plains Cree and Blackfoot, 1840–1880." MA thesis, McGill University, 2009.

Ginzburg, Carlo. *The Cheese and the Worms: The Cosmos of a Sixteenth-Century Miller*. Translated by John and Anne Tedeschi. Markham, ON: Penguin Books, 1982.

———. "Microhistory: Two or Three Things That I Know about It." *Critical Inquiry* 20, no. 1 (Autumn 1993): 10–35.

Giraud, Marcel. "Foreword." In *The New Peoples: Being and Becoming Métis in North America*, edited by Jacqueline Peterson and Jennifer S.H. Brown, xi–xiii. Winnipeg: University of Manitoba Press, 1985.

Giraud, Marcel. *Le métis canadien: Son rôle dans l'histoire des provinces de l'Ouest*. 2 vols. Paris: Institut d'ethnologie, 1945.

Goldman, Shalom. *God's Sacred Tongue: Hebrew and the American Imagination*. Chapel Hill: University of North Carolina Press, 2004.

Goldring, Philip. "Religion, Missions, and Native Culture," *Journal of the Canadian Church Historical Society* 26, no. 2 (October 1984): 43–49.

Goossen, N. Jaye. "William Mactavish." *Dictionary of Canadian Biography Online*, vol. 9 (1861–1870). http://www.biographi.ca/en/index.php.

Goossen, Norma Jaye. "The Relationship between the Church Missionary Society and the Hudson's Bay Company in Rupert's Land, 1821 to 1860, with a Case Study of the Stanley Mission under the Direction of the Rev. Robert Hunt." MA thesis, University of Manitoba, 1975.

Grabowski, Jan, and Nicole St-Onge. "Montreal Iroquois *engagés* in the Western Fur Trade, 1800–1821." In *From Rupert's Land to Canada*, edited by Theodore Binnema et al., 23–58. Edmonton: University of Alberta Press, 2001.

Grant, John Webster. *Moon of Wintertime: Missionaries and the Indians of Canada in Encounter since 1534*. Toronto: University of Toronto Press, 1984.

Gray, Robert. *Cardinal Manning: A Biography*. New York: St. Martin's Press, 1985.

Gresko, Jacqueline. "Creating Little Dominions within the Dominion: Early Catholic Indian Schools in Saskatchewan and British Columbia." In *Indian Education in Canada: The Legacy*, edited by Jean Barman et al., 1:88–109. Vancouver: University of British Columbia Press, 1986.

———. "Everyday Life at Qu'Appelle Industrial School." In *Western Oblate Studies 2—Études oblates de l'ouest 2*, edited by Raymond Huel, 71–94. Edmonton: Edwin Mellen Press, 1992.

———. "The 'Serfs of the System?' Oblate Brothers and the Sisters of Saint Ann in British Columbia Schools, 1858–1920." In *Western Oblate Studies 4—Études oblates de l'ouest 4*, edited by Raymond Huel, 119–41. Edmonton: Western Canadian Publishers, 1996.

Hall, Catherine. "Of Gender and Empire: Reflections on the Nineteenth Century." In *Gender and Empire*, edited by Philippa Levine, 46–76. Oxford History of the British Empire Companion Series. New York: Oxford University Press, 2004.

Hamelin, Jean, and Nicole Gagnon. *Histoire du catholicisme québécois: Le XXᵉ siècle, 1898–1940*. Edited by Nive Voisine. Montréal: Les Éditions du Boréal Express, 1984.

Harries, Patrick. "Anthropology." In *Missions and Empire*, edited by Norman Etherington, 238–60. Oxford History of the British Empire Companion Series. Oxford: Oxford University Press, 2005.

Honouring the Truth, Reconciling for the Future: Summary of the Final Report of the Truth and Reconciliation Commission of Canada. Winnipeg: Truth and Reconciliation Commission of Canada, 2015.

Hsia, R. Po-Chia. *The World of Catholic Renewal 1540–1770*. New York: Cambridge University Press, 1998.

Huel, Raymond J.A. *Archbishop A.-A. Taché of St. Boniface: The "Good Fight" and the Illusive Vision*. Edmonton: University of Alberta Press and Western Canadian Publishers, 2003.

———. "Gestæ Dei Per Francos: The French Canadian Experience in Western Canada." In *Visions of the New Jerusalem: Religious Settlement on the Prairies*, edited by Benjamin G. Smillie, 39–53. Edmonton: NeWest Press, 1983.

———. "La mission Notre-Dame-des-Victoires du lac la Biche et l'approvisionnement des missions du Nord: le conflit entre Mgr V. Grandin et Mgr H. Faraud." In *Western Oblate Studies 1—Études oblates de l'ouest 1*, edited by Raymond Huel, 17–36. Edmonton: Western Canadian Publishers et l'Institut de recherche de la Faculté Saint-Jean, 1990.

———. "The Life Cycle of an Early Oblate Establishment: St. Peter's Mission, Reindeer Lake." *Vie Oblate Life* 53, no. 3 (December 1994), 235–65.

———. "The Oblates of Mary Immaculate and the Hudson's Bay Company: A Mutuality of Interests in the Interior of the Canadian North-West." *Vie Oblate Life* 57, no. 3 (December 1998), 439–66.

———. "The Oblates, the Métis, and 1885: The Breakdown of Traditional Relationships." *Canadian Catholic Historical Association, Historical Studies* 56 (1989): 9–29.

———. *Proclaiming the Gospel to the Indians and the Métis: The Missionary Oblates of Mary Immaculate in Western Canada, 1845–1945*. Edmonton: University of Alberta Press and Western Canadian Publishers, 1996.

———. "Vital-Justin Grandin." *Dictionary of Canadian Biography Online*, vol. 13 (1901–1910). http://www.biographi.ca/en/index.php.

———. "Western Oblate History: The Need for Reinterpretation." In *Western Oblate Studies 3—Études oblates de l'ouest 3*, edited by Raymond Huel, 13–39. Edmonton: Western Canadian Publishers, 1994.

Hughes, Katherine. *Father Lacombe: The Black-Robe Voyageur*. Toronto: McClelland and Stewart, 1920.

Hutchinson, Gerald M. "British Methodists and the Hudson's Bay Company 1840–1854." In *Prairie Spirit: Perspectives on the Heritage of the United Church of Canada in the West*, edited by D.L. Butcher et al., 28–43. Winnipeg: University of Manitoba Press, 1985.

Indigenous and Northern Affairs Canada. http://www.ainc-inac.gc.ca/index-eng.asp. Accessed 18 May 2016.

Innis, Harold A. *The Fur Trade in Canada: An Introduction to Canadian Economic History*. Toronto: University of Toronto Press, 1999.

Jarvenpa, Robert. "The Hudson's Bay Company, the Roman Catholic Church, and the Chipewyan in the Late Fur Trade Period." In *"Le castor fait tout": Selected Papers of the Fifth North American Fur Trade Conference, 1985*, edited by Bruce G. Trigger et al., 485–517. Montreal: Lake St. Louis Historical Society, 1987.

Jarvenpa, Robert, and Hetty Jo Brumbach. *Ethnoarcheological and Cultural Frontiers: Athabascan, Algonquian, and European Adaptation in the Central Subarctic.* New York: Peter Lang, 1989.

———. "The Microeconomics of Southern Chipewyan Fur-Trade History." In *The Subarctic Fur Trade: Native Social and Economic Adaptations,* edited by Shepard Krech III, 147–84. Vancouver: University of British Columbia Press, 1984.

Jonas, Raymond. *France and the Cult of the Sacred Heart: An Epic Tale for Modern Times.* Berkeley: University of California Press, 2000.

Jonquet, E. *Mgr Grandin: Oblat de Marie Immaculée, premier évêque de Saint-Albert.* Montréal: Archevêché de Montréal, 1903.

Jordan, Mary V. *To Louis from Your Sister Who Loves You, Sara Riel.* Toronto: Griffin House, 1974.

Julia, Dominique. "La pesée d'un phénomène." In *Histoire de la France religieuse: Du Roi Très Chrétien à la laïcité républicaine,* edited by Jacques Le Goff and René Rémond, 3:190–200. Paris: Éditions du Seuil, 1991.

Kennedy, Jacqueline. "Qu'Appelle Industrial School: White Rites for the Indians of the Old Northwest." MA thesis, Carleton University, 1970.

Kerbiriou, Anne-Hélène. "Le corpus photographique des missionnaires Oblats dans le Nord-Ouest canadien, 1880–1930: Un document historique." In *Western Oblate Studies 3—Études oblates de l'ouest 3,* edited by Raymond Huel, 41–63. Edmonton: Western Canadian Publishers, 1994.

———. *Les Indiens de l'ouest canadien vus par les Oblats, 1885–1930.* Sillery: Les éditions du Septentrion, 1996.

Kermoal, Nathalie. "Métis et marginalité: Le cas de Saint-Paul-des-Métis." In *La francophonie sur les marges,* edited by C.J. Harvey and A. MacDonell, 41–51. Saint-Boniface: Les Presses universitaires de Saint-Boniface, 1997.

Kirsch, Stuart. "Lost Tribes: Indigenous Peoples and Social Imaginary." *Anthropological Quarterly* 70, no. 2 (April 1997): 58–67.

Klassen, Henry C. "Life in Frontier Calgary." In *Western Canada: Past and Present,* edited by Anthony W. Rasporich, 42–57. Calgary: McClelland and Stewart West, 1975.

Knowles, Norman. *Winds of Change: A History of the Roman Catholic Diocese of Calgary since 1968.* Calgary: Roman Catholic Diocese of Calgary and St. Mary's College, 2004.

Koester, Charles Beverley. *Mr. Davin, M.P.: A Biography of Nicholas Flood Davin.* Saskatoon: Western Producers Prairie Books, 1980.

Kowalsy, Nikolaus. "Mgr de Mazenod et l'Œuvre de la Propagation de la Foi." *Études oblates* 11 (1952): 238–60.

Krech, Shepard, III. "The Influence of Disease and the Fur Trade on Arctic Drainage Lowlands Dene, 1800–1850." *Journal of Anthropological Research* 39, no. 1 (Summer 1983): 123–46.

Krehbiel, Edward Benjamin. *The Interdict: Its History and Its Operation, with Especial Attention to the Time of Pope Innocent I.* Charleston, SC: BiblioBazaar, LLC, 2009.

Lacombe, Guy. *Anecdotes du vécu.* Edmonton: Les Éditions Duval, 1993.

Lacombe, Guy, and Raymond Huel. "L'épopée des oblats dans l'ouest canadien." *Francophonies d'Amérique* 1 (1991): 99–109.

Laframboise, Ronald. "Eugène de Mazenod et les pauvres: Une question récurrente." *Vie Oblate Life* 58, no. 1a (April 1999): 203–7.

Lamirande, Émilien. "À propos des premières missions d'Eugène de Mazenod et de ses confrères (1816–1823). Inspiration et accomplissement." *Vie Oblate Life* 60, no. 2 (2001): 1–30.

———. "Les pauvres et les âmes les plus abandonnées d'après Mgr de Mazenod." *Études oblates* 20 (1961): 3–19.

Lamothe, Dawn Adèle, "The Oblate Construction of the Métis Other: *Mission Ambulante* among *Les Hivernants*, 1830–1880." MA thesis, University of Alberta, 2002.

Langlois, Claude. "Politique et religion." In *Histoire de la France religieuse: Du Roi Très Chrétien à la laïcité républicaine*, edited by Jacques Le Goff and René Rémond, 3:125–43. Paris: Éditions du Seuil, 1991.

———. "Une France duelle? L'espace religieux contemporain." In *Histoire de la France religieuse: Du Roi Très Chrétien à la laïcité républicaine*, edited by Jacques Le Goff and René Rémond, 3:211–329. Paris: Éditions du Seuil, 1991.

Lapointe, Richard. *100 noms*. Regina: Société historique de la Saskatchewan, 1988.

Le Chevallier, Jules. *Batoche: Les missionnaires du Nord-Ouest pendant les troubles de 1885*. Montréal: L'Œuvre de presse dominicaine, 1941.

———. *Esquisse sur l'origine et les premiers développements de Calgary*. Calgary: La Paroisse Sainte-Famille, 1936.

Le Roy Ladurie, Emmanuel. *Montaillou: The Promised Land of Error*. Translated by Barbara Bray. New York: Vinatge Books, 1979.

Leflon, Jean. *Eugene de Mazenod: Bishop of Marseilles, Founder of the Oblates of Mary Immaculate*. Translated by Francis D. Flanagan. 4 vols. New York: Fordham University Press, 1966.

Legal, Émile J. *Short Sketches of the History of the Catholic Churches and Missions in Central Alberta*. Edmonton: Archdiocese of Edmonton, 1915.

Leighton, Douglas. "A Victorian Civil Servant at Work: Lawrence Vankoughnet and the Canadian Indian Department, 1874–1893." In *As Long As the Sun Shines and Water Flows: A Reader in Canadian Native Studies*, edited by Ian A.L. Getty and Antoine S. Lussier, 104–19. Vancouver: University of British Columbia Press, 2000.

Lesage, Germain. *Capitale d'une solitude*. Ottawa: Éditions des Études oblates, 1946.

———. *L'Évêque errant*. Ottawa: Les Éditions de l'Université d'Ottawa, 1950.

Levasseur, Donat. *Histoire des Missionnaires Oblats de Marie Immaculée: Essai de synthèse*. 2 vols. Montréal: Maison provinciale, 1983.

———. "La venue des Oblats de Marie Immaculée en Amérique." In *Western Oblate Studies 2—Études oblates de l'ouest 2*, edited by Raymond Huel, 13–29. Edmonton: Edwin Mellen Press, 1992.

———. *Les Oblats de Marie Immaculée dans l'ouest et le nord du Canada, 1845–1967*. Edmonton: University of Alberta Press and Western Canadian Publishers, 1995.

Levine, Philippa. "Introduction: Why Gender and Empire?" In *Gender and Empire*, edited by Philippa Levine, 1–13. The Oxford History of the British Empire Companion Series. New York: Oxford University Press, 2004.

———. "Sexuality, Gender, and Empire." In *Gender and Empire*, edited by Philippa Levine, 134–55. The Oxford History of the British Empire Companion Series. New York: Oxford University Press, 2004.

Lindsay, Debra. "The Hudson's Bay Company-Smithsonian Connection and Fur Trade Intellectual Life: Bernard Rogan Ross, A Case Study." In *"Le castor fait tout": Selected Papers of the Fifth North American Fur Trade Conference, 1985*, edited by Bruce G. Trigger et al., 587–617. Montreal: Lake St. Louis Historical Society, 1987.

———, ed. *The Modern Beginnings of Subarctic Ornithology: Correspondence with the Smithsonian Institution, 1856–1868*. Winnipeg: Manitoba Record Society, 1991.

———. "Science in the Sub-Arctic: Traders, Trappers and the Smithsonian Institution, 1859–1870." PhD diss., University of Manitoba, 1989.

Lundlie, Lise. "Les oblats et le Collège Mathieu." In *Western Oblate Studies 4—Études oblates de l'ouest 4*, edited by Raymond Huel, 103–17. Edmonton: Western Canadian Publishers, 1996.

Macdougall, Brenda. "'The Comforts of Married Life': Metis Family Life, Labour, and the Hudson's Bay Company." *Labour/Le Travail* 61 (Spring 2008): 9–39.

———. "The Myth of Metis Cultural Ambivalence." In *Contours of a People: Metis Family, Mobility, and History*, edited by Nicole St-Onge, Carolyn Podruchny, and Brenda Macdougall, 422–64. Norman: University of Oklahoma Press, 2012.

———. *One of the Family: Metis Culture in Nineteenth-Century Northwestern Saskatchewan*. Vancouver: University of British Columbia Press, 2010.

———. "Socio-Cultural Development and Identity Formation of Metis Communities in Northwestern Saskatchewan, 1776–1907." PhD diss., University of Saskatchewan, 2005.

———. "Wahkootowin: Family and Cultural Identity in Northwestern Saskatchewan Metis Communities." *Canadian Historical Review* vol. 87, no. 3 (September 2006): 431–62.

MacGregor, James G. *Father Lacombe*. Edmonton: Hurtig Publishers, 1975.

Maclean, John. *James Evans, Inventor of the Syllabic System of the Cree Language*. Toronto: William Briggs, Wesley Buildings, 1890.

Macleod, Roderick Charles. "James Farquharson Macleod." *Dictionary of Canadian Biography Online*, vol. 12 (1891–1900). http://www.biographi.ca/en/index.php.

McNally, Vincent J. *The Lord's Distant Vineyard: A History of the Oblates and the Catholic Community in British Columbia*. Edmonton: University of Alberta Press, 2000.

Madill, Dennis F.K. "Treaty Research Report: Treaty Eight (1899)." Ottawa: Indian and Northern Affairs Canada, 1986.

Marchildon, Greg, and Sid Robinson. *Canoeing the Churchill River: A Practical Guide to the Historic Voyageur Highway*. Regina: Canadian Plains Research Center, 2002.

Martel, Gilles. *Le messianisme de Louis Riel*. Waterloo, ON: Wilfrid Laurier University Press, 1984.

Mayeur, Jean-Marie. "Jules Ferry et la laïcité." In *Jules Ferry, fondateur de la République*, edited by François Furet, 147–60. Paris: Éditions de l'École des Hautes Études en Sciences Sociales, 1985.

McCarthy, Martha. "The Founding of Providence Mission." In *Western Oblate Studies 1—Études oblates de l'ouest 1,* edited by Raymond Huel, 37–49. Edmonton: Western Canadian Publishers et l'Institut de recherche de la Faculté Saint-Jean, 1990.

———. *From the Great River to the Ends of the Earth: Oblate Missions to the Dene, 1847–1921.* Edmonton: University of Alberta Press and Western Canadian Publishers, 1995.

———. "The Missions of the Oblates of Mary Immaculate to the Athapaskans, 1846–1870: Theory, Structure and Method." PhD diss., University of Manitoba, 1981.

———. *To Evangelize the Nations: Roman Catholic Missions in Manitoba, 1818–1870.* Winnipeg: Manitoba Culture, Heritage and Recreation Historical Resources, 1990.

McGrath, Ann, and Winona Stevenson. "Gender, Race and Policy: Indigenous Women and the State in Canada and Australia." *Labour/Le Travail* 38 (Fall 1996): 37–53.

Mellor, Alec. *Histoire de l'anticléricalisme français.* Paris: Mame, 1966.

Miller, J.R. "Anti-Catholicism in Canada: From the British Conquest to the Great War." In *Creed and Culture: The Place of English-Speaking Catholics in Canadian Society, 1750–1930,* edited by T. Murphy and G. Stortz, 25–48. Montreal and Kingston: McGill-Queen's University Press, 1993.

———. "Denominational Rivalry in Indian Residential Education." In *Western Oblate Studies 2—Études oblates de l'ouest 2,* edited by Raymond Huel, 139–55. Edmonton: Edwin Mellen Press, 1992.

———. *Shingwauk's Vision: A History of Native Residential Schools.* Toronto: University of Toronto Press, 1996.

———. *Skyscrapers Hide the Heavens: A History of Indian-White Relations in Canada.* 3rd ed. Toronto: University of Toronto Press, 2000.

———. "The State, the Church, and Indian Residential Schools in Canada." In *Religion and Public Life in Canada: Historical and Comparative Perspectives,* edited by Marguerite Van Die, 109–29. Toronto: University of Toronto Press, 2001.

Mills, Hazel. "Negotiating the Divide: Women, Philanthropy and the 'Public Sphere' in Nineteenth-Century France." In *Religion, Society and Politics in France since 1789,* edited by F. Tallett and N. Atkin, 29–54. London: Hambledon Press, 1991.

The Missionary Diocese of Athabasca. Toronto: The Literature Committee of the Missionary Society of the Church of England in Canada, 1907.

Mitchell, Estelle. *The Grey Nuns of Montreal and the Red River Settlement, 1844–1984.* Montreal: Éditions du Méridien, 1987.

Morice, A.G. *History of the Catholic Church in Western Canada: From Lake Superior to the Pacific, 1659–1895.* 2 vols. Toronto: Musson Book Company, 1910.

Morton, Arthur S. *A History of the Canadian West to 1870–71.* Toronto: University of Toronto Press, 1973.

———. *Under Western Skies.* Toronto: Thomas Nelson and Sons, 1936.

Mulhall, David. *Will to Power: The Missionary Career of Father Morice.* Vancouver: University of British Columbia Press, 1986.

Mullet, Michael A. *The Catholic Reformation.* New York: Routledge, 1999.

Neatby, Leslie H. "François Beaulieu." *Dictionary of Canadian Biography Online,* vol.10 (1871–1880). http://www.biographi.ca/en/index.php.

Ortolan, Théophile. *Les Oblats de Marie Immaculée durant le premier siècle de leur existence.* 4 vols. Paris: P. Lethielleux, Libraire-Éditeur, 1909.

Ouellet, Joséphine. "Mgr Albert Pascal, o.m.i. (1848–1920): Cheville ouvrière du diocèse de Prince-Albert." In *Western Oblate Studies 1—Études oblates de l'ouest 1,* edited by Raymond Huel, 89–103. Edmonton: Western Canadian Publishers et l'Institut de recherche de la Faculté Saint-Jean, 1990.

Painchaud, Robert. "Les exigences linguistiques dans le recrutement d'un clergé pour l'ouest canadien, 1818–1920." In *Sessions d'études—1975: Étude présentée au congrès annuel de la Société canadienne d'Histoire de l'Église catholique,* 50–64. L'Université de Sudbury, le 21 septembre 1975.

———. *Un rêve français dans le peuplement de la Prairie.* Saint-Boniface: Éditions des Plaines, 1987.

Pannekoek, Frits. "The Anglican Church and the Disintegration of Red River Society, 1818–1870." In *The Prairie West: Historical Readings,* edited by R. Douglas Francis and Howard Palmer, 100–15. Edmonton: Pica Pica Press, 1985.

———. *A Snug Little Flock: The Social Origins of the Riel Resistance of 1869–70.* Winnipeg: Watson and Dwyer Publishing, 1991.

Pariseau, Jean. *Les Oblats de Marie-Immaculée dans les paroisses canadiennes-françaises de la région de Rivière-la-Paix, 1912–1967.* Edmonton: Western Canadian Publishers, 1992.

Parliament of Canada. www.parl.gc.ca. Accessed 18 May 2016.

Payment, Diane Paulette. *"Les gens libres—Otipemisiwak": Batoche, Saskatchewan, 1870–1930.* Ottawa: Études en archéologie, architecture et histoire, 1990.

———. "Un aperçu des relations entre les missionnaires catholiques et les Métisses pendant le premier siècle de contact (1813–1918) dans l'Ouest canadien." In *Western Oblate Studies 3—Études oblates de l'ouest 3,* edited by Raymond Huel, 139–58. Edmonton: Western Canadian Publishers, 1994.

Pereiro, James. *Cardinal Manning: An Intellectual Biography.* Oxford: Clarendon Press, 1998.

Perin, Roberto. *Rome in Canada: The Vatican and Canadian Affairs in the Late Victorian Age.* Toronto: University of Toronto Press, 1990.

Persson, Diane. "The Changing Experience of Indian Residential Schooling: Blue Quills, 1931–1970." In *Indian Education in Canada: The Legacy,* edited by Jean Barman et al., 1:150–68. Vancouver: University of British Columbia Press, 1986.

Pielorz, Joseph. "La Congrégation OMI était-elle fondée le 25 janvier 1816?" *Vie Oblate Life* 54, no. 2 (August 1995): 161–82.

Plongeron, Bernard. "Affirmation et transformations d'une 'civilisation chrétienne' à la fin du XVIIIe siècle." In *Civilisation chrétienne. Approche historique d'une idéologie. XVIIIe– XXe siècle,* edited by Jean-René Derré et al., 9–22. Paris: Beauchesne, 1975.

Podruchny, Carolyn. "Baptizing Novices: Ritual Moments among French Canadian Voyageurs in the Montreal Fur Trade, 1780–1821." *The Canadian Historical Review* 83, no. 2 (June 2002): 165–95.

———. *Making the Voyageur World: Travelers and Traders in the North American Fur Trade.* Lincoln: University of Nebraska Press, 2006.

Porter, Andrew. "Religion, Missionary Enthusiasm, and Empire." In *The Oxford History of the British Empire*. Vol. 3, *The Nineteenth Century*, edited by Andrew Porter, 222–46. New York: Oxford University Press, 1999.

———. "Trusteeship, Anti-Slavery, and Humanitarianism." In *The Oxford History of the British Empire*. Vol. 3, *The Nineteenth Century*, edited by Andrew Porter, 198–221. New York: Oxford University Press, 1999.

"Prairie Grass to Mountain Pass": History of the Pioneers of Pincher Creek and District. Pincher Creek, AB: Pincher Creek Historical Society, 1974.

Quéré, Martin. "La correspondance de Mgr de Mazenod avec les missionnaires." *Kerygma* 24 (1975): 178–91.

———. "Monseigneur de Mazenod et le missionnaire oblat." *Études oblates* 20 (1961): 237–70.

Ray, Arthur J. *Indians in the Fur Trade: Their Role as Trappers, Hunters, and Middlemen in the Lands Southwest of Hudson Bay, 1660–1870*. Toronto: University of Toronto Press, 1974.

Ray, Arthur J., Jim Miller, and Frank Tough. *Bounty and Benevolence: A History of Saskatchewan Treaties*. Montreal and Kingston: McGill-Queen's University Press, 2000.

Rémond, René. *La droite en France de la première Restauration à la Ve République*. Paris: Aubier, 1968.

———. *L'anti-cléricalisme en France de 1815 à nos jours*. Paris: Fayard, 1976.

Rivère, Edmond. *Jean-Charles Pandosy, missionnaire et pionnier du Nord-Ouest*. Presses de Bras-d'Apic, 2013.

Robb, Andrew. "David Laird." *Dictionary of Canadian Biography Online*, vol. 14 (1911–1920). http://www.biographi.ca/en/index.php.

Roberto, Claude. "Quelques réflexions sur les relations entre les Oblats, les populations autochtones et le gouvernement avant et après la signature des traités 6, 7 et 8." In *Western Oblate Studies 4—Études oblates de l'ouest 4*, edited by Raymond Huel, 71–82. Edmonton: Western Canadian Publishers, 1996.

Rodgers, J.A. "Lac du Brochet." *The Beaver* (March 1945): 11–13.

Rogers, Rebecca. "Retrograde or Modern? Unveiling the Teaching Nun in Nineteenth-Century France." *Social History* 23, no. 2 (May 1998): 146–64.

Sawchuk, Joe, Patricia Sawchuk, and Theresa Ferguson. *Metis Land Rights in Alberta: A Political History*. Edmonton: Metis Association of Alberta, 1981.

Semple, Neil. *The Lord's Dominion: The History of Canadian Methodism*. Montreal and Kingston: McGill-Queen's University Press, 1996.

Silver, A.I. "French Canada and the Prairie Frontier, 1870–1890." *The Canadian Historical Review* 50, no. 1 (March 1969): 11–35.

Slobodin, Richard. *Metis of the Mackenzie District*. Ottawa: Canadian Research Centre for Anthropology, Saint-Paul University, 1966.

———. "The Subarctic Metis as Products and Agents of Culture Contact." *Arctic Anthropology* 2, no. 2 (1964): 50–55.

Smandych, Russell and Anne McGillivray. "Images of Indigenous Childhood: Contested Governance in the Canadian West to 1850." In *Empire and Others: British*

Encounters with Indigenous Peoples, 1600–1850, edited by Martin Daunton and Rick Halpern, 238–59. Philadelphia: University of Pennsylvania Press, 1999.

Smith, Derek G. "The 'Policy of Aggressive Civilization' and Projects of Governance in Roman Catholic Industrial Schools for Native Peoples in Canada, 1870–95." *Anthropologica* 43, issue. 2 (2001): 253–71.

Smith, Donald B. "A History of French-Speaking Albertans." In *Peoples of Alberta: Portraits of Cultural Diversity*, edited by Howard and Tamara Palmer, 84–108. Saskatoon: Western Producer Prairie Books, 1985.

———. *Honoré Jaxon: Prairie Visionary*. Regina: Coteau Books, 2007.

Smith, Donald, and Henry Klassen. "Onward! Calgary in the 1890s." In *Centennial City: Calgary 1894–1994*, 1–12. Calgary: The University of Calgary, 1994.

Sœur de la Providence, Une. *Le Père Lacombe: "L'homme au bon cœur."* Montréal: Le Devoir, 1916.

Spry, Irene M. "The Métis and Mixed-Bloods of Rupert's Land before 1870." In *The New Peoples: Being and Becoming Métis in North America*, edited by Jacqueline Peterson and Jennifer S.H. Brown, 95–118. Winnipeg: University of Manitoba Press, 1985.

———. "William Joseph Christie." *Dictionary of Canadian Biography Online*, vol. 12 (1891–1900). http://www.biographi.ca/en/index.php.

Stanley, George F.G. "Alberta's Half-breed Reserve Saint-Paul-des-Métis,1896–1909." In *The Other Natives: The Métis*, edited by Antoine S. Lussier and D. Bruce Sealey, 2:75–107. Winnipeg: Manitoba Métis Federation Press, 1978.

Staum, Martin. "Nature and Nurture in French Ethnography and Anthropology, 1859–1915." *Journal of the History of Ideas* 65, no. 3 (2004): 475–95.

———. *Labeling People: French Scholars on Society, Race, and Empire, 1815–1848*. Montreal and Kingston: McGill-Queen's University Press, 2003.

Stepan, Nancy. *The Idea of Race in Science: Great Britain, 1800–1960*. London: Macmillan Press, 1982.

Stocking, George W. Jr. *Victorian Anthropology*. New York: The Free Press, 1987.

St-Onge, Nicole. "'He Was Neither a Soldier Nor a Slave: He Was Under the Control of No Man': Kahnawake Mohawks in the Northwest Fur Trade, 1790–1850." *Canadian Journal of History / Annales canadiennes d'histoire* 51, no. 1 (2016): 1–32.

———. *Saint-Laurent, Manitoba: Evolving Métis Identities, 1850–1914*. Regina: Canadian Plains Research Center, 2004.

———. "Uncertain Margins: Métis and Saulteaux Identities in St-Paul des Saulteaux, Red River 1821–1870." *Manitoba History* 53 (Oct. 2006): 2–10.

Sylvain, Philippe. "Charles-Auguste-Marie-Joseph de Forbin-Janson." *Dictionary of Canadian Biography Online*, vol. 7 (1836–1850). http://www.biographi.ca/en/index.php.

Talbot, Robert J. *Negotiating the Numbered Treaties: An Intellectual and Political Biography of Alexander Morris*. Saskatoon: Purich Publishing, 2009.

Thévenin, René, and Paul Coze. *Mœurs et histoires des Indiens peaux-rouges*. Paris: Payot, 1928.

Thomas, L.G. "The Church of England and the Canadian West." In *The Anglican Church and the World of Western Canada, 1820–1970*, edited by Barry Ferguson, 16–28. Regina: University of Regina, Canadian Plains Research Center, 1991.

Thompson, John Herd. "Nicholas Flood Davin." *Dictionary of Canadian Biography Online*, vol. 13 (1901–1910). http://www.biographi.ca/en/index.php.

Tierney, Brian. *Origins of Papal Infallibility, 1150–1350: A Study of the Concepts of Infallibility, Sovereignty and Tradition in the Middle Ages.* Leiden, Netherlands: E.J. Brill, 1972.

Titley, Brian. "Dunbow Indian Industrial School: An Oblate Experiment in Education." In *Western Oblate Studies 2—Études oblates de l'ouest 2*, edited by Raymond Huel, 95–113. Edmonton: Edwin Mellen Press, 1992.

Tobias, Michael. "The Anthropology of Ascent." *Mountain* 44 (July–August 1975): 31–36.

Tough, Frank. *"As Their Natural Resources Fail": Native Peoples and the Economic History of Northern Manitoba, 1870–1930.* Vancouver: University of British Columbia Press, 1996.

Trottier, Alice. "Les Oblats et la colonisation en Alberta." In *Western Oblate Studies 1— Études oblates de l'ouest 1*, edited by Raymond Huel, 107–16. Edmonton: Western Canadian Publishers, 1990.

Truth and Reconciliation Commission of Canada: Calls to Action. Winnipeg: Truth and Reconciliation Commission of Canada, 2015.

Van Kirk, Sylvia. "John Rowand." *Dictionary of Canadian Biography Online*, vol. 8 (1851–1860). http://www.biographi.ca/en/index.php.

———. *Many Tender Ties: Women in Fur-Trade Society, 1670–1870.* Norman: University of Oklahoma Press, 1980.

Vanast, Walter. "Compassion, Cost and Competition: Factors in the Evolution of Oblate Medical Services in the Canadian North." In *Western Oblate Studies 2—Études oblates de l'ouest 2*, edited by Raymond Huel, 179–95. Edmonton: Edwin Mellen Press, 1992.

Venini Byrne, M.B. *From the Buffalo to the Cross: A History of the Roman Catholic Diocese of Calgary.* Calgary: Calgary Archives and Historical Publishers, 1973.

Verhelst, Daniël. *La Congrégation du Cœur Immaculé de Marie (Scheut).* Louvain, Belgium: Presses universitaires de Louvain, 1986.

Wade, Mason. *The French Canadians, 1760–1967.* 2 vols. Toronto: Macmillan of Canada, 1955.

Waite, P.B. "Frederick Arthur Stanley." *Dictionary of Canadian Biography Online*, vol. 13 (1901–1910). http://www.biographi.ca/en/index.php.

———. "Thomas White." *Dictionary of Canadian Biography Online*, vol. 11 (1881–1890). http://www.biographi.ca/en/index.php.

Wartelle, Jean-Claude. "La Société d'anthropologie de Paris de 1859 à 1920." *Revue d'histoire des sciences humaines* 1, no. 10 (2004): 125–71.

Weekes, Mary. *Trader King as Told to Mary Weekes.* Regina and Toronto: School Aids and Textbook Publishing Company, 1949.

Young, Egerton Ryerson. *The Apostle of the North: Rev. James Evans.* New York: Fleming H. Revell Company, 1899.

Zemon Davis, Natalie. *The Return of Martin Guerre.* Cambridge, MA: Harvard University Press, 1983.

INDEX

A

Aborigines' Protection Society, 45–46

Aquinas, Saint Thomas, 7, 131n33, 195n43

aggressive civilization, 65

Agnès, Sister (Marie-Rose Caron): arrives at Saint-Jean-Baptiste, 26, 143n89; and convent boarding school, 27, 67–68, 73, 76; on spring mission, 194n42

Alacoque, Marguerite-Marie, 36, 77–78, 180n68

alcohol, 50, 51–52, 60, 162n48

Anglicanism, 17, 46, 52–55, 75, 88–89, 158n6, 159n14

Annales de la Propagation de la Foi, Les, 13, 14, 25, 80–81

Aubert, Pierre, 18, 140n52

Ayamihew-Okima, Chief, 48

B

Beaulieu, François, 74, 176n48

Bellecourt, Georges-Antoine, 137n19

Bermond, François-Xavier, 140n56

Bienheureuse-Marguerite-Marie mission, 57, 99–100, 107. *See also* Canoe Lake

Boisramé, Louis, 25

Boucher, Philomène, 26, 68, 143n89

Bourget, Ignace, 7

Bowes, Patrick, 25, 33, 36, 167n90

Brabant, Marguerite, 90

Bruce, James, 70

C

Caër, Jean-Marie, 32, 72, 75–76, 179n63

Campbell, Robert, 54

Canada, Government of: exclusion of Métis from treaty system, 117; and missionary schools policy, 172n2; perceived bias toward Anglican schools, 88–89, 185n111; petitioned for funding of schools by Oblates, 36, 83–86, 88, 90–91; petitioned to disallow free trade in English River District, 58; role in setting up residential schools, 65, 187n124; and Saint-Paul-des-Métis, 115; use of Oblate information on Indigenous peoples, 5, 94

Canoe Lake, 38, 39, 57, 99, 156n202. *See also* Bienheureuse-Marguerite-Marie mission

Capitale d'une solitude (Lesage), 16

Carrière, Gaston, 94

Catherine, aged (Chipewyan language teacher), 99, 193n33

Charlebois, Ursule Cécile, 76–77

Chipewyan speakers: 17–18, 51; at biannual missions, 49, 56–57, 100–101; danger to from impious métis, 110–11; at Île-à-la-Crosse, 8; missionary-made category of, 101–2, 126; Oblates struggle to learn language of, 97–99; poverty, 57–58, 69; at Reindeer Lake, 20; work in transcribing prayers, 101

Chipman, Clarence C., 59

Choquette, Robert, 4, 44–45, 157n6

Christian civilization. *See* civilizing mission of Oblates

Christie, William Joseph, 50–51, 162n51, 184n103

civilizing mission of Oblates: failure of Saint-Bruno in, 72–76, 116; as focus of Saint-Jean-Baptiste, 10–12, 95–96; métis as positive influence for, 86–87, 184n105; orphans and, 90–91; as part of search for funding, 80–85; as purpose of convent boarding school, 66–68;